D1527376

Professional Military Education
in the United States

Professional Military Education in the United States

A Historical Dictionary

Edited by
WILLIAM E. SIMONS

Robin Higham, Advisory Editor

Greenwood Press
Westport, Connecticut • London

355.0071
P964

Library of Congress Cataloging-in-Publication Data

Professional military education in the United States : a historical dictionary / edited by
William E. Simons.
    p.   cm.
  Includes bibliographical references and index.
    ISBN 0–313–29749–5 (alk. paper)
    1. Military education—United States—History—Encyclopedias.   I. Simons, William E.
U408.P78   2000
355'.0071'073—dc21   99–043507

British Library Cataloguing in Publication Data is available.

Library of Congress Catalog Card Number: 99–043507
ISBN: 0–313–29749–5

First published in 2000

Greenwood Press, 88 Post Road West, Westport, CT 06881
An imprint of Greenwood Publishing Group, Inc.
www.greenwood.com

Printed in the United States of America

The paper used in this book complies with the
Permanent Paper Standard issued by the National
Information Standards Organization (Z39.48–1984).

10 9 8 7 6 5 4 3 2 1

Contents

Preface

Calling on the expertise of a number of different scholars, this volume presents in encyclopedic format a panorama of the growth of professional military education (PME) in the United States. Arranged in alphabetical order, each entry tells a separate piece of the story, and most provide source information for the reader who wants to explore that subject in more detail. Although many of the institutions and practices originating in Europe that provided the inspiration and models for American adaptation are included, the bulk of the entries are devoted to institutions of PME that emerged here, together with the personalities, concepts, academic practices, contentious issues, and key locations that have been instrumental in their development since the early 19th century.

Introducing the collection of entries is a brief historical narrative that ties together most of the topics chronologically and explains many of their interrelationships. It begins with French influences on early American recognition of the need for professional military education and on the formative years at West Point and traces the subsequent evolution of different forms of officer preparation and postcommissioning education in both the U.S. Army and Navy. It concludes with PME developments following World War II, including those within the newly independent Air Force and the steadily increasing emphasis on joint education under the aegis of a now-statutory Joint Chiefs of Staff organization.

The following entries were selected for their relevance to professional military education provided for officers. In this respect, I have used the distinction between military education and training made in John Masland and Laurence Radway's *Soldiers and Scholars: Military Education and National Policy* (Princeton U. Press, 1957): "[T]raining identifies instruction that is oriented to a particular military specialty and that is designed to develop a technical skill. . . . Education . . . implies instruction or individual study for the purpose of intellectual development and the cultivation of wisdom and judgment. It prepares a man to deal with novel situations." Thus, with the exception of the U.S. Army's artillery and engineer schools, which are included to provide historical continuity with pioneering predecessor institutions, this volume contains none of the service branch schools since they are devoted largely to training a young officer for the beginning duties and weapons of his initial specialty. While the Marine Corps's Basic School resembles a branch school in many respects, it is included because it also performs a broader, socializing function much like that of a service academy, schooling the young officer in the traditions, professional ethos, and unique ways of his chosen service.

The contributors were not asked to adhere to any preconceived scheme of analysis when dealing with their topics; nor were they asked necessarily to render evaluative judgments. Rather, the only order imposed was strictly historical: In what ways did it contribute to PME? Why? However, the compilation of the following entries, several of which present unfamiliar details and insights regarding their subjects, seems worthy of some sort of conclusions, findings, or assessment. Hence, I have ended the volume with a statement, called "Editor's Postscript," of what can best be characterized as (hopefully) informed opinion. The judgments presented in this final section are, of course, mine, although I am quite certain that some at least are shared by others.

Throughout the volume, the views expressed are those of the individual authors whose names appear beneath their entries and should not be considered as those of the organizations with which they are affiliated. Entries with no contributor's name have been prepared by the editor and represent views for which I am entirely responsible. An asterisk appearing after a topic first mentioned in an entry indicates a cross-reference to another entry.

This volume could not have been put together without the generous and thoughtful effort of the contributors who volunteered their knowledge and took valuable time from their busy schedules to prepare the original essays that appear here. A gratifying number of them, some perfect strangers in the beginning, prepared two or more. All responded to my invitation out of personal belief in the important contribution made by PME to our defense establishment and nation and out of respect for the role their respective subjects have played in it. Obviously I cannot name all the contributors in these pages, but I wish to express my deep appreciation for their scholarly efforts and their trust. Many of them have made significant contributions to the professional literature in their own right and gratify the project by their participation.

Special recognition, however, is merited by a few individuals: Ray Bowers, USNA classmate and onetime USAFA colleague, lent his scholarly skills to the production of a wide variety of original entries and offered timely critiques as the project advanced. Alan Gropman, longtime friend and Air Force colleague, saw early merit to the project and helped get it going by recruiting a number of other contributors. Robin Higham, as advisory editor, lent his wide-ranging knowledge of military topics and sources and provided invaluable assistance in identifying possible contributors for many of these. Shirley Lithgow, formerly my secretary at RAND, provided timely and valuable clerical assistance.

William E. Simons

Acronyms and Abbreviations

AAF	Army Air Forces (World War II)
ACSC	Air Command and Staff College
ACT	American College Testing
ACTS	Air Corps Tactical School (pre–World War II)
AEF	American Expeditionary Force (World War I)
AFB	Air Force Base
AFIT	Air Force Institute of Technology
AFROTC	Air Force Reserve Officers' Training Corps
AFSC	Armed Forces Staff College; also Air Force Specialty Code
ANSCOL	Army-Navy Staff College (World War II)
ASTP	Army Specialized Training Program (World War II)
ASW	Anti-submarine warfare
ATC	Air Training Command
ATO	Air Training Officer
AU	Air University
AWC	Air War College or Army War College
CGSC	Command and General Staff College (U.S. Army)
CHDS	Center for Hemispheric Defense Studies
CinC	Commander-in-Chief
CJCS	Chairman of the Joint Chiefs of Staff
CNO	Chief of Naval Operations
CONAC	Continental Air Command
CRES	Command Readiness Exercise System (U.S. Air Force)
CSS	Confederate States Ship

DA	Department of the (U.S.) Army
DAU	Defense Acquisition University
DoD	Department of Defense
ERB	Educational Requirements Board (U.S. Air Force)
FIP	Flight Instruction Program
GSS	General Service Schools (pre–World War II)
ICAF	Industrial College of the Armed Forces
ICBM	Intercontinental ballistic missile
INSS	Institute for National Strategic Studies
IOC	Infantry Officers Course (U.S. Marine Corps)
IRMC	Information Resources Management College
JAWS	Joint AFSC War-gaming System
JCS	Joint Chiefs of Staff
JCSOS	Joint and Combined Staff Officer School
JICM	Joint Integrated Contingency Model
JLASS	Joint Land Aerospace Sea Simulation
JSO	Joint Specialty Officer
KUVNAS	Course for the Perfection of Senior Officers (USSR)
MAAG	Military assistance advisory group
MAJCOM	Major (Air) command
MCWAR	Marine Corps War College
MECEP	Marine Corps Enlisted Commissioning Education Program
MGO	Master General of Ordnance (U.K.)
M.I.T.	Massachusetts Institute of Technology
M.MAS.	Master of Military Arts and Science
M.MS.	Master of Military Studies
MOS	Military occupational specialty
M.S.	Master of Science
MTM	Military Theater Model (U.S. Army)
NAS	Naval Air Station
NATO	North Atlantic Treaty Organization
NCO	Non-commissioned officer
NDU	National Defense University
NPS	Naval Postgraduate School
NROTC	Naval Reserve Officers' Training Corps
NWC	National War College or Naval War College
OCS	Officer Candidate School

OJT	On-the-job training
PAJE	Process for the accreditation of joint education
Ph.D.	Doctor of Philosophy
PME	Professional military education
RAF	Royal Air Force (U.K.)
RAFC	Royal Air Force College (U.K.)
RFC	Royal Flying Corps (U.K., World War I)
RKKA	Workers and Peasant Red Army (USSR)
RMA	Royal Military Academy (U.K.)
RMC	Royal Military College (U.K.)
ROTC	Reserve Officers' Training Corps
RSAS	RAND Strategy Assessment System
RUSI	Royal United Services Institution (U.K.)
SAAS	School of Advanced Airpower Studies (U.S. Air Force)
SAC	Strategic Air Command
SAM	School of Aerospace Medicine (U.S. Air Force); also surface-to-air missile
SAMS	School of Advanced Military Studies (U.S. Army)
SAT	Scholastic Assessment Test
SAW	School of Advanced Warfighting (U.S. Marine Corps)
SHAPE	Supreme Headquarters Allied Powers Europe (NATO)
SIWS	School of Information Warfare and Strategy
TBS	The Basic School (U.S. Marine Corps)
TRADOC	Training and Doctrine Command (U.S. Army)
TWX	Theater Warfare Exercise (U.S. Air Force)
U.K.	United Kingdom
UNAAF	United Action Armed Forces (pre–World War II)
U.S.	United States
USA	U.S. Army
USAAF	U.S. Army Air Forces (World War II)
USACGSC	U.S. Army Command and General Staff College
USAF	U.S. Air Force
USAFA	United States Air Force Academy
USCGA	United States Coast Guard Academy
USMA	United States Military Academy
USMC	U.S. Marine Corps
USMMA	United States Merchant Marine Academy

USN	U.S. Navy
USNA	United States Naval Academy
USRC	United States Revenue Cutter
USS	United States Ship
VMI	Virginia Military Institute

Introduction: A PME Panorama

Education developed specifically for the military profession is one of the significant features characterizing Western civilization. It emerged in the United States beginning in the early 19th century with the founding of the Military Academy at West Point. This institution, like several of those to follow in America, borrowed from many of the practices already established in the professional military schools of Europe. Civilian educators and military officers alike visited these schools on several occasions during the 19th century and brought back concepts and materials that were then adapted to the unique political conditions and social attitudes extant during different periods of the U.S. experience.

The earliest European influences on PME in the United States were French. Much of the existing professional literature was written in French; and the military reputation established by French armies in the Napoleonic Wars, coupled with America's philosophical attraction to France's revolutionary spirit, made its military literature particularly appealing. Moreover, the impressive performance of French military specialists and the overall contribution of French forces to the American Revolution were still fresh in the national conscience. Hence, when public-spirited citizens and professional soldiers of the newly independent American republic recognized the shortcomings of their embryonic national defense establishment, they naturally looked toward French concepts and practice for help.

As one of Europe's major continental powers and having developed one of the better-organized central administrative structures among European governments, France had in place perhaps the most extensive and systematic patterns of military schools to train officers in the early 19th century. Having pioneered in the development of mathematics and mathematically based education, useful in serving an extensive system of public works, France also led Europe in the systematic schooling of military engineers. It had established its first military engineering schools during the 17th century and its national school, at Mézières, in 1749. It had also applied its scientific talent to the development of Europe's most highly regarded artillery professionals. The royal government had established a series of early artillery schools in a number of major garrison towns and, in 1756, had created an advanced, central artillery college at La Fère. (Ironically, France's Royal Army did not always utilize this expertise to tactical advantage, largely because of the subordination of small artillery units to individual infantry regiments.)

After a few years of the anti-intellectual policies of France's early revolutionary governments, leaders of the Convention recognized that nation's need for basic scientific education and, in 1794, founded what soon became l'École Polytechnique. A central college of basic engineering studies, the Polytechnic launched the careers of generations of canal and harbor planners, road and bridge builders, and designers of military fortifications. After 1795, young men aspiring to artillery careers also received their basic scientific education at this institution.

Under Napoleon, the provision of a basic military education for all officer candidates became more routinized, and a system was established whereby newly commissioned officers could pass directly into military schools of application for more advanced study. The Polytechnic became more military in character, and a parallel precommissioning institution for aspiring infantry and cavalry officers was provided at St. Cyr. The separate schools of application for artillery and military engineering were combined in one central institution at Metz, and a similar facility for advanced cavalry training was established at Saumar. A school to train army officers for the staff corps was added after restoration of the Bourbon monarchy.

By contrast, in the U.S. Congress, there still existed considerable hostility to the idea of a standing army of professionals and, hence, resistance to continuous federal provision for institutions to educate military officers. Despite vigorous advocacy of a military academy that would serve as the intellectual foundation for a professional officer corps, from national figures such as George Washington and Alexander Hamilton, early congresses were willing only to provide for a professional Corps of Artillerists and Engineers. In that same spirit, in 1802, the Congress authorized conversion of this body, already located at West Point, to a Corps of Engineers to include ten cadets and "constitute a military academy," with the Chief Engineer to act as its superintendent. Clearly, the Congress then was intent on not providing an educational institution for the Army as a whole. This attitude was manifest even by the Secretary of War, 1808–1813, who failed to order newly appointed cadets to report for duty and dispersed many of those already at West Point, along with their instructors, to perform service elsewhere.

By the time James Madison took office as President in 1813, America's only military school had been suffering from administrative neglect. Facilities at West Point were barely adequate and textbooks practically nonexistent. In April 1812, perhaps in a surge of wartime fervor, Congress had provided for permanent professorships in mathematics, natural philosophy, and engineering and directed that the teaching staff no longer be detailed to duties away from the academy. It had also increased the authorization of cadets to 250. But much more was needed to improve the teaching program.

Significant improvement came via France. In 1815, President Madison detailed two American Army officers to France for two years to study educational practices there and to assemble a collection of military textbooks and other teaching materials for use at West Point. One of these was Brevet Major Sylvanus Thayer, who, upon his return, would be assigned as its new superinten dent. Trained as an engineer by contemporary American standards, Thayer's primary interest was in l'École Polytechnique. Returning to the Military Academy in 1817, he instituted many new program features modeled after Polytechnic academic routine and classroom practices. Before leaving France, Thayer and his companion, a Lt. Colonel McRee, also visited and studied the curriculum and routines of the School of Application for Artillery and Engineering, at Metz.

Whereas French practices had a prompt influence at West Point, their impact on American interest in military schools of application was much less immediate. Despite some U.S. civilian and military officials questioning openly the adequacy of training provided for the young nation's military leaders following the clash with Britain in 1812–1813, even the Army's leadership was not motivated to provide advanced professional education for its commissioned officers. It was not until General Theodore Jesup, the service's Quartermaster General, convinced Secretary of War John C. Calhoun of the need that steps were taken in that direction. In a 1823 letter to Calhoun, he wrote, "The importance of a school of practice is too obvious to require demonstration. Without such an establishment, uniformity of discipline cannot be expected, nor can the government be sufficiently acquainted with the character, capacity, and attainments of its officers to be able to employ them to advantage in the event of war."

Jesup's plea struck a responsive chord in Calhoun, himself an advocate of a professionally trained officer corps. In the following April, ten of the Army's companies of artillery were ordered to Fortress Monroe—protecting the harbor at Norfolk, Virginia—and reformed as America's first military school of application. Two years later, a similar school of infantry was established when four companies of the Army's Third Infantry regiment were ordered from Wisconsin to join several companies of the Sixth Infantry at Jefferson Barracks, Missouri. Unlike the Artillery School of Application, however, the infantry school, commanded by Colonel Henry Leavenworth, was short-lived. Nearly a month *before* Leavenworth was notified that a shipment of textbooks was being sent to the school, most of the garrison at Jefferson Barracks was deployed to the Upper Missouri territory for duty on the frontier.

Although no other Army schools were established until after the Civil War, the U.S. Navy created a permanent institution to educate and train its young officers. Unlike the Army's schools, the Navy's inspiration and program concepts were homegrown. Brought to a head by the hanging in 1842 of a mutinous midshipman in training aboard the brig *Somers*, public support swelled for the establishment of a permanent naval school. The strength of this support came from the influential eastern seaboard states whose sons were the main beneficiaries of the Navy Department's midshipman appointments. Within the Navy itself, the growing support was accelerated by recognition of the changing professional demands brought by the gradual introduction of steam propulsion for naval ships. The program model for the U.S. Navy's venture into professional education was West Point.

First at the Naval Asylum in the naval yard at Philadelphia and, after 1845, at the new Naval School in Annapolis, Maryland, the academic curriculum provided for young midshipmen appeared very similar to that given the Army Engineer Corps cadets along the banks of the Hudson. Until after the Civil War, the Naval Academy (as it was officially named in 1850) had as its major distinction attention to seamanship and navigation and the substitution of marine engineering for civil engineering. Another related difference was that until 1851, when the school became a four-year institution, much of the instruction was aimed primarily at preparing some of the midshipmen for their promotion examinations to the rank of lieutenant. After that date, the Naval Academy became wholly dedicated to the precommissioning mission.

Following the Civil War, a new emphasis on professional military instruction affected the educational institutions of both U.S. services. Both service academies took on a decidedly more professional military character, with West Point severing its formal relationship with the Corps of Engineers (1866) and the Naval Academy subjecting the control and some of the content of its instructional program to greater professional naval influence. But the new emphasis resulted also in the growth of professional education programs for officers already commissioned.

In the Army, this growth was helped greatly by the enthusiastic support of General William T. Sherman, who was Commanding General from 1869 to 1883. Sherman respected theory and was familiar with the works of some European writers such as Baron Antoine de Jomini and Sir Edward Hamley, but he regarded field experience and practical instruction as more important in the preparation of an officer. Partly in response to his urging, while commander of the Division of the Missouri Territory, the Artillery School of Application was reopened at Fortress Monroe in 1868. As Commanding General, a year later, he presented diplomas to the first graduating class.

His practical bent drew Sherman's attention to the career of Emory Upton, a young West Pointer who had distinguished himself during the Civil War and who had developed a new manual of infantry tactics soon after. Sherman saw to it that Upton was appointed commandant of cadets and instructor in tactics at his alma mater in the early 1870s, during which period Sherman talked occasionally with Upton about tactical options that might be effective in combating the Indians on the Western plains. Sherman thought that the British experience in their military campaigns in India might provide some valuable insights and arranged for Upton and two other officers to tour Asia following his duty at

West Point to see firsthand how Asian armies were organized and employed. Following the Prussian victories over the armies of Austria (1864) and France (1871), Sherman had also developed a strong interest in Prussian military organization and methods and instructed Upton and his party to return from the Orient by way of Europe. Upton's enthusiasm over his observations of Prussia's system of mobilization and its provisions for the professional education of its officer corps helped move Sherman toward some decisions that affected significantly the future of the military profession in the United States.

What had impressed Upton so strongly about the Prussian military education system was the careful articulation among the different levels of instruction and between formal schooling and the evolution of an officer's career. Officer candidates were first chosen on the basis of their performance on a highly discriminating qualifying examination following a broad general education conducted either in the public schools or in cadet houses administered by the military. Then, after completion of a year's service with a regiment or, in some cases, of two years at the Upper Cadet School in Berlin, chosen candidates entered a year of intensive preparation in military studies prior to the officer's precommissioning examination. Line officers then entered into duty with an assigned regiment while artillery and engineer officers completed two more years of combined theoretical and practical studies. After three years' duty with their respective regiments, officers from both the line and scientific corps were encouraged to compete for admission to the Kriegsakademie, a senior war college program, completion of which was necessary for appointment to the general or field staff. In this senior school, both advanced military studies—theoretical *and* practical—and general studies were provided.

Not long after Upton's return from Europe, Sherman issued a series of command directives that expanded markedly the officer education efforts of the U.S. Army. Wary of the determination of post–Civil War congresses to keep the Army small and on short rations, Sherman was careful to avoid requesting congressional authorization for new schools. Each was to be operated within the limitations of regular garrison funds. High on Sherman's priority list was the newly reopened Artillery School, to which he appointed Emory Upton as "superintendent of theoretical instruction" following that officer's return in 1877. Next came the School of Application for Infantry and Cavalry which he established at Fort Leavenworth, Kansas, in 1881, following a series of petitions from Maj. General John Pope pointing out the advantages provided by the size of this large post and the presence of cheap federal prison labor. To assure that its tactical concepts became disseminated throughout the Army, Sherman ordered each regiment of cavalry and infantry to assign one of its lieutenants to the new school every two years. Meanwhile, a group of engineer-officers at Willetts Point, New York, had organized a technical society to perpetuate the study of military engineering now that West Point had been taken away from the Corps. Sherman encouraged their efforts and helped the growth of this enterprise toward becoming a full-fledged educational institution; it was formally designated the Engineer

School of Application in the second year following Sherman's retirement. By the turn of century, these innovations were followed by the establishment of several other army specialized branch schools and schools of application.

The U.S. Navy's sole school of application during this period was the Torpedo School at Newport, Rhode Island, but its atmosphere was rather like that of a factory and the focus was highly technical rather than professionally military. In fact, the Navy's educational concerns following the Civil War were directed mainly at technical matters—principally the problems created by the Navy's gradual transition to steam propulsion. Even before the war's end, Congress had authorized a course at the Naval Academy for Assistant Engineers, to be selected by competitive examination from young men 18 to 22 years of age with some previous scientific training and experience in the fabrication of steam engines. In 1866, a class of two acting third assistant engineers were ordered to the academy for instruction, but several years elapsed before the provisions of the 1864 act were implemented again. The academy experimented for more than twenty years with special "engineer" programs before abolishment of the Navy's Engineer Corps dictated that all line officers also be qualified for engineering duties. In the meantime, the demand for technical expertise had moved beyond that reasonably anticipated from a typical junior officer. Beginning in the 1870s, a few officers annually were sent to Britain's Royal Naval College to study naval construction, and the growing requirement for more advanced technical instruction began to generate appeals for a naval school to satisfy it.

Meanwhile, largely through the vision and persistence of Commodore Stephen B. Luce, the Navy was moving ahead toward formal study of the broader science of naval warfare. Luce had been assigned to the Atlantic squadron, home-ported in Norfolk, Virginia, during the period of Emory Upton's tour at Fortress Monroe, and they had become good friends. Luce had become intrigued by Upton's enthusiastic descriptions of Prussian military institutions, and the latter officer had encouraged Luce in his interests in a program of professional education suitable as preparation for higher naval command. Through Luce's urging, the Naval War College was established at Newport, Rhode Island, and he was named its first president. Despite his bringing in such outstanding military scholars as Alfred Thayer Mahan and the Army's Tasker Bliss as professors, however, Luce fought an uphill battle to set the institution on a steady course. Opposition was strong within the naval officer corps, among those responsible for personnel assignments, and among the naval secretaries' closest advisors, almost resulting in the school's abolishment in 1893. Even though the War College was preserved, naval education had not yet attained the same degree of acceptance as the counterpart activities in the Army.

While the nation's regular armed forces were developing their programs of professional education and training, important events had also been taking place at the level of state government.

In the academy's early years, West Point graduates were primarily expected to become citizen-soldier officers, who would train the nation's reserve forces in peacetime and then lead America's citizen-soldier armies to victory in times of war. By 1820, however, this notion had all but died. Consequently, the task for educating reserve officers, as envisioned by the leaders of the new republic, settled on the shoulders of the civilian colleges of the individual states. The first example of this trend occurred in New England, in many respects a result of improvements made at the Military Academy.

In 1819, not long after Captain Alden Partridge was replaced as the West Point superintendent by Major Sylvanus Thayer, Partridge founded the American Literary, Scientific, and Military Academy at Norwich, Vermont. This first private institution for military education in the United States served as a model for other institutions advocated by Partridge in a plan called the American System of Education. Acting out of his newly heightened conviction that standing armies represent potential threats to civil liberties and republican institutions, he promoted his conception vigorously through speaking engagements and private correspondence with members of Congress and other influential citizens. In a political era dominated by Jacksonian views, Partridge found receptive audiences. Nearly twenty schools implementing his plan and following the Norwich model came into existence throughout the United States. Not all survived, but several did.

The most notable Norwich-like schools surviving the Civil War were the Virginia Military Institute (founded in 1839) and The Citadel (1842). In the mid-1830s, Partridge had helped cultivate state legislative support for both institutions by delivering lectures and meeting with state officials in Virginia and South Carolina (as well as other southern states). Both schools based their early programs on the concept of combining "literary, scientific, and military education" embodied in the Partridge concept of a proper education for the citizen-soldier. Other southern military colleges, with one exception, were not reopened following the war. The exception, the State Seminary of Learning and Military Academy, founded near Alexandria, Louisiana, in 1855, reopened at Baton Rouge as the Louisiana State University in 1869.

In its new identity, the Louisiana institution was one of the beneficiaries of new national legislation authorizing federal assistance to support at least one college in each state that included instruction in agriculture, mechanical arts, and military tactics. The Morrill Land Grant Act of July 1862, named for its sponsor, Congressman Justin Morrill from Partridge's Vermont, provided for grants of public lands that could be used by the states "to endow and support" such institutions. The Civil War's demonstrated need for trained officers for the North's hastily raised militia units was a major motivation for this wartime legislation. While the proportion of academy graduates in the tiny Regular Army officer corps had grown from 15 percent in 1817 to 76 percent by 1860, very few ever served in the militia. Postwar legislation (1869) strengthened the initial law by giving the President the authority to assign an Army officer to each land-grant institution to provide the military instruction. In 1890 Morrill himself, then a senator, sponsored new legislation to increase the federal government's annual support and make it available also to colleges specifically established for African-American students.

The turn of the century brought significant changes to the education of Regular Army officers as well. Alarmed by the confusion and ineptitude shown in organizing and supporting a multidivisional army and deploying it overseas in the Spanish-American War, President William McKinley's (and later, Theodore Roosevelt's) Secretary of War, Elihu Root, recognized the need for several staff and command reforms. Convinced of the merit of changes being advocated by disciples of the late Emory Upton, he initiated internal executive actions and obtained the necessary legislation to reorganize the Army, provide for a trained reserve, and create a general staff. Root also established an Army War College, located in Washington, D.C., and organized an articulated system of PME that provided appropriate preparation for the different stages of an officer's career. The latter included restructuring of the Fort Leavenworth schools to provide for a full-fledged General Service and Staff College, in which selected Reserve officers as well as Regular graduates of the Army's School of the Line could receive a second year of professional education. All this was accomplished between 1899 and 1904.

The provision for some advanced military education for Reserve officers reflected a basic weakness in the contemporary provisions for a trained national reserve force. The Land Grant Act of 1862 had, in effect, passed responsibility for the precommissioning education of reserve officers to the states and their basically civilian institutions. And the quality of this education varied widely, depending on the local curricular policies and the teaching competence and organizational skills of the local instructor. Despite the President's authority to assign Regular Army officers to each of the land-grant schools, fewer than 100 were ever assigned. In the spirit of preparedness, which developed in the years prior to U.S. entry into World War I, congressional recognition of the shortcomings in the nation's unofficial reserve training provisions led to passage of the National Defense Act of 1916. Among other provisions, this act enabled federal authorities to manage reserve officer training in the colleges at a national level, to award Reserve commissions at the time of graduation, and to pool the graduates in the Officer Reserve Corps for potential call-up in a national emergency.

Full implementation of the authority to form a Reserve Officers' Training Corps (ROTC) for the Army awaited the end of "the war to end all wars." Beginning in 1920, ROTC units were established in 135 colleges, with Regular Army officers and noncommissioned officers assigned to them as well as many secondary schools as instructors and administrative staff. Similar authority to establish a naval ROTC program was provided in 1925. By the time Pearl Harbor was bombed in 1941, the Army's program—which included Army Air Corps units—had turned out the bulk of over 106,000 Reserve officers estimated as available for active service. The Naval ROTC had graduated reservists from 27 different campuses and had established cooperative relationships with the civilian higher-education community that would enable the Navy to establish other campus-based officer training programs later in the war.

Meanwhile, the professional education programs of both services had been modified to reflect the rapid development of their respective weapon system technologies. The Navy was first to be confronted with the problem. The advantages demonstrated by steam-propelled vessels in Civil War blockade and riverine operations had indicated the importance of that technology for the future development of naval power. And although the postwar congresses had been reticent to commit the funds for new steam-powered construction, the Navy leadership responded to the need for officers trained in steam engineering.

The Navy's first approach, during the early 1870s, was to assemble annual classes of cadet-engineers at the Naval Academy to study special concentrations of applied mathematics and engineering subjects. These classes were kept apart from the regular cadet-midshipmen until 1874 when the program was expanded to four years and the cadet-engineers (now 25 annually) were incorporated into the regular battalion of officer candidates and some common classes. In 1882, however, Congress intervened by abolishing the "midshipman/engineer" distinction and insisting that all students admitted to the academy enter through the regular congressional appointment system—just one of several provisions to the Naval Personnel Act of 1882 that were crafted to deal with a growing surplus of commissioned officers. One result, however, was the reinstatement of a common academy curriculum and a necessary reduction of engineering studies, ironically just at the time when Congress authorized construction of the U.S. Navy's first all-steel hulled cruisers. This situation was relieved somewhat in 1889, when the academy was permitted to offer a special senior-year curriculum for those "naval cadets" opting for careers in the Navy's Engineer Corps, but this provision ceased ten years later with Congress's disestablishment of that organization.

With the advances in naval technology developing faster than a common-purpose academy's capacity to provide sufficient instruction in all its current elements, the Navy looked to supplementary approaches to the problem. Not long after the Personnel Act of 1882, naval officers were selected for specialized engineering studies in civilian universities. The Navy had already begun the practice of sending two or more Naval Academy graduates annually to study in the advanced ship-building course at Britain's Royal Naval College; so the precedent for special postgraduate educational assignments had been established. In 1893, Rear Admiral Stephen B. Luce, by then retired from the active Navy, arranged for the creation of a school for naval architecture at the Massachusetts Institute of Technology that provided advanced education for officers in the Navy's technical corps. Four years later, the same year in which the British Admiralty decided to no longer admit foreign students to its naval college, a postgraduate course in naval architecture was established at the U.S. Naval

Academy for selected members of its graduating cadet-engineers. That program, along with the naval architecture course, ended with elimination of the Navy's Engineer Corps in 1899.

Meanwhile, debate was under way within the Navy Department whether advanced technical education in civilian universities or in the Navy's own schools would best serve its needs. With Congress by then committed to the construction of a modern, much-enlarged navy, the issue was resolved by 1909, when a School of Marine Engineering was established at the Naval Academy for a class of ten officers. At first under the direction of regular academy department heads, it was redesignated the Postgraduate Department in 1912 and began assembling a separate faculty and expanding its course offerings. Closed for two years during World War I, it reopened in 1919 as the Naval Postgraduate School and was given responsibility for administering naval use of civilian university programs as well as its own resident instruction.

Advanced technical education for U.S. Army officers began in the Corps of Engineers and the Signal Corps early in the 20th century with officers selected for study in civilian universities. But it was the development of military aviation and growth of the Army Air Service following the First World War that gave impetus to provision for advanced technical instruction within the Army's system of PME. Within less than three weeks following the Armistice, the chief of the Air Service's Airplane Engineering Division recommended to the service's director-general that an Air School of Application be established at McCook Field, Dayton, Ohio, to provide career pilots with the engineering knowledge appropriate to their profession. The recommendation was approved early in 1919, and the first class of seven officers entered training in November. The one-year course included aerodynamics, thermodynamics, electrical engineering, materials, and a number of maintenance-oriented practical studies. As became a frequent practice in subsequent years at the Ohio school, a few outstanding students were selected for additional engineering study in civilian institutions.

In 1920, another Air Service school was established at Langley Field, Virginia, to provide air officers with a more general military education appropriate for their specialty. This course also imparted some knowledge of technology important for airmen but was designed primarily to prepare experienced air officers for operational command functions. Ten years after its founding, with the creation of the Army Air Corps, this school was moved to Maxwell Field, Alabama, where it became the Air Corps Tactical School. It was at this school that the concepts of strategic bombardment and tactical ground support applied during World War II were developed more fully into air power doctrine.

During the war, most of the PME institutions were closed for the period of emergency, with a few exceptions, as the services placed primary emphasis on short-term training activities. Both the Army and Navy greatly expanded their pilot training programs, opening new flight schools to augment the traditional programs conducted at Randolph Field, Texas, and Pensacola, Florida. Relying heavily on Reserve officers commissioned through its peacetime ROTC programs as instructional cadre, the Army created a number of officer candidate schools beginning in July 1941 to officer its rapidly expanding force structure. It also accelerated the basic courses at its established branch schools for the newly commissioned officers and created new branch schools for armor, tank destroyer, and anti-aircraft artillery training.

The Navy, whose increased officer personnel requirements were less immediate and geared to an extended ship construction schedule, followed a somewhat different course. Having met its early fleet expansion needs with commissioned Naval ROTC graduates and selection of qualified college graduates for precommissioning training in newly created Naval Reserve midshipman schools, the Navy had by mid-1942 also turned to the nation's colleges for help. By year's end, it announced formation of the V-12 program whereby a pool of young men selected as Navy or Marine Corps officer candidates would be made draft exempt, study in regular college undergraduate programs—receiving minimal military instruction—and prepare for timely entrance to one of several reserve midshipman schools for their precommissioning training.

Meanwhile, all the services began to plan for the postwar era as the conflict moved toward a close. In September 1944, the Headquarters, U.S. Army Air Forces (USAAF) elaborated on a study of future educational requirements for air officers prepared several months earlier by its training command and submitted its recommendations to the War Department. In July of that year, a board of senior naval officers and civilian educators headed by Rear Admiral William Pye reported to the Secretary of the Navy on its study of postwar education for career naval officers. Besides recommending comprehensive systems of periodic PME for their respective officers' career development, both reporting bodies went beyond their respective service needs and proposed creation of a new institution for selected officers from all the services to focus on the joint employment of all military arms.

One of the few PME institutions which remained active during the war—in fact, created in June 1943—was the Army-Navy Staff College (ANSCOL), established at the urging of USAAF Chief, General "Hap" Arnold to prepare officers from all services for command and staff functions associated with joint commands and joint operations. Shortly before the war ended, the ANSCOL staff was charged by the Joint Chiefs with drawing up a plan for joint military education in the postwar era. Its submission provided the basis for the Joint Chiefs' own plan, which provided for joint education at all levels of officer PME. It called for at least 30 percent of the student rosters in PME courses made available to officers after both six and twelve years of commissioned service to consist of officers from services different than that of the school itself. At the highest level of PME, the Chiefs' plan cited ANSCOL as a model for a new, permanent Army-Navy institution in Washington to provide "a broad appreciation of the inter-relationship between national and international policy and the military force by which such policies are sustained and enforced." The plan also called for a joint industrial college and recommended a close association between the Army-Navy college and a school for foreign service officers should the State Department decide to establish one.

In November 1945, the War Department appointed a board of general officers, the Gerow Board, to develop a plan for the postwar education of Army officers. It requested separate plans for schools appropriate for each of the major commands and for officers serving at even higher command levels. Reporting in February 1946, the board recommended a three-tiered structure with the bottom tier controlled respectively by the ground forces, air forces, and service forces and offering alternative schools within each for officers of different branches and career specialties. For the middle tier, the board recommended an "Armed Forces College" for officers of all Army branches, hopefully also to include naval officers, to prepare for command and staff duties associated with combined arms and joint operations.

At the top the Gerow Board called for a "National Security University" consisting of five equal-status schools: a national war college; an industrial college; an administrative college; an intelligence college; and a State Department college. All were to maintain a joint-service focus in their respective programs. Notably, the middle-level college, three from the top tier, and the overarching university structure would actually come to pass in subsequent years, albeit with somewhat different names and under control of a permanent Joint Chiefs organization made subordinate to a civilian Secretary of Defense.

The emphasis on joint education is one of three major developments in the character of PME during the postwar period. The other two are the broadening of curriculum content in the senior-level schools and the abandonment of a totally prescribed curriculum at the service academies. Certainly, there has been substantial ferment as well in the lower and middle-tier institutions for service-oriented officer education, which resumed operation following World War II, as will be demonstrated in a number of the essays that follow. But many of these changes were short-lived or later modified and represented little change in the basic purposes of the schools themselves.

The importance attached to joint PME emerged directly from wartime experience and gained strength during a number of more limited conflicts and crisis-response episodes of the cold war era. By the late 1940s, experience with joint operations and close interaction with allies had convinced General Dwight D. Eisenhower and other wartime leaders of the need for greater attention to joint matters in the Army's professional schools. Their influence was reflected in the reports of the Army's Gerow Board and of the wartime Chiefs of Staff. The Navy was not as enthusiastic regarding joint initiatives, in spite of the recommendation of its own Pye Board, probably more of a reflection of its larger postwar concern over the prospects of losing independent cabinet status and certain administrative functions to a single, controlling secretary of a department of defense. Still, it did quickly endorse the establishment of a high-level joint institution, the National War College.

Key events occurred quickly. The National War College (NWC) came into existence on February 5, 1946, almost before the ink was dry on the Gerow Board's report. Two months later, the Army's industrial college—reopened in 1943 and operating in the Pentagon—became the joint Industrial College of the Armed Forces (ICAF) and joined the war college within the grounds of Fort Lesley McNair. By August, the Navy had endorsed the Army's concept of a permanent mid-level institution to prepare officers from all services for joint staff assignments and even offered to house the new Armed Forces Staff College (AFSC) at its operating base in Norfolk, Virginia. Thus, within a year from Japan's surrender ending World War II, the United States had established three colleges dedicated to joint PME. Both the NWC and AFSC were placed under supervision of the *wartime* Joint Chiefs of Staff.

The basic structure for effective joint education was in place even before the defense establishment itself was restructured through the National Security Acts of 1947 and 1949 and the creation of a Department of Defense (DoD). Indeed, both developments stemmed from similar sets of concerns about the demonstrated need for better interservice cooperation and joint combat operations. But soon-to-develop squabbles over service roles and missions, accentuated by continuing competition for the lion's share of limited defense expenditures, convinced numerous observers over the years that the availability of joint schools was not sufficient to bring about the harmony and effective interaction desired. Competition for combat missions continued in Washington and in the theater during the Vietnam War and affected both strategy and operations. Crises requiring rapid military responses in the late '70s and early '80s revealed critical shortcomings in the U.S. ability to assemble and employ appropriate joint capabilities effectively. Structural features within the DoD that permitted the services to take harmful unilateral actions and encouraged parochial attitudes were seen to be at fault.

Knowledgeable members of Congress set out to remedy the situation, resulting in the DoD Reorganization (Goldwater-Nichols)Act of 1986. This act limited or constrained the operational advisory and force-programming roles of the service Chiefs and strengthened the operational planning and joint command roles of the JCS chairman and the theater commanders-in-chief (CinCs). In effect, the JCS chairman was made military czar of all joint matters, including joint education. Moreover, Goldwater-Nichols established requirements for service in joint duty assignments before any officer could advance to a senior leadership position and mandated new procedures for the selection, education, and assignment of joint duty officers. All intermediate and senior PME institutions operated by the services were required to include substantial units of joint subject matter in their curricula, and the programs of the joint colleges were to be reviewed regularly by the Secretary of Defense, assisted by the JCS chairman, to effect needed enhancement of their preparation of student-officers for joint assignments.

Implementation of these statutory requirements resulted in procedures, administered by elements of the Joint Staff, for examining and certifying PME institutions relative to their meeting the prescribed standards for joint education. The DoD was assisted in this process by a special panel on military education (Skelton Panel) of the House Committee on Armed Services that surveyed the entire range of intermediate and senior PME institutions and recommended measures for DoD consideration. Many of these measures were adopted as elements of departmental PME policy and became operative in the 1990s.

The strengthening of joint elements in their programs was the most recent development in the general broadening of the senior PME curricula in the post–World War II era. But the broadening process itself began not long after the war colleges reopened, in part because of recognition that the United States would be immersed as never before in the politics and economic recovery actions of postwar international security initiatives. The process began also because of the experience of senior officers assigned to positions in government agencies where the main concerns were not even primarily military. It had become quite evident that the traditional war college curriculum dealing with service-oriented operational issues, combined arms employment, military command, leadership skills, consumer logistics, and even Defense Department and broader national security organization would no longer provide adequate preparation for senior-level responsibilities.

In the early 1950s, two political scientists at Dartmouth College, John Masland and Laurence Radway, undertook a detailed study of military education as part of their continuing interest in the role of the military in government. While proving important historical background on the growth of military participation in primarily civilian governmental offices, they focused particularly on those elements of existing PME programs intended to prepare officers for duties requiring them to participate in the formulation of national policy.

By the mid-1950s these scholars had found that "[t]he War Colleges now define the responsibilities of the senior professional officer in a broad context of political, economic, and social relationships" and had developed curricula accordingly. In varying degrees, all the senior colleges considered operational plans and military policy questions in terms of employing all the nation's resources and of their political, economic, and social implications. In addition to the more traditional studies, the subject matter of the college programs now included national strategy, supplier logistical considerations, international relations, American government and politics, and some consideration of economics, although most of these curricular elements were devoid of much attention to historical perspective.

More recently, the war colleges have given considerable emphasis also to military history, particularly following the 1989 report and recommendations of the Skelton Panel. In varying degrees, their emphasis has included attention to past military mistakes as well as successes, often requiring attention to the broader contextual factors operating at the time, thus incorporating historical perspective on nonmilitary considerations as well. This curricular trend has been facilitated by reducing the reliance on visiting lecturers and providing students with more opportunity for elective courses within the regular college programs.

With a general broadening of war college curricula, a demand was created for a different and better academically qualified faculty. Rather than, as Masland and Radway observed, faculty members serving primarily as planners and administrators of program units and seminar groups, the colleges needed more academically trained subject matter specialists. Even the college staffs themselves acknowledged in the mid-1960s that their heavy reliance on formal, plenary-session lecturers, even including the usual opportunity for student questions, was far from ideal (a finding also reached by a number of different reviewing groups). With due regard for the administrative problems necessarily entailed, the war colleges and their sponsoring agencies have responded to the demand for better faculty in a significant way. Instead of the token number of civilian academics found by Masland and Radway at a few of the war colleges, some of whom were visiting scholars brought on to advise and to present occasional lectures (a scene not very different from the numbers and pattern of utilization observed by the Skelton Panel 30 years later), well-qualified academics now substantially populate the war college faculties. At the Naval War College which, unlike the others, has had civilian faculty hiring authority since 1957, over one-third of its faculty is civilian. The Air War College, which has had that authority only since Goldwater-Nichols, now has 30 civilian professors, all but three of which hold the Ph.D. Both the National War College and the Industrial College have faculties that are nearly 60 percent civilian.

The third major PME development of the postwar era occurred at the service academies, within the academic portion of their curricula. The professional military instruction at each of the schools underwent changes as well, as new equipment and techniques were introduced in their respective services; but these changes did not alter the fundamental nature and purposes of this precommissioning indoctrination and training.

The impetus for academic change began even before the Second World War as heightened admissions standards and world conditions brought larger numbers of better-prepared students to both West Point and Annapolis. By 1939, for example, over 52 percent of West Point's Corps of Cadets had completed at least one year of civilian college. Following the war, the problem of challenging young officer candidates who arrived with substantial academic backgrounds continued, but movement toward an effective solution got a major boost with the establishment of a brand-new institution, the U.S. Air Force Academy (USAFA).

Although highly controversial in the early postwar years, the idea of providing yet another service academy received a strong recommendation from the Service Academy (Stearns) Board in 1949. Board members, a substantial number of whom were civilian career educators, were unanimous in their opinion that a four-year undergraduate academy was essential to each military service for motivating young officer candidates for full careers of national service and for defining the ethical and professional standards for the service at large. However, the program of site selection and construction for the new academy were delayed until after the Korean War and the presidency of Dwight Eisenhower, who had served as deputy chairman on the Stearns Board. Meanwhile, the fledgling U.S. Air Force continued to obtain its newly commissioned officers from graduates of West Point, the Naval Academy, and the Air Force ROTC and, in needed skill-areas, through direct entry.

While the Air Force Academy's original curriculum, drawn up by a series of Air Force planning boards, was modeled largely after that at West Point, steps were taken to move away from the traditional, totally prescribed series of courses before its first operative academic year had been completed. Plans were made in the spring of 1956 for a program of curriculum enrichment to begin that fall. At first consisting of accelerated versions of required courses, enrichment in the second semester of 1956–57 made available a few electives in both mathematics and the humanities for academically qualifying volunteers that were in addition to their regular courses. By the following year, arrangements were in place whereby advanced students could choose among a larger variety of electives to replace regular courses of which they had validated their mastery through examinations or for which they had transferred credits from civilian colleges. By the time the Air Force Academy's first cadet-class graduated, plans were completed to offer qualified students from subsequent classes a limited number of academic majors.

The chief architect of the new academy's program of curriculum enrichment, Dean Robert McDermott, Brig. General, USAF, who had reflected upon his own frustration while a West Point cadet, perceived a wastage of human capital and stifled potential in forcing all students into a common, lock-step curriculum, regardless of their past academic achievement.

Meanwhile, the older academies, both of whom had experimented with alternative course options for upperclassmen and had relied on sectioning-by-merit to enable accelerated progress through prescribed subject matter, were taking notice of the program developments in Colorado. Many of their junior-year students had spent exchange weeks at the Air Force Academy, an annual practice, and reported their observations. A newly appointed superintendent at the Naval Academy and a faculty/staff committee from West Point visited USAFA to observe and discuss the operation of the enrichment program. And, since 1958, all the academy superintendents and key staff members were gathering annually to confer on common problems.

As a consequence, as the enrichment process gradually evolved, both the Air Force Academy and the Naval Academy were offering full-fledged academic majors to all students by academic year 1969–70. West Point, for its own reasons, was more cautious in its move away from the traditional service academy approach. It had nonetheless made electives available to all cadets throughout the 1960s and encouraged their grouping in significant subject-matter concentrations by the end of that decade. It too moved to full academic majors in academic year 1983–84.

Although not affecting the academic programs of the service academies or the nature of their military training programs, one other development of the postwar decades made significant changes in the cadet and midshipman communities—and in the American military services in general. The U.S. Congress, in October 1975, enacted legislation providing for the admission of young women in all federal service academies beginning with the following academic year. Accordingly, as the classes of 1980 reported to their respective academies in the summer of 1976, each included a female contingent. Only the Coast Guard had provided training for women officer candidates at its academy previously, as a temporary wartime measure. So each had to make available the necessary physical accommodations and plan for the inclusion of women in its training regime. Moreover, each of the services had to make appropriate faculty and staff personnel adjustments; for example, the Air Force decided to detail 15 female junior officers to the Cadet Wing to serve as surrogate upperclassmen and role models for the entering women cadets. Despite several adjustments of living conditions, controversy over appropriate training standards, and patterns of discrimination by their male counterparts in the early years, women cadets and midshipmen have become established and significant members of the student bodies at each of the service academies, undergoing the same regimen as their male counterparts.

Professional military education in the United States has truly evolved in significant ways since the early 19th century. This does not mean, however, that all the controversies that have arisen over the years have been put to rest. Solutions have been applied, some more effective than others, but some of the earlier criticisms, albeit with new labels, are still alive. The entries that follow describe the evolution in more detail and shed needed light on some of the controversies.

THE DICTIONARY

A

AIR COMMAND AND STAFF COLLEGE. The U.S. Air Force's intermediate service school, charged with preparing midcareer officers to employ air and space power at the operational level of war and for service in higher-level command and staff positions. The Air Command and Staff College (ACSC) is part of the Air University, at Maxwell Air Force Base, Alabama.

With the successful conclusion of World War II, General Henry H. Arnold,* General Carl A. Spaatz, and the leadership of the U.S. Army Air Forces anticipated the creation of not only a separate service but also a distinct professional military education (PME) organization for air force officers. This new PME system, known as Air University,* featured a three-tiered structure for officer education. ACSC's antecedent, the Air Command and Staff School, comprised the middle rung and enrolled its first class of 103 officers on September 3, 1946. The school's first commandant was Maj. General Earl W. Barnes, who had commanded the XIII Fighter Group in the Pacific war.

Although originally intended as a single comprehensive nine-month course, the Command and Staff School went through a number of organizational changes during its early years of operation. Some of the changes were a response to outside events; others were part of the process of aligning the various PME schools within the Air University; still others stemmed from the recommendations of civilian and military oversight panels. With the outbreak of the Korean War, the academic year was reduced to fourteen weeks, as the school was directed to teach a number of Special Staff School courses. In 1954, the nine-month program was restored, and five years later the Command and Staff School was redesignated Command and Staff College, with a final name change (to the present ACSC) taking place in 1962.

The curriculum at ACSC also underwent considerable revision. The initial course of study was understandably influenced by the recent wartime experience. The program was divided among seven academic "divisions" (Operations, Logistics, Army, Navy, Intelligence, New Developments, and Military Management), reflecting the march of aviation technology, the presumed primacy of strategic air operations, and the need for developing staff and management skills. The 1946 mission statement spoke not only of the need to prepare officers for "command of groups, wings, and for staff duties" but also to "stimulate constructive thought" about the employment of military aviation. It also aspired to impart an awareness of the "capabilities and limitations" of ground and naval forces, and to "acquaint officers with world affairs which may influence military thought." With only cosmetic modifications, this mission statement has remained essentially unchanged.

From 1950 to 1954, the school's curriculum changed drastically as part of the Air Force's response to the exigencies of the Korean War. Air Command and Staff School took responsibility for two shorter staff courses as well as a number of specialized courses, taken by (for example) intelligence or logistics officers in lieu of the general Field Officer Course. It was not until 1954 that the school returned to a single generalized course for midcareer officers.

From 1954 to 1963, the curriculum emphasized the bipolar world of the intensifying cold war. Two broad curriculum phases, Air Power Fundamentals and USAF Operations, contained smaller blocks of instruction such as The Enemy, The Free World, Military Doctrine, and Technological Developments, with staff-skills courses (speaking, writing, and problem solving) distributed throughout. In 1963, yet another curriculum reorganization allocated increased attention to the principles and techniques of military management.

Increased U.S. involvement in Southeast Asia left its mark on ACSC in a number of ways. Although the curricular focus remained on "conventional" and "strategic" (i.e., nuclear) air warfare, the emphasis on counterinsurgency operations noticeably increased. In 1971, for example, the course devoted 50 hours to the study of counterinsurgency (as compared with 55 hours for Strategic Offensive and Defensive Forces). Several critics of ACSC and Air Force PME in general have cited a failure to study the lessons of the Vietnam War; for some years after U.S. withdrawal from Southeast Asia, there was little in the way of substantive post-Vietnam reassessment in the Air Force's PME system. Many saw the failure to craft an air power strategy appropriate for the war and reliance on questionable measures of success such as "sortie generation" and truck-kill statistics as stemming in part from an overemphasis on "managerial" values within the Air Force. Even commentators who were not sympathetic to this particular line of reasoning noted a need to "put 'war' back into the war colleges."

Air University in general, and ACSC in particular, received congressional scrutiny in the late 1980s from a House subcommittee headed by Rep. Ike Skelton (D–Missouri). The report of the Skelton Panel* recommended a general raising of academic standards, increased study of military history and classical theory, and an improvement in military and civilian faculty expertise. At ACSC, these efforts were aided by internal reform, initially by two successive commandants, Brig. General Charles D. Link (1989–90) and Brig. General Phillip J. Ford (1990–91). They initiated significant changes to the ACSC curriculum, including a renewed emphasis on military history and air power theory, and inaugurated its first campaign planning course.

The coalition air operations against Iraq during operations Desert Shield and Desert Storm indirectly touched off the most recent major curriculum revision. The catalyst was the arrival as commandant in summer 1992 of Colonel John A. Warden III, the architect of the initial Gulf War air campaign plan, with a mandate from USAF leaders to completely redesign the curriculum: to emphasize the application of the operational art in air warfare and systematic analysis of target systems and (most notably) to expand student reading loads and their use of computers. Accordingly, academic year 1998 provided ten integrated courses, organized around the thought process required to effectively apply air and space power in the emerging international environment. The courses addressed issues from objective formulation through conflict resolution and emphasized the evolution of air power theory, its role in support of the joint forces commander, the capabilities of sister services, the joint planning processes, international relations, and the future of warfare. AFSC students could also take specialized elective courses and were required to complete a thesis project as a graduation requirement. In addition to the resident program, ACSC has always offered a "nonresident," or correspondence, program, to be completed by officers serving in other duty assignments. Formerly a traditional paper product, the nonresident program in 1996 became available on CD-ROM.

In addition to the seminar and lecture program, the school has made extensive use of war game simulations as a teaching tool. In the 1940s and 1950s the school employed "map" or "illustrative" problems, using large mapboards laid out on classroom floors. More sophisticated war games followed. In 1965, a counterinsurgency exercise known as Quick Stitch appeared, followed in 1967 by the more conventional Big Stick war game, in which students were given the opportunity to conduct simulated employment of the latest weaponry. Improvements in computer simulations in the 1980s and 1990s made possible simultaneous play by many seminars against Red Team adversaries at the Air Force Wargaming Institute, often focusing on the Korean Peninsula or the Middle East, reflecting timely national security concerns.

In addition to preparing its graduates for subsequent command and staff assignments, ACSC has, at various times during its existence, played a role in the evolution and refinement of air power doctrine. Indeed, the 1959 school mission statement explicitly included "contribut[ing] to the development of sound Air Force Command and Staff doctrine and practice." ACSC faculty made substantive inputs to the various editions of *Air Force Manual 1–1* (Basic Doctrine), as well as other service and joint doctrine publications. There have also been periodic attempts to use the students and faculty of the school as a "think tank" for solving contemporary air power problems. In 1967–71, ACSC personnel participated in the Air Staff's attempt to analyze the effectiveness of air power in the war in Southeast Asia. More recent attempts by senior Air Force leadership to harness the intellectual resources of ACSC include a 1994 effort to define future space warfare issues, and a 1996 Chief of Staff–sponsored study of the future of air and space power.

Sources:

Michael F. Burke, "History of the Air Command and Staff College: Twenty-fifth (Silver) Anniversary Command Edition," HQ Studies Series No. 41, 1971, unpublished command history in Air University Library, Maxwell AFB, AL.

Marvin I. Cohen and Richard H. Jackson, *History of the Air Command and Staff College* (Maxwell AFB, AL: Office of Information, Headquarters Air University, 1966).

Jerome A. Ennels and Wesley Phillips Newton, *The Wisdom of Eagles: A History of Maxwell Air Force Base* (Montgomery, AL: Black Belt Press, 1997).

James A. Harrold, "A Historical Analysis of Basic Air Force Doctrine Education Within the United States Air Force Air Command and Staff College, 1947–1987," 1987, unpublished thesis in the Air Force Institute of Technology, Wright-Patterson Air Force Base, OH.

Richard R. Muller

AIR CORPS SCHOOL OF ENGINEERING. Founded in 1919 as the Air School of Application, renamed the Air Service School of Engineering in 1920, and given its lasting name in 1926, the Air Corps School of Engineering offered a yearlong program of technological and engineering education for benefit of selected air officers of the U.S. Army. Situated in Dayton, Ohio, it became the direct forerunner of the Air Force Institute of Technology.*

During World War I many leading civilian engineers served in the Air Service's Airplane Engineering Division at McCook Field, Ohio. The division's chief after the Armistice was Colonel Thurman H. Bane, an officer-pilot who had recently headed the Air Service's Technical Section in Washington. On November 30, 1918, Bane sent an official recommendation that an Air School of Application be established within the Engineering Division at McCook, to offer technical training to permanent officers of the Air Service. Bane offered that future graduates might either return to line-officer careers or serve as administrators of engineering activities. Contrasting the widespread lack of engineering knowledge among air officers to the more favorable situation in the Army Corps of Engineers and the Ordnance Department, Bane wrote, "No branch of the service wants nor should have men who are merely executives."

The idea was supported by Colonel M. E. Davis, Air Service chief of training, who pointed out that it was time for the young air arm to turn to professional, as opposed to wartime, education. General Charles T. Menoher, director of Military Aeronautics, approved establishment of the school in early 1919. The first class enrolled on November 10, 1919, under Bane, who served as commandant until retiring in 1922. For admission, an officer needed the airplane pilot's rating plus either (1) a degree from the U.S. Military Academy,* the U.S. Naval Academy,* or a recognized technical college or (2) demonstrated versatility in calculus, theoretical mechanics, and advanced physics and chemistry.

Annual classes of about a dozen officers experienced a vigorous 50-week curriculum, which included heavy doses of aerodynamics, thermodynamics, electrical engineering, and other theoretical studies, along with more-practical topics like maintenance, armaments, "scientific management," and shop work. Design was addressed in a general way. The year ended with a course in performance and flight testing. Specialists and other technical people of the Engineering Division served as lecturers and guided the students in their studies, which when feasible followed the "applicatory method," emphasizing independent problem solving and self-study. Students sometimes tested their solutions in flight. (Having surmounted all the above, according to the *Air Service News Letter* of October 8, 1920, all members of the initial class celebrated their graduation by parachuting from a Martin Bomber at 2,500 feet.) It was widely agreed that the school fostered mutually beneficial understanding, not only between the student officers and the Engineering Division but also, in the longer term, between the technical and the line-oriented parts of the Air Service.

An influential forerunner of the school had been the Army and Navy School of Aeronautical Engineering, held at Massachusetts Institute of Technology (M.I.T.) during World War I. Links to civilian engineering schools thereafter remained strong. Scholars from the graduate schools often served as guest lecturers, and the students used many of the same textbooks used in the universities. While most graduates returned to the line, a few went on to graduate study at M.I.T. or elsewhere. (James Doolittle, a 1923 graduate of the Air Service School of Engineering, completed the Ph.D. in aeronautical engineering at M.I.T. two years later, leading to his remarkable achievements in development and flight testing prior to World War II.)

The school moved from McCook to Wright Field, also in Dayton, in 1927. (Classes were suspended in 1927–28.) Thereafter, emphasis gradually shifted toward the training of young officers for duty within the Engineering Division. The applicatory method was less heavily used, and steps were taken to create a permanent faculty. The school shut down soon after Pearl Harbor, having by then produced over 200 graduates, many of whom would hold high-level responsibilities during World War II. The school reopened in 1944 for a series of short courses, and it closed finally upon organization of the Army Air Forces Institute of Technology in September 1946.

The School of Engineering and the Air Corps Tactical School,* which included a lesser dose of aviation technological education, both fit into the pattern of the Army's other branch schools for professional officers between the wars. The School of Engineering, by its existence and the nature of its curriculum, reflected broad recognition within the air arm of the critical importance of technology in air warfare.

Sources:

Chief of Air Service, *Annual Reports*, 1921–26.

History, *U.S. Army Air Forces Institute of Technology, 1946–1947*. Microfilmed documentary materials at Office of Air Force History, Washington, DC.

John J. Powers, "Founding of the Air Force Institute of Technology," *Air University Review* (September–October 1964).

Ray L. Bowers

AIR CORPS TACTICAL SCHOOL. During the interwar years, the U.S. Army's Air Corps Tactical School (ACTS) served as the educational and doctrinal center for the fledgling Army Air Service (later Army Air Corps and then U.S. Army Air Forces). Virtually all the senior Army Air Force leadership in World War II attended ACTS and were indoctrinated into American air power theory there.

Following World War I, air-minded officers recognized the importance of the air arm and the need for officers educated in the employment of military aircraft. With the creation of the Air Service as a separate combat arm in 1920 (previously Army aircraft had been assigned to the Signal Corps), the Air Service Field Officers School was established at Langley Field, Virginia. Several name changes and a change of locale were to follow: the school was redesignated as the Air Service Tactical School in 1922, then as the Air Corps Tactical School in 1926. In order to be more removed from Washington and War Department politics, ACTS moved to Maxwell Field in Montgomery, Alabama, in 1931.

The mission of ACTS was to educate and train air corps officers (a few from other combat arms and services also attended) in the strategy, operations, and tactics of air power. Since there was little to no established body of knowledge or doctrine for air power as compared to the long histories of armies and navies, ACTS emerged as the center of doctrinal development in the Air Corps and became the highest educational institution for airmen. The school's motto was a reflection of air power's relative lack of history, Proficimus More Irretenti (We Make Progress Unhindered by Custom). Emerging from World War I, air power had been limited but of growing significance and had demonstrated even greater potential. Upon that potential, air power theory and doctrine developed—not upon any body of significant evidence. Entering World War II, the Army Air Forces had a highly coherent conception of how to apply air power. That vision had been largely developed by the faculty and students at ACTS.

As airpower theory developed, it also became the raison d'être justifying the airmen's call for a separate air force. Inspired by Billy Mitchell's outspoken plea during the 1920s for a separate air force, coequal with the Army and the Navy, Air Corps leadership continued to push for independence after Mitchell's court-martial in 1926. Air leaders reasoned that the strongest case for an independent air force would be the realization of a unique mission for air power. Strategic bombardment theory and doctrine developed at ACTS became that unique mission. In the 1920s, the ACTS curriculum had advocated a balance between the many possible air combat missions. By 1930, the focus shifted to strategic bombardment. As the technological capability of bombers and bombsights improved through the decade, the cadre at ACTS refined their bombing doctrine through various tests and planning exercises.

Upon the United States entry into World War II, ACTS had bequeathed a highly coherent vision of strategic bombardment doctrine which the U.S. Army Air Forces leadership was eager to test against its enemies. The core tenets of ACTS theory featured high-altitude, unescorted, daylight, precision, strategic bombardment of the vital centers of the enemy's industrial web. ACTS theory viewed industrial societies as a fragile web—if the right, key industries were hit (i.e., electric power grids or ball bearing plants), then the rest of the web would unravel or be paralyzed. An enemy society would then be incapable of replenishing its combat forces. This view reflected American moralism and a desire to avoid striking civilians directly in contrast to bombardment advocates in other countries. ACTS thinkers believed B-17 *Flying Fortress* bombers would be able to fly far above most enemy fighters in self-defending formations, and the Norden bombsight would allow pinpoint bombing accuracy.

Unfortunately, ACTS testing had been conducted in ideal conditions and failed to account for the fog and friction of real war. ACTS theorists underestimated potential enemy capabilities and overestimated American capabilities. German industry was not fully mobilized and proved quite ingenious at finding workarounds when damage and losses occurred. B-17s proved incapable of protecting themselves without escort fighters from highly capable German fighters. The Norden bombsight (tested in the California desert with ideal weather conditions) did not prove very accurate when faced with the winds, clouds, and weather of Europe. Smoke and debris clouds from the first bombs striking further obscured targets for subsequent bomb crews. Heavy fighter attacks and anti-aircraft fire (flak) also made it difficult for bomber crews to conduct accurate bombing runs. Army air forces leadership proved slow to change its doctrine and tactics despite evidence that change was warranted.

Resistance to change might in part be attributed to the thorough training the air leadership received at ACTS. Nearly all the senior air force leaders had attended ACTS and were inculcated in bombardment doctrine. In 1939–40, ACTS shortened its curriculum to 12-weeks and pushed four classes through that year instead of the usual one class per year. This was part of an effort to ensure educated senior officers in a rapidly expanding Army Air Corps. Former students and instructors carried their knowledge into their post-ACTS jobs. In August 1941, Harold L. George, Kenneth N. Walker, Haywood S. Hansell, Jr., and Laurence S. Kuter formed the planning team that produced Air War Planning Division 1 (AWPD-1), the blueprint for the strategic bombing campaign against Germany. All four men had been prominent instructors and bomber advocates at ACTS.

In June 1940, the last of the 12-week courses finished, and the Air Corps Tactical School suspended operations. Rapid expansion required knowledgeable officers for senior command and staff positions. ACTS staff members were prime candidates for such jobs. A series of U.S. Army Air Forces–applied tactical schools filled the breach in part, providing short, specialized training geared toward the exigencies of war. After the war, the newly born U.S. Air Force established the Air University* at Maxwell Air Force Base to educate its officer corps in the mold of ACTS.

The legacy of ACTS is manifold. The debate about the efficacy and proper role of air power continues. The strategic bombardment theory born at ACTS still strongly influences current Air Force thinking and doctrine. Notably, some thinkers view ACTS, strategic bombardment theory, and its execution as excellent case studies in the dangers of dogmatic thinking and rigid adherence to untested theory and doctrine.

Sources:

Robert T. Finney, *History of the Air Corps Tactical School, 1920–1940* (Washington, DC: Center for Air Force History, 1992).

Thomas H. Greer, *The Development of Air Doctrine in the Army Air Arm, 1917–1941* (Washington, DC: Office of Air Force History, 1985).

Michael S. Sherry, *The Rise of American Airpower: The Creation of Armageddon* (New Haven, CT: Yale University Press, 1987).

Barry D. Watts, *The Foundations of U.S. Air Doctrine: The Problem of Friction in War* (Maxwell Air Force Base, AL: Air University Press, 1984).

Capt. Theodore A. Kracht, USAF

AIR FORCE INSTITUTE OF TECHNOLOGY. The Air Force Institute of Technology (AFIT), since its founding in 1946 as the Army Air Forces (AAF) Institute of Technology, has offered professional education in engineering, logistics, and management to thousands of U.S. Air Force officers enrolled in resident programs at Wright-Patterson Air Force Base, Ohio. AFIT also has administered the studies of Air Force personnel in civilian institutions and with private industry.

The lineage of AFIT reaches back to the prewar Air Corps School of Engineering* at Dayton, Ohio. In July 1945, looking ahead to "a new era in aeronautics, both military and civil," General Hugh Knerr, commanding Air Technical Service Command at Dayton, called for planning to expand the engineering school and add air logistics and maintenance to its curricula. Authorized in late 1945, the AAF Institute of Technology opened in ceremonies on September 3, 1946.

Initially, the institute was part of Air Technical Service Command, shortly renamed Air Materiel Command, and was under the "educational coordination" of a new Army Air Forces University, soon renamed the Air University,* at Maxwell Air Force Base (AFB), Alabama.* To encourage a universitylike atmosphere, deans, department heads, and many of the institute's faculty members were to be civilians, expected to conduct research on topics related to AAF problems. In fall 1946, nearly 250 students were enrolled in the institute's initial two colleges—the College of Engineering and Maintenance and the College of Logistics and Procurement. Each college had a one-year graduate-level course and a two-year undergraduate program. The mission, as reaffirmed in 1947, was to conduct "educational courses primarily in the field of Engineering sciences and industrial administration, at undergraduate and graduate level, for AAF officers, to improve and maintain at a high level the technical competence of the AAF."

Upon creation of United States Air Force in 1947, AFIT acquired more of the general features that would color its future history. Its permanent home, Wright-Patterson AFB, was formed by the merger of Wright Field, with its engineering research facilities, with neighboring Patterson Field, center of Air Force supply and procurement activities. The civilian institutions program, transferred briefly to Maxwell, was returned to AFIT in 1948. On April 1, 1950, AFIT became part of Air University, thus ending its direct link to Air Materiel Command. Meanwhile the creation of an Air Research and Development Command, initially at Wright-Patterson but distinct from Air Materiel Command, would lead to endless opportunities for productive research by AFIT faculty and students.

Graduate-level studies soon overshadowed undergraduate and refresher offerings at AFIT, and by 1951, in-residence graduate-level programs, many of them tailored to meet the needs of Air Research and Development Command, ranged from aeronautical engineering and electronics to industrial and engineering administration. The civilian institutions program came to include the education of Air Force medical and dental officers. A graduate-level residence program in nuclear engineering was added in 1953, yielding extensive research using the reactor of the Nuclear Engineering Center until its closing nearly two decades later.

Reflecting the generally acknowledged quality of AFIT's resident offerings, federal legislation in 1954 authorized the institute to grant master's degrees contingent on accreditation by a nationally recognized accreditation authority. The Engineers Council for Professional Development conferred accreditation on AFIT's master's-level engineering programs in 1955, and the institute awarded its first degrees in March 1956—22 M.S. degrees in electrical engineering and nuclear engineering. Accreditation of the institute's business-related programs by the American Association of Collegiate Schools of Business followed in spring 1958; the graduate logistics program was accredited by the North Central Association of Colleges and Schools in 1963. The School of Engineering awarded its first doctoral degrees in June 1969, after preliminary accreditation of its doctroral program by North Central.

In 1958, following the successful Soviet orbiting of *Sputnik*, AFIT initiated a master's-level astronautics program. Courses began in July at Massachusetts Institute of Technology and in September at the resident School of Engineering. Graduates of the resident program received some of the first M.S. degrees in astronautics ever awarded, in August 1960. Of the many Air Force astronauts in projects Mercury, Gemini, and Apollo, virtually all were graduates of an AFIT residence offering or had studied at a civilian university under AFIT administration.

Over the years, as might be expected, the institute underwent sundry internal reorganizations. In 1959, for example, there existed five main elements—the School of Engineering, the School of Logistics, the School of Business, the Civil Engineering Center, and the Civilian Institutions Program. Having experienced several minor name changes, in 1962 the institute reacquired what was to be its lasting name, Air Force Institute of Technology. Permanent buildings gradually replaced the several scattered facilities at Wright-Patterson AFB, and a complex approximating a single AFIT campus emerged. Growth continued, such that the student quota for 1970 was 1,843 officer-students, including 1,510 in graduate programs, all in addition to the Minuteman effort, discussed below, and an airman's education and commissioning program.

The Minuteman venture was a long-enduring AFIT program with Strategic Air Command (SAC), where personnel serving in remote Minuteman missile sites studied toward advanced degrees. The effort began in 1962 as an AFIT School of Engineering extension center at Malmstrom AFB, Montana. An individual could, after about three years of half-time study at Malmstrom followed by ten weeks in residence at AFIT, obtain a master's degree in aerospace engineering. The venture was soon expanded to other bases and to include offerings in business administration and industrial management, as well as programs at the undergraduate level. The University of Montana and other universities provided faculty members and varied support under contracts. Until transferred to SAC in 1987 amid planning for early shutdown, AFIT's Minuteman program yielded important benefits not only in broadening the technical education of the officer corps but also in helping recruit and retain personnel for missile duty.

Budget stringencies slowed expansion in the 1970s and led to phasedown in the AFIT undergraduate effort and airman's program. The Air Force's need for educated engineering personnel, however, continued to grow in hand with the accelerating pace of technological advances in air weaponry. The nation's supply of scientific and engineering graduates was meanwhile tightening—one 1984 study noted that many high schools no longer offered the work in mathematics needed as preparation for college engineering studies. In reply, the Air Force attracted new college graduates by promising them immediate graduate study at AFIT or, in some cases, a second baccalaureate—typically in electrical engineering, reflecting the surging influence of computers in all technology. New graduates of Air Force ROTC* and the Air Force Academy* were placed directly into graduate professional schools, and existing Air Force personnel were given incentives to study for conversion into needed fields of engineering and physical sciences, all under AFIT administration.

Relatively new technologies of the 1980s became strongly evident in the content of course offerings and in faculty and student research projects. Such areas included laser technology, artificial intelligence, stealth technology, robotics, and, of course, computer and software engineering. Much research was at least loosely related to the nation's Strategic Defense Initiative, including very-large-scale integrated circuitry, directed-energy weapons, and tracking technologies. As student quotas decreased amid a scaling-down Air Force, the AFIT staff enlarged its consulting activities, helping other Air Force and Defense Department agencies find solutions. Boards of visitors* consisting of outside scholars and leaders in industry annually reviewed AFIT's activities.

The tradition inherited from before World War II was never entirely lost— that the institute and its schools existed mainly to foster a broad, technically literate officer corps rather than to produce research scientists and engineers. But as science and technology themselves became over more specialized, so too did AFIT's offerings. Officers studied to prepare for future roles in Air Force laboratories, for responsibilities in the administration of research and development activities, or for duties in specific technical career fields. Besides the graduate programs, AFIT offered various relatively short courses of "professional continuing education," designed to upgrade practitioners of particular engineering or logistics disciplines in new developments of their fields. AFIT proposals to provide broader offerings designed to raise the technological knowledge of nonspecialist officers were generally unfruitful, as they appeared to duplicate similar offerings at the other Air University professional schools.

AFIT in the mid-'90s reported that over its history more than 250,000 students had been enrolled in its programs, including more than 900 from other countries. Roughly a third of the Air Force's generals had studied in AFIT-sponsored programs. One study, which looked at the Air Force in 1967, found that of the 14,000 line officers having master's degrees, 48 percent had obtained their degrees through an AFIT program. By the mid-'90s, the Graduate School of Engineering had granted more than 8,500 degrees, including some 200 doctorates in fields ranging from engineering physics to computer engineering and operations research. Of the school's 110 faculty members, about half were military officers, including some on extended tours beyond the usual four years. Faculty patterns were similar in the smaller Graduate School of Logistics and Acquisitions Management, which produced about 100 master's graduates annually in such fields as software management, systems management, and logistics management.

As the Air Force decreased in size during the 1990s, the cost-effectiveness of AFIT's residence programs came into question. When Air Force officials in 1997 moved to close the AFIT schools at Wright-Patterson, members of Congress took up active opposition. In April 1998, Acting Secretary of the Air Force F. Whitten Peters announced his decision that AFIT should continue operating as currently structured. It remained clear that, regardless of AFIT's future, the Air Force's future activities in basic and applied research, acquisition, and logistics required a corps of leaders having strong and diverse educational backgrounds in science and technology.

Sources:

Annual histories of Air University and the Air Force Institute of Technology, and other microfilmed materials at Office of Air Force History, Washington, DC.

Captain Sanders A. Laubenthal, "The Air Force Institute of Technology," in Lois E.
    Walker and Shelby E. Wickam, eds., *From Huffman Prairie to the Moon: The
    History of Wright-Patterson Air Force Base* (Wright-Patterson Air Force Base,
    OH: Air Force Logistics Command, 1984).
Barbara Ann Wechsler, "History, AFIT," AUOI-H Study Series Number 9, 1966, Air
    University, Maxwell Air Force Base, AL.

Ray L. Bowers

AIR FORCE RESERVE OFFICERS' TRAINING CORPS (AFROTC). The
U.S. Air Force's ROTC, the branch's oldest and largest commissioning program,
headquartered at Maxwell Air Force Base, Alabama,* recruits, educates, and
trains officers for the United States Air Force. It also conducts the Air Force's
Junior AFROTC program, which teaches citizenship, promotes community service, develops character, and provides instruction in air and space fundamentals
for high school cadets.

The AFROTC program has its roots in the Morrill Act of 1862 (also known
as the Land Grant Act). This act, among other things, established at least one
college in every state that taught military tactics as an integral part of its curriculum. Subsequent legislation authorized the use of military personnel, rifles,
uniforms, and other equipment at these and other educational institutions that
voluntarily conducted military training. During World War I, the National Defense Act of 1916 established the Reserve Officers' Training Corps* as a source
for the newly authorized Officers' Reserve Corps, but the program was temporarily discontinued in 1918. It resumed operations in the fall of 1919 and
remained in existence until 1932, when the program was again phased out,
primarily for budgetary reasons. In 1946, the Army reactivated the ROTC program that included, for the first time, Army Air Forces ROTC units at 78 institutions.

During the years that followed, the program expanded rapidly and experienced
numerous organizational changes. Though initially assigned to Air Training
Command, the program was transferred to the Continental Air Command
(CONAC) in December 1946. When the U.S. Air Force became a separate
branch of the military in September 1947, the unit's name also changed to
Air Force ROTC (AFROTC). Shortly thereafter, the Air Force decided that
AFROTC "constituted the first step in the officer education ladder" and, "in the
interest of continuity and integration of the educational programs," should be
assigned to the USAF major command (MAJCOM) responsible for this functional area. As a result, in August 1952 the Air Force reassigned the AFROTC
program to its center for professional military education known as Air University* (AU). For the next three decades, AFROTC remained an AU subordinate
unit in spite of Air University's loss of MAJCOM status and realignment under
Air Training Command.

Air University moved quickly to reduce the AFROTC program's span of
control and altered its method of operation. Initially, field supervision for the

program had been the responsibility of the various CONAC numbered air forces. Though this arrangement worked well, it failed to provide a separate and distinct agency for developing, coordinating, and administering AFROTC policy, plans, and programs. As a result, in August 1952, Air University established Headquarters AFROTC to provide centralized control over the program and to ensure its overall continuity of operation. In addition, Air University divided the program into geographical areas across the nation and assigned a liaison team to each of them for field supervision and inspections.

The initial four-year AFROTC curriculum consisted of two courses of study. The basic course contained instruction in such general subjects as world political geography, air power concepts, and exercise of command and was taught during the first two years of the program. An advanced course during the final two years focused on more specialized instruction in air operations, Air Force supply systems, military publications, and specialized training. After receiving a commission, AFROTC graduates were assigned to a reserve pool that permitted them to enter active duty during any period of mobilization. Experience later proved that further training was necessary before the newly commissioned officer could truly be productive. Consequently, Air University introduced a new four-year AFROTC course of study in the fall of 1953 designed to provide AFROTC graduates with a higher level of understanding of the military and improved growth potential. It included such new areas of study as elements of aerial warfare, applied air science and techniques, the Air Force in operation, and concepts of leadership and airpower.

By August 1956, Congress had passed Public Law 879, which authorized the establishment of a Flight Instruction Program (FIP). An integral part of the AFROTC curriculum, this was designed primarily to provide a screening and motivational device for determining whether seniors who applied for pilot training possessed the basic aptitude to become successful pilots. Prior to FIP's establishment, the AFROTC Cadet Flying Indoctrination and Orientation Program had been the primary screening and motivational device for cadets interested in becoming pilots. However, increasing difficulties in obtaining airlift support for the program and the adverse impact of base closures seriously limited participation in this activity.

Another major revision of the AFROTC program structure occurred in October 1964 with the passage of the ROTC Revitalization Act. This act, in addition to continuing the traditional four-year program, established a new two-year program that allowed students with two years remaining in school (either at the undergraduate, graduate, or a combination of both levels) to compete for commissions. The two-year program significantly increased AFROTC's flexibility and the pool of students eligible for commissions, since the four-year program had precluded thousands of junior college and transfer students from entering the program. This act also authorized financial assistance for students participating in the four-year program and instituted a new six-week field training program, the first of which was held at Keesler AFB, Mississippi, during the summer of 1965. In addition, the new law established a prerequisite for enrollment in the advanced Professional Officers Course and created the Junior AFROTC Program for thousands of high school students across the nation.

Following Air University's return to MAJCOM status in July 1983, the Air Force realigned AFROTC under Air Training Command (ATC). It remained there until July 1993 when AU was once again brought under ATC (re-designated Air Education and Training Command), and AFROTC again became an AU subordinate unit. To further consolidate USAF officer acquisition efforts, in February 1996, Air University established the Air Force Officer Accession and Training Schools and realigned both AFROTC and the Officer Training School under this new organization. In spite of these changes, the AFROTC program remained divided among four regions (Northeast, Northwest, Southeast, and Southwest), had nearly 150 detachments at various colleges and universities, and had cross-town agreements at more than 700 other institutions. In addition, the Air Force Junior ROTC program continued to operate at over 500 high schools and had over 65,000 students enrolled in the program.

Sources:

AFROTC Office of Information, "Historically Speaking on Air Force ROTC," Maxwell
    Air Force Base, AL, 1968.
Air University Catalog, 1997 (Maxwell Air Force Base, AL: Air University Press, 1997).
Headquarters AFROTC, "The AFROTC Program: A Speaker's Resource Guide," Air
    University, Montgomery, AL, undated.
Price D. Rice, "The History and Development of the Air Force Reserve Officer's Training
    Corps Program," unpublished master's thesis, American University, 1951.

Jerome A. Ennels

AIR UNIVERSITY. The military education center of the United States Air Force at Maxwell Air Force Base, Alabama, operates colleges, schools, institutes, and other organizations aimed at educating and developing the USAF's future planners and leaders. It also conducts the Air Force's air power research and doctrinal development programs as well as USAF Reserve commissioning activities.

The roots of Air University (AU) can be traced to the U.S. Army Reorganization Act of 1920, which established the U.S. Air Service as a combatant arm of the Army. Most of the officers assigned to this newly established branch were poorly trained in air tactics and techniques, lacked actual aerial combat experience, and had little knowledge of the principles of employing the new air arm. Hence, the Air Service quickly realized that its principal need was for an efficient school system for training and educating officers to command and staff air units and for developing aerial concepts and doctrines. As a result, in February 1920, the Army established several general and specialized schools for educating and training air officers, including an institution at Langley Field, Virginia, which became known as the Air Corps Tactical School.*

Throughout its existence, the Tactical School was the intellectual center of the pre–World War II Army air arm. Though its basic mission was to educate air officers in the strategies, tactics, and techniques of air power employment, the school, by necessity, also became inextricably involved in the development of air doctrine. In fact, doctrinal development subsequently emerged as one of the school's primary missions, and for more than 20 years, this institution served as the sounding board for ideas concerning the critical issue of the role of air power in war. The school moved to Maxwell Field in 1931, where it remained until the wartime requirements for officers of the caliber of those associated with the institution led to the suspension of classes in June 1940 and to the discontinuation of the school two years later.

By the end of World War II, leaders of the Army Air Forces (AAF) realized that the decision to close the Tactical School, while deemed necessary, had essentially been shortsighted. As a result, they established Air University in March 1946 to fill the void left by the Tactical School's inactivation and to correct many of the problems and deficiencies of the Air Corps's prewar education system. Schools constituting the old system had operated independently and were poorly coordinated in terms of scope, doctrine, and curriculum. Air University consolidated these activities into a centralized educational system and eliminated the traditionalism, rigidity of thought, and the formalization of instruction that had often characterized military education in the past. The new institution was a progressive, forward-looking PME system designed to keep the Air Force's thinking fresh and projected at least five years in the future.

This far-reaching educational system became operational in April 1946, when the School of Aviation Medicine at Randolph Field, Texas, became one of its subordinate units. The AAF Special Staff School joined the AU family three months later. Air University's PME resident schools opened in the fall of 1946, when classes began at the Air War College* (AWC) and Air Command and Staff College.* The Air Tactical School, later replaced by the Squadron Officer School, began classes the following year at Tyndall Field, Florida. Other institutions like the Air Force Institute of Technology,* the Eaker College for Professional Development, the AU College for Research, Doctrine, and Education, and the College of Enlisted Professional Military Education joined the AU family during the years that followed. In time, the Air Force Reserve Officers' Training Corps (AFROTC)* and Officer Training School also became AU subordinate units and were subsequently merged under the Air Force Officer Accessions and Training School. Similarly, all academic support organizations, including the Academic Instructors School, International Officers School, the Extension Course Institute, and the Air University Library, were subsequently combined under AU's Office of Academic Support.

Numerous changes occurred in the AU school curricula during that time. Most were evolutionary in nature and aimed at ensuring that students were kept abreast of current technologies, international situations, and military concepts and capabilities. Others were somewhat radical and more profound. At the senior

PME school, for example, the emphasis had drifted away from how to fight an air war toward high-level policy and decision making. As a result, in the mid-1970s Air University launched a three-year campaign of curriculum review and overhaul refocused on how to fight an air war and the use of military history to accomplish this. The command also increased the number of civilian scholars on the AWC and ACSC faculties and implemented new student selection policies to ensure the Air Force's best officers attended these schools in residence. Later, in 1986 following the Goldwater-Nichols Department of Defense Reorganization Act,* Air University again revamped the AWC and ACSC curricula to increase their focus on joint matters, particularly joint war fighting. Commensurately, more Army and Navy officers were added to the faculties, staffs, and students of both schools as a prerequisite for awarding Phase 1, Joint PME credit. Air University also developed a course of instruction aimed at increasing the student's level of education in strategic thinking and jointness.* The resulting one-year program of the School of Advanced Airpower Studies* was designed to create soldier-scholars who would have the ability to develop, evaluate, and employ air power.

Air University's organizational status also changed several times during its history. Although AU operated as a MAJCOM throughout most of its existence, the Air Force realigned it in May 1978 under Air Training Command, reducing the organization to a level comparable to a numbered air force. The change was short-lived, however, and in July 1983 Air University once again became a major command. Several years later, funding shortages and military restructuring again brought the AU organizational status under review. As a result, in July 1993, Air University was once again realigned under Air Training Command with the latter redesignated Air Education and Training Command. In spite of the loss of MAJCOM status, Air University continued as the professional military education center of the U.S. Air Force, the think tank for ideas, concepts, and doctrine regarding the development and employment of U.S. air power.

Sources:

Suzanne Budd-Gehri, "Study War Once More: Teaching Vietnam at Air University," a CADRE paper presented at the Southeast Conference of Asian Studies at Duke University, January 19, 1985.

George N. Dubina, "Fifty Years of Aviation History at Maxwell Air Force Base, 1910–1960" (Maxwell Air Force Base, AL: AU/HO Study No. 18. n.d.).

Jerome A. Ennels, "A Short History of Air University" (Maxwell Air Force Base, AL: AU/HO Study, 1995).

Jerome A. Ennels and Wesley P. Newton, *The Wisdom of Eagles: A History of Maxwell Air Force Base* (Montgomery, AL: Blackbelt Press, 1997).

Jerome A. Ennels

AIR UNIVERSITY QUARTERLY REVIEW. See *AIR UNIVERSITY REVIEW/ AIRPOWER JOURNAL.*

AIR UNIVERSITY REVIEW/AIRPOWER JOURNAL. Since 1947, the official professional journal of the United States Air Force: redesignated as *Airpower Journal* in 1987.

When the U.S. Air Force was founded in 1947, most of its initial cadre of officers had been officers of the U.S. Army. In its first decade, the USAF also received a substantial input of officers from the U.S. Naval Academy.* Thus, the professional publications of both the Army and the Navy served as precedents for the *Air University Quarterly Review,* named for the Air Force major command [See Air University.*] established to oversee its professional schools. Many branches of the Army, like ordnance, had their own private associations that started producing magazines in the aftermath of World War I. The principal journal of the Army aviators was *U.S. Air Service,* which began in February 1919. Although it tried to expand to incorporate airmen from the other services from its earliest days and even attracted articles from Assistant Secretary of the Navy Franklin D. Roosevelt and other naval persons, it never did escape its army coloration and expired in 1956 when its longtime editor died. Among the other *Quarterly Review* precedents was *Air Corps Newsletter,* which was published under various titles from September 21, 1918, until 1958.

The first issue of the *Air University Quarterly Review* was published as a government document under the editorship of Captain Harry Moore in the spring of 1947, even before the USAF officially came into existence. Ever since then, under various titles, it has been quartered at Maxwell AFB, Alabama, for its entire life. It was issued in a saddle stitch (pamphlet style) format during the early years but eventually grew into a perfect binding (book style). It remained a quarterly until 1963 when, under General Curtis LeMay, it expanded to a bimonthly and consequently changed its name to the *Air University Review.* For most of its life, the editor has been a USAF colonel or lieutenant colonel.

In the late 1970s, the *Review* was authorized to expand to an additional signature (36 pages), and it then reached its zenith in terms of size—a bimonthly of 128 pages. At that time, its staff included its own copy editors, layout and design personnel, and a financial manager. Later, it was moved into a larger organization, the College for Aerospace Doctrine, Research and Education. Thenceforth, the copy editing, design, and financial functions were assumed by personnel of Air University Press. From 1949 onward, occasional versions in Spanish and Portuguese have been published. They usually have not been complete translations, but rather only selections of some of the best articles from the English version.

The *Air University Review* fell into difficulties in the mid-1980s and briefly went out of publication. A part of the reason seems to have been that it had lost its focus on the main concerns of the Air Force profession and thus lost its funding support. The last issue of the *Review* was that of January–March 1987.

However, Air University soon created another publication in its place: *The Airpower Journal.* The purpose was to more tightly focus the work on the operational level of war. It was also substantially reduced from what the *Review*

had been, going to a quarterly instead of a bimonthly cycle and to three sig-
natures for a total of 96 pages instead of the 128 in the last years of the *Review*.
Since then, the flow of good articles has justified a return to 128 pages. Recently,
the *Airpower Journal* staff has developed an electronic version that includes
many of its articles and more that can be downloaded through the Internet. It
is named *Air Chronicles*, and the address is www.cdsar.af.mil/airchronicles.html.

While it would be too much to assert that the Air Force's professional journal
has had a definitive effect on the intellectual life of the service, perhaps it is
fair to call it a "significant factor." Chiefs of Staff Thomas White (4 articles),
Curtis LeMay, Charles Gabriel, Merrill McPeak (2 articles), and Ronald Fogle-
man, among many other USAF general officers, have contributed. So, too, have
any number of lieutenants and some enlisted people. Many prominent author-
scholars from the United States and abroad have also contributed, including
Richard K. Betts, Bernard Brodie, John Erickson, Raymond L. Garthoff, Colin
S. Gray, Morris Janowitz, Charles C. Moskos, Peter Paret, George H. Quester,
Thomas C. Schelling, Russell F. Weigley, and Gill Robb Wilson. Among the
political leaders writing for the journal have been Secretary of Defense Harold
Brown (before his tenure), Lawrence J. Korb, and Ambassador John Patrick
Walsh.

The magazine's influence outside the service has also grown, having been
often cited in periodicals ranging from *International Security* to *Wilson Quarterly*. The staff maintains a liaison with the editors of the professional journals
of the other services including *Military Review,* * *Parameters,* * and *Naval War
College Review.* * The editor of the lattermost is a sitting member of the *Air
Power Journal*'s editorial board, which meets periodically and reports its findings to the commander of Air University and the Chief of Staff of the Air Force.

The Air Force professional journal has published its own index plus one
supplement, ed. Michael A. Kirtland, *Air University Index, 1 May 1947–March
1987*. However, it is more easily accessed through a CD ROM, *U.S. Government
Periodicals Index* or the *Air University Library Index of Military Periodicals*.
The lattermost covers the entire life of the journal, but the former deals only
with the most recent years.

David R. Mets

AIR WAR COLLEGE. The senior service school of the U.S. Air Force, devoted to teaching senior officers in the Air Force and other government agencies
about strategy, the global environment, and the deployment and employment of
air and space power in a joint context.

Founded in March of 1946, dedicated on September 3, 1946, the Air War
College was located in the former home of the Air Corps Tactical School* that
had moved to Maxwell Air Force Base (AFB), Alabama, in 1931. Its first commandant was Maj. General Orville A. Anderson, and it enrolled 55 officers from
the Army Air Forces, other branches of the U.S. Army, the Navy and Marine
Corps and two RAF officers for a year-long course of study. The AWC had as

its original mission statement "consideration of the broad aspects of air power by selected officers to determine the most effective development and employment of the Army Air Forces as a whole, and to prepare these officers to command and employ large Air Force units." The focus was on war fighting, and the faculty consisted of senior USAAF colonels experienced in military arts and science and command. The curriculum included such topics as the study of strategy, tactics, logistics, technology, intelligence, command and management from a USAAF, later U.S. Air Force, perspective.

The Air War College had a large impact on the newly independent U.S. Air Force created by the National Security Act of July 26, 1947. It became the first of a series of professional military education schools to be located at Maxwell AFB as a part of the Air University.* The class of 1948 became heavily involved in writing basic doctrine for the newly independent U.S. Air Force. For a number of years, a small number of students were kept on after completing the course to continue working on doctrine issues. What eventually emerged was *Air Force Manual (AFM) 1-1, Air Force Basic Doctrine*, finally published in March of 1953 after a six-month hiatus caused by the Korean War when classes at the AWC were suspended.

Classes resumed on January 8, 1951, but the ten-month academic year was restored and has been in place ever since. Also in 1951, a board of advisors made the first of a series of recommendations that civilian Ph.D.s be hired as AWC faculty. It would take 35 years, until 1986, for this recommendation to be implemented to place more than a handful of civilian academics on the faculty. The curriculum was divided into three phases consisting of ten weeks devoted to International Relations, twenty weeks on Air Warfare, and a concluding ten weeks on Global Strategy. A thesis was required, and the focus on doctrine continued. The first civilian graduate from the Air War College was a member of the class of 1953, and the tradition of admitting civilians, six to twelve a year, from various government agencies has continued ever since.

The Air War College went through several changes in its mission statement and modifications of its curriculum (1952 and 1958) before major changes were undertaken in the 1960s. In 1960, "air power" in the mission statement was changed to "aerospace power." The first formal evaluation program of students was instituted, and the Air War College Associate program (alternately Seminar Course) was added to the already existing Correspondence Course (alternately Extension Course). The curriculum was extensively revised in 1961, and the George Washington University graduate program was begun at the AWC, awarding 63 graduates in that first class an M.A. in international affairs. Also in the same year, the college began to publish the "Air War College Supplement," containing lectures given by guest speakers, exceptional student papers, and articles by the faculty and staff. The class of 1964 showed a large increase in numbers of students with 274 rather than the 185 of the previous class. Class size has averaged in the 200 to 260 range ever since save for the period 1968–72 during the Vietnam War. During the remainder of the decade, leadership and management issues came to supplant some of the emphasis on war fighting, as "U.S. National Security Policy" became redefined as "Defense Management and DOD Decision Making." The term 1967–68 saw the introduction of the first electives program whereby students could select courses other than follow a totally prescribed core curriculum.

In the period of the 1970s, the college reflected in its own way the change swirling about the nation and society, both at home and abroad. The first woman officer graduated in the class of 1970. The first African-American officer since Benjamin O. Davis (1950) graduated in the class of 1972. Although international officers had been part of each class since the inception of the Air War College, they had been limited to close, English-speaking allies, principally from the Royal Air Force and eventually from other NATO allies. The first non-NATO international officer, from Australia, graduated in 1973. The first international officer from outside this group—Iran—graduated in the class of 1974. There are now forty or more international officers from roughly 40 countries in each AWC class.

Both in the 1970s, with the Clements Commission and in the 1980s, with the Skelton Panel,* the AWC curriculum has been taken to task for allowing itself to drift away from its primary mission. The Clements Commission concluded that far too much of the curriculum had been reoriented from war fighting to management issues, behavioral studies, and other non–war fighting subjects. Congressman Ike Skelton (D–Missouri) made similar charges in the late 1980s in the Skelton Report on Military Education. It suggested a greater emphasis on military history, more rigorous grading of all course activities, and a better prepared and higher quality faculty as antidotes to what had become a rather lackluster program.

As a consequence of these recommendations, both the commanders of Air University and the Air War College had mandates for reform. They strove to increase the number of Ph.D.s on the faculty from a half-dozen or so to nearly four times that number, increase academic rigor, and improve curriculum content. Students were already expected to produce a major research paper, the Defense Analytical Study, take some electives as well as the core, and participate in a series of exercises and war games, including a two-week capstone, National Defense Exercise, at the end of the year. Added to these features in 1989 was a study of various world regions followed by a field seminar on location, where students meet with U.S. country team personnel, foreign officials, academicians, and journalists to gain a sense of local cultural underpinnings and a different view of regional security issues.

Other reforms involved a renewed emphasis on air warfare and space operations in the curriculum and efforts to gain accreditation from the Joint Chiefs of Staff (JCS) in providing Phase One of Joint Military Education. They included the grading of all student performance during the academic year and requirements for more frequent and more rigorous writing assignments. The Air War College also hired its first civilian academic dean and appointed civilian department heads for the first time in its history. Indications of the resulting increased academic quality of its programs are perhaps to be found in the number of AWC graduates winning and earning commendation in the JCS Strategy Essay Competition among all the U.S. military intermediate and senior service schools. In the past seven years, the AWC has had two winners of the competition and a significant proportion of those chosen as Distinguished Essays.

The Air War College runs the largest open enrollment correspondence program for a senior service school of any of the services. At its peak, in 1983, it had nearly 10,000 students enrolled. The length of the course has gone from two years to one year and back again. When the program had to be completed in a single year, enrollment dipped to 1,175. The program appears to have settled into a two-year program on nonresident studies with 4,000–5,000 students enrolled at any one time. In the late 1990s, a major effort was undertaken to improve this portion of the AWC's activities through the use of computer-assisted instruction and the Internet.

In the more than fifty years since its inception in 1946, the Air War College has produced nearly 11,000 graduates of the resident program and over 33,000 officers and civilians from its nonresident program. Among them are hundreds of general officers, both American and foreign, and a number of Chiefs of Staff of the armed forces of our nation and those of friends and allies. The professional military education of airmen the world over has been greatly enhanced by this institution.

Grant T. Hammond

THE AMERICAN MILITARY ENLIGHTENMENT. Term coined by Samuel P. Huntington to characterize a uniquely fertile period (1832–1846) of early United States history for the creation of military thought and southern educational institutions.

The fifteen years from the end of Jackson's first administration to the beginning of the Mexican War saw an outpouring of military thought and writing which was, in many respects, unique in American history. Military societies sprang into being; military journals led brief but active lives; military offices published significant—and original—books; the idea of a military profession was expounded and defended. This eruption may be appropriately termed the American Military Enlightenment. Many factors contributed to its appearance, but the intellectual wells from which it was fed were predominantly Southern. Peculiarly enough, the Enlightenment ceased almost as abruptly as it had begun. The 1850s were as barren of significant military thought as the 1820s. Moreover, this military flowering was exclusively one of awareness and articulation. It was singularly void of lasting institutional reforms. The ideas of the Enlightenment, however, molded the form which professionalism in practice was to take after the Civil War.

The causes of the Enlightenment were complicated. The natural course of military development induced officers increasingly to recognize a "military science" distinct from technical specialties and civil pursuits. The initial, embryonic institutions of military professionalism, particularly West Point,* also contributed. The Military Academy had only begun to function effectively in 1817; consequently, it did not become capable of reproducing its kind until a couple of decades later. Dennis Hart Mahan,* the leading figure of the Enlightenment, for instance, was graduated in 1824 and, returning to teach in 1830, expounded the gospel of professionalism to successive generations of cadets for forty years. The thinking of the Enlightenment was also stimulated by the developing interest in science which spread through Europe and America in the 1830s and 1840s.

In this respect, the Enlightenment was rather closely linked to the intellectual currents of the day. Significantly, both Mahan and Matthew Fontaine Maury,* the leading naval figure, made their initial reputations as technical specialists, the former as an engineer and the latter as an oceanographer. The military journals generally had more technical articles than professional ones on the art of war. A military society, such as the United States Naval Lyceum founded by officers at the Brooklyn Navy Yard in 1833, sponsored scientific and technical researches and, at times, seemed more preoccupied with meteorology, zoology, botany, and mineralogy, than with more strictly naval subjects. The political conditions of the time also tended to stimulate professional activity. The Jacksonian attack on military institutions forced the officer to produce an *apologia pro vita sua.* The advanced outpouring of military thought was thus not unrelated to the backward state of military institutions. The same blanket hostility of a liberal society, which stimulated Federalists and Southerners to political theory, drove the advocates of military professionalism to sophisticated thought and pungent expression.

The principal positive impetus to the Military Enlightenment came from Southern conservatism. Southerners dominated the serious thought and discussion of military affairs. Military periodicals flourished during the 1830s and 1840s as they had never done before and as they were not to do again until the 1890s. The *Military and Naval Magazine* was published from 1833 to 1836, the *Army and Navy Chronicle* from 1835 to 1844, and the *Military Magazine* from 1839 to 1842. Preeminent among the journals interested in military affairs, however, was the great magazine of the South, the *Southern Literary Messenger. The Messenger* consistently devoted extensive attention to military and naval matters. By 1844, it had become the closest thing the country had to an army and navy journal. The two outstanding military writers and thinkers of the Enlightenment, Mahan, and Maury, were both Virginians; Maury went South in the Civil War and Mahan was sorely tempted to do so. Southern interest in the study of the military art was also manifest in the creation of local military schools. Virginia Military Institute* was established in 1839, the Citadel* and the Arsenal set up in South Carolina in 1842, Kentucky Military Institute in 1845. By 1860, every Southern state, except Florida and Texas, had its own state-supported military academy patterned on the models of West Point and VMI. With the notable exceptions of VMI and the Citadel, most of the Southern schools, like the military journals, did not survive the Civil War. Nonetheless, while they existed, they gave the South a unique sectional system of military education, which was absent in the north and west.[1]

AMPHIBIOUS WARFARE SCHOOL. The second tier of the four-tiered Marine Corps professional military education system offering a one-year course of study of career-level professional education and training for captains.

The contemporary mission of the Amphibious Warfare School is to provide

[1]Reprinted by permission of the publisher from THE SOLDIER AND THE STATE by Samuel P. Huntington, Cambridge, Mass.: Harvard University Press, Copyright © 1957 by the President and Fellows of Harvard College, renewed © 1985 by Samuel P. Huntington. (Asterisks added.)

career-level PME with an emphasis on warfighting skills, tactical decision making, combined arms operations, and the employment of Marine air–ground task forces in expeditionary operations, so as to prepare graduates to function as commanders and staff officers at appropriate levels within the Fleet Marine Force. In practice, the focus of instruction is on service-unique military operations at the battalion/squadron, regiment/group, and Marine Expeditionary Unit levels.

The origins of the Amphibious Warfare School can be traced to the Marine Officers Training School, one of two initial post–World War I schools at Quantico, Virginia.* Founded in March 1919, its initial class convened for a 22-week course of instruction in the autumn of 1919. Its size varied, as demobilization and postwar adjustments resulted in officers arriving and departing. Students ranged in grades from second lieutenant to captain. This institution was dissolved with the establishment of the Marine Corps Schools on September 1, 1920. Experienced instructors and course materials helped lay part of the foundation of the Marine Corps Schools, and its course of instruction became the forerunner of the Company Officers Course.

The Company Officers Course was founded in concept on September 1, 1920, as the second-level school in the then new three-tiered professional military education system of the Marine Corps. However, it did not receive its first students until 1921. This was due to problems the Corps had in deciding who would receive company grade regular commissions and then their seniority on the ensuing lineal list. Classes were disrupted in 1927 and canceled in 1928 because of Marine Corps overseas commitments in Nicaragua and China (Shanghai). Renamed the First Year Class in 1934, the curriculum and staff organization was restructured and modeled after that of the newly formed Fleet Marine Force, i.e., personnel, intelligence, operations, and logistics, with the course of study focused primarily on amphibious warfare. In 1936, the course was renamed again, with it being titled the Junior Course. The one-year course of instruction was suspended during World War II. The 1940–41 class graduated in January 1941, with the staff and students sent to Fleet Marine Force units or assigned to screen officer candidates in the reserve officers course or train newly commissioned second lieutenants at the Basic School.*

Students in this period ranged in rank from first lieutenant to major; however, they were normally senior first lieutenants and captains. Class size was small between 1920 and 1941, ranging from lows of 18 in 1929–30 and 19 in 1933–34, to a high of 53 in the 1924–25 and 1925–26 academic years. No army officers attended, and only in three consecutive classes were there naval officers: in the 1933–34 to 1935–36 academic years. In this period no international officers were in either the classes or the staff. By the closing of the school in 1941, 655 officers had attended it: Marine Corps—594; Marine Corps Reserve—47; U.S. Navy—14. Many of the Marine regimental commanders of late World War II were graduates of this course or served on the faculty of the Marine Corps Schools and hence instructed in it.

In the 1920s, the curriculum was modeled after that of the U.S. Army Infantry

School at Fort Benning, Georgia. In the 1930s, reflecting the shift within the Marine Corps Schools and the course of study of the Field Officers Course (now called the Command and Staff College*), the curriculum emphasized amphibious warfare. By 1940, the primary emphasis was on the assault as opposed to advanced base defense, but at a lower tactical level than its senior sister school. A conscious effort was made to link the course of study, paralleling the focus of the Marine Corps, to the U.S. Navy and Marine operations in support of a naval campaign. Operational problems were set in the Central Pacific and focused on the amphibious assault.

Between 1941 and 1944, the needs attendant to a major and rapid expansion of the Corps took precedence over any type of long- or short-term broad education or training for career officers. However, by 1944, with an unprecedented Marine Corps expansion, the need became apparent for trained company grade officers in ground and aviation matters beyond that in their initial training. This was further aggravated by the basic reality that most officers in the Marine Corps had no military experience prior to the war. Hence, in February 1944 the Aviation-Ground Officers School was established within the Marine Corps Schools at Quantico, Virginia. Initially, the school trained ground officers for nonflying duties with aviation units. The new school was an outgrowth of a program begun in 1943 to provide such a capability. The initial course was eight weeks in length, and 90 percent of the graduates proceeded to further specialist training. Subsequently, the school was renamed the Marine Air-Infantry School on January 30, 1945, and expanded to 13 weeks. It also had an expanded mission: prepare both aviation squadron and infantry battalion officers in the administration and tactical employment of air and ground units. This emphasized the need for cooperation between air, ground, and sea forces for success in combat. The five classes of this school graduated 399 students during the war. In 1946 the short Marine Air-infantry School course was dissolved.

In the autumn of 1946, the Corps revived its professional military education program for career officers. The course for captains was now called the Junior School, its name from 1946 to 1964, when it changed to the Amphibious Warfare School. As with its prewar predecessor, it had a course one academic year in length, except during the Vietnam era, when two six-month courses were taught per annum. The rank of the students generally remained that of captain, with international officers becoming part of the student body in the post–World War II years. Sister service representation was always a goal, although the number of U.S. Army, Navy, and Air Force officers was not as large as desired. The focus of the curriculum after World War II was amphibious operations, at the battalion and regimental levels.

The Amphibious Warfare School now has approximately 200 students per class, generally of the grade of captain. Each class has sister service representation, generally officers from the U.S. Army and U.S. Navy. International officers are a regular part of the student body, generally numbering between 12 and 18 per course. The curriculum remains one academic year in length, lasting from August to May. The methods of instruction include lectures; seminars; staff rides; and field, practical application, and war game simulation exercises. Each summer the school has also taught a two-week reserve officer course and has a nonresident course that parallels the resident curriculum.

In the late 1990s, several major innovations were under consideration. A possible name change to emphasize the more comprehensive nature of Marine Corps capabilities and possible future commitments was examined but rejected. However, the summer reserve course is being replaced with a two-week nonresident course offered by Marine Corps's College of Continuing Education. Its students will be both regular and reserve officers enrolled in either an offensive or defensive warfare concentration, offered in alternate years. Finally, a possible change to something like the Vietnam-era program, which could alter the length and increase the number of officers being offered resident course instruction in the future, was still under active study as the year 2000 began.

In 1989, the 39th commandant of the Marine Corps, General Alfred M. Gray, in describing the Amphibious Warfare School course, praised its accomplishments and called it the equivalent of "a junior staff course." However, the school stresses that it is more than a staff planning course. The faculty assumes that the graduates will know the appropriate tactical procedures and operational techniques. Rather, the conceptual focus is on the total Marine concept, emphasizing warfighting, leadership, and the decision-making process associated with the profession of arms. The technique is for students to come to a decision, explain the thought process leading to it, and then have the decision critiqued by fellow officers and the faculty. Stated differently, the approach and atmosphere is a collegial one that emphasizes both the education of the mind and the training of each officer, as appropriate.

Sources:

Colonel Kenneth Clifford, USMCR, *Progress and Purpose: A Development History of the United States Marine Corps* (Washington, DC: Marine Corps Historical Center, 1974).
1st Lieutenant Anthony Frances, USMCR, "History of the Marine Corps Schools, 1945," unpublished manuscript in the Archives, Marine Corps Research Center, Quantico, Virginia.
National Archives, RG 127. Marine Corps Muster Rolls, 1918 to 1941.

Donald F. Bittner

ANNAPOLIS. *See* U.S. NAVAL ACADEMY.

ANNAPOLIS, MARYLAND. Significant seaport in colonial America and the U.S. Federal period, located at the juncture of the Severn River and the Chesapeake Bay, 27 miles east of Washington, D.C.; Maryland's capital since 1694 and the site of the U.S. Naval Academy.

Blessed with a fine harbor, the early tobacco planters on the western bank of Maryland Colony's Seven River soon found themselves on the outskirts of a rapidly growing town. Accession to the English throne by the Dutch King William in 1688 brought about the appointment of a new Protestant governor for the colony who, in 1694, moved his capital from Catholic St. Mary's to Anne Arundel's Town, already the official residence for the colony's shipping coordinators and the royal tax collectors. The governor, Francis Nicholson, prompted development of a plan for his capital city, the central elements of which still focus much of the commercial life and the formal state activities of Annapolis today. In 1696, honoring the heir apparent to the throne, Princess Anne, the name Annapolis was adopted.

By the mid-18th century, Annapolis had grown into one of the most important and vibrant cities in the thirteen colonies. Moreover, as a colonial capital and an active seaport with relatively frequent communication with England, it had come to acquire a certain patina. As one author claims, "there was not a community in all Britain of the size of Annapolis which could have shown such splendor of living." The jumping-off point for significant tobacco commerce, the city had become the location of luxurious town houses for the wealthy planters. Their homes were furnished with items brought from England by ships' captains on their return voyages, and their families were adorned in London's latest fashions. The winter season, when the planters moved into town, was characterized by a series of "dinners, balls, and receptions" and a theater season, active enough by 1771 to warrant construction of a new, permanent theater building.

Toward the end of the winter season of 1755, Annapolis was visited by British Maj. General Edward Braddock and a group of officers from his expeditionary force, preparing in Virginia for its ill-fated attempt to capture Fort Duquesne. Apart from their quest for necessary provisions and the arrival for consultations of Colonel George Washington of the Virginia militia, who would help guide the expedition, the British arrival set off a week-long round of plays and banquets. The scarlet coats of the British officers entranced the young ladies of Annapolis, and they "danced and flirted" into the wee hours. Braddock, naive about his anticipated route of march, purchased a handsome coach from Governor Sharpe in which he expected to ride toward the country beyond the Alleghenies.

The coming of the Revolution had divisive effects on Annapolis society. Although three of its leading citizens—Charles Carroll, William Pace, and Samuel Chase—were signers of the Declaration of Independence, others remained loyal to the British Crown. Some had their property seized and were forced to move elsewhere in Maryland or flee to England. However, Annapolis itself, whose harbor prompted erection, in 1776, of four fortified earthworks, was untouched by the war. (Even in 1814, the two remaining and permanently strengthened fortifications, one of which was Fort Severn, were ignored by Admiral

Cochrane's squadron as it made its way up the Chesapeake to attack Fort Mc-Henry.)

Following the War of 1812, as the growth of other East Coast ports detracted from Annapolis, Fort Severn was accorded less regard by the War Department. Both it and its companion battery on the Severn's north shore were placed under command of an Army captain, with a total compliment of only 108 men. In 1817, the President and Congress were approached about incorporating the structure in a new Navy depot to take fuller advantage of the harbor, but the initiative failed to gain support, and the fort's garrison continued to dwindle.

Thus the land and facilities occupied by Fort Severn had little significance in the Army's plans when Secretary of the Navy George Bancroft* decided in 1845 to establish a permanent school to train young naval officers. By convincing his War Department counterpart to transfer the site, he established a relationship between Annapolis and the U.S. Navy that, with one four-year exception during the Civil War, was to become permanent. Officially renamed the United States Naval Academy* in 1850, Bancroft's creation was temporarily relocated northward to Newport, Rhode Island,* in 1861, to permit the Army to reactivate Fort Severn's protective battery for the war's duration.

Since the academy's return to Annapolis in 1865, the city's public identity has been essentially twofold: the site of Maryland's state government and the Naval Academy.

Sources:

Ruby R. Duval, "Fort Severn: Forerunner of the United States Naval Academy," *Shipmate* (October 1958).

W. O. Stevens, *Annapolis: Anne Arundel's Town* (New York: Dodd, Mead, 1937).

ARMED FORCES STAFF COLLEGE. A branch in Norfolk, Virginia, of the National Defense University, Washington, D.C. consisting of three programs: the Joint and Combined Staff Officer School, the Joint and Combined Warfighting School, and the Joint Command, Control, and Information Warfare School.

General Dwight D. Eisenhower, then Army Chief of Staff, suggested in an April 17, 1946, memorandum that "[T]here is a need for a school which will conduct short courses of approximately five months duration in joint staff technique and procedures in theaters and joint overseas operations." The Armed Forces Staff College was the result.

The Joint Chiefs of Staff formally announced AFSC's establishment on August 19, 1946, effective retroactively to August 13. The commandant was a three-star admiral or general assisted by a staff of senior officers and a multiservice faculty. The scope of instruction included study of the organization, composition, and functions of theaters and major joint task forces and their responsibilities (strategic, tactical, and logistical).

The AFSC faculty began instruction in late August 1946 as five subject-matter divisions: Intelligence, Operations, Logistics, Communications, and Special Subjects, each headed by a colonel or navy captain. A faculty board was responsible for the curriculum, selection of lecturers, research and analysis, and implementation of special studies or recommendations requested by the Joint Chiefs of Staff.

Periodic reviews of the curriculum over the years considered, but rejected, lengthening or shortening the 22-week course and assessed its relevance to the mission of the college and future requirements of its graduates. The curriculum changed only in minor ways and remained focused primarily on joint planning and the operational art* of war. However, it was regularly updated with influences of nuclear warfare, revisions in the U.S. joint and combined command structure, post–World War II military and political alliances, and other special topics as they became important to national security. About 25 percent of the curriculum was divided among the subjects of management, executive fitness, communicative arts, and electives. Among the electives were such subjects as The Commander and the Media, designed to teach staff officers how to interact with television and print media.

During its first 35 years AFSC was an independent school responsible to the Joint Chiefs of Staff. Then in 1981, AFSC became a component college of the National Defense University* (NDU), composed of the National War College* and the Industrial College of the Armed Forces*—both at Fort Lesley McNair* in Washington, D.C.—and also operating under the Joint Chiefs of Staff. Thereafter, the college's administrative organization included a deputy commandant who assisted the two-star commandant in college affairs, an executive officer, an editor, an international affairs advisor, and a public affairs officer. The faculty and staff continued as before in six departments, three of which focused solely on the seminars and course content of the Joint and Combined Staff Officer School (JCSOS). Since 1985, a fourth department has managed a separate Joint Command, Control, and Electronic Warfare School. Two others have supported the functioning of both schools.

A series of actual and perceived failures of interservice cooperation from 1980 to 1983 led to greatly increased congressional attention to joint matters, and on October 1, 1986, the Goldwater-Nichols Act* was signed into law. Title IV, delineating the designation Joint Specialty Officer (JSO) and specifying the training of officers, had the greatest impact on AFSC as the only joint staff college for midgrade officers. The act required that the Department of Defense improve its education and officer assignment policies and required that all new general or flag officers complete a joint duty assignment.

As a follow-up action, the House Armed Services Committee's Panel on Military Education (Skelton Panel*), in 1987, examined the ten intermediate and senior professional military education schools to assess the Defense Department's ability to develop officers competent in joint and strategic matters. The panel recommended a two-phased approach to the education of JSOs. Phase I, required of all officers at each intermediate or senior service school, would offer a broad overview of all services' capabilities and limitations, an introduction to joint planning, and a study of the role of service components in a unified command. Phase II would "concentrate on the integrated deployment and employment of multi-service forces," focus on joint doctrine, use "case studies in both developed theaters and undeveloped contingency theaters," promote better understanding of each service's culture and perspectives, and facilitate "developing joint attitudes and perspectives." Phase II training, offered only at AFSC, would be given to Phase I graduates on their way to assignment as J3Os.

Dramatic changes were made at AFSC after Title IV of Goldwater-Nichols was enacted and as the Joint Chiefs of Staff implemented the recommendations of the Skelton Panel. Course content during this period began to reflect the needs of individual theater commanders as well as sponsors in various directorates within the Joint Chiefs of Staff. Moreover, changing from a five-and-a-half-month permanent change of station assignment to a 12-week temporary duty school cut the class hours nearly in half. Despite the necessary changes, however, AFSC has remained loyal to its original educational philosophy of teaching interservice teamwork.

JCSOS classes in 1998 concentrated about 50 percent of their time on the topic of joint and multinational operation planning, including a detailed computer-assisted exercise/war game. (In mid-1996, AFSC added a Directorate of Educational Technology to manage the war-gaming functions and other applications of information technology.) Approximately 35 percent of class time was devoted about equally to studies of the joint perspective, strategic synchronization, and the operational art of war. Within the studies on the joint perspective was a requirement for teams of three or four officers from different services to write a collaborative research paper on a joint issue. A little less than 10 percent of the remaining class time was devoted to focused studies dealing with such matters as the detailed organization and responsibilities of the various commanders-in-chief for whom the graduates will eventually work. Administrative matters were reduced to less than 5 percent of class time.

Grading individual student performance, as recommended by the Skelton Panel, has been problematic in AFSC courses for two reasons: First, having students with differing ranks and experience levels enrolled in the same class makes direct comparison difficult. Secondly, the mission of the school and learning objectives for each block are thought to be best served by fostering a cooperative attitude among students. Competition for top grades and class ranking might defeat the course purpose of producing top-notch staff officers ready for joint and combined duty. Methods of evaluating students at AFSC changed in the mid-1970s to a form still in use as of 1996. Rather than measuring individual achievement, seminar aggregate scores document the effectiveness of instruction.

The mission of the Armed Forces Staff College evolved at the beginning of the Information Age into the challenge to educate staff officers and other leaders in joint operation planning and warfighting in order to instill a primary commitment to joint and combined teamwork, attitudes, and perspective. The college's commitment to quality education, collaboration rather than competition, personal and professional growth, and the highest professional standards indicates that the United States can have full confidence in the college's ability to perform its mission with continued excellence and flexibility.

Kenneth W. Fritz

ARMY COMMAND AND GENERAL STAFF COLLEGE. The crucible of command for the World War II generation of U.S. Army leaders, most of whom attended the staff school at Fort Leavenworth, Kansas, during the 1920s and 1930s and in the postwar era a principal source for development and dissemination of the Army's combined arms doctrine.

Leavenworth reopened its regular schools in 1919 and initially continued as before World War I with two separate professional courses—the first-year School of the Line and the second-year General Staff College. But in 1923, to accommodate the large "hump" of officers who entered the service during World War I and who had no schooling in the duties of the general staff or high command, the War Department reduced the program to one year and redesignated it as the Command and General Staff School. This nearly doubled the size of the annual graduating classes. By 1929, the wartime hump had been reduced, and the curriculum was lengthened to two years. Seven classes graduated from the two-year course between 1930 and 1936, with all students attending both years. By the mid-1930s, the War Department again determined a need for more trained general staff officers. Consequently, the Leavenworth course from 1936 to 1940 reverted to a single year.

The interwar Leavenworth classes were considerably larger than those of the prewar school; most of the one-year courses graduated nearly 250 officers, with the two-year courses about half of that. Although students normally were majors and senior captains, instruction sought to prepare them for positions two to three ranks above their current grades. The 1920 National Defense Act made attendance at the interwar Command and General Staff School a defining experience of an officer's career. Graduation from Leavenworth was required for qualification for the General Staff Eligible List, a prerequisite for attendance at the Army War College,* service on the War Department General Staff,* and ultimately higher command. The World War II leadership of the Army and Army Air Forces, from Henry Arnold II,* Dwight Eisenhower, Omar Bradley, Jacob Devers, Carl Spaatz, to army, corps, and division commanders, nearly all were products of the interwar Command and General Staff School. During World War II, the school continued to function, graduating over 20,000 officers from three dozen ten-week, specialized general staff and service staff classes. Upon graduation most officers immediately went to a staff position in one of the newly mobilized divisions or other major units.

In 1946 the Army resumed the regular one-year course at Leavenworth, with one major change. Immediately following the end of the war, the Army War

College was not yet reopened; Leavenworth was thus responsible for covering in one year what it and the War College formerly had done in two. When the Army reopened the War College in 1950 as its capstone school, Leavenworth's area of responsibility again narrowed.

During the 1950s and 1960s the Command and General Staff College became the Army's premier tactical school, concentrating on warfighting skills at division and corps level. Although traditional tactics and logistics dominated the course, additional offerings on such topics as nuclear weapons and security assistance and internal defense also appeared. Throughout this period class size steadily grew, from about 400 to over 1,300 during the years of the Vietnam War. Most students were majors, and each class included sizeable contingents of foreign officers and those from other U.S. services. Graduates during this period were perceived as generalists, but with particular tactical competence for division operations.

The major curriculum revisions in the post–World War II era occurred in the early 1970s, largely as a result of recommendations of the 1966 Board to Review Army Officer Schools (the Haines Board*) and the 1971 Review of the Army Educational System (the Norris Board). In order to meet the changing needs of an increasingly complex army, these boards perceived a need for the role of the college to evolve from a one-course, one-curriculum institution to that of the professional university of the Army. Beginning with the 1972–73 academic year, therefore, Leavenworth introduced a significant electives program to the course. All students would pursue a traditional CGSC core curriculum (about 60 percent of instruction time) emphasizing problem solving, command and staff procedures, and tactics and logistics of combined arms units division size and larger. Professional electives, in the general area of military art and science, constituted the remaining 40 percent of instruction time and would be offered during the second half of the academic year. The electives would give an infantry major, potentially preparing to be an operations staff officer or for battalion command, the opportunity to take additional courses on tactics and combined arms operations, while his ordnance classmate could improve his skills and knowledge in such areas as "planning, programming, and budgeting" and advanced logistics. Because most graduates did not immediately join the Army in the field, the college also broadened instruction to include more on Department of the Army, joint, and combined staffs, and on other support, logistic, and administrative functions. The effect was a broadening of the general curriculum and a lowering of the instructional center of gravity for tactics to include battalion and brigade operations.

As a result of the electives program, in 1976 the North Central Association of Colleges and Schools accredited the college, thereby allowing Leavenworth to grant a Master of Military Art and Science (M.MAS.) degree to students who took additional course work and wrote a thesis. The electives program has changed and expanded in ensuing years, with dozens of course offerings in subjects like leadership, military history, area studies, force development, and operational art. Similarly, the M.MAS. program continues to graduate several dozen officers annually who have successfully written an independent thesis based on original research relating to some aspect of military art and science.

In the 1990s the Command and General Staff College arguably remains the single most important professional educational experience for Regular Army officers, about half of whom attend. It continues as a doctrinal center for the service, particularly in drafting, updating, and promulgating the Army's principal doctrinal manual, *FM 100–5, Operations*.

Sources:

Boyd L. Dastrup, *The U.S. Army Command and General Staff College: A Centennial History* (Manhattan, KS: Sunflower University Press, 1982).

Timothy K. Nenninger, *The Leavenworth Schools and the Old Army: Education, Professionalism, and the Officer Corps of the United States Army, 1881–1918* (Westport, CT: Greenwood Press, 1978).

————, "Leavenworth and Its Critics: The U.S. Army Command and General Staff School, 1920–1940," *Journal of Military History* 58 (April 1994).

John W. Partin (ed.), *A Brief History of Fort Leavenworth, 1827–1983* (Fort Leavenworth, KS: Combat Studies Institute, U.S. Army Command and General Staff College, 1983).

Timothy K. Nenninger

ARMY FIELD ARTILLERY SCHOOL. Since 1911, a school at Fort Sill, Oklahoma, to educate and train field artillerymen within the War Department's progressive system of professional military education (PME). It has also developed tactics, doctrine, and force structure and helped design new equipment.

On June 5, 1911, the War Department issued General Order Number 73 that authorized the establishment of the School of Fire for Field Artillery. Modeled after the German Artillery School at Juterbog, the School of Fire set out to teach a new procedure of fire direction, called indirect fire that was rapidly supplanting direct fire in European armies. Before any concrete accomplishments could be achieved, however, the Mexican Revolution caused the War Department to close the school in the spring of 1916.

Following the United States entrance into World War I, the War Department reopened the School of Fire late in 1917 and dispatched Colonel William J. Snow to be commandant. Snow, who later served as Chief of Field Artillery for the War Department, initiated an ambitious construction program, restructured the course of instruction, and enlarged and reorganized the staff and faculty. Equally important, Snow and his wartime successors, Colonel Adrian S. Fleming and Brig. General Laurin L. Lawson, taught field artillery soldiers mobile warfare tactics in addition to indirect fire to make the school more than the gunnery school it had been prior to the war.

During the 1920s and 1930s, the school, renamed Field Artillery School in 1919, added another critical mission. Besides broadening its PME teaching commitment by adding more courses of instruction in the 1920s, the school embarked on a long-range program in the 1930s to improve field artillery mobility, gunnery, and equipment. Innovative directors of the Gunnery Department, Major Carlos Brewer, Major Orlando Ward, Lt. Colonel H.L.C. Jones, and others with support from school commandants, created the fire direction center to centralize command and control and to facilitate massing fire. They also pushed the adoption of motor vehicles as prime movers to replace the horse and introduced new tactics and organization. By the time the United States entered World War II, in December 1941, the Field Artillery School had developed a field artillery branch that was preeminent throughout the world.

Besides expanding its training load during World War II, the Field Artillery School continued to be a leader in field artillery developments. To take advantage of long-range field guns that were being introduced and to support the other combat arms more effectively, the school promoted organic air observation for field artillery. Influenced by the school and the Chief of Field Artillery, Major General Robert M. Danford, the War Department finally approved organic air observation for field artillery in June 1942 after testing had affirmed its soundness. The Department of Air Training in the school, created in 1942 and led by Colonel William W. Ford, trained pilots to be adept at taking off from and landing on short, uneven fields, often surrounded by obstacles such as trees and wires. Using techniques developed and taught at the school, organic air observers in light aircraft provided liaison, reconnaissance, observation, and target acquisition which enabled field artillery units to bring massed fire down on the enemy.

After World War II, the Field Artillery School experienced dramatic organizational changes over a period of several years. In November 1946 the War Department consolidated all artillery training and equipment development, including a new Antiaircraft and Guided Missile School at Fort Bliss, Texas, under the Artillery Center at Fort Sill as part of a cost-saving measure. The center was composed of the Artillery School (formerly the Field Artillery School) and all Army ground force units at Fort Sill. The reorganization forced the Artillery School (by July 1957, renamed U.S. Army Artillery and Missile School) to teach anti-aircraft artillery subjects and to be involved in air defense artillery (as it was named after 1957) developments for nearly 23 years. In 1969, the Department of the Army redesignated the U.S. Army Artillery and Missile School as the U.S. Army Field Artillery School and gave Fort Bliss total responsibility for air defense artillery instruction and developments.

In the midst of the organizational turmoil, the Fort Sill school still retained its primary mission. It trained officers and enlisted personnel to employ missile, rocket, and cannon field artillery and played a seminal part in the development of tactics, doctrine, organization, and equipment for conventional and atomic field artillery. For example, in 1953 school personnel fired the first atomic field artillery piece, the 280-mm gun, at Frenchman's Flat, Nevada. During the 1950s, school personnel also participated in the development of rockets and missiles that were capable of carrying a nuclear warhead, such as the *Honest John* rocket, the *Corporal* missile, and the *Redstone* missile. In 1963, the school tested aerial rocket artillery, a helicopter equipped with a rocket system, to determine its ability to furnish fire support on the modern battlefield. In the 1960s, aerial rocket artillery demonstrated that it could follow the contour of the land, uninhibited by terrain, and furnish effective fire support in the jungles, mountains, and deltas of South Vietnam. In the meantime, the school cooperated in the development of the Field Artillery Digital Automated Computer that significantly reduced after 1967 the time required to calculate fire direction data.

After the Vietnam War, when training requirements had been dramatically increased, the Field Artillery School shifted its attention back to combat in Europe. In response to the massive rearmament of Soviet and Warsaw Pact military forces during the 1960s and early 1970s, the Field Artillery School, under the guidance of progressive commandants, initiated far-reaching modernization programs. Over a period of sixteen years, beginning in 1974, the Field Artillery School substantially reshaped field artillery tactics, doctrine, equipment, organization, and training. It participated in the development of the Multiple-Launch Rocket System, the *Paladin* 155-mm self-propelled howitzer, and other field artillery systems. Simultaneously, as befits a PME institution, the school helped to write AirLand Battle doctrine, redesigned field artillery force structure, and revamped field artillery training to make it more effective and more realistic.

With the budget and the force structure reductions that accompanied the end of the cold war early in the 1990s, the Field Artillery School had to be more innovative in order to meet the needs of a force-projection military force. The school leveraged advanced technology to ensure that officers and enlisted personnel in the active Army, the Army National Guard, and the Army Reserve would be trained to the same standard. The school also worked to automate field artillery systems and continued developing doctrine, tactics, techniques, and procedures for the new weapon systems being introduced.

With the exception of the pre–World War I years, the Field Artillery School played an active role in shaping American field artillery. Without a doubt the school made American field artillery a critical combat arm on the battlefields of the twentieth century.

Sources:

Boyd L. Dastrup, *King of Battle: A Branch History of the U.S. Army's Field Artillery* (Fort Monroe, VA: Office of the Command Historian, U.S. Army Training and Doctrine Command, 1992, reprinted by the U.S. Army Center of Military History, 1994).

History of the Field Artillery School (4 vols.) (Fort Sill, OK: U.S. Army Field Artillery School, 1942–67).

Wilber S. Nye, *Carbine and Lance: The Story of Old Fort Sill* (Norman: University of Oklahoma Press, 1937, reprinted in 1969).

Melvin L. Whitely, "History of the Field Artillery School," unpublished manuscript in
the Morris Swett Technical Library, U.S. Army Field Artillery School, Fort Sill,
OK.

Boyd L. Dastrup

ARMY GENERAL STAFF. *See* WAR DEPARTMENT GENERAL STAFF.

ARMY INDUSTRIAL COLLEGE. Institution created in 1924 to train Army
officers needed to plan for industrial mobilization and avoid repeating the ineffectiveness of practices followed in the United States during World War I.

Despite the fact that World War I had been raging for 32 months when the
United States declared war, notwithstanding the large numbers of war orders
received by U.S. industry to arm the French and the British, and despite the
National Defense Act of 1916 (which, among other things, established a rudimentary mechanism for mobilizing American industry), U.S. ground and air
forces that fought in World War I were largely supplied with French and British
munitions. This was because U.S. industrial mobilization had been so inefficient.

Because of that ineffectiveness, Congress passed legislation to build an apparatus to ensure that if the United States went to war again, it would be better
mobilized industrially. The National Defense Act of June 4, 1920 delineated
responsibilities in the Office of the Secretary of War for procurement and industrial mobilization. It charged an assistant secretary with "supervision of the
procurement of all military supplies . . . and the assurance of adequate provision
for mobilization of materiel and industrial organizations essential to war-time
needs."

In October 1921, the assistant secretary established a procurement division to
supervise "procurement of all military supplies and other business of the War
Department pertaining thereto . . . and the assurance of adequate provision for
the mobilization of materiel and industrial organizations essential to war-time
needs." The division was subdivided into a current supply branch and a planning
branch, both under the direction of an Army colonel. The Planning Branch was
responsible for planning for wartime procurement and industrial mobilization
and was also the agency that dealt with the Navy Department and all other
government departments on "all matters pertaining to the allotment of industrial
facilities and materials required for war."

For the next decade the Planning Branch was the only government agency
engaged in industrial mobilization planning. The Army and Navy Munitions
Board was founded in 1922 to deal with potential logistical frictions between
the Army and Navy, but it was ineffective for more than a decade.

Soon after both these organizations were founded it became apparent to War
Department leaders that there was no formal schooling for the people who would
staff the Planning Branch. Several Planning Branch staff officers lobbied for an
institution to educate officers for their organization. Their efforts bore fruit in
1924 with the establishment of the Army Industrial College. In 1924 the

Secretary of War issued a general order establishing "A college, to be known as the Army Industrial College . . . for the purpose of training Army officers in the useful knowledge pertaining to the supervision of all military supplies in time of war and to the . . . mobilization of material and industrial organizations essential to war-time needs."

The college was assigned to the assistant secretary of the department for direction rather than the War Department General Staff* (which supervised all other professional military education including the Army War College*). The first course lasted four months, with only nine army officers in its student complement. But within a year of the college's founding, small numbers of Marine and naval officers began attending. It is important to note that from the beginning the focus of the curriculum was on general logistics and not just procurement.

The motivations of the school's founders went beyond just understanding the mechanics of procurement and industrial mobilization. These men hoped to educate military officers about industry to the point that such educated people could control industrial mobilization and in fact direct war industries. These officers believed it had been a mistake to leave control of war industries in the hands of civilian financiers and industrialists like Bernard Baruch (chairman of the World War I War Industries Board) during World War I, and they thought that military control would yield greater efficiency. The officers of the Planning Branch believed their interests differed from those of businessmen: that the former would concentrate on the military mission and require effectiveness; the latter would focus on efficiency and profits. The former understood the need for profits but did not believe the two entities could become effective partners— thus creating the necessity for military officers to be in control.

The staff officer most involved in fostering the creation of the Army Industrial College, Major James H. Burns, wrote: "While actual production was essentially the task of industry, planning and control . . . of the production of War Department supplies were primarily military responsibilities." He argued that the "authority" to plan and control "should not be surrendered" to agencies outside of the War Department and that the Army should be organized to supervise industry in wartime. He believed that "military men should be thoroughly trained in the [mobilization] plan so that they could man the key positions in time of war." Once war production was well under way, "these men could be replaced by 'Captains of Industry' working as part of the War Department organization." The assistant secretary of war in 1924 shared this view and believed the college would "fit officers for the mobilization and direction of the industrial power of the country."

As it turned out, the notion that industrial mobilization was too important to be left to civilian industrialists—that soldiers could master industry after a relatively short training program—was a premise that the commander-in-chief did not accept. When the Congress declared war in 1941, President Franklin D. Roosevelt found such an arrangement absurd and refused to implement the industrial mobilization plans written by the Planning Branch and the Army and

Navy Munitions Board (and critiqued by the Army Industrial College) that gave the military essential control over business.

Before then, the Army Industrial College had slowly gained in prestige and in size. For the first three years the college ran a five-month course, and in 1927 it began to conduct a ten-month course. That was the mode until World War II began in Europe; then the college began rushing large numbers of students through the course several times each year to enlarge the body of officers with education in industrial mobilization. The first three classes had 9, 13, and 30 students respectively, and the classes in the early 1930s matriculated student bodies in the 40s and 50s. There were two classes in 1940 and four in 1941. More than one-quarter of all Army Industrial College graduates matriculated in that one year. Incidentally, Major Dwight D. Eisenhower served in the Planning Branch in the early 1930s, was a part-time faculty member at the college for four years, and considered himself to be a member of the Industrial College class of 1933. By December 1941, when the Army Industrial College ceased to operate because of the war emergency, it had trained about 1,000 officers of whom about 15 percent were from the Navy and Marine Corps.

Despite the efforts of such distinguished strategists as Eisenhower, the number of graduates did not come close to fulfilling the needs of the Army. During the height of the war there were 25,000 officers in Army procurement branches, and no more than 2 percent of these could have been Industrial College graduates. Those who were had intensely studied industry, examined the activities of the World War I War Industries Board and other World War I mobilization agencies, and also analyzed mobilization problems from that war. Students also provided analytical support and criticism to the Planning Branch and to the Army and Navy Munitions Board when these organizations wrote the various industrial mobilization plans. Perhaps Donald M. Nelson summed up the benefit of the Army Industrial College best. Nelson had worked inside the initial mobilization agencies that Roosevelt appointed before December 1941 and was the first director of the War Production Board, a gigantic mobilization bureaucracy that came into existence in mid-January 1942. He wrote that the Army Industrial College had produced a "reserve of practical experience and research" that his 20,000-person bureaucracy could use. Beyond that, however, he refused to go.

Sources:

Terrance J. Gough, "Soldiers, Businessmen and U.S. Industrial Mobilization Planning Between the World Wars," *War & Society* 9, no. 1 (May 1991).

Alan L. Gropman, *Mobilizing U.S. Industry in World War II*, McNair Paper 50 (Washington, DC: National Defense University Press, 1996).

Marvin A. Kreidberg and Merton G. Henry, *History of Military Mobilization in the United States Army, 1775–1945* (Washington, DC: Headquarters, U.S. Army, 1955).

J. M. Scammell, "History of the Industrial College of the Armed Forces 1924–1946," unpublished manuscript, National Defense University Library.

Alan L. Gropman

ARMY RESERVE OFFICERS' TRAINING CORPS (ROTC). Federally legislated organization, authorized in 1916, that gave structure and support to programs previously administered by the individual states for training civilian college students to become officers in the state militias and Federal Reserve forces.

The concept of the Army Reserve Officers' Training Corps originated from the visions of George Washington, Thomas Jefferson, Frederick von Steuben, and George Clinton. In 1783, New York Governor George Clinton was the first to develop a plan that called for the introduction of military instruction at one civilian college in each state of the Union. Under this plan, students, after completing their degree and the prescribed course of military instruction, would be commissioned and serve a short tour of active duty. Upon returning to civilian life, they would form a trained officer reserve pool that would be available in time of emergency. A system of inspections and reports was to give coherence and uniformity to this officer education program.

Norwich University,* in Vermont, and the University of Virginia were two of the first civilian institutions of higher learning in the United States to actually incorporate military education into their curricula. The American Literary, Scientific and Military Academy—now Norwich University, founded by Captain Alden Partridge* in 1819, is where the modern Army ROTC traces its heritage. Captain Partridge intended the military training at Norwich to "constitute an appendage" to a cadet's civil education, only one element in a curriculum designed to educate young Americans for the dual role of the citizen-soldier: engineers, businessmen, or teachers during peace and combat commanders in the event of war. Thomas Jefferson also supported the citizen-soldier concept. Upon founding the University of Virginia in 1825, Jefferson made tactical drill and training an important supplementary aspect of the college curriculum. Limited military instruction, he hoped, would produce qualified officers for the military reserve and, in time, develop as a proper field of study throughout the entire academic community.

Meanwhile, 20 other private military schools of the Norwich model were established across the eastern United States before the outbreak of the Civil War (1861–65). But with no visible threat to national security and a general indifference of most Americans for military education, few of these institutions survived the antebellum period. Some state governments organized military colleges similar to Norwich, including the Virginia Military Institute* in 1839 and the South Carolina Military Academy (the Citadel*) in 1842. Although the influence of West Point* soon became apparent, the curriculum of these military colleges retained the Norwich inclination to prepare young men for civilian careers as well as for the duties of military leadership. Clearly, the concept of collegiate military education had already taken root when Americans faced their first modern war in 1861.

Almost immediately, the mass army demands of the Civil War compelled

United States legislators to make some provision for the education of military leaders on a grand scale. The need for approximately 20,000 trained Army officers provided a tangible justification, among others, for using federal land grants to assist in financing the creation of agricultural and industrial colleges. Representative Justin S. Morrill* of Vermont sponsored this legislation, which fully espoused the citizen-soldier theory. The Land Grant College Act was passed in 1862, allowing for the establishment of an unofficial reserve officer training program at the state level. It entitled every state to receive 30,000 acres of public land for each of its members in Congress, the sale of which would generate funds to establish at least one "agricultural and industrial college" per state. The act stipulated that "military tactics" be included in the curriculum of such institutions.

During the period between the Civil War and World War I (1865–1917) the true potential of this unofficial reserve officer training program was never realized because of a lack of quality control and centralized management. With the Land Grant Act the Congress had relinquished its authority for administering reserve officer training to the state governments. As a result, uniform national standards did not exist for collegiate precommissioning education, nor did the federal government hold supervisory authority to regulate such training. While the President was authorized to detail Regular Army or retired officers as military instructors, fewer than 100 were ever assigned. By 1914 the Army had assigned barely enough officers to teach military tactics and drill at eleven civilian military colleges, 52 land-grant colleges, and eleven other collegiate institutions. As a result, the quality of military instruction at civilian institutions varied from good to poor depending on the competence of the instructor and the number of years and number of hours per week prescribed for graduation. A mere 100 or so students who participated in college military training during this period were commissioned in the Regular Army (almost all Regular Army commissions went to West Point graduates). Only 1,500 served as officers during the Spanish-American War, and approximately 9,000 mobilized with the Army for World War I.

Precommissioning education at civilian institutions improved with the full implementation of the official ROTC program in 1920. This resulted from a provision of the National Defense Act of 1916, which granted the federal government jurisdiction to manage reserve officer training at civil institutions on the national level, to award Reserve officer commissions upon graduation, and then pool ROTC graduates in the Officers Reserve Corps for call-up in an emergency. During the interwar period Regular Army officers and enlisted men were assigned as ROTC cadre to approximately 135 institutions of higher learning, as well as military junior colleges and high schools. The branch affiliation of each ROTC institutional unit determined its on-campus curriculum and summer camp training. Some schools supported several different types of ROTC units (infantry, cavalry, artillery, engineer, etc.).

In the wars of the mid-20th century, Reserve officers assumed the leadership of mobilizing units, trained the Army to combat readiness, and then led America's soldiers to victory on several battlefields. Approximately 120,000 ROTC graduates were called to officer duty during World War II and the Korean War (1951–53). During actual hostilities, however, the ROTC could not train new officers fast enough, causing the Army to rely on officer candidate school (OCS) programs in meeting the production demands for an additional 152,000 officers. Nonetheless, the solid combat record of Reserve officers during these conflicts and the cost effectiveness of ROTC officer production encouraged the federal government to also develop the ROTC program as the primary source of commissions for the active (Regular) Army in the decades that followed.

In 1948, the Army introduced the Distinguished Military Graduate program, which awarded Regular Army commissions to ROTC cadets of superior performance. The Reserve Officers Act of 1955 committed ROTC graduates to either two years of active duty or six months of active duty for training, depending on the needs of the Army. The Army maintained senior ROTC units at 190 institutions with a cadet enrollment of nearly 100,000. After 1955 between 70 and 85 percent of all active duty Army second lieutenants were products of the ROTC. Meanwhile, ROTC graduates increasingly infiltrated the ranks of the Regular Army officer corps and by 1989 constituted almost 70 percent of its field grade officers and nearly 60 percent of its generals.

The growing importance of the ROTC to the active Army developed in spite of the program's lagging management structure, which up until the mid-1960s administered the program in a very decentralized, haphazard manner. When the inefficiencies of the administrative process failed to meet the demands of the peacetime buildup during the cold war (1947–90), the federal government responded by gradually improving, centralizing, and standardizing the program. A General Military Science curriculum was introduced during the late 1950s and early 1960s to replace the chaotic branch specific courses. Congress passed the Reserve Officers' Training Corps Vitalization Act of 1964, which authorized 5,500 two- and four-year scholarships, and introduced a "two-year program," allowing certain students to earn a commission in two years after successfully completing a six-week basic summer camp. In 1967 the monitoring agency for the ROTC was expanded from a headquarters staff division to a directorate. Six years later, replacing the directorate, the Office of the Deputy Chief of Staff for ROTC was formed within the new Headquarters, U.S. Army Training and Doctrine Command (TRADOC) to supervise the program through four ROTC region commands.

Following the Vietnam War (1965–73), the improved ROTC management system faced the challenges of recruiting officer candidates in an environment of indifference, without the inducements of the past: the draft and the compulsory military training of the land-grant colleges. Problems in both quantity and quality plagued the program, causing the Army to place increased emphasis on ROTC recruiting efforts and the Congress to raise scholarship authorizations to

12,000. When General William R. Richardson assumed command of TRADOC in 1983, he acted to resolve the problems in quality. He decided to improve the caliber of Reserve officer graduates by raising standards and by granting the ROTC the command status necessary to enforce them.

The activation of the Headquarters, U.S. Army Cadet Command, on April 15, 1986, signaled the beginning of a new era in Army precommissioning training. Under the direction of its first commander, Maj. General Robert E. Wagner, the new organization implemented major initiatives to standardize on-campus and summer camp training, tighten commissioning standards, and transition leader development programs to meet the national security challenges of the future. The creditable performance of newly commissioned ROTC graduates in Operation Just Cause (Panama) and Operation Desert Storm (Persian Gulf) during the period 1989–91 demonstrated the positive effects of these reforms on the Army's combat readiness. During its first ten years, the Cadet Command awarded almost 53,000 commissions, bringing the total of officers produced through the ROTC program since 1920 to nearly 600,000.

The concepts of America's Founders for Army officer training were well realized through the standardization brought about by the Cadet Command at the end of the 20th century. After 200 years of evolution, the United States had developed a civil-military process capable of training competent officers, at low cost, for the entire Army from the complete spectrum of academic institutions across the nation.

Sources:

Arthur T. Coumbe and Lee S. Harford, Jr., *U.S. Army Cadet Command: The 10-Year History* (Fort Monroe, VA: U.S. Army Cadet Command, 1996).

James T. Currie and Richard B. Crossland, *Twice the Citizen: A History of the United States Army Reserve 1908–1995*, Department of the Army Pamphlet 104–10, Washington, DC, 1989.

Marvin A. Kreidberg and Merton G. Henry, *History of Military Mobilization in the United States Army, 1775–1945* (Washington, DC: Center of Military History, 1989).

Gene M. Lyons and John W. Masland, *Education and Military Leadership: A Study of the R.O.T.C.* (Princeton, NJ: Princeton University Press, 1959).

Lee S. Harford, Jr.

ARMY WAR COLLEGE (1901–40). The capstone institution of the U.S. Army's system for officer professional military education, first established in 1901, at Washington Barracks (now Fort Lesley McNair).

While the creation of an Army war college may have been the logical outgrowth of earlier professional military education institutions (the Army's Artillery School, Fort Monroe, Virginia,* 1824; the Infantry and Cavalry School, Fort Leavenworth, Kansas,* 1881; and the Naval War College, Newport, Rhode Island,* 1884), it nonetheless originated with the Secretary of War, Elihu Root,* in 1899. Emerging from a disappointing display of military incompetence in the Spanish-American War, the Army War College was officially commissioned by General Order Number 155 on November 27, 1901. This general order established a progressive system of officer professional education to be supervised by a War College Board. The board was formed with Maj. General Samuel B. M. Young as the president, and hence he became the college's first commandant.

With the passing of the General Staff Act in 1903, the college itself was formed as an adjunct to the War Department General Staff;* Maj. General Young became the first Chief of Staff of the U.S. Army and Brig. General Tasker Bliss* succeeded him as the president of the Army War College. The primary function of the board and the college was to prepare both organizationally and intellectually for the creation and activation of the General Staff Corps. The first college class of six captains and three majors began work on November 1, 1904, in a temporary location across the street from the White House, at 22 Jackson Place.

The period between 1901 and 1940 marks the first two of four discernible stages in the history of the Army War College. Each stage similarly emerged out of lessons learned from a major 20th-century conflict and was subsequently shaped largely to accommodate the external pressures of the times. The "first Army War College" spanned the period from 1901 to 1917, from its inception following the Spanish-American War to the beginning of World War I. The "second Army War College" emerged during the period of 1919 to 1940, from the end of World War I to the beginning of World War II. The "third Army War College" spanned the period 1950 to 1990, from the end of World War II to the end of the cold war. And the "fourth Army War College" has begun to emerge in the aftermath of the cold war and in response to the expected challenges of the 21st century. Although not official names, these numbered designations are useful for understanding the War College's evolution.

From June 1907, until its closing to accommodate pre–World War II mobilization in 1940, the college was located in Theodore Roosevelt Hall, its first official schoolhouse, at Washington Barracks—now known as Fort McNair—in Washington, D.C. In February 1903, at ceremonies commemorating the laying of the cornerstone of this magnificent structure, founding father Elihu Root's dedication speech included two visionary statements that would guide the college for the rest of the century. First, he said that the purpose for the Army War College was "not to promote war, but to preserve peace by the intelligent and adequate preparation to repel aggression." He went on to say that in order to achieve this high purpose the college must commit itself to "study and confer on the great problems of national defense, of military science and of responsible command." An interesting aspect of the history of the Army War College is how, in response to the needs of the Army and the nation, the college has shifted the emphasis among these three great problems with respect to its central purpose and curriculum.

Before World War I, the War College student body ranged from 12 to 22 students, made up almost exclusively of line Army officers and a few Marines. Students were selected from a pool of applicants for a limited number of seats aimed primarily at the duties of higher command in war and, in peace, preparing for war. The student body of the second Army War College grew to between 75 and 90 students selected by the chiefs of the respective arms and services, within assigned quotas and policy guidelines.

In the beginning, the War College was dedicated primarily to producing officers for general staff duties within the War Department and the major subordinate commands. From these beginnings Tasker Bliss decided that the college, as an adjunct to the general staff, would not conduct academic instruction per se, but rather students would "learn things by doing things" through the "applicatory method" of instruction. This was to become the early forerunner to what the college would later refer to as "experiential learning." By emphasizing primarily war planning duties throughout this period, the prevailing teaching methodology was referred to as the "collegium," drawing upon a close mentoring/teaching role for the faculty relative to their novice students.

The focus of study (really staff action) during this early period was largely on contingency planning, which combined the tactical employment of higher-level formations with Army and Navy cooperation so obviously lacking throughout the Spanish-American War. Actual staff actions were supplemented with map exercises, command post exercises, and historical staff rides—all designed to sharpen the staff skills and critical thinking skills of the prospective graduate. In its formative stages the War College was significantly influenced by the workings of the German (Prussian) General Staff* system, the program of the Naval War College and the Infantry and Cavalry School at Fort Leavenworth, Kansas. In 1910 the college's coat of arms was officially approved with the motto Prudens Futuri (providing for the future) emblazoned upon it. While still in its formative years the War College was well on its way in building the firm foundation that would characterize it over the upcoming decades—always providing for the future.

Following a two-year interruption from 1917 to 1919, the second Army War College emerged out of lessons learned from "the war to end all wars." As in 1900, following the Spanish-American War, World War I revealed obvious weaknesses in the defense establishment's ability to effectively mobilize the nation for a major conflict. In response to this deficiency, the college consolidated its role as an educational institution, and the presentation of formal instruction began to replace the staff action and planning so characteristic of its formative years. The role of command, in conjunction with the impact of economic, political, and social considerations, formed the centerpiece of the curriculum. Mobilization and campaign planning for the operation of field armies and higher formations were a primary focus, and the third Root imperative of "responsible command" was officially added to the curriculum. While map maneuvers, command post exercises, and war games continued to provide for practical application, emphasis was also placed on historical and analytical studies. Guest lecturers were also introduced to provide the context of nonmilitary subjects. While the German General Staff system had strong influence on the first War College, it was the French General Staff organization that was most influential during its second period.

The National Defense Acts of 1916 and 1920 also played defining roles in the life of the Second War College; the former severed the college's adjunct relationship to the War Department General Staff, and the latter reorganized the War Department and established specific educational requirements for General Staff officers. "Preparation for war" and the "conduct of war," from the tactical to the operational levels, best describe the focus of instruction, and students were being prepared to perform both command and staff functions as the onset of World War II began to take form. Essentially the college had begun to mature its program from an emphasis on staff actions and the tactical art to one which, in the third stage of its history, would be marked even more by command and staff functions and the practice of the operational art.*

Sources:

Harry P. Ball, *Of Responsible Command: A History of the U.S. Army War College* (Dallas, TX: Taylor Publishing Company, rev. ed., 1994).

Richard A. Chilcoat, "The 'Fourth' Army War College: Preparing Strategic Leaders for the Next Century," *Parameters* (Winter 1995–96).

George S. Pappas, *Prudens Futuri: The U.S. Army War College 1901–1967* (Marceline, MO: Walsworth Publishing Company, for the Alumni Association of the U.S. Army War College, 1968.)

Robert A. Brace

ARMY WAR COLLEGE (1950–). The contemporary U.S. Army War College (USAWC), located since 1951 in Carlisle Barracks, Pennsylvania, after reopening temporarily at Fort Leavenworth following a 10-year closure in 1940.

As World War II came to a close in 1946 General Dwight D. Eisenhower, in close collaboration with his predecessor, Army Chief of Staff George C. Marshall, offered the original Army War College facilities at Fort Lesley McNair,* Washington, D.C., as the home for the newly created National War College.* This "joint" war college was established to address shortcomings in interservice coordination and cooperation experienced by both Marshall and Eisenhower during the war.

In 1950, coincidental with the start of the Korean War, Army Chief of Staff General J. Lawton Collins moved to fill an educational gap he believed existed between the Army's intermediate-level Command and General Staff College* and the new joint-oriented senior-level National War College. Accordingly, he reestablished the Army War College. Moreover, given the limited number of student-spaces available to Army officers in the prestigious joint college, it was determined that completion of the Army War College course would count equally among the criteria for senior officer promotions. The first class was assembled in Grant Hall at Fort Leavenworth, Kansas,* as an interim location, but in October 1951 the War College moved to occupy facilities being prepared on the military garrison of Carlisle Barracks,* 125 miles north of the nation's capital.

This reopening marked the third of four distinct periods in the college's history, each generally succeeding the major conflicts of the 20th century. As these transitions have occurred, the central emphasis of the War College has matured somewhat sequentially and progressively through the three levels of warfare— beginning initially with a strong focus on the tactical art, transitioning during the middle two periods primarily to the operational art,* and finally in recent years focusing more squarely on the strategic art. The "third Army War College" emerged out of the strategic level lessons learned from World War II and the emerging Cold War. From 1950 to 1990 the college's primary emphasis was focused on cold war relations with the Soviet Union, and its curriculum began to reflect more fully all three of the "great problems of national defense, military science, and responsible command" identified initially by its founder, Elihu Root.*

The National Security Act of 1947 and the defense reorganization it articulated had an obvious significant influence on the college during the early portion of this period. So did the Vietnam War during the period's middle years. The curriculum, for example, was adjusted to cast army combat support activities in the broader context of national security concerns; it focused on the role of the military in national policy formulation, exploring the relationships between the Joint Chiefs, the Secretary of Defense, the National Security Council, and the Congress. Later in the period, it gave particular emphasis to the scientific management techniques introduced by Secretary of Defense Robert McNamara and to the strategy of counterinsurgency. The Haines Board,* which reviewed the Army's officer education system in 1967, recommended adding electives to the resident course of instruction and encouraged a two-year corresponding studies course, designed to correspond directly to the resident program, but in a nonresident, distance education format. This initiative doubled the size of the student body, heretofore about 200 residents, the first year and tripled it for the future.

Maj. General DeWitt Smith, whose two tours totaling five years during the mid- and late 1970s made him the longest serving commandant, engendered a "collegial," collaborative style of leadership and academic acumen that established him as the contemporary father of the college. Under his influence, the instructional methodology began to embrace the contemporary principles of adult education, very much in keeping with the college's original concepts of learning by doing introduced by Tasker Bliss* in 1901. The seminar group became the crucible for learning in an environment marked by an abiding sense of collegiality. In this atmosphere he encouraged a strengthening of the bonds among the students as they interacted in their seminar groups and between the students and the faculty, who by then found themselves collaborating on studies directed by the Army Chief of Staff. Several of these would significantly influence the future of the Army.

From 1986 to 1990 the Goldwater-Nichols Defense Reorganization Act* of 1986 and the follow-on PME study launched by Missouri Congressman "Ike" Skelton had profound effects on the shape of the curriculum. A strong strategic emphasis was firmly implanted within the curriculum along with a driving emphasis on "jointness,"* the underlying theme to the Reorganization Act. The act also set up Defense department–wide procedures leading eventually to the accreditation of PME institutions by the Joint Staff. The Army War College was initially accredited for joint education in May of 1993.

But the cold war occupied the central focus of the curriculum, which during this period alternated between emphasizing founder Elihu Root's imperatives of "national defense" and "military science," with special emphasis on the operational art, and later giving particular attention to "responsible command" in the form of command, leadership studies and management studies. Finally, near the end of this period, the curriculum stabilized somewhat with a more balanced focus on all three of Root's imperatives accompanied by strong emphasis on jointness and the strategic-level of war.

With the fall of the Berlin Wall in 1989 and the subsequent end to the cold war, marked especially by the breakup of the Soviet Union, the end of a bipolar world, and recognition of the United States as the world's only superpower, the Army War College once again modified its program. The contemporary focus is one of preparing selected military, civilian, and international leaders for strategic-level responsibilities given the uncertainties of a "new world order/disorder" and the anticipated challenges of the 21st century. The curriculum has evolved to embrace in full measure the practice of the "strategic art," defined as the skillful coordination and integration of ends, ways, and means to preserve and defend the national interests at home and abroad. If the first three stages of the Army War College's history were in large measure defined by the Industrial Age and the global conflicts emerging therefrom, the fourth Army War College has been defined by the dawn of the Information Age and the technologies combined with the conflicts arising out of this transitional period in world history. Information and education technology, spurred by the advent of digitization and the microprocessor, are not only revolutionizing how the college teaches and students learn, but more importantly it is changing the fundamental ways in which human and materiel resources will be managed to fight future wars. Though focusing more broadly, the Army War College still maintains its unique "land power" perspective. Strategic-level leadership to effect strategic employment of land power is the fundamental focus of the contemporary and future Army War College.

The USAWC has dedicated itself to the vision of becoming "the nation's preeminent center for strategic leadership and land power . . . a learning institution and installation of excellence . . . preparing today's leaders for tomorrow's challenges . . . by pursuing the mastery of the strategic art through education, research and outreach." Built on the firm foundation provided by founder Elihu Root, the current Army War College is focused squarely on its motto of providing for the future.

Sources:

Harry P. Ball, *Of Responsible Command: A History of the U.S. Army War College* (Dallas, TX: Taylor Publishing Company, rev. ed., 1994).
Maj General Richard A. Chilcoat, "The 'Fourth' Army War College. Preparing Strategic Leaders for the Next Century," *Parameters* (Winter 1995–96).
John W. Masland and Laurence I. Radway, *Soldiers and Scholars: Military Education and National Policy* (Princeton, NJ: Princeton University Press, 1957).
George S. Pappas, *Prudens Futuri: The U.S. Army War College 1901–1967* (Marceline, MO: Walsworth Publishing Company, for the Alumni Association of the U.S. Army War College, 1968).

Robert A. Brace

ARMY WAR COLLEGE COMMENTARY. *See PARAMETERS.*

ARNOLD, HENRY H. Henry Harley (Hap) Arnold (born 1886, died 1950), General of the Air Force (1949), a graduate of the U.S. Military Academy, Army Industrial College, and the U.S. Army's General Service School, is considered the father of the U.S. Air Force and an early advocate of professional military education for airmen.

From his initial flight training at Wilbur and Orville Wrights' school in Dayton, Ohio (1911), as the ranking airman in Washington, D.C., working to build the Air Service for World War I, through the arduous years between the wars, then finally as commander of the Army Air Forces during World War II, Arnold's career is the embodiment of early American airpower. His impact on professional military education, largely indirect, took many forms, and his influence on military and political leaders and the general public regarding the formulation and propagation of airpower theory cannot be denied.

Arnold possessed a global vision of airpower. He believed air forces could do anything, anytime, anywhere; whether it be an auxiliary function for the Army or Navy or an independent function such as humanitarian airlift or strategic bombing. Furthermore, he believed air forces should be commanded by airmen who are schooled in and understand the unique requirements of organizing, training, equipping, and employing the air arm. He recognized early that much of what made airpower unique was its synergistic mix of professional aviators, technology, and industry. He advanced these ideas through three primary means: (1) example, (2) mentoring, and (3) policy.

Arnold demonstrated his personal concern about the maintenance, supply, and production aspects of aircraft as well as his convictions about their employment. As a flight instructor in College Park, Maryland (1912), he familiarized himself with the Wrights' production lines, could disassemble and reassemble his own airplane, and wrote the first military technical manual for aircraft. As the Assistant Director of Military Aeronautics during World War I, he understood that the Air Service's foremost challenge was to overcome the "complete absence of materiel, especially airplanes," and he built lasting relationships with civilian scientists and industrialists. Later, he demonstrated the operational potential of air forces by successfully leading a flight of ten Martin B-10 bombers on an 18,000-mile round-trip flight from Washington, D.C., to Fairbanks, Alaska (1934). But the most dramatic measure of his belief in airpower came when Arnold put his own career on the line by supporting and defending Brig. General William Mitchell* during Mitchell's very public and personally vicious court-martial proceedings (1926).

Arnold was careful to share his convictions about airpower with other promising leaders. Carl Spaatz learned the importance of technology and civilian scientists to airpower and applied these lessons as the USAF's first Chief-of-Staff. Ira Eaker, also a ranking combat commander in World War II, co-authored three books with Arnold, intended to educate the general public, prospective pilots, and air-ignorant military men concerning airpower.

As chief of the Army Air Corps (1938), determined to ensure that a larger number of air officers attend the Air Corps Tactical School* (ACTS), Arnold directed that a study be made to examine the feasibility of substantially shortening the course. The school enacted the change in the 1939–40 academic year, providing the Air Corps with a healthy cadre of air-minded officers during the expansion for war. In 1943, as chief of the AAF, he was instrumental in bringing about creation of the Army-Navy Staff College to train officers of all services for joint operations. This school became the direct antecedent, three years later, of today's Armed Forces Staff College.*

Arnold's all-embracing approach to airpower theory and his forceful influence on professional military education, provided the U.S. Air Force with the legacy of a global outlook that is especially valid today.

Sources:

Henry H. Arnold, *Global Mission* (New York: Harper & Brothers, 1949).
H. H. Arnold and I. C. Eaker, *Winged Warfare* (New York: Harper & Brothers, 1941).
Thomas M. Coffey, *Hap: The Story of the U.S. Air Force and the Man Who Built It, General Henry H. "Hap" Arnold* (New York: Viking Press, 1982).
Dik Daso, "Origins of Airpower: Hap Arnold's Early Career in Aviation Technology, 1903–1935," *Airpower Journal* (Winter 1996).

Capt. George L. Stamper, Jr., USAF

ARTILLERY SCHOOL AT FORT MONROE. First military school of application in the United States (1824) and, after West Point, the U.S. Army's second-longest-functioning institution of professional education, finally closing in 1950.

For the widely dispersed U.S. Army of the early 19th century, the use of artillery was judged to be too technical in nature to continue training under the traditional method of instruction by the officers and NCOs of the individual regiments and companies. Interest in the formation of a school of application for artillery began by the early 1820s. In 1823, Quartermaster General Theodore Jesup wrote to the Secretary of War stating, "no man is fit to command a regiment, or even a company of infantry, unless he have some knowledge of fortification, and be well versed in every branch of artillery duty. There are now no means of obtaining that knowledge, nor can the means be furnished in any other way than by establishing an artillery school of practice." The idea took hold, and on April 5, 1824, the Adjutant General of the Army issued General Orders Number 18. This order directed "that ten companies of artillery be stationed at Fortress Monroe, to be organized as a regiment, and will be called the 'artillery corps for instruction.' " In addition to setting the general framework of the school, the order also set the staff and named Colonel John Rogers Fenwick of the Fourth Artillery as the commander. The course of instruction was to be two years long, with entire artillery companies rotating through so that both officers and enlisted men would become acquainted with their technical duties as well as the routine of garrison life.

Colonel Fenwick's other duties prevented him from taking command in person. The actual work of establishing the school thus fell to the second in command, Lt. Colonel Abraham Eustis. Colonel Eustis set about the work of organizing the school and arranging its curriculum. The daily routine, as set in Artillery School of Practice Orders Number 113, dated December 12, 1824, included drill as infantry, both company and battalion; manual of artillery and mechanical maneuvers; laboratory instruction in ordnance; and routine drills, parades, inspections, and guard duties.

In 1826, as the two-year course of instruction came to an end for the first set of companies, their place was taken by eight others. At this time, the Commanding General of the Army, Maj. General Jacob Brown, commented as follows about the new school: "Among [the benefits] may be noted . . . habits of uniformity and accuracy in the practical routine of service, fresh incitement to the cultivation of military knowledge, emulation and *esprit de corps* among the troops, and mutual conformity and general elevation of individual character among the officers."

In spite of its good reputation, the school began to suffer from the effects of the small size of the U.S. Army and the many campaigns of the 1830s. Lack of funds and limits on personnel and facilities also took a toll. After ten years of operation, during which 25 out of 36 artillery companies had formally completed the course, the school was allowed to close down. Adjutant General Office General Orders Number 31 of 1834 transformed the Artillery School of Practice into the post of Fort Monroe.

Just prior to the Civil War, the Army once again looked to the education of its artillery soldiers. On October 30, 1856, Headquarters of the Army General Orders Number 9 directed three companies to form at Fort Monroe the School of Practice in garrison, seacoast, and siege artillery. Lt. Colonel Harvey Brown, of the Second Artillery, was appointed commandant in December 1857 and directed to "proceed immediately" to organize the school. By the following January, a board of officers established a new two-year course of instruction. Subjects taught were to include drawing, mathematics, engineering as it related to artillery, ordnance relating to pyrotechny and the construction of artillery carriages and equipment, drills with the different pieces of artillery, gunnery, transportation, surveying and topography, and saber drills. During the summers, there would be an encampment for practice in camp and field duties. As before, entire companies would attend the course. By May 1858 the school received its official name, The Artillery School. By September 1860, however, the approach of the Civil War caused the instruction to be suspended.

After the end of that conflict a permanent artillery board was established (January 30, 1866), and it was ordered to submit plans for the reestablishment of an Artillery School at Fort Monroe. Its recommendations were published on November 13, 1867. The school would be for both officers and enlisted men. All newly appointed artillery second lieutenants, whether from civil life or the ranks of the Army, and all graduates of the U.S. Military Academy* commissioned in the artillery were to attend the course. Later, officers from other branches as well as the Navy and Marine Corps also were permitted to attend. "The application of artillery . . . the duties of artillery troops in campaigns and sieges . . . military law and military history" were added to the subject matter of the prewar curriculum, although the course of instruction was designed to last for only one year. As before, the officers were expected to also perform all the routine garrison duties and drills. In 1869, the first class was graduated, with General William T. Sherman* presenting the diplomas. In his report of 1871, the commandant, Brevet Maj. General William F. Barry, noted that already a total of 54 lieutenants, or nearly half of the artillery officers of that grade, had graduated from the course. It operated continuously for the rest of the century.

Many improvements were made in these decades. The course was lengthened to two years, and new courses in such subjects as signaling and reconnaissance were added to the curriculum. Over time, it was realized that not all the information needed for instruction was contained in the textbooks, and the staff began a program of publication of detailed monographs on technical subjects. By the 1880s the school was organized into separate departments, to include engineering, military art and science, military history and geography, law and administration, tactics and practical instruction, applied sciences and ballistics. In 1892, the *Journal of the United States Artillery* began publication to provide another vehicle for the discussion of artillery-related topics.

The Spanish-American War brought a temporary end to the operations of the school. It also provided the needed impetus for changes recommended by a reviewing board in 1885. In spite of these recommendations, the seacoast defenses of the United States had been allowed to remain dependent upon the old muzzle-loading weapons that had been standard since the Civil War. New advances in technology and metallurgy had not been incorporated into the artillery during the 1880s and 1890s, and the school was still teaching the use of out-moded weapons while the rest of the world had long turned to breech-loading rifles. Soon after the war with Spain, a new system of construction began at Fort Monroe and elsewhere, designed to incorporate new rifles in a series of detached batteries that would provide greater defense to the Hampton Roads area. When the school reopened in 1900, much of this new construction was in progress.

The focus on coast defense was reflected in subsequent events. The school's new curriculum included instruction in electricity, mines, seacoast engineering, coast defense, and chemistry. Courses were also offered for enlisted men. By the regulations issued in 1906, the school would focus solely on coast artillery. By that time, the Army, in one of its periods of reorganization, recognized that the artillery had progressed to a point in which there were actually two branches. In 1907, the Coast Artillery and Field Artillery branches separated, with the school at Fort Monroe becoming the Coast Artillery School. This last form of the school continued to serve the Army through two world wars at Fort Monroe. The school was finally moved from Fort Monroe to Fort Winfield Scott in 1946 and disbanded in 1950, when the Coast Artillery was disestablished.

Throughout its long history, the artillery school at Fort Monroe had many outstanding and famous officers among its students or on its faculty. These included Abraham Eustis, Robert Anderson, William F. Barry, Emory Upton,* William T. Sherman, Royal T. Frank, John C. Tidball, James M. Ingalls, Peyton March, and Lyman Lemnitzer. Its effects were measured not only in the number of soldiers it educated, but in being a source of professional thought and growth for the artillery branch. As the first of the Army's branch schools, it left a legacy for the U.S. Army Training and Doctrine Command, the major command housed at Fort Monroe today.

Sources:

Robert Arthur, *The Coast Artillery School: 1824–1927* (Fort Monroe, VA: The Coast Artillery School Press, 1928).

John Wands Sacca, "An Unrivaled Education: The Professional Preparation of Noncom-missioned Officers for Coast Defense at Fort Monroe and Willets Point, 1867–1908," unpublished paper in the collections of the Casemate Museum, Fort Monroe, Virginia.

Richard P. Weinert and Robert Arthur, *Defender of the Chesapeake: The Story of Fort Monroe*, 3rd rev. ed. (Shippensburg, PA: White Mane Publishing Co., 1989).

Dennis P. Mroczkowski

ARTILLERY SCHOOL OF APPLICATION. *See* ARTILLERY SCHOOL AT FORT MONROE.

B

BANCROFT, GEORGE. George Bancroft (born 1800, died 1891), graduate of Harvard College and a noted historian, was Secretary of the Navy (March 1845–September 1846) under President James Polk and established the U.S. Naval Academy.

After graduating from Harvard in 1817, Bancroft studied at Gottingen, where he received a Ph.D. in 1820. He returned to the United States in 1822, spent a year tutoring Greek at Harvard, and then joined Joseph Green Cogswell in founding the noted Round Hill School in Northampton, Massachusetts. He sold his interest in the school in 1830 and devoted himself to writing his *History of the United States*, the first volume of which appeared in 1834. Meanwhile, he became . . . one of the leaders of the western, or agrarian wing of the [Democratic] party in opposition to the Boston, or urban, wing. . . .

[In 1844] Bancroft . . . captured the Bay State delegation to the Baltimore Convention for Van Buren. When it became clear that Van Buren could not be nominated, however, he led the stampede to Polk. . . . [However], his selection as Secretary of the Navy was less a personal reward than an attempt to placate Van Buren. Bancroft's nomination, sent to the Senate on 5 March 1845, was confirmed ten days later. . . .

Following the President's expressed wishes, Bancroft sought to revamp the Service's systems of education and promotion and to inculcate a high code of conduct. . . .

One of Bancroft's first official functions was to select the commander for the naval force that was to carry Alexander H. Everett to China with the ratification copy of the Treaty of Wanghia. On 17 March 1845, Commodore James Biddle accepted the appointment. Bancroft's orders . . . directed him to proceed to China via the Cape of Good Hope, land Everett at Macao, or closer to Canton if possible, and then carry him to such ports as he wished. Once treaty ratifications had been exchanged, Biddle's ships were to secure firsthand information about the Treaty Ports. . . .

Biddle left New York on 4 June 1845. By he time he reached Rio de Janeiro, however, Everett had been taken sick and was forced to return home, leaving Biddle to complete the mission. . . .

With relations between the United States and Mexico deteriorating in consequence of the joint resolution of 1 March 1845 annexing Texas [former] Secretary Mason had ordered Commodore David Conner's Home Squadron to concentrate at Veracruz, [and] diverted Commodore Robert F. Stockton's squadron from a projected cruise to the Mediterranean to Texas. . . . After Mexico broke diplomatic relations, in April, the administration issued preparatory orders to General Zachary Taylor to move into Texas. In mid-June, Bancroft instructed Stockton to consider Texas a part of the United States as soon as the Republic accepted annexation and to treat any invasion accordingly. . . .

Following Texan acceptance of annexation, General Taylor, supported by Conner's squadron, moved his force into Corpus Christi on 25 July. Late in August, after Bancroft reminded the Bureau chiefs involved to provide coal and provisions at Pensacola for Conner's vessels, Conner received precautionary war orders. . . . he was to blockade the Mexican east coast except for disaffected states such as Yucatan and Tampico. . . .

On 23 October, Conner notified Bancroft that the administration's earlier proposal to negotiate had been accepted by Mexico. To contribute to the success of the negotiations and in compliance with Mexican desires, he withdrew the squadron from Mexican waters, a move for which Bancroft highly commended him. . . .

Bancroft also moved toward . . . the founding of a naval academy. Until his day, Congress had opposed establishing such an academy on four main grounds: 1) doubt that formal academic training had any value to a military officer, 2) conviction that the United States was immune from war, 3) fear of any extension of executive power, and 4) dislike of the patronage and preferment associated with West Point.* . . .

When the annual board for the examination of midshipmen convened at the Naval Asylum* [in Philadelphia] on 2 June 1845, Bancroft asked them to advise him on . . . the suitability of Fort Severn at Annapolis, Maryland,* as a site for an academy; the course to be offered; and the choice of three experienced officers to assist in planning the school. The board considered Fort Severn a suitable site, and it suggested the establishment of the grade of cadet and a program calling for two years at the school, three at sea, and one on a practice ship. . . .

The next step was to ask Secretary of War William I. Marcy to transfer the fort to the Navy. Marcy readily agreed, and on 15 August 1845, the post became the property of the Navy. Bancroft then ordered those midshipmen not attached to ships to report to the fort in October along with a small instructional and administrative staff headed by Commander [Franklin] Buchanan.* By placing eighteen of the Navy's twenty-five professors of Mathematics on waiting orders at reduced pay, Bancroft secured the $28,200 needed to begin operating the school. . . .

The Naval School* opened on 10 October with two groups of students. The larger consisted of midshipmen ordered there on their return from sea. Most of these . . . were eligible for promotion once they passed their examinations. The second group were men who came voluntarily as acting midshipmen holding letters authorizing their appointments as midshipmen but who had yet to put in their sea duty. By the beginning of 1846, some fifty-six students had reported and the school was safely under way. Soon thereafter, when Bancroft had to approach Congress for money to repair Fort Severn, . . . his success in establishing the school within the normal appropriation for education helped with support . . . of the powerful Chairman of the House Ways and Means Committee. . . .

Along with education, Bancroft championed merit promotion and economy. On 8 July 1845, he promulgated regulations prepared by Engineer in Chief Charles H. Haswell that provided for a board to convene to examine and arrange engineers according to merit. . . .

Bancroft had so economized that the estimates he provided in his annual report for 1845 were only about two-thirds as large as Mason's were a year earlier. . . .

An interesting commentary on Bancroft's report is that the President took a much stronger stand in favor of enlarging the Navy than the Navy Secretary. When the Senate asked him how many steamers he desired, Bancroft secured an estimate from his bureau chiefs. . . . Bancroft promptly cut the number to three steam frigates, five steam sloops, and two smaller steamers. . . . [H]e believed that merchant ships could substitute for coastal steamers and that no foreign steam navy could possibly attack the United States. . . .

By mid-January 1846, the Mexican situation had darkened again. . . . On the seventeenth, therefore, the cabinet agreed to the occupation by the Army of the disputed territory north of the Rio Grande and the concentration of Commodore Conner's vessels at Veracruz. On the twenty-fourth, the frigate *Cumberland*, intended for the African Squadron, was sent to reinforce Conner, who nevertheless continued to believe that the Mexicans would not resort to hostilities and to decline Bancroft's suggestion that because of his poor health he return home. . . .

Commodore Conner's sanguine expectations of peace with Mexico were shattered when he learned of Mexican orders for an attack on General Taylor's forces which President Polk on 13 January had ordered to the Rio Grande. Conner sailed from Veracruz on 4 May in the vain hope of preventing a collision. . . .

Bancroft's most important orders went to Conner, who was directed to impose a blockade, seize Mexican vessels and, where possible, ports, and also to give assistance to the Army. By the time the orders reached him, Conner had already taken these actions. . . .

Meanwhile, on 21 July, Bancroft appointed a board of twenty-one senior officers to consider promotion by merit. . . . The board's majority voted for promotion by merit and made the recommendations Bancroft requested. To express its disapproval of the merit system, however, the Senate refused to confirm the nominees and its strong reaction killed the innovation for a long time. . . .

Four days after the Appropriations Act became law, Bancroft used its authorization to pay passed midshipmen as masters when they did duty in that rank, and also issued a General Order providing for the filling of masters' vacancies by examining passed midshipmen and promoting those found "worthy of advancement." Three days later, he established appointment examinations for naval constructors, boatswains, gunners, carpenters, and sailmakers as well.

These two orders were Bancroft's swan song. Having decided to honor Bancroft's oft-repeated request for a foreign post, on 1 August Polk sounded out Mason on returning to the Navy Department. After Mason agreed to do so, on 9 September Bancroft resigned to accept appointment as Minister in London.[2]

BARNARD, HENRY. Henry Barnard (born 1811, died 1900), graduate of Yale College, a noted American educator who was a member of the legislature and Superintendent of Common Schools in the state of Connecticut and became the first U.S. commissioner of education. Just prior to the Civil War, he studied

[2]Excerpted, with permission, from K. Jack Bauer, "George Bancroft, 11 March 1845–9 September 1846," in Paolo E. Coletta, ed., *American Secretaries of the Navy, Vol. I, 1775–1913* (Annapolis, MD: Naval Institute Press, 1980), Copyright 1980 by the United States Naval Institute. (Asterisks added.)

many of the military schools of Europe and, later, reported on their educational practices.

Following his graduation from Yale College in 1830, Barnard became a teacher and studied law. Soon after being admitted to the Connecticut bar in 1835, he was elected to the Connecticut legislature, where he served three terms. Barnard became a forceful and vocal advocate for free public schools, both elementary and secondary, in the state—a cause that he championed nationally and to which he devoted much of his life. The opposition of political forces who feared the tax consequences of Barnard's proposals terminated his legislative career, and he moved to neighboring Rhode Island in 1845 and became secretary to that state's board of education. Four years later, however, he was brought back to Connecticut to serve as Superintendent of Common Schools and, later, as head of the state's teacher training institution.

In 1855, as part of his advocacy of publicly supported education, Henry Barnard embarked on a publishing venture that was to lead him into the special universe of military education. As editor of the new *American Journal and Library of Education*, Barnard promised in his first announcement of this publication to "provide an account of the Military and Naval Schools of different countries" as perspective on the issue of extending and improving similar institutions in the United States. He had been asked to undertake this task by Samuel Colt, founder of the Colt Patent Firearms Factory in his native Hartford, who supported the collection of necessary data for the project. Colt sought the information to assist in planning for a school of mechanical engineering, which he intended to establish in Hartford, and in which he intended to include military instruction. Barnard corresponded with the appropriate government ministries in many European countries and collected numerous reports and documents on their military schools and on those in the United States.

Barnard's reports were published in a variety of forms. The first increment, "Military Schools in France and Prussia," was released as an issue of the *American Journal and Library of Education* in 1862. Later that year, material from the same text appeared as part 1 of a series, featured in successive issues of the same journal, on different countries' instruction in the science and art of war. This, of course, occurred early in the Civil War, after it had become clear that the nation was in for a long and bloody conflict; and Barnard, as a result of the early articles, received "numerous letters [asking] for information and suggestions" from persons urging additional American schools for military instruction. In response, he incorporated the series of articles plus material for forthcoming articles into a single volume, the first edition (1862) of *Military Schools and Courses of Instruction in the Science and Art of War*. Initially given the relatively innocuous title "Papers on Military Education," the original book included material on Austria, England, France, Prussia, Sardinia, Switzerland, and the United States. In 1872, with the support of Samuel Colt's widow, Barnard published a revised edition, in which he added chapters on "Bavaria, Saxony, Holland," on the newly united Italy, on Russia, and on Sweden and incorporated

new material on naval schools and on changes in educational institutions that
followed the Austro-Prussian War. The new edition was published in New York
by E. Steiger.

Meanwhile, following the Civil War, Barnard had been appointed the first
U.S. commissioner of education, a post he held for three years. At age 59, he
returned to his beloved *American Journal of Education*, which he published
intermittently until 1882.

Sources:

Henry Barnard, *Military Schools and Courses of Instruction in the Science and Art of
War*, rev. ed. (New York: Reprinted by Greenwood Press, 1969).
The Encyclopedia Americana, International Edition, Vol. 3 (Danbury, CT: Grolier, 1997).

THE BASIC SCHOOL. Marine Corps institution that provides initial professional military education and training for newly commissioned second lieutenants and warrant officers, regardless of their source of commission. Founded in
1891 as the School of Application for newly commissioned second lieutenants,
it assumed its current name in 1922.

The Basic School (affectionately called TBS) is a combined training, educational, and "regimental," i.e., Marine Corps, socialization program. As such, it
provides proper training and initial PME for young officers, socializes him/her
into the Corps, and is a rite of passage for newly commissioned lieutenants.
Stated another way, it gives all marine officers, regardless of rank, age, or military occupational specialty (MOS), a common shared experience while also
laying the foundation for their subsequent careers in the Corps.

The School of Application marked a major departure in traditional Marine
Corps officer training policy. Many traditionalists at the time opposed "schooling" for officers; such individuals believed that the profession of arms could be
learned only by doing, i.e., on-the-job training. In the early years, the school
suffered from overseas commitments that affected its functioning and the rapidly
changing technology of the era that influenced its curriculum. The school was
closed during the Spanish-American War, the Philippine Insurrection, and the
Boxer Rebellion. In 1903 it relocated to the Marine Barracks, Annapolis, Maryland,* and remained there until 1908.

Renamed the Marine Officers School in 1908, it was moved to the Marine
Barracks, Naval Station, Port Royal (now Parris Island), South Carolina. Two
years later, its home changed yet again, to the Marine Barracks, Norfolk, Virginia. With the approach of World War I, the long course of study (at one time
two years in length) proved impractical as immediate demands precluded a
lengthy period of initial officer training. In July 1917, the remnants of the school
moved to the new base at Quantico, Virginia.* However, a different type of
training, conducted through the Marine Corps Officers Training Camp, was implemented to meet the pressing needs of an expanding Marine Corps and prepare
newly commissioned second lieutenants for their duties associated with the

World War I era. This forced the suspension of entry-level, career officer training and education for Marines until after that conflict.

With peace and an excess of officers, the Marine Officers School were reestablished at Quantico, albeit with a different focus than its prewar predecessor. It tried to draw upon the lessons of the war to prepare officers for the future needs of the Corps. In March 1919, the name Marine Officers Training School was adopted and a class assembled in the autumn of that year. Then, in January 1920, a second school was organized: the Marine Officers Infantry School These new and changing schools, with their overlapping names, curricula, and ranks of students, reflected the confusion of the time and the uncertainty of the Marine Corps as the service attempted to adjust to postwar needs, strength, organization, and missions. All of this is reflected in the history and lineage of The Basic School, as it claims the postwar schools in its ancestry.

Order emerged from chaos in the summer of 1920 when Colonel John C. Beaumont, USMC, assumed command of a consolidated Marine Officers School. He designed and implemented what became in that year a conceptual three-tiered system of Marine Corps Professional Military Education.* In a major innovation for the Corps, it founded three separate and distinct courses/schools, each with different missions, soon to be called The Marine Corps Schools: The Basic School, the Company Officers Course (now called the Amphibious Warfare School*), and the Field Officers Course (now called the Marine Corps Command and Staff College*). However, students arrived at each in a staggered sequence: 1920 for the Field Officers Course, 1921 for the Company Officers Course, and 1922 for The Basic School.

Peacetime training and education for newly commissioned officers were resumed with the opening of The Basic School at the Marine Barracks, Quantico, Virginia, in 1922. However, in the interwar years, because of space limitations, it did not remain there long. Thus, in 1924, The Basic School moved yet again—this time to the Marine Barracks, Philadelphia Navy Yard. It remained there until 1945, when it returned to Quantico, where The Basic School has been ever since. It occupied a number of different sites there until finally moving, in 1958, to its current location at Camp Barrett. At the latter site, TBS is housed in a modern, permanent facility as part of the Marine Corps Combat Development Command.

The Basic School used to produce marine officers with the officially designated skills to command an infantry platoon or company. In those days, for officers with the infantry MOS, the course for newly commissioned second lieutenants was the only infantry school they attended. However, more recently it provides officers with only an infantry orientation—and officers with the infantry MOS attend the Infantry Officers Course (see below) after graduation. In recent years, all newly commissioned marine officers (regular and reserve, male and female, air and ground), almost all of whom are university graduates, have attended the infantry-oriented basic course.

The Basic School now consists of three courses: The Basic Officer Course, which all Marine Corps second lieutenants attend, lasts for approximately six months. After it, the lieutenants then proceed to military occupational specialty schools, which range in length from twelve weeks (supply, logistics, and motor transport), to eighteen months (aviation flight training). Officers with the infantry MOS attend the Infantry Officers Course (called IOC) at The Basic School. IOC was established in 1977 to provide in-depth training for those officers assigned the infantry occupational specialty. Each class in IOC is approximately ten weeks in length and has the task of preparing an officer for duty as a platoon commander within an infantry or reconnaissance battalion. The Basic School also teaches a Basic Warrant Officers Course of approximately three months' duration. This is for noncommissioned and staff noncommissioned officers appointed to rank of WO-1. Warrant officers of the grade of WO-2 with the infantry MOS attend the Infantry Officers Course.

For the past quarter of a century, the Basic Officer Course for second lieutenants has generally been six months in length. Although tactics, techniques, and weapons systems have changed over the years, the course has remained fairly constant in concept over the decades, as its purpose remains to train, educate, and socialize the newly commissioned officer in infantry skills and the duties and responsibilities of a Marine Corps officer. Thus, officers from the 1930s to the 1990s have a shared common experience, regardless of rank, MOS, or length of service, based on a curriculum that still focuses on basic infantry skills (warfighting, time on the rifle and pistol ranges, land navigation, and communications); weapons and their employment; offensive and defensive tactics (all oriented from the fire team through the company levels); scouting and patrolling; physical training; leadership; combat service support; administration and military law; nuclear-biological-chemical defense; Marine Corps and military history, and expeditionary and amphibious operations. As an initial young officer training institution, the focus is primarily upon training; however, a foundation in professional military education is now part of the curriculum, to include an emphasis on professional reading—which, like physical training and leadership, has become one of the foundation building blocks of an officer's (and all marines) career from initial entry to final departure from active or reserve duty with the Corps.

Sources:

1st Lieutenant Anthony Frances, USMCR, "History of the Marine Corps Schools," 1945, unpublished manuscript in the Archives, Marine Corps Research Center, Quantico, Virginia.

Jack Shulimson, "Daniel Pratt Mannix and the Establishment of the Marine Corps School of Application, 1889–1894, *Journal of Military History* (October 1991).

U.S. Marine Corps Lineage of The Basic School, December 28, 1984.

Donald F. Bittner

BLISS, TASKER H. Tasker Howard Bliss (born 1853, died 1930), a graduate of the U.S. Military Academy and the Army's Artillery School of Application, and briefly the Army's chief of staff, taught at the Naval War College and shaped the early program of the Army War College during two tours as its president.

He was born to George Ripley Bliss and Mary Ann Raymond Bliss, both the descendants of old New England families, on December 31, 1853, in Lewisburg, Pennsylvania. His father was a professor of Greek at Lewisburg College, later Bucknell University, which young Bliss attended for two years, until family finances forced him to seek a free education at the U.S. Military Academy.* Admitted in the summer of 1871, he graduated number eight of 43 members in the class of 1875. He achieved this standing without overexerting himself and while pursuing a vigorous extracurricular reading program in military history. His classmates regarded him as their intellectual leader, but in the process, he also gained the reputation as a man whose theoretical understanding exceeded his ability to translate theory into practice. This reputation pursued him through-out his service career. Nevertheless, his first choice of branch was the cavalry. He learned that this selection would prevent one of his classmates with lower class standing, James G. Sturgis, from obtaining a cavalry assignment that he passionately wanted. Bliss immediately shifted his preference to the artillery, a circumstance that proved both personally and professionally fortuitous. Sturgis died the next year with Lt. Col. George Armstrong Custer at the Little Big Horn. For his part Bliss entered the artillery at a time when the revolution in the speed, armor, and armament of naval vessels was producing a corresponding revolution in coast defenses. In particular, fire control for the large caliber, breech-loading, automatic recoil guns consisted of a system of observed indirect fire that in-volved computing the target's estimated location at the time the shells arrived. Such a system placed a high premium on gunners possessing mathematical abil-ities of a high order—which Bliss certainly exhibited in abundance.

Assigned as a second lieutenant to the 1st Artillery, Bliss spent very little time with his regiment (and troops) during the first twenty-three years of his service. Instead he occupied a succession of increasingly important educational and staff billets. From 1876 until 1880 he was an instructor of modern languages at West Point, where his intelligence and broad learning caught the attention of the superintendent, Maj. General John M. Schofield. Bliss attended the Artillery School of Application at Fort Monroe, Virginia,* during the 1883–84 academic year, graduating with honors. He spent the following year on the school's staff. In 1885 he became an instructor at the new Naval War College* at Newport, Rhode Island.* During his three-year tour, he received the assignment to study the military education systems of the major European powers. He spent one summer in Germany, France, and Great Britain collecting detailed information.

Schofield, the newly promoted commanding general, appointed Bliss his aide in 1888, with the assignment to inspect small arms and artillery. Schofield also secured Bliss's transfer to the commissary department (with an accompanying promotion to captain), although the new captain's duties remained the same. Schofield's retirement in 1895 led to Bliss's assignment as special assistant to Secretary of War Daniel Lamont. Bliss drafted Lamont's final annual report which included a call for greatly enhanced coastal defenses. In 1897 Bliss accompanied the new American minister to Spain, Steward L. Woodford, and took up the duties of military attaché in Madrid. Having Woodford's complete confidence, Bliss became involved at a high level with the ultimately futile attempts by the McKinley administration to head off a war with Spain. With the American declaration of war, he returned to the United States and became chief commissary of the I Corps (and a temporary colonel), mobilizing at Chickamauga, Georgia. Subsequently appointed chief of staff of the 1st Division of that corps, Bliss eventually saw some skirmishing in Puerto Rico. Although he missed the decisive actions in Cuba and the Philippines, this lack of combat experience did not harm his career. Bliss became the collector of Cuban customs, a position that was key to the effective performance of the American military government on the island. He reformed and rationalized the Cuban customs service, which brought his abilities to the attention of Secretary of War Elihu Root.* Bliss became a brigadier general in the Regular Army on July 21, 1902.

Secretary Root, then in the midst of his fight to create a general staff, on his own authority established the War College Board as a halfway house to his objective. He appointed Bliss to the board. When Congress created the War Department General Staff,* Bliss became one of the first members as well as president of the Army War College* in Washington, D.C. He conceived of the new institution as "a collegium," in which student officers, with already prepared minds, would learn the functions of a general staff by drafting war plans and policy papers—essentially acting as an adjunct to the staff itself. Bliss's plan for the Army War College (heavily influenced by his experiences at the Naval War College) dovetailed closely with the ideas of his friend and classmate Colonel Arthur Wagner, for the School of Application for Infantry and Cavalry* at Fort Leavenworth, Kansas.* Wagner, who had been the driving force behind the intellectual renaissance at Leavenworth before the war with Spain, wanted to elevate it yet another notch to "a true war college." It did not happen.

Two years after Bliss departed Washington in 1905 for a succession of commands in the Philippines (the same year that Wagner died), a new Chief of Staff, Maj. General J. Franklin Bell, redirected the Army War College toward training officers—as a temporary expedient until the Army had a sufficient number of Leavenworth-trained officers to draw upon. Temporary became permanent because Bliss's concept of using the student officers to supplement the work of the General Staff drew the War College into the conflict between the Chief of Staff and the adjutant general for primacy in the War Department. The National Defense Act of 1916, heavily influenced by a former adjutant general, Maj. General (Ret.) Fred C. Ainsworth, effectively excluded the War College from acting as an adjunct to the General Staff.

Even though Bliss served an additional tour as president of the Army War College from June until November 1909, he did nothing to reverse this trend. In fact, Bell was so impressed by his loyalty in carrying out Bell's policies that he recommended Bliss for the post of Chief of Staff of the Army. Bliss did not achieve this position for another eight years, serving in the interim as a department commander and, beginning in 1915, as assistant to the Chief of Staff—with promotion to major general to date from November 20, 1915. Shortly after the United States's entry into World War I, Bliss became acting and then Chief of Staff and was promoted to full general on October 6, 1917. It was not his finest hour. Although very intelligent and still capable of working long hours despite his 63 years, he required a very long time to reach decisions. He was much better suited to act as a wise counselor in the sphere of military diplomacy, a skill he first demonstrated during Colonel Edward M. House's mission to Europe (October 28 to December 17, 1917).

Bliss retired from active duty for age on December 31, 1917. President Woodrow Wilson immediately recalled him to active duty and sent him back to France to serve as the American permanent military representative at the Supreme War Council, where he steadfastly supported General John J. Pershing's efforts to employ an independent American army on the Western Front. Following the Armistice, Bliss became a member of the American delegation to the Versailles Peace Conference. The failure of the U.S. Senate to ratify the Versailles Treaty led Bliss, now finally retired, to become one of the founding members of the Council on Foreign Relations. He spent the last years of his life attempting to educate the American people on the nation's role in the 20th-century world. He died on November 9, 1930, in Washington, D.C.

Bliss's most important contribution to military education was his role in the founding of the Army War College. The attempt to use the student officers to reinforce the planning capacities of the General Staff—which Root espoused—demonstrated a shrewd appreciation of the weaknesses of the original legislation. At the same time, Bliss's concept of the college as a collegium seriously underestimated the intellectual preparation of his fellow officers and the political liabilities it imposed on the Army. On the other hand his lofty expectations set a standard of excellence that helped elevate the Army War College from its establishment. Bliss, who seemed out of joint with his times in many ways, proved simply to be two generations ahead of them. His abilities to work closely without rancor with a sister service and with allies on the highest political-diplomatic-military levels proved a harbinger of the kinds of skills high-ranking American military leaders would have to possess in the last six decades of the twentieth century and beyond.

Sources:

Harry P. Ball, *Of Responsible Command: A History of the U.S. Army War College* (Carlisle Barracks, PA: Alumni Association of the U.S. Army War College, 1984).

Todd R. Brereton, "An Impractical Sort of Officer: The Army Career of Arthur L. Wagner, 1875–1905," unpublished Ph.D. dissertation, Texas A&M University, 1994.

Frederick Palmer, *Bliss, Peacemaker: The Life and Letters of Tasker H. Bliss* (New York: Dodd, Mead & Co., 1934).

David F. Trask, *The AEF and Coalition Warmaking, 1917–1918.* Modern War Studies,
Theodore A. Wilson, ed. (Lawrence: University Press of Kansas, 1993).

Edgar F. Raines, Jr.

BOARDS OF VISITORS/ADVISORS. Panels of interested citizens, usually
containing a number of educators and/or military retirees having previous association with military education, appointed by the President, the Congress, a
service department, or other higher authority periodically to observe and critique
the operation of a particular professional military educational institution and
report publicly to the appointing authority.

Before the United States became engulfed in its Civil War, all of the major
powers of Western Europe and North America were supporting a number of
professional military schools; and several governments had established reviewing boards, some of which included civilian members, to monitor school operations and recommend desirable change. The earliest institution of its kind to
receive advice from such a board was the U.S. Military Academy,* which was
first observed by a board of visitors in 1815. Annual appointments of a board
by the President did not begin until 1819, under Superintendent Sylvanus
Thayer,* who invited public scrutiny of the institution. A similar provision was
made for the newly established U.S. Naval Academy* in 1850.

The concept of having boards of interested citizens appointed by high-level
civil authority to review military instruction appears to have been uniquely
American. According to Henry Barnard,* the first reported reviewing body for
military schools in Europe may have been in Prussia. Since the reforms of 1844,
a central board of studies operated under the authority of an inspector-general
of military education. This standing board of both experienced military officers
and civilian professors reviewed all the schools periodically and advised the
inspector-general accordingly. A similar Council of Military Education was authorized by the British Parliament as part of that country's military reforms
following the Crimean War; however, its only civilian member (of five) was a
clergyman. Europe's closest approximation of American practice was a one-time
commission appointed by France's "legislative assembly" in 1850 to examine
the programs of instruction at l'École Polytechnique* and "recommend all need-
ful changes in the studies of the students."

The American practice of annual reviews by appointed boards of private citizens provides benefits for both the public interest and the school authorities as
well. Not being connected directly with the schools being reviewed or their
sponsoring agencies, the members often are able to perceive conditions needing
improvement and suggest reasonable solutions that local authorities may find
difficult to acknowledge. The efforts of successive Naval Academy boards of
visitors, for example, described elsewhere in this volume (see Competitive Admissions*), helped influence the Navy Department to raise academic admissions
standards in the 1920s and '30s. Similarly, the West Point board of 1906 recommended that an academic department of English and history be separated

from the teaching of law to enable better mastery of course material by the academy's history instructors. This innovation was approved by the internal Academic Board two years later, leading to other improvements in both English and history instruction.

The foregoing example also illustrates another potential benefit of independent boards of review, namely to strengthen the case for worthy changes desired by local officials. In the 1906 example, the new department was desired by Super-intendent Albert L. Mills but resisted initially by West Point's entrenched board of permanent department heads. Similar support was provided by West Point's 1921 board of visitors for Superintendent Douglas MacArthur's* request that newly assigned military instructors first study their subject at a civilian univer-sity. Though stymied initially by the War Department's inability to provide the necessary tuition funds, the practice gained limited implementation later in the decade and full implementation following World War II. At Annapolis, repeated board of visitors' criticism in the early 1930s lent support to the pleas from civilian faculty members, who dominated most of the departments offering the-oretical and cultural studies, in opposition to the Navy Department's inter-war policy of steadily reducing the civilian faculty numbers. However, in this case, it took the onset of another world war and the rapid expansion of the U.S. fleet finally to arrest the trend.

Although the practice of providing for a board of visitors originated with the service academies (since 1948, the composition of all federal service academy boards has been standardized by law to include five senators and five congress-men), it has been adopted by other PME institutions as well. State military colleges modeled after Thayer's West Point copied the practice early in their existence; the Virginia Military Institute's* first board of visitors was appointed in 1837 with a former West Point professor, Claudius Crozet,* as its president. Many of the PME schools provided for experienced officers also have made such a provision, including both the National War College* and the Industrial College of the Armed Forces.*

Among the individual services, the Air Force has made the most widespread use of visiting boards. Its administrative center for PME, the Air University,* has had a board of visitors since its original organization as the Army Air Forces University in 1945. Reporting annually to the Air Force Chief of Staff, following visits of four or five days at the university's headquarters, Maxwell Air Force Base, Alabama, the board is authorized by the Chief to "inquire into the organi-zation, management, policies, curriculum, methods of instruction, [and] physical equipment . . . of the Air University." Before preparing its reports, advisory sub-committees also make several-day visits to the university's subordinate schools, such as the Air War College* (also at Maxwell) and the Air Force Institute of Technology* in Ohio. AFIT's visiting board is composed of scholars from a number of the nation's civilian engineering faculties and leaders of industry.

Although the Army schools have made use of occasional advisory boards, neither the Army War College* nor the Army Command and General Staff

College (USACGSC)* had provided for regular visitations until required by law. Both had preferred to organize outside boards (not to be confused with the series of Department of the Army review boards, e.g., Gerow,* Eddy, Haines,* etc.) for specific reviewing purposes and to select their membership accordingly. Since 1973, however, the Army War College and CGSC have been visited annually by different subcommittees of the Army Educational Advisory Committee, a body appointed by the Secretary of the Army in accordance with the Federal Advisory Committee Act of October 1972.

Both the Naval War College* and Naval Postgraduate School* are reviewed annually by boards of advisors appointed by the Secretary of the Navy. Annual reviews have served the former institution since 1967 and the latter since the following decade.

Sources:

Henry Barnard, *Military Schools and Courses of Instruction in the Science and Art of War*, rev. ed. (New York: E. Steiger, 1872) (New York: Reprinted by Greenwood Press, 1969).

Sydney Forman, *West Point: A History of the United States Military Academy* (New York: Columbia University Press, 1950).

John W. Masland and Laurence I. Radway, *Soldiers and Scholars: Military Education and National Policy* (Princeton, NJ: Princeton University Press, 1957).

William E. Simons, *Liberal Education in the Service Academies* (New York: Bureau of Publications, Teachers College, Columbia University, 1965).

BUCHANAN, FRANKLIN. Franklin Buchanan, Rear Admiral, U.S. Navy (born 1800, died 1874), the first superintendent (1845–47) of the U.S. Naval Academy.

Charles Lee Lewis, a Buchanan biographer, states that he was "the founder of its traditions of sound practical scholarship and rigid discipline; . . . [the] captain of Commodore Matthew Calbraith Perry's flagship in the famous expedition to Japan; . . . the highest officer in the rank in the Navy of the Confederate States of America and the first commander of an ironclad to engage in battle [CSS Virginia in the battles in Hampton Roads, 8–9 March 1862]."

Buchanan in concert with Secretary of the Navy George Bancroft* were directly responsible for the founding of the Naval School at Annapolis, Maryland,* in 1845. It was started on a shoe string by scraping funds and staff positions from other Navy accounts. It was up to Buchanan to set the course for the school in establishing the curriculum, placing the school in a naval operational and institutional setting, and providing the basis for inculcating in the midshipmen the moral values and competence for naval service. The institutions he established and the moral tone he set were the underpinnings of the U.S. Naval Academy* for the next two centuries.

Buchanan was a line officer, not an educator, but he had a keen interest in looking after the professional education of his subordinates both at sea and at the new academy. Among his accomplishments were: (1) the establishment of the academy's Academic Board charged with establishing the curriculum of the school and judging the educational, physical, and professional fitness of its midshipmen, (2) recruiting a faculty balanced between civilian academics and naval officers, and (3) developing and promulgating the Rules and Regulations for the Internal Government of the Naval School. In various forms all these institutions and practices endure to the present. He had the foresight to have the academy's rules and regulations approved by the Secretary of the Navy, thus strengthening his hand when it was necessary to deal with deficient, but politically connected midshipmen.

While the new school under Buchanan's leadership borrowed heavily from techniques, textbooks, and practices of its older sister institution at West Point, New York,* Buchanan put his own stamp on the naval school's environment. The emphasis was on education and personal discipline, not group drill. In its early days the midshipmen had few military duties and indeed did not always wear uniforms or participate in military drill. Buchanan, anticipating opposition from old school naval officers, insisted on a high practical content in the instruction. Midshipmen were rotated to sea duties and then returned to the academy to prepare for their lieutenant's examinations. The balance of the practical with theory was to be the hallmark of the naval academy's curriculum then and in future years.

Buchanan paid particular attention to the moral development of his midshipmen and insisted on the highest principles of honor and sobriety in the discharge of duties. The seeds of the academy's honor code are to be found in Buchanan's lectures to and his disciplining of midshipmen.

After his service in the Confederate States Navy during the Civil War, he retired to his home near Easton, Maryland. He was the first president (1868–69) of the Maryland Agricultural School, the direct predecessor of today's University of Maryland (Buchanan resigned this post over political interference in a tenure dispute).

Sources:

John E. Jessup (ed. in chief), *Encyclopedia of the American Military* (New York: Scribners, 1994).

Charles Lee Lewis, *Admiral Franklin Buchanan: Man of Action* (Baltimore, MD: The Norman Remington Co., 1929).

Jack Sweetman (revised by Thomas J. Cutler), *The United States Naval Academy: An Illustrated History* (2nd ed.) (Annapolis, MD: Naval Institute Press, 1995).

Charles Todorich, *The Spirited Years: A History of the Antebellum Naval Academy* (Annapolis, MD: Naval Institute Press, 1984).

James A. Winnefeld

C

CADET SCHOOLS. Institutions of precommissioning education that emerged in many European states during the 17th and 18th centuries. Primarily for the sons of noble families and of deceased or serving military officers, cadet schools in some states and during particular periods occasionally also admitted members of the bourgeoisie.

Cadet schools came into existence as one means by which the ruling houses of Europe bound the nobility to their will and gained their loyal support. Under the older feudal system, the noble estate had often been at loggerheads with a local ruler and, through collective effort, frequently frustrated his intentions. With the growth of the modern centralized state, whether ruled by a vested monarch or by a local princeling, rulers sought ways of controlling the restless nobility and of insuring that their ultimate instrument of control—a loyal standing army—was competently led. What more effective means for a ruler to encourage these outcomes than—borrowing John Moncure's phrasing—"taking future officers from their parents at a young age and undertaking their training himself in military schools"?

Cadet schools first appeared in number among the smaller German states during the early years of the Thirty Years' War: Nassau in 1617; Hesse in 1618; Friedland in 1624. Not always the first to innovate but ready to borrow the successful practices of others, the monarchs of Europe's larger states soon established similar schools of their own. Determined to prevent future repetitions of the kind of depredations Brandenburg towns had suffered from the Swedes and Imperial troops during the Thirty Years' War, Frederick William, "the Great Elector," set out to establish a standing army. He founded his first school for approximately 60 sons of landowning Junker families in 1645, in Berlin. To this were added new cadet schools of similar size at Kolberg and at Magdeburg in 1653, each provided primarily for sons of deceased officers to bind the nobility of new territory acquired in the Treaty of Westphalia (1648).

Although all of these schools closed near the end of the century, the tradition was established for the new Kingdom of Prussia (1701). King Frederick I quickly reopened the cadet school in Berlin and the one in Kolberg, both of which resumed their earlier curriculum of riding, fencing, fortifications, mathematics, and French. In 1704 and 1705, respectively, a new school was opened in Brandenburg and a second in Berlin that taught law, diplomacy, and natural philosophy as well as military subjects. Frederick's son, Frederick William I, merged the original cadet schools to form a single "corps of cadets," which by 1720 had grown to 200 officers' sons, selected personally by the king. In 1730, he appointed his own son, the future Frederick the Great, as chief of the cadet corps. By the end of the Seven Years' War (1763), with Frederick now on the Prussian throne, the number of cadets had outgrown the Berlin facility. Two new junior schools were established in towns well to the east of Berlin to provide the basic education and to ensure that the boys arriving in Berlin for their last few years of schooling were adequately prepared to do the work. This system of lower schools feeding qualified students into a central institution to finish their training became entrenched in Prussian and German military practice well into the 20th century.

Despite the growth and reorganization of the French army in the 17th century, permanent institutions for the education of young cadets were not established until the 18th. During his administration as war minister, Louvois had formed companies of cadets which received schooling as part of their overall training regimen, but this institution had not survived beyond 1692. It was not until the administration of minister d'Argenson, in 1751 under King Louis XV, that a regular cadet school, l'École Royale Militaire, came into existence in Paris. It admitted boys as young as eight years from families who could establish at least four generations of noble blood. In 1777, borrowing a practice of France's recent opponent, the Paris school was converted to a central cadet finishing academy that accepted the best students from ten regional, cadet preparatory schools created in the previous year. Called *colleges*, these schools were located in provincial towns such as Auxerre, La Flèche, Sorrèze, and so on and were administered by ecclesiastics until all schools were suppressed by the Revolution; Napoleon began his military career at one of these colleges, in Brienne. After he became first consul, new cadet colleges were opened in Paris, Versailles, St. Germain, and Fountainebleau, comprising the Prytanée Francaise. In 1803, Napoleon converted the Fountainebleau school to l'École Spéciale Militaire* which, like its royal predecessor, capped the military education of the better students from the other schools.

Prior to the American Revolution, the British army maintained only one institution that provided schooling for cadets, the Royal Military Academy* at Woolwich. Founded in 1741 to provide instruction for the officers and men then serving in the engineers and in England's Regiment of Artillery, its cadet activity began very modestly. At the time, most cadets were the sons of the officers serving in the artillery companies, which were authorized only five cadets each.

Not until 1744 were the cadets placed in uniform and subjected to military control; in that year they were organized into a separate company, administered by two officers. Until 1752, cadets obtained their own quarters, many living with their fathers. By 1782 the cadet company had grown from 20 to 60 boys, and by 1798 to 100. Throughout the 18th century, the main subject of classroom instruction was mathematics.

By the time the tiny United States Army was formed, military schools for young cadets had become a well-established tradition among the major European powers, including the two nations with early influence on the shaping of American culture. It is not surprising, therefore, that the founding fathers of this young republic—Washington, Hamilton, John Adams, and others—should have thought in terms of a military academy to train American youths for military service when their minds turned to providing for the necessary instruments of national defense.

Sources:

Henry Barnard, *Military Schools and Courses of Instruction in the Science and Art of War* (rev. edition, originally 1872) (New York: Reprinted by Greenwood Press, 1969).
Andre Corvisier (trans. Abigail T. Siddall), *Armies and Societies in Europe, 1494–1789* (Bloomington: Indiana University Press, 1979).
John Moncure, *Forging the King's Sword: Military Education Between Tradition and Modernization: The Case of the Royal Prussian Cadet Corps, 1871–1918* (New York: Peter Lang, 1993).

CALHOUN, JOHN C. John Caldwell Calhoun (born 1782, died 1850), graduate of Yale College, was Secretary of War, 1817–1825, in the administration of President James Monroe, and first in that office to advocate the growth of professionalism in the officer corps through a concerted program of professional military education.

Calhoun did this by supporting both the reformation of the U.S. Military Academy* at West Point, New York, and by envisioning a structure of advanced schools, such as the Artillery School of Application* at Fortress Monroe. These actions flowed from his conviction that a well-officered force of regulars, rather than citizen-soldier militia, should be the nation's first reliance for defense.

Calhoun is, of course, most famous as the great spokesman for the cause of states' rights for the South. An early and intense nationalist in the Democratic-Republican Party of Thomas Jefferson, he was a War Hawk member of Congress in the War of 1812. He served as Vice President of the United States, 1825–1832, and later (1843–1845) as Secretary of State.

But it was his years as U.S. senator from South Carolina that most markedly reflected his championship of the southern cause. In a nation whose political and economic course has generally been that of classical liberalism, Calhoun stands out as a stalwart theorist of conservative political thought. Two works, the *South Carolina Exposition and Protest* and *A Disquisition on Government*, expressed his views of the rights of states within the federal compact. He was ever the bitter political rival of fellow South Carolinian Andrew Jackson. In conflict with that former War of 1812 general, now President, Calhoun led the fight against the so-called Tariff of Abominations during the nullification crisis of 1833.

In espousing the cause of officer professionalization and advancement of PME, Calhoun essentially had to part company with his own political party. West Point had been founded during Jefferson's presidency, but Jefferson continued to place his faith in the capacity of citizen-soldier militia; he regarded standing armies of regulars with animus and suspicion. But the War of 1812 presented Calhoun with conflicting examples of what the American pattern of military preparation should be, a dichotomy that would mark the nation's defense structure for the rest of the century. One example was the American victories at Lundy's Lane and Chippewa in 1814, when well-trained and well-led American regulars carried the day against equal numbers of redcoats. Yet these victories had come only after poorly prepared and ill-disciplined bodies of American troops, many of them militia, had suffered a long string of humiliating defeats at the hands of relative handfuls of British regulars.

Andrew Jackson's victory at the Battle of New Orleans at the end of the war offered a far different example. At that battle, a polyglot American army prevailed over British regulars who themselves had beaten some of Bonaparte's best. The British were, in the words of Jackson, "cut down by the untutored courage of the American militia" and intense, accurate fire.

Becoming Secretary of War during the nationalistic Era of Good Feelings, Calhoun believed the former example was the correct one. He recognized further that quality of officers, rather than mere lengthy training of forces per se, was the crucial ingredient. To that end he worked tirelessly to support Brevet Major Sylvanus Thayer* when that officer was named superintendent of West Point. The academy had previously been plagued by maladministration and conflicts over curriculum, discipline, and mission. But Calhoun backed Thayer to the hilt, adding professors, raising admission and curricular standards, improving governance, and advancing overall the prestige of the institution. West Point thus eventually emerged as the essential incubator of a professional ethos in the officer corps of the U.S. Army.

Calhoun's other interest was in advanced schools of instruction capable of turning out officers, presumably graduates of the reformed academy, highly competent in the areas of artillery and engineering. This was particularly because Calhoun believed that the nation would have to rely upon a small but "expansible" regular army, to whose peacetime skeleton could be added additional companies on short notice. Such an army would need artillery and engineering arms of very high quality to assist the infantry if victory were to be achieved.

Calhoun thus departed from the traditional militia concept. Instead, he chose to place his faith in the regulars first, with the standing army, using his expansible plan, as the central military resource of the United States. Officers well prepared by a structure of PME were essential to the success of what he proposed. Only barely, during the era of hostility toward a professional officer corps that followed during Jackson's presidency, did his ideas survive in a strong West Point and schools such as the Artillery School at Fort Monroe.*

Calhoun's death, along with that of his old fellow War Hawk Henry Clay of Kentucky, and the political self-destruction of Daniel Webster of Massachusetts, marked the end of the old system of compromise that had held the country's sections together in tension since 1820. Set in motion was the coming of the terrible Civil War in which would be tested both the American citizen-soldier militia model as well as the professional officers whom Calhoun had worked so hard to produce.

Sources:

Samuel P. Huntington, *The Soldier and the State: The Theory and Politics of Civil-Military Relations* (New York: Vintage/Random House, 1957).

Allan R. Millett, *Military Professionalism and Officership in America* (Columbus, OH: Mershon Center, 1977).

Russell F. Weigley, *History of the United States Army* (New York: Macmillan, 1967).

Charles M. Wiltse, *John C. Calhoun, Nationalist, 1782–1828* (Indianapolis, IN: Bobbs-Merrill, 1944).

John W. Gordon

CALVERT, JAMES F. James Francis Calvert (born 1920) graduated from the U.S. Naval Academy and the National War College, served on the staff of the Armed Forces Staff College, and from 1968 to 1972 was superintendent of the U.S. Naval Academy,* where he effected major improvements and implemented significant academic reform.

James Calvert was born in Cleveland, Ohio, and attended Oberlin College for two years before being admitted to the Naval Academy in 1939. Graduating from the academy after completing the wartime three-year program, he attended Submarine School in New London, Connecticut,* and, in September 1942, joined USS *Jack* (SS-259) as torpedo data computer operator. Participating in nine war patrols, including eight aboard the *Jack*, Calvert served in every officer capacity except commanding officer and received several citations for "conspicuous gallantry" and "extraordinary heroism."

After World War II, Calvert served in various submarine officer positions and, in 1955, was selected for duty in the relatively new nuclear propulsion program. In November 1956 he was assigned to command USS *Skate*, still under construction, which he commissioned thirteen months later. Under Calvert's command, *Skate* set transatlantic speed and submerged endurance records and conducted two extensive cruises under the Arctic ice. In February 1959 she became the first submarine ever to surface at the North Pole.

Following several other command or staff assignments, including study at the

National War College,* the now Rear Admiral Calvert was named superintendent of the U.S. Naval Academy. Calvert arrived to find the academy in ferment.
His predecessor, Rear Admiral Draper Kauffman, who had inherited a near-
revolt by civilian faculty members over a standardized grading policy three years
earlier, had dampened the crisis somewhat through a number of administrative
adjustments, including establishing a 58-member Faculty Forum. However, the
basic tensions between the improved faculty's desire to continue the academic
reforms begun a decade earlier and the naval leadership's conviction that the
academy's professional military mission needed greater emphasis were still in
evidence. Calvert saw merit in both points of view and started immediately to
lead both efforts forward.

Regarding military professionalism as the distinctive contribution of a service
academy, Calvert focused on the honor system and the summer training cruises
as particularly valuable influences on the young midshipmen. In John Lovell's
paraphrasing Calvert told incoming faculty members that "[t]he key . . . lay in
tapping latent idealism from the midshipmen's earliest days at the Academy,
and then progressively cultivating his sense of discipline, responsibility, and
willingness to be accountable for his actions." Having observed a need for more
thorough indoctrination in the concept of honor, which Calvert regarded as a
"core value" in an officer's preparation, a "comprehensive review" of the honor
system was undertaken at his insistence. He also changed the routine for the
midshipmen's first summer cruise to assure a higher quality of this critical training. Whereas, formerly, the younger midshipmen had been scattered, like the
upperclassmen, among a number of different ships in the fleet and subject to
the respective attitudes and procedures of a variety of commanding officers,
Calvert arranged for two special training ships in both the Atlantic and Pacific
fleets that would provide a more systematic and uniform training experience.

Concurrently, Admiral Calvert saw the Navy benefiting from enabling midshipmen to pursue academic studies of particular interest to them to productive
levels of concentration. Encouraging free expression of ideas in the Faculty
Forum, whose meetings he made a point of attending regularly, he soon became
sympathetic to the development of a wider variety of elective courses and provisions for academic majors for all students. Accordingly, in his second year as
superintendent, Calvert implemented a reduction of the required common curriculum—except for its professional core, which he doubled—by requiring only
a minimum number of choices among electives in each of three broad disciplines: mathematics, the physical sciences, and the social sciences and humanities. Building on his or her individual selections, each midshipman was then
required to elect from among 24 available majors. Overall enrollment in particular majors was capped by navy priorities. To enhance the effectiveness of these
changes, Calvert increased emphasis on faculty research, supported upgrading
of the academy's computer system and required its use by midshipmen, and
secured final approval and funding for construction of the Nimitz Library and
the Engineering Studies Complex.

Calvert, who was promoted to vice admiral in August 1970, authored three books during his career: *Surface at the Pole* (1960), concerning his under-the-ice cruises; *A Promise to Our Country* (1961), a patriotic, inspirational book for youngsters; and *The Naval Profession* (1965), about the life of a naval officer.

Sources:

John P. Lovell, *Neither Athens Nor Sparta?: The American Service Academies in Transition* (Bloomington: Indiana University Press, 1979).

"REAR ADMIRAL JAMES F. CALVERT, UNITED STATES NAVY, 46th Superintendent, 20 July 1968 =," Public affairs release (mimeo., U.S. Naval Academy, July 1968.

Jack Sweetman, revised by Thomas J. Cutler, *The U.S. Naval Academy: An Illustrated History, 2nd ed.* (Annapolis, MD: Naval Institute Press, 1995).

CAPSTONE: JOINT EDUCATION FOR FLAG AND GENERAL OFFI-CERS. The CAPSTONE Course, attended by newly selected flag and general officers from all military services, is the highest level of joint professional military education conducted by the National Defense University. Those attending the course are called CAPSTONE Fellows.

The need for the course was recognized because each service conducts its own selection process for promotions based largely on mastery of each service's core competencies, e.g., commanding ships, employing aircraft, or leading soldiers and marines. Problems arose, however, when senior officers were assigned to joint commands without backgrounds that acquainted them with the capabilities and limitations of the other components. Early attempts at jointness,* which consisted of little more than pie slicing to ensure that every service had a piece of the action, produced the dismal results of Koh Tang Island and the unnecessary casualties of Desert One and made a powerful argument to find a more effective means to share knowledge.

On May 26, 1982, the Joint Chiefs of Staff (JCS) directed that the National Defense University* establish a course of joint PME for flag and general officers. Two pilot programs of eleven weeks each were conducted in 1983. While the goals of the new CAPSTONE Course met with general acceptance, differences remained over the structure and methods to be used. Despite a recommendation from the House Armed Services Committee that a six-month curriculum be developed, the JCS opted for two eight-week courses and then, in July 1986, for a six-week course, given to four classes per year.

The course remained optional until the 1986 Department of Defense Reorganization Act (Goldwater-Nichols*) became law. It required "each officer selected to promotion to the grade of brigadier general, or in the case of the Navy, to rear admiral (lower half) . . . to attend a military education course designed specifically to prepare them to work with the other armed forces." (Officers such as medical, veterinary, nurse, chaplain, etc., were exempted.) Officers were to complete the course within two years of their promotion.

Having determined, through a combination of experimentation and legislative fiat, that four courses per year were still adequate, planners judged that important questions of content and methodology remained. Everyone concurred with placing the principal emphasis on the highest levels of national strategy. Initially, the curriculum included lengthy readings and wargames designed to illustrate strategic issues and illustrate how various service capabilities could be integrated to craft the best solutions. This was done with the help of highly respected, retired four-star officers from all services. Known as Senior Fellows, they are selected for their demonstrated mastery of joint and combined issues. While their mentoring role has continued, the content of the course has evolved away from extensive readings into more active exchanges. The 40 fellows in each class meet with "those who do," i.e., the Chairman of the Joint Chiefs, every service Chief, the commanders-in-chief of all nine unified commands, as well as numerous other senior officials from the National Security Council, Department of Defense, the Department of State, and Congress.

The CAPSTONE curriculum is reviewed and approved annually by the Chairman of the Joint Chiefs. Each chairman in turn has shaped it, and it is not surprising that the curriculum is taking on an increasingly interagency orientation. This reflects the fact that very few, if any, contemporary problems will yield to purely military solutions. In addition to the inclusion of civilian leaders, such as the Director of the Central Intelligence Agency, as presenters, a few senior State Department officials join the classes each year as fellows and provide a useful balance to the discussions.

The speed of communications in the late 1990s has enabled the United States and its allies to respond in timely fashion to world crises, but in turn, this can limit the time available to today's senior military leaders for assembling and deploying appropriate response forces. Accordingly, NDU president Lt. General Chilcoat has shaped the curriculum to better enable CAPSTONE Fellows to rapidly assume command of joint organizations that are established in response to crisis situations.

The course necessarily involves a good deal of travel. In general, the first week is spent in Washington, meeting principally with the leaders of the Joint Staff and senior intelligence officials. The next two weeks are spent visiting representative bases of each of the services within the continental United States, including talks with each of the commanders-in-chief of the unified commands, and in preparations for the overseas trips that follow.

Recognizing the importance of allies and coalition partners, the fellows are divided into three groups for their overseas travel—typically, one to the Asia-Pacific region, one to Europe, and one to the Western Hemisphere. All trips are targeted on U.S. national security interests but intended to provide understanding of regional perspectives and cultures. The latest major change was made in 1997, when countries of Southeast Asia and Southwest Asia were included. Upon return, the various groups brief each other on lessons learned.

The sixth week reflects the cutting edge of joint PME by including meetings with the Secretary of Defense, each service Chief, futurists, business leaders, and experts in transnational threats, such as terrorism and weapons of mass destruction. The focus expands to include different paradigms of national security; for example, if our tanks are ready but a hacker is able to take down the New York Stock Exchange, do we really have effective national security?

The outlook for the future is fluid. Officers selected for flag/general officer today increasingly have had some joint experience earlier in their careers. Having largely bridged the divide between service identities, we may now find ourselves needing to bridge a cultural divide between military professionals and their political masters outside the Department of Defense. The goal remains the same: educating senior military officers on the incorporation of all elements of national power to achieve national security objectives.

Sources:

Les Aspin Letter to General R. E. Dougherty, USAF (Ret.), Chairman, Senior Military Schools Review Board, March 5, 1987.

Chairman of the Joint Chiefs Instruction 18001.01, Appendix H to Enclosure F: "General/Flag Officer Joint Learning Objectives for the Capstone Course."

Public Law 99–433, 10 USC 663, "Goldwater-Nichols Department of Defense Reorganization Act of 1986," 99th Congress, 2d sess., October 1, 1986.

Charlie Schill, "DoD, Hill at Odds Over Time in Flag Officer Course," *Navy Times*, July 10, 1989.

Lt. Colonel A. James Diehl, USMC

CARLISLE BARRACKS, PENNSYLVANIA. Carlisle Barracks is the United States's oldest, still active military post, located approximately 125 miles north of Washington, D.C. and 25 miles west of Harrisburg, Pennsylvania. At one time it was the site of the Carlisle Indian School and, since 1951, has been the location of the U.S. Army War College.

Carlisle Barracks, Pennsylvania, antedates West Point, New York,* as the oldest, still occupied military garrison in the United States. Located in the middle of Pennsylvania's Cumberland Valley, the garrison is on the northeast side of the town of Carlisle, Pennsylvania. The post was founded on May 30, 1757, by British Colonel John Stanwix, who came to the area to protect the local settlers from Indian tribes during the French and Indian War.

Carlisle Barracks enjoys a rich history that closely parallels that of the nation itself. In its earliest times it served as an outpost for the westward movement and as a garrison in support of the Revolutionary War, principally for the production of ordnance materials and ammunition. For a while it also served as a prison for Hessian soldiers captured by General George Washington at the Battle of Trenton. The Hessian Gunpowder Magazine, constructed in 1777, remains today as the oldest surviving structure on Carlisle Barracks. During the period 1778 to 1781 the barracks, then known as Washingtonburg, was the home of the American Artillery School, the nation's first formal military training institution. Over the course of its history Carlisle Barracks would come to be home of some ten different army schools. In 1794, in an effort to quell the Whiskey Rebellion of farmers to the west, President George Washington came to Carlisle and became the only president in American history to don the military uniform as the nation's commander-in-chief and review troops who were preparing to advance against potentially hostile resistance.

The post gained its current name of Carlisle Barracks in 1807, six years after the old post was finally and officially purchased from the heirs of William Penn. From 1838 to 1870 the barracks was the home of the School of Cavalry Practice, the forerunner to the armor branch school. In the Civil War, Regular Army recruits as well as some volunteers and draftees were inducted at Carlisle Barracks. During the Gettysburg campaign, Confederate infantry occupied the post, June 27–30, 1863. The following day, two brigades of New York and Pennsylvania militia held the borough of Carlisle against shelling by Maj. General J.E.B. Stuart's cavalry. The federal defense perimeter, however, did not include Carlisle Barracks, and Stuart occupied the military installation without resistance overnight July 1–2, burning most of it prior to moving south to join the battle at Gettysburg.

A particularly poignant period in the history of Carlisle Barracks dates from 1879 to 1918 when the barracks was the home of the Carlisle Indian Industrial School. This noble idea of then Lieutenant (later Brig. General) Richard H. Pratt was designed "to educate not subjugate" the American Indian by providing both academic and vocational skills to help assimilate Indian children into American society. Athletics were a major part of the program, and there emerged several American athletic legends from the Carlisle Indian School: such names as Jim Thorpe and Louis Tewanima, heroes of the 1908 and 1912 Olympics; Chief Bender, famous baseball pitcher for Philadelphia; and Glenn "Pop" Warner, who coached the school's football team to national prominence when it defeated the powerhouses of the day such as Army and Notre Dame. In 1918 the War Department repossessed Carlisle Barracks from the Department of the Interior and established General Hospital 31 on the post. From 1920 through the Second World War, the Army Medical Field Service School was then located on the installation. Between 1946 and 1951 the garrison served intermittently as the home of the School for Government of Occupied Areas, the Adjutant Generals School, the Chaplains School, the Military Police School, the Army Security Agency School, and the Armed Forces Information School.

In 1951 after temporarily reopening in 1950 at Ft. Leavenworth, Kansas, the United States Army War College* moved to Carlisle Barracks. In 1962 the Army's Combat Developments Command Institute of Advanced Studies (renamed the Strategic Studies Institute in 1971) was established there; it was subsequently merged into the Army War College in 1973. In 1967 the Military History Research Collection (renamed the Army Military History Institute in 1977) was formed on the post. Designated as the Army's central historical repository in 1970, the institute, with its vast holdings of military history books, manuscripts, and photos was fully integrated into the Army War College in 1994. In 1976 the Army's Physical Fitness Research Institute was established as part of the War College, and likewise in the fall of 1993 the Peacekeeping Institute was created as part of the emerging state-of-the-art gaming and simulation Center for Strategic Leadership. July 1994 marked the opening of J. Lawton Collins Hall, the new home for the Center for Strategic Leadership and the Army's first educational facility designed specifically for the 21st century, providing the college, the Army, and the nation with "information-age" capabilities for strategic level war-gaming, modeling, simulation, and experiential learning using the most modern information and educational technology.

Sources:

Harry P. Ball, *Of Responsible Command: A History of the U.S. Army War College* (Dallas, TX: Taylor Publishing Company, 1984, rev. ed., 1994).
"Historic Carlisle Barracks Pennsylvania," U.S. Department of Army, Headquarters, U.S. Army Garrison, Carlisle Barracks, PA, February 1, 1995.
Lt. Colonel Thomas Grant Tousey, *Military History of Carlisle and Carlisle Barracks* (Richmond, VA: Dietz Press, 1939).

Robert A. Brace

CHAUVENET, WILLIAM. Professor William Chauvenet (born 1820, died 1870), graduate of Yale College, headed the school at the Naval Asylum in Philadelphia (1842–1845), where he developed a two-year plan for a permanent naval academy. When Annapolis was chosen as the new site for the Naval School, Chauvenet became the academy's first professor of mathematics, a post from which he exerted great influence on the academy's development.

William had the advantages of an excellent training in his youth. . . . He attended the best boys' preparatory school in Philadelphia and his mathematical genius was soon recognized by Dr. Samuel Jones, the school director. Dr. Jones . . . convinced William's father that his gifted son should be sent to Yale College. . . .

Though but sixteen years of age when he entered Yale, William had mastered the entire four-year course in mathematics prior to his entrance to the college. He was the only member of his class to pursue the special optional course in mathematics, and in his senior year he astonished his instructor by originating numerous mathematical techniques for solving difficult problems. . . .

Soon after his graduation from Yale, William was invited by Professor Alexander Dallas Bache to assist in a series of important magnetic observations at Girard College in Philadelphia. Professor Bache, head of the college, and later Superintendent of the U.S. Coast Survey . . . was a leading figure in American science. He and William Chauvenet developed a lifelong friendship and Doctor Bache later used his powerful influence to assist William in the establishment of the Naval Academy.* . . .

[In 1841, Chauvenet] was appointed a professor of mathematics in the United States Navy. Professor Chauvenet served for a brief period on board the U.S. Steamer *Mississippi* . . . Although Professor Chauvenet realized that there were certain advantages in sending midshipmen on board ship at an early age, he soon became convinced that the system of shipboard teaching then in vogue was totally inadequate for the proper training of future naval officers.

[I]n April 1842, Professor Chauvenet was made head of the Naval Asylum School.* The young professor, with an unusual combination of intellectual and physical vitality, began to exert on naval officer education as great an influence as Colonel Sylvanus Thayer* had exerted on military education at West Point.* ...

The midshipmen at the Asylum School responded to Professor Chauvenet's efforts and the school became so successful that it was decided to close the other [shore] schools gradually and concentrate all shore instruction at Philadelphia. In spite of the professor's youth, his students were inspired and motivated by his immense knowledge, his unusual teaching ability, his dignified manner, and his strong personal character. The professor was encouraged but he realized that the course of study was too brief and that the subjects covered were too limited to suffice for the proper education of a naval officer. He drew up a plan for an expanded school in which all the subjects conceived to be indispensable to a naval officer would be taught by competent instructors.

He realized that it was virtually impossible to get Congress to pass a bill authorizing a naval academy; many such attempts had failed over the previous forty-year period. ... his plan was to initiate a successful course of study and then to ask Congress to support it. He suggested to several secretaries of the navy that they already had the power to assign professors and naval officers to an expanded Naval Asylum School.

In 1843–44 Professor Chauvenet drew up a two-year course of study which Secretary of the Navy David Henshaw approved. ... The summer months were to be devoted to practical instruction aboard a small vessel under command of the professor of gunnery and tactics.

Secretary Henshaw ordered the Naval Asylum School to initiate the new course in September 1844 but, unfortunately, the order was rescinded by one of Secretary Henshaw's successors ... who did not feel that the midshipmen could be spared from service at sea for a two-year period. ...

George Bancroft* became Secretary of the Navy in March 1845. With renewed hope Professor Chauvenet called Mr. Bancroft's attention to his plan for an academy. He enlisted the support of Dr. Bache, whose influence at the Navy Department was considerable. ... In a master stroke of diplomacy, Mr. Bancroft then asked the Board of Examiners, scheduled to meet at the Naval Asylum School in June 1845, to report to him on a plan for a naval academy and the desirability of locating such an academy at Fort Severn in Annapolis [Maryland].*

The Board ... confined their deliberations to the plan for organization and the issue of the academy's location ... [and] recommended to Mr. Bancroft that Annapolis be chosen. Thus Mr. Bancroft obtained the direct sanction of a very influential board of senior navy officers. ... The transfer of Fort Severn from the Army to the Navy was arranged by Mr. Bancroft and Mr. William L. Marcy, Secretary of War and father of [one of Chauvenet's instructors].

Secretary Bancroft had already appointed Commander Franklin Buchanan* ... the first superintendent of the Naval School* at Annapolis. In a famous letter dated 7 August 1845 the Secretary outlined for Commander Buchanan a plan for the establishment and development of the new Naval School. This letter ... followed closely the plan originally suggested by Professor Chauvenet. ...

The Naval School in Annapolis opened on 10 October 1845. William Chauvenet was the first Head of the Department of Mathematics, the first Naval Academy* Librarian, and a member of the first Academic Board. He submitted the first program of studies which was adopted by the Board. During the next fourteen years he worked unceasingly to make the Academy the greatest institution of its kind in the world. Increasing awareness of his stature as a mathematician and a scientist notably enhanced the reputation of the Academy. Always the most prominent member of the faculty, he was the guiding spirit of the institution. . . . Historians agree that Professor Chauvenet did more than any other individual to establish the institution on a firm and scientific basis and that he raised the calling of the United States naval officer to a position of distinction.[3]

THE CITADEL, THE MILITARY COLLEGE OF SOUTH CAROLINA. A state institution, established in 1842, whose graduates are expected to provide leadership across a full range of civil and community life and, in time of war, in volunteer or militia/reserve forces.

The Citadel combines academic education realized through its comprehensive liberal arts college (with some nineteen degree programs) and a military framework that offers a rigorous program of professional military education. Its historical significance within the American pattern of PME is that the college, as a higher-education entity of the state of South Carolina rather than a federal service academy, serves primarily to educate and equip graduates to serve as citizen-soldier leaders as well as those choosing to follow the profession of arms as a career. Save for the seventeen years of its being closed after the Civil War, it has carried out this role since the beginning.

The name "The Citadel" precedes the actual establishment of the college and comes from both the location and the design of the building constructed on the site of a Revolutionary War rampart. Founded in Charleston on ground used since the 18th century for military purposes by a succession of colonial, state militia, British, Continental, and federal forces, The Citadel, the Military College of South Carolina, is an institution whose graduates have distinguished themselves in many walks of life. Of those following a full-time military career, many have achieved flag or general officer rank, four of them in the Confederate States Army, 1861–1865. From the outset the practice of scholarships for "beneficiary or State Cadets"—meritorious young men not able to bear the full expense of tuition—reflected the college's dedication to egalitarian principles of education.

The Citadel originated because of the state's need for educated citizens and the practical requirement both to train officers for the militia and to maintain guard over arms and ammunition stored in two main arsenals. One of these was in the oldest city in the state, Charleston. Stretching across that city's peninsula from river to river, a line of fortifications was constructed during the American Revolution. Of this line, its central feature was the "Hornwork," which guarded the outskirts of the city. The Citadel was a target of intense British bombardment

[3]Reprinted, with permission, from John A. Tierney, "William Chauvenet—Father of the Naval Academy," *Shipmate*, September/October 1969, Copyright 1969 by the United States Naval Academy Alumni Association. (Asterisks added.)

during the siege of 1780, and President Washington later reviewed troops there; and, in the early 19th century, federal and militia forces were assigned to guard the new Spanish Moorish–style "Citadel" erected as an arsenal. It was in this building, now converted to commercial use, that the state stored the substantial quantity of arms that would be used should the militia have to be called into service to meet some future emergency.

The educational concept itself reached back to the previous century. Washington himself, with the experience of the Continental Army fresh in his mind, had early in his presidency conceived a sort of Swiss-militia concept that called for highly trained citizen-soldier forces and regional military academies to train officers. While his proposal did not survive in the Militia Act of 1792, the idea of combining officer training and higher education gained ground thereafter with the creation of both the U.S. Military Academy* and Norwich University.* But for South Carolina, it was the Nullification Crisis of 1832 that more than any other historical force served as the main catalyst for the establishment of an institution for military education. War talk within the state during that period of tension over federal government policy played a direct role in leading key political figures to urge legislative creation of the "Citadel Academy" and, in Columbia, a companion institution called the "Arsenal Academy." The Arsenal, burned during the occupation by General William Sherman's* forces in 1865 and never reopened, was to serve as the location for first-year cadet training.

Arrival of the first cadets in early 1843 marked the initial or antebellum and Civil War period of PME, in which the curriculum, influenced by both West Point and Norwich, was a mix of both academic and PME studies. Cadets received instruction in "the duties of the soldier, the schools of the company and of the battalion, the science of war, the evolutions of the line, and the duties of commissioned officers." Drill by squads, companies, and so on employed the line-and-column tactics evolved during the Napoleonic era and as yet unmodified by the introduction of the mass-produced single-shot rifles that would make the Civil War so lethal. They also, with the onset of the Mexican War just four years after the college's founding, actively trained the companies comprising the Palmetto Regiment, a unit of state volunteers embarking for Mexico. The cadets received praise for their effectiveness in this work, and certainly the Palmetto Regiment acquitted itself well, being first to carry its colors over the walls of Mexico City.

But a far sterner test of that proficiency lay ahead—the Civil War and literally the shots that opened the conflict. South Carolina, politicized since nullification days to the cause of secession, had pledged to leave the Union should Lincoln win the presidency in 1860. But federal forces continued to hold Fort Sumter, guarding the mouth of Charleston harbor. When it appeared probable that Sumter might be resupplied by sea, Citadel cadets were promptly dispatched to fire at any Union ship that so attempted. Thus it was that the cadets, manning a battery of four guns positioned on an island commanding the channel, opened fire on the steamer *Star of the West* as that vessel tried to slip by to the fort.

With the cadets firing in earnest, the ship turned away, reversed course, and stood out to sea, its mission a failure.

Thereafter, as this state-federal incident led the way into full-scale conflict, Citadel cadets continued their education, trained volunteer units as they had in the Mexican War, and fought during the Civil War as a unit of the Confederate army in fully eight more engagements. But in early 1865, with Sherman approaching from Savannah and with still more federal forces poised at the mouth of the harbor, the Confederates—to include the cadets—evacuated Charleston lest they be trapped in the city. The cadets were thus in the field on active service when the last units of the Confederate army surrendered. Meanwhile, federal forces occupying Charleston moved into The Citadel—to remain there for just as many years as the college had existed previously. Of Citadel graduates eligible to serve the Confederacy, one in five had perished from wounds or service-related disease.

Its reopening after Reconstruction initiated a second period of PME. Training continued in much the same pattern as before, but with graduates now able, as the century drew to a close, to apply for commissions in the federal forces. By the Spanish-American War and not counting those in state forces, twenty-two Citadel graduates held War Department commissions in United States volunteer troops or in the Regular Army. Of these last, three achieved general officer rank by career's end. Such opportunities increased in the early years of the new century, when the so-called Root Reforms (after Secretary of War Elihu Root*) made possible commissions in the regular forces upon passing a competitive qualifying examination.

Still another era of PME began with the National Defense Act of 1916. This act, which established the Reserve Officers' Training Corps (ROTC),* improved, standardized, and expanded the process of officer training and set The Citadel's PME role squarely within a formal relationship to the federal government. Until the start of World War I, Citadel cadets could also attend the Citizens' Military Training Camps held at Plattsburg, New York, which gave officer training to civilian volunteers. By the end of that war, nearly 300 Citadel graduates held Army, Navy, or Marine Corps commissions. And of those graduating between the end of the war with Spain and U.S. entry into World War I, thirteen eventually achieved general officer rank.

In that same period, the college won the right to grant the bachelor's degree, to offer academic majors, to expand faculty, and create academic departments. Between the two world wars, it divided its cadet corps into artillery and infantry-oriented units, and graduates were commissioned into the Officers' Reserve Corps, a resource for providing the Army with combat arms officers. With the start of World War II, however, full mobilization of the nation's manpower led to a decision to discontinue ROTC after mid-1943 and use the resources elsewhere. After the class of 1943 graduated, cadets were permitted to enlist in the Enlisted Reserve Corps, where they were able to complete some of their studies before being shipped off to basic training and probable assignment to Officers'

Candidate School. The Citadel was left to carry on with only a nucleus corps of cadets as its classes of 1944, 1945, and 1946 were mobilized or as their members chose to compete for aviation cadet slots with the Navy or the Army Air Forces. Enlisted members of the Army Specialized Training Program were housed in the barracks in 1944–1945. Of those Citadel cadets graduating between World War I and the end of World War II, more than forty would eventually achieve general officer rank.

The standard ROTC program through which The Citadel had accomplished its PME effort since early in the twentieth century was resumed after World War II. Such effort was expanded, first, after the creation of the U.S. Air Force as a separate branch and the addition of ROTC for that service; and, twenty-some years thereafter, with a Naval ROTC* unit by which to prepare cadets for commissioning in the Navy and the Marine Corps. Today, graduates can receive commissions in the active Army, Navy, Marine Corps, and Air Force, or in the Reserve and National Guard. Likewise, when the Marine Corps created its Enlisted Commissioning Education Program (MECEP), in the early 1970s, The Citadel welcomed these handpicked NCO-officer candidates to the campus. They, wearing Marine uniform to all college functions with the cadets, interacted well within the NROTC unit. So also did the officer candidates participating in the Navy's Enlisted Commissioning Education Program interact well with the cadets seeking Navy commissions through NROTC, bringing a seasoning element of service gained in the fleet.

Army ROTC meanwhile greatly expanded opportunities for cadets to attend ranger-challenge, airborne, ranger, and air assault training, cadet professional development, and other special opportunities. The termination of the draft and the provision of scholarships awarded on a competitive basis in this and the other services indicate the focus of ROTC as a specialized, high-quality program oriented to producing both career officers as well as citizen-soldier leaders who would serve in local Reserve and Guard units in addition to their normal civilian careers. The Citadel thus requires that each cadet, irrespective of citizenship and formal commitment to accept a commission, take one semester of ROTC each of the eight semesters of attendance at the college, thus deriving substantial benefit from the leadership component of its PME offerings. Access to study abroad programs of up to one semester, as well as access to summer programs in Australia, France, Germany, Spain, and the United Kingdom, serve to complement The Citadel's academic and PME programs, as does the program for student internships in the state's House of Representatives and Senate delegation offices in Washington, these last occurring either in the summer or for an academic semester.

The Citadel's Greater Issues series regularly brings to the campus figures of international reputation and standing who speak on issues that provide context to PME activities. Its College of Graduate and Professional Studies has, since 1966, offered degrees up to the master's level in several disciplines (two of them joint M.A. programs with the University of Charleston), and uses the same faculty, laboratory, and lecture facilities as does the cadet program. Guest lecturers brought to the campus under the auspices of this program are likewise available to the cadets while serving to enrich both PME and academic programs.

In 1996, The Citadel's board of visitors* voted unanimously to admit women. Both the women who matriculated after that decision and those who are attending now or will attend later, to include female members of the MECEP program mentioned above and presently enrolled, are assured of having full access to the program of PME that has been a hallmark of The Citadel since the beginning.

Cadets today, as has been the practice certainly throughout this century, are organized into company and battalion units, where selection of cadet leaders is by peer evaluation, an order-of-merit list that includes academic and other factors, and by appearance before a board for interview. Life in the corps of cadets is in a very real way a 24-hours-a-day leadership laboratory whose pillars are academic, athletic, and spiritual. A well-established honor system builds in each graduate a sense of honor for life.

Sources:

Gary R. Baker, *Cadets in Gray: The Story of the Cadets at the South Carolina Military Academy and the Cadet Rangers in the Civil War* (Columbia, SC: Palmetto Press, 1989).

Oliver J. Bond, *The Story of The Citadel* (Greenville, SC: Southern Historical Press, reprinted, 1989).

John P. Thomas, *The History of the South Carolina Military Academy* (Charleston, SC: Walker, Evans and Cogswell, 1893).

Russell F. Weigley, *The History of the United States Army* (New York: Macmillan, 1967).

John W. Gordon

CLAUSEWITZ. General Carl Philipp Gottlieb von Clausewitz (born 1780, died 1831), Prussian soldier and military philosopher who is widely acknowledged as the greatest of all the classical military theorists.

The meaning and practical impact of Clausewitz's theories remain subjects of hot debate, and the lessons taken from his works vary dramatically depending on the times and on the interpreter. Nonetheless, Clausewitz continues to exercise a powerful influence on military doctrine, on the writing of military and political history, and on professional military education.

Entering the Prussian army at the age of thirteen, Clausewitz served throughout the Wars of the French Revolution and Napoleon. Although a Prussian patriot and a die-hard opponent of the French, Clausewitz recognized the social and political, as well as the military, significance of the French Revolution. He believed, along with the other reformers who ultimately saved Prussia, that the state would have to make radical reforms in all three areas if it was to survive. As a result, despite his long and close association with the royal family, his liberal political views were a cause of suspicion and often an obstacle to his advancement. Through sheer intellectual ability and professional competence, however, Clausewitz rose from humble beginnings to positions of significant responsibility. He fought in the early campaigns of 1793–95, in the disastrous Jena-Auerstädt campaign of 1806, in the campaign of 1812 in Russia (as an officer in the Russian army), and throughout the War of Liberation in 1813–14. During the Waterloo campaign in 1815 he was chief of staff of a Prussian army corps that fought at Ligny and Wavre. After the wars, he served as administrative head of the War College in Berlin. He was recalled to field service during the emergency caused by revolutions in France and Poland in 1830, serving as chief of staff of Prussia's army on the Polish frontier. Engaged in that mission, he died of cholera in 1831.

Clausewitz is most renowned for his great theoretical work *On War (Vom Kriege)*, published posthumously in 1832. Clausewitz was a prolific writer, however, and a number of his other works have had a significant impact in the English-speaking world. Chief among these other works is his *Principles of War*, written in 1812 as a tutorial for the 16-year-old Prussian crown prince. This short book is often mistakenly described as a summary of *On War*, which was written much later and reflects a very different outlook. Although an extensive review of *On War* was published in both Britain and the United States in 1835, the full text of Clausewitz's magnum opus was not available in English until publication of Colonel J. J. Graham's translation in 1873. Even this version was not widely available until 1908, when F. N. Maude published an edited version of Graham's work. Maude unfortunately inserted a great many notes containing his own social-Darwinist views, which have served to distort the Prussian writer's reputation ever since. The standard English-language version since 1976 has been the superb translation by Michael Howard and Peter Paret.

It is impossible to summarize either *On War* or its influence on readers. Clausewitz wove together a great many concepts and insights, treating not only tactics and strategy (by which he often meant what we now call the operational level of war) but also the relationship of military affairs to domestic and international politics; military analytical techniques; the proper writing and use of military history; and problems of military education. He is most famous for his statement that "War is a continuation of policy by other means." The actual meaning of this phrase, however, goes well beyond its usual interpretation— usually by writers not truly familiar with Clausewitz's work—as a purely rational explanation of war as an instrument of national policy. In fact, Clausewitz's approach emphasizes the interplay between rational calculation; emotional, psychological, and moral forces; and the elements of friction, chance, and probability that characterize the real world. So rich is Clausewitz's thought that readers are often able to grasp only those parts of it that seem immediately relevant to contemporary events. As a result, he has been seen quite differently in different periods. Writing in the 1920s and 1930s, for example, Basil Liddell Hart characterized Clausewitz as the "Mahdi of Mass" and the "Apostle of Total

War." Writing in the nuclear era, political scientists like Robert Osgood saw him instead as "the preeminent military and political strategist of limited war in modern times."

Clausewitz was known and studied in British military schools even before the Prusso-German victory over France in 1870–71 made the German military model preeminent. British interest was stimulated in part because of the Duke of Wellington's famous response to the Prussian writer's comments on the Battle of Waterloo in his study *The Campaign of 1815 in France*. In the United States, however, there is little firm evidence that Clausewitz was used in military education before the 1890s. When the young John McAuley Palmer (later an A.E.F. brigade commander in France and an outstanding General Staff officer) stumbled across *On War* around 1892, he was immensely surprised to read Clausewitz's famous statement about the relationship of war and politics. "This truth was so startlingly simple that I could not grasp it at first. But it gradually dawned upon me that here was a fundamental military concept which I had never heard about in my four years at West Point.*" Whatever influence Clausewitz had on American military education before World War I came largely through German and British writers like Colmar von der Goltz, Spenser Wilkinson, and the naval theorist Julian Stafford Corbett. These writers drew intelligently on Clausewitz, but they applied his ideas in very different ways and often disagreed violently among themselves.

Neither is there much evidence that *On War* was directly utilized in American PME during the interwar years, even though the school year at the Army War College* was divided into two parts based on a distinction made by Clausewitz: Preparation for War (September to February) and Conduct of War (February to June). U.S. Army doctrine explicitly rejected Clausewitz's emphasis on the subordination of strategy to politics, saying, "Politics and strategy are radically and fundamentally things apart. Strategy begins where politics end. All that soldiers ask is that once the policy is settled, strategy and command shall be regarded as being in a sphere apart from politics." Of the 785 officers who wrote Leavenworth papers between 1928 and 1935, not a single one selected option #388, "Clausewitz—His Influence on Principles and Doctrines of Modern Warfare." In 1928, Navy Captain George Meyers published a book entitled *Strategy* that was very Clausewitzian and intended as a textbook for the Army and Navy War Colleges,* but it was little used. *On War* still exerted a powerful influence on PME curricula through its impact on other writers, and large sections of Clausewitz's study of the campaign of 1806 were translated and used at the Army's Command and General Staff School [College].* Probably the most important route for Clausewitz's influence on PME, however, was through the individual efforts of officers like Eisenhower and Patton, both of whom are known to have made extensive study of *On War* on their own time.

During World War II, a great deal of new material on Clausewitz was published in the United States, mostly by expatriate German writers like Hans Rothfels and Herbert Rosinski. O. J. Matthijs Jolles, another German refugee from

Nazism, published the first "American" translation of *On War* in 1943. Roth-fels's essay in Edward Meade Earle's *Makers of Modern Strategy: Military Thought from Machiavelli to Hitler*, published the same year, was the first truly sophisticated discussion of Clausewitz widely available to American military educators. Rosinski lectured extensively in the senior PME schools in the 1950s. Unfortunately, Rosinski's lectures tended to baffle his students and were dis-continued for that reason in 1957. Clausewitz's reputation in PME circles through the 1950s—as evidenced by West Point's 1951 training pamphlet *Jom-ini, Clausewitz, and Schlieffen*—tended to be that put forward by Liddell Hart: he was viewed as a bloody-minded proto-Nazi bent on mass offensive warfare and world conquest.

That absurd view of the military philosopher was only gradually displaced by the insights of writers like Samuel Huntington, who stressed Clausewitz's in-sistence that military professionals accept their subordination to the political leadership; Robert Osgood, who emphasized the "limited war" component of *On War*'s theories; and Henry Kissinger, who applied Clausewitz's rational anal-ysis to the problems of nuclear warfare. Although military educators' interest in the Prussian theorist was stimulated by limited wars like that in Korea, by the nuclear arms race, and by Clausewitz's impact on communist military thought, it was the military-political debacle in Vietnam that brought Clausewitz to center stage in American PME. Clausewitz's ideas underlie the most influential state-ments of the military lessons learned from Vietnam: Colonel Harry Summers's seminal 1981 study, *On Strategy: A Critical Analysis of the Vietnam War* (orig-inally written at the Army War College), and the "Weinberger doctrine," first expressed by Secretary of Defense Caspar Weinberger in 1984. *On War* was adopted as a key text at the Naval War College in 1976, the Air War College* in 1978, and the Army War College in 1981. It has always been central at the U.S. Army's School for Advanced Military Studies* at Leavenworth (founded in 1983). The U.S. Marine Corps's brilliant little philosophical field manual *Warfighting* (1989/1997) is essentially a distillation.

It was *On War*'s explication of the relationship between policy, politics, and military operations that first drew the attention of American officers who had experienced defeat in Vietnam. However, other aspects of Clausewitz's analysis soon attracted operational thinkers. Clausewitzian concepts like the "center of gravity" and the "culminating point of the offensive" thus came to occupy a central place in American doctrine, both single-service and joint. Victory in the 1991 Persian Gulf War and the collapse of communism tended to lessen the emotional pressures that had driven a generation of American officers to wrestle with Clausewitz's notoriously challenging philosophical examination of war. Nonetheless, his place in American military education is secure.

Sources:

Christopher Bassford, *Clausewitz in English: The Reception of Clausewitz in Britain and America, 1815–1945* (New York: Oxford University Press, 1994).

Carl von Clausewitz, *Historical and Political Writings*, Peter Paret and Daniel Moran,
    ed. and trans. (Princeton, NJ: Princeton University Press, 1992).
Carl von Clausewitz, *On War*, trans. Michael Howard and Peter Paret (Princeton, NJ:
    Princeton University Press, 1976).
Peter Paret, *Clausewitz and the State: The Man, His Theories, and His Times* (Princeton,
    NJ: Princeton University Press, 1976).

Christopher Bassford

COMMAND AND GENERAL STAFF SCHOOL. *See* ARMY COMMAND
AND GENERAL STAFF COLLEGE.

COMMAND OF THE AIR. Concept that first winning the air battle would
enable military commanders to achieve success in all other phases of a war that
had a dominant influence on the curricula of professional military educational
institutions operated by the U.S. Air Force and its predecessors.

General Giulio Douhet, an early advocate of air power, titled his famous 1921
book *The Command of the Air* and admitted in its pages that Alfred Thayer
Mahan* was a part of its inspiration. Mahan was at the height of his fame at
the onset of the First World War; and the notion that once command of the sea
were established all else would follow, central to his theory, no doubt caught
Douhet's attention. Douhet was at the time immersed in the war in Italy and
authored his tome in the immediate aftermath.

Ideas like Douhet's certainly had some influence on the American airmen in
Europe with Pershing—particularly the concepts espoused by leaders of Britain's Royal Flying Corps. After they returned, the U.S. Army Air Service established a specialized school for its officers at Langley Field, Virginia, in 1920,
soon after naming it the Air Service Field Officers School. General Billy Mitchell* returned from Europe in 1919 and became the assistant chief of the Air
Service. From the beginning, he was a major influence in the development of
the school's curriculum. But there were several others who played important
roles, including the commandant, Colonel Thomas De Witt Milling, and Major
William Carrington Sherman, one of the instructors. Both Mitchell and Sherman
wrote books on the subject of air power, and a central theme of both was that
the first mission of air power was to achieve command of the air. Sherman was
later on the faculty at the Command and General Staff School* at Fort Leavenworth,* and Mitchell was a frequent lecturer at the U.S. Army War College*
in the early 1920s.

The original demand for command of the air in World War I had arisen among
the ground generals. Therefore, there was not much of an argument on the
subject between the Army General Staff* and the airmen. The argument in the
early twenties had more to do with the exploitation of command of the air and
the methods of achieving it in the first place. Many of the airmen at the school
and all over the Air Service asserted that centralized control by an airman was
necessary to win air supremacy or superiority and that usually its exploitation

by autonomous or independent air operations would be more productive than work in direct support of ground units. The General Staff asserted that the ground support mission was more important than autonomous work, and because of that air units should be under the direct command of the various field commanders. The argument became more and more heated, and the result was the court-martial of General Mitchell in late 1925. He subsequently resigned, and in 1926 the congressional act establishing the Army Air Corps was a direct outcome of the debate. Some airmen thought that it was a step forward; others argued that it was just a sop and that the only real change was that the Field Officers School was renamed the Air Corps Tactical School.*

In the early 1920s, Giulio Douhet had generally argued that command of the air could be best achieved by attacking enemy airpower on the ground and that consequently the bomber arm was the most important. Billy Mitchell and his followers at that time asserted that a part of the battle for air superiority had to take place in the air and that, therefore, the pursuit (fighter) arm was the preeminent part of an air force. After the court martial, though, the thinkers at the Air Corps Tactical School became increasingly dedicated to the notion that the major part of the air battle would be the bomber attack on enemy airfields, aircraft factories, fuel supplies, and the like. Thus they were moving toward Douhet. Mitchell himself, by then a civilian, moved in the same direction. Though neither the pursuit nor the ground attack courses of instruction ever disappeared from the Air Corps Tactical School curriculum before World War II, it is clear enough that the bomber program was considered the most important—and that is the principal notion that most airmen carried to Europe and the Pacific.

The Air Corps Tactical School was shut down during World War II, and the combat experience suggested rather strongly that a Douhet-type attack was not the ultimate answer—that air forces had to be prepared to win supremacy aloft through an air battle perhaps supplemented with an attack of the enemy air assets on the ground. But one of the revolutionary effects of the coming of nuclear weapons was the undermining of that idea.

The Air University* and three of its constituent schools—the Squadron Officers School, the Air Command and Staff College,* and the Air War College*—were established during the nuclear era, in the later 1940s. From their founding at least until the middle of the Vietnam War, the dominant idea in all three curricula was that a future major war was likely to be a short, total one employing nuclear weapons at an early stage. This meant that there would be little time for an air battle at all and that nuclear weapons were so overwhelmingly powerful that such a battle would be irrelevant in any event. The addition of nuclear-tipped intercontinental ballistic missiles (ICBMs) seemed to reinforce the Douhet approach because there could be no defense against them except some sort of a preemptive attack.

Korea had been seen by many as an aberration, but when the second limited war (Vietnam) came along, it changed the schools' perceptions of command of the air. In neither Korea nor Vietnam was it possible to mount a full-blooded attack on enemy air power on the ground. If command of the air was to be achieved at all, it would have to be done largely through a battle aloft and through a battle rising from the ground in the form of surface-to-air missiles (SAMs) combined with radar-directed anti-aircraft fire. From the mid-1970s onward, then, the vision of the future at the Air Force professional military schools was that in all cases except perhaps an unlikely nuclear war, command of the air would have to be achieved by some combination of air battle and air-to-surface attack on air power resources on the ground.

Sources:

Robert T. Finney, *History of the Air Corps Tactical School* (reprint, Washington, DC: Center for Air Force History, 1992).
Alfred F. Hurley, *Billy Mitchell: Crusader for Airpower* (new ed., Bloomington: Indiana University Press, 1964, 1975).
David R. Mets, *Master of Airpower* (Novato, CA: Presidio, 1988).
David R. Mets, "To Kill a Stalking Bird," *Airpower Journal 12* (Fall 1998).

David R. Mets

COMPETITIVE ADMISSIONS. The use of competitive examinations in selecting candidates for American precommissioning education became an issue during the 19th century and remained an issue well into the 20th. That it became an issue at all reflected yet another aspect of the influence of European practice on PME in the United States.

In comparing the French and Prussian military school systems in 1869, an English Military Education Commission commented that "the most marked point of contrast" between the two "consists in the thoroughly competitive character of the [French system]." The same law in 1794 that established l'École Polytechnique,* during the period of the French Directory, also created a plan for a system of competitive examinations leading to admission to the various civil and military services supplied with graduates by the school. Very quickly, certainly by the time of Sylvanus Thayer's* visit, competitive examinations also were instituted for the 16- to 20-year-old candidates to determine admissions to both the Polytechnic and St. Cyr.* Reflecting the different curricula at the two schools, the exams required of St. Cyrians were "much less severe" than those for the Polytechnic. Competition was a prominent feature of the programs of instruction at other French military schools as well—including the schools of application. An academic order of merit, one of the French program features adopted by Thayer for West Point,* determined not only the assignment of graduates from these schools but also the preference for course selections when curriculum alternatives were made available.

In the United States, the possibility of competitive admissions to the service academies became a contentious issue. Many members of Congress regarded this prospect as a threat to their control over service academy appointments and to the value of appointments as a form of political patronage. Accordingly, once appointed, candidates for admission to both the military and naval academies were required only to pass a qualifying examination.* Since the Congress insisted that all congressional districts have equal opportunity for representation in the student bodies, the qualifying standard was kept quite low—reflecting the wide range of public education made available among the different states of the young American republic.

With the heightened interest in military affairs brought on by the Civil War, public interest in the professional military practices of other countries led to close inspection of the education being provided for military leaders among the great powers of Europe. American observers, like the distinguished educator Henry Barnard,* reported on the competitive nature of admissions to the military schools of France and England. The latter had introduced competition for the first time in 1855, with respect to the Royal Military Academy at Woolwich,* in response to a large demand for skilled artillerists and engineers during the Crimean War. But by the time of Barnard's first report, seven years later, the practice had been extended to some of the other British military schools as well.

Observations of European practice prompted several attempts to impose competitive admissions on service academies in the United States. In its report of 1863, West Point's board of visitors* recommended that "all appointments of cadets be made from a list established by competitive examinations . . . according to an order of merit assigned by the examiners." In 1864, a similar recommendation was made by the board of visitors to the Naval Academy.* On May 18 of that same year, in a Senate debate accompanying action on the annual appropriation bill for the U.S. Military Academy,* Senator Anthony (Rhode Island), sought an amendment that would require such a procedure: "I submit that we may safely in this republican country give our young men the privileges that are conceded in Imperial France and aristocratic England that we may safely place competition against patronage, and give to modest merit a chance with pretentious imbecility." However, even in wartime, Congress balked at the idea of requiring admissions based on competition, and the reliance on relatively elementary qualifying examinations continued throughout the 19th century.

During the 20th century, the accelerated development of new military technology created a need for more and more advanced knowledge among service academy graduates. Satisfying this need meant either lengthening the academies' courses of study or demanding that candidates for admission already demonstrate more basic knowledge than had been demanded in years past. Illustrative of the need for change in admissions standards is the fact that in 1903, only 43 percent of the entrants to West Point had completed requirements for a high school diploma. The student body at the U.S. Naval Academy* was even less well prepared; not until 1903 was the minimum age for admission raised to 16, and the elementary nature of the Annapolis curriculum prompted three successive boards of visitors (1917, 1918, and 1919) to urge that entrance requirements be raised to require demonstration of at least a high school equivalency.

Educational variances among the states continued to fuel congressional resistance to the academies' use of competitive examinations, but both schools raised considerably their standards for admission by the late 1930s. Both employed rather stiff qualifying examinations in a broad range of subjects or, alternatively, a "substantiating examination" in English and mathematics for graduates of approved high school programs. Admission to an accredited college, based on proficiency in an acceptable range of units on the College Entrance Examination Board (CEEB) tests, was also acknowledged as a valid qualification for an appointee.

Congressional appointments based on each legislator's own criteria for ranking his candidates, together with a combination of alternative means of meeting minimum qualifying standards, continued as the U.S. service academies' method of admission in the years following World War II. However, during the immediate postwar period, more and more members of Congress utilized the competitive results of examinations in various subjects administered by the U.S. Civil Service as one of their ranking criteria.

In the more recent postwar decades, several new competitive elements also have modified the process. Since 1958, the service academies have abandoned their own locally produced entrance examinations and, instead, have relied on the standard examinations utilized by the admissions boards of most colleges. Moreover, the academies have been granted more direct control over the final admissions selections. Members of Congress may nominate as many as ten candidates for each of their appointment vacancies, giving each academy's board of admissions the opportunity to select among them, as follows: Either among all ten or among nine alternate nominees, the congressman or senator having already designated his or her principal nominee. Or, the nominating member, as traditionally, may rank all of the nominees himself. In either case, each admissions board has a veto authority over a particular candidate if he or she fails to meet the academy's scholastic, medical, and physical aptitude standards.

In cases of special appointments, such as those of the president, those from within active and reserve military ranks, or those from the appropriate Reserve Officers' Training Corps (ROTC),* the service academy admissions boards have complete selection authority. This provision applies also to the nominations allocated to children of servicemen killed in line of duty, of those suffering 100 percent disability, and of those listed as prisoners of war (POW) or missing in action (MIA).

Sources:

Henry Barnard, *Military Schools and Courses of Instruction in the Science and Art of War* (rev. ed.) (New York: E. Steiger, 1872).

William E. Simons, *Liberal Education in the Service Academies* (New York: Bureau of Publications, Teachers College, Columbia University, 1965).

United States Naval Academy, 1997–98 Catalog, Annapolis, MD: Naval Academy, 1997.

CORPS OF ARTILLERISTS AND ENGINEERS. Element of the new U.S. national army, established in 1794, which incorporated a military school at its garrison location at West Point and served as an early forerunner of the U.S. Military Academy.

A diplomatic crisis with Great Britain stemming from a resumption of war between Britain and France in 1793 provoked Congress to confront the prospect of warlike acts threatening U.S. shores. The British navy was ignoring American protests regarding the rights of neutrals to free passage of commerce on the high seas, and British troops still occupied strategically located forts along the northwest frontier. Congress reacted in March 1794 by passing the Naval Act for the construction of new ships and by authorizing the construction of coastal fortifications and additional sites for storing munitions. In May, at President Washington's urging, it voted to establish a Corps of Artillerists and Engineers consisting of four battalions—eventually to man the new forts—incorporating the existing battalion of artillery within it. The same legislation authorized the appointment of 32 cadets to the corps. After a year of recruitment, the three new battalions were assembled at West Point, New York* to garrison that post and train for their intended duties, under the corps commander, Lt. Colonel Stephen Rochefontaine.

George Washington had long advocated formal instruction to prepare young men for military leadership. In his message to Congress in 1793, for example, he asked the members to consider whether "a material feature" in the improvement of measures for national defense "ought not to be to afford opportunity for the study of those branches of the military art which can scarcely be obtained by practice alone." Once the Corps of Artillerists and Engineers had been authorized, he directed his Secretary of War to form a school for instruction of the corps, with Rochefontaine as its head, and to support it with proper books and apparatus. As Russell Weigley explains, Washington "hoped to escape the dependence on foreigners for the technical skills of those branches that had characterized the Revolution and was still evident in the leadership of the West Point school." Both field officers serving under Rochefontaine at corps headquarters, Major Louis de Tousard and Major J.J.U. Rivardi, were also French.

Not much is known about the conduct and program of the original school, except that all cadets and junior officers of the corps were expected to attend. The school records and the stone building where classes took place were destroyed in a fire of mysterious origin in 1796. But the effort was not abandoned.

Reacting to tensions produced by the quasi war at sea with the French Directory and that government's apparent designs on Louisiana, Congress, in 1798, appropriated over $1 million for additional harbor fortifications and arms, created a Navy Department, and authorized increases in the size of the existing infantry regiments. It also authorized a doubling of the Corps of Artillerists and Engineers and authorized President John Adams to appoint four civilian teachers in "the arts and sciences" for the school. The following year, it authorized an increased number of cadets for the corps, and the President began an unproductive search for someone to head a proper military academy like those being proposed by several prominent figures. In 1800, just two years before Congress acted to establish the U.S. Military Academy,* Adams encouraged his new Secretary of War to implement the existing authorizations for instructing the artillerists and engineers, indicating his willingness to appoint 64 cadets and a number of instructors. As Sidney Forman has shown, however, "Adams was handicapped by the insuperable difficulty of finding qualified American teachers" and was reluctant to hire foreigners. Accordingly, it wasn't until January 1801, virtually on the eve of Adams's departure from office, that he finally appointed George Baron as a teacher of mathematics and reactivated the instruction at West Point. However, Baron soon found it difficult for a civilian to instill study discipline in a group of young military men, and he abandoned his position early in 1802.

By this time Thomas Jefferson had taken office, and in the midst of several foreign policy problems that conceivably could have led to issues of national security he resolved to set officer instruction on a firmer footing. On February 16, 1801, he designated Major Jonathan Williams as Inspector of Fortifications and Superintendent of the post at West Point. In April his Secretary of War named Louis de Tousard the Army's Inspector of Artillery, in effect dividing administration of the corps into two separate entities. In May, Williams was ordered to "to direct the necessary arrangements for the commencement of [a military] school" that the President had decided to establish for 20 to 30 officers and cadets. Legislation formally creating a Corps of Engineers that would "constitute a military academy" was proposed to the Congress and finally enacted in March 1802.

Sources:

Edward C. Boynton, *History of West Point* (New York: D. Van Nostrand, 1863).
Sidney Forman, *West Point: A History of the United States Military Academy* (New York: Columbia University Press, 1950).
Russell F. Weigley, *History of the United States Army* (New York: Macmillan, 1967).

CROZET, CLAUDIUS. Claudius Crozet (born 1789, died 1864), attended l'École Polytechnique (1807) and the School of Application for Artillery and Engineers at Metz (1809). Crozet had a prominent role as an engineering and mathematics teacher and advisor at both the United States Military Academy (USMA) and the Virginia Military Institute (VMI). He introduced the teaching of descriptive geometry in America and brought the scientific thinking of the l'École Polytechnique from Napoleonic France to the United States.

Crozet ranked 21 among 56 students who graduated from the prestigious l'École Polytechnique* in 1807. He studied at the land artillery program at Metz before earning a commission as a second lieutenant in the Imperial Artillery Corps. Crozet supervised bridge work during the battle of Wagram. However, his main wartime service was with Marschal Michel Ney's division of the Grande Armée as it invaded Russia. Crozet became a captain of the artillery train of the Imperial Guard and became a prisoner during the battle of Borodino. He decided to emigrate to the United States after Napoleon's fall from power.

Crozet was able to secure letters of recommendation from the Marquis de Lafayette and other distinguished French gentlemen whom he met on the ship crossing the Atlantic Ocean. One of these gentlemen was Simon Bernard, a 1797 École Polytechnique graduate. This newly commissioned brigadier general of the U.S. Army Corps of Engineers and member of the board of visitors* of the U.S. Military Academy* helped Crozet. The combined influence of these French gentlemen led to Crozet's being appointed a professor of civil and military engineering (1816–23) at the USMA.

Superintendent Sylvanus Thayer* of the academy was just starting to modernize the curriculum and stabilize the administration. He welcomed the experienced former French officer. Crozet recommended the textbooks of instructors he had studied under while at École Polytechnique. The better-written and more advanced French textbooks supplanted the current English mathematics and science books of the day. Crozet's approach was to overcome the curriculum shortcomings by teaching descriptive geometry, calculus, principles of artillery, grand tactics, and topography. He taught with the help of blackboards, which he introduced to America. Crozet brought over all his drawings and books with him to America.

The resulting modernization of the entire mathematics curriculum led West Point's board of visitors, in its 1822 report, to state that "Captain Crozet is by far the best mathematician in the United States." However, bitter feelings developed between him and Thayer over differences of opinion concerning the ways in which certain subjects should be taught and how the classroom routine should be conducted. Crozet, the teacher, thought Thayer's concept of instruction to be too authoritarian, and he resigned his teaching post after only seven years.

Crozet next became the principal engineer and Surveyor of Public Works for the state of Virginia. He supervised this first state transportation department planning canal and railway construction. He engineered what was then the longest railroad tunnel in the United States, through the Blue Ridge Mountains, in 1858. He also promoted military education in Virginia as the first president of the board of visitors of the Virginia Military Institute* (1837–45). Although he never taught a class at VMI, Crozet molded the character of the new school in Lexington. He developed the curriculum, recommended textbooks, and suggested cadet rules and regulations.

Crozet was a professional engineer when tradition-bound amateurs dominated the field. He became an expert builder of roads and railroads in Virginia. His influencing the transfer of Napoleonic French military and civil engineering to West Point and VMI brought the spirit of the École Polytechnique to the United States.

Sources:

Edwin L. Dooley, Jr., "Claudius Crozet: Disseminator of French Technical Education to the United States," *The Consortium on Revolutionary Europe, 1750–1850: Proceedings*, 1984, 1986.

Robert F. Hunter and Edwin L. Dooley, Jr, *Claudius Crozet: French Engineer In America, 1790–1864* (Charlottesville: University Press of Virginia, 1989).

M. L. Welch, "Early West Point French Teachers and Influences," *American Society of Legion of Honor Magazine* (Spring 1955).

Alan C. Aimone

D

DANIELS, JOSEPHUS. Newspaper editor and publisher (born 1862, died 1948) who served as Secretary of the Navy in the administrations of President Woodrow Wilson (1913–21) and as ambassador to Mexico (1933–41). Daniels became the editor of the Raleigh *News and Observer* and made it into one of the leading newspapers of the South.

A southern political progressive during the post-Reconstruction era and also a religious fundamentalist, he became identified with William Jennings Bryan but demonstrated strong support for Wilson during the election of 1912 and afterward as a cabinet member. During his early years as Secretary of the Navy, Daniels manifested great concern for the education of the naval officer corps and enlisted sailors, devoting considerable time to various extensive reforms. He wanted to make the Navy "a great university," a reflection of the progressive faith in education as a key to personal growth, advancement, and responsible citizenship as well as solicitude for those in the lower orders of society. His zeal for education aroused much opposition in naval circles, traditionally conservative in outlook, but it also engendered praise elsewhere.

Daniels interested himself in enlisted personnel, seeking to minimize spare time and to fill it with educational activity. Setting up academic departments everywhere at sea and ashore, he decreed that recruits would be required to receive mandatory instruction for the first two years of enlistment during off-duty hours. Later activity would be voluntary. Although this program encountered considerable initial opposition, it immediately attracted many students. The Army and the Marines later set up comparable schooling systems.

Daniels was surprised to discover that only a few students were in attendance at the Naval War College,* an institution in Newport, Rhode Island,* charged with training senior officers for important staff and command assignments. The Board of Navigation was reluctant to assign officers to the college because they were needed to man ships at sea. Nevertheless, Daniels soon established quotas for attendance and made completion of the War College course, either by attendance or by correspondence, a prerequisite for the promotion of senior officers. These measures soon involved many officers in programs of study, and the course-completion requirement continued on in later years.

Daniels also criticized the curriculum of the U.S. Naval Academy,* arguing that it dealt effectively with technical subjects but inadequately with the humanities. One solution to this problem was to introduce civilians as the heads of humanities programs at Annapolis. This policy continued to the present, distinguishing the Naval Academy from its counterparts in the other services. To broaden the educational outlook of the academy, he reorganized the board of visitors,* appointing distinguished civilian educators to it.

Although Daniels endured much criticism, his efforts to strengthen naval education later received approbation and emulation both in the U.S. services and abroad. Educational improvements were an essential element in the creation of a navy second to none between 1916 and 1945. Whatever their social significance, they made invaluable contributions to the efficiency of the U.S. Navy during World War II and after.

Sources:

Paolo E. Coletta, ed., "Josephus Daniels," *American Secretaries of the Navy, Vol. 2* (Annapolis, MD: Naval Institute Press, 1980).

E. David Cronon, *The Cabinet Diaries of Josephus Daniels, 1913–1921* (Lincoln: University of Nebraska Press, 1963).

Josephus Daniels, *The Wilson Era* (2 vols.), (Chapel Hill: University of North Carolina Press, 1944, 1946).

David F. Trask

DAVIDSON, GARRISON H. Garrison Holt Davidson (born 1904, died 1992), Lt. General, U.S. Army, graduate of the U.S. Military Academy (USMA), served as commandant of the Army Command and General Staff College (CGSC), 1954–56, and as superintendent of USMA, 1956–60.

General Davidson influenced the Command and General Staff College* to change its emphasis from training to education, and reformed the academic, military, and physical programs at West Point to broaden opportunities for all cadets. With his penchant for organizational reform, he began an evolutionary process at the U.S. Military Academy (USMA)* that eventually transformed a completely prescribed standard curriculum into the multiple electives and majors offered today. In both cases his aim was to provide the Army with more competent and versatile officers.

Commissioned a second lieutenant of Engineers upon graduation from USMA, he remained there for a decade in a number of roles, including service as an instructor in the Department of Natural and Experimental Philosophy (later the Department of Mechanics) and a successful stint as head football coach. He handled construction projects in the early days of World War II but made his mark as General George S. Patton's chief engineer in North Africa and Sicily. He remained as the Seventh Army engineer from the landings in Southern France until the end of the war, when he became president of the first mass trial of war criminals at Darmstadt. After a number of peacetime staff assignments, he came to the attention of General Matthew Ridgway in Korea while serving as the assistant division commander of the 24th Infantry Division and preparing defensive lines around Seoul and Pusan. When Ridgway became Army Chief of Staff in 1954, he appointed Davidson commandant of CGSC.

Davidson had never had time to attend Army schools after West Point, but he quickly showed the insight and organizational skills that would make him such a successful educational reformer. He established study groups to look at all facets of the college's operations, including an Educational Survey Commission made up of distinguished senior educators, both civilian and military, with the mission to examine the whole academic curriculum. Davidson concluded that CGSC needed to get more involved in the creation of army doctrine, and that the academic program needed to emphasize education designed to create flexible decision makers instead of training to memorize standard principles. He obtained additional staff authorizations to establish a doctrinal division that later would become the Combat Developments Command, and he redesigned the curriculum to have students think and reason through complex problems and case studies. As Davidson was being reassigned, the findings of the Educational Survey Commission reinforced the need to make CGSC more of a college and less of a training school, and his successor, Maj. General Lionel McGarr, would take the process even further.

Davidson had requested the West Point assignment from Ridgway's successor, General Maxwell Taylor, and he arrived with a number of concerns gleaned from his own experience at the academy as well as from observations during his service away from it. By the end of his first year he had formulated a strategy to accomplish reform that was very similar to that he used at CGSC. He established a number of study groups to look at future academic requirements and curriculum, the honor system, and the development of military leadership. Never before had so many of the staff, faculty, alumni, and cadets been involved in such a thorough review of academy programs. Davidson's strategy not only furnished planners a wealth of information, it also co-opted possible opposition groups by giving them input into the evaluation process. Many superintendents, such as Douglas MacArthur,* who had tried to force change at West Point by decree, found much of their work undone as soon as they were reassigned. Davidson's changes, by and large, were much more permanent.

He reduced the emphasis on football and spread the benefits of athletic and physical training more widely throughout the Corps of Cadets. He also expanded military leadership training during the summer to give cadets increased hands-on experience leading more-junior classes and spending a few weeks as a "third lieutenant" with active Army units. However, his main impact on USMA was in shaping the future course of the academic curriculum. He managed to persuade the Academic Board to permit advanced instruction to challenge the most talented cadets, and to allow each senior to take one elective in each semester. A reduction in engineering requirements also freed up a third elective, but that reform did not last. Nevertheless, Davidson had proved the need for a more challenging and flexible curriculum, and his successors continued to move away from the completely standardized course offerings he had inherited.

Though he attempted to extend his tour at West Point, he was reassigned to command the Seventh and First Armies before his retirement in 1964. He later served in a number of administrative positions in California higher education, but never lost his devotion to the Military Academy he had done so much to shape.

Sources:

Theodore J. Crackel, *The Illustrated History of West Point* (New York: H. N. Abrams, 1991).

Boyd L. Dastrup, *The U.S. Army Command and General Staff College: A Centennial History* (Manhattan, KS: Sunflower University Press, 1982).

Garrison H. Davidson, "Grandpa Gar: The Saga of One Soldier as Told to His Grandchildren," unpublished manuscript in the USMA Library Special Collections Division, West Point, NY, 1974.

John P. Lovell, *Neither Athens nor Sparta?: The American Service Academies in Transition* (Bloomington: Indiana University Press, 1979).

Lt. Colonel Conrad C. Crane, USA

DEFENSE ACQUISITION UNIVERSITY. Educational consortium, chartered by Congress in 1990, to educate and train Department of Defense professionals for effective performance in the acquisition of U.S. defense systems.

In 1990, Congress passed the Defense Acquisition Workforce Improvement Act, Public Law 101–510. The act was intended to stimulate the Department of Defense to improve the quality of its acquisition workforce. It required the establishment of career development and personnel management programs for the DoD's acquisition professionals; creation of a senior acquisition corps; and improvements in the overall education, training, and experience of the department's acquisition workforce. Among the act's provisions was specific direction to establish a school of application for acquisition within the DoD.

The Defense Acquisition University (DAU) was established by DoD Directive 5000.57 with the mission to educate and train professionals for effective service within the defense acquisition system. The DAU opened its doors on August 1, 1992. It operates as a consortium of DoD education institutions and training organizations offering courses for more than 100,000 military and civilian personnel serving in 11 specific acquisition career fields. These fields include: acquisition logistics, auditing, business/cost estimating/financial management, communications and computer systems, contracting, industrial contract property management, program management, manufacturing/production/quality assurance, procurement and purchasing, system planning/research/development/engineering, and test and evaluation.

The Defense Acquisition University oversees a wide range of acquisition education and training activities. Through its education and training consortium, the DAU sponsors basic, intermediate, and advanced acquisition courses designed to infuse the DoD acquisition workforce with practical knowledge. Normally, DAU students take a core acquisition course before enrolling in mandatory functional training. Throughout their careers, acquisition professionals take additional consortium courses to enhance their general understanding of the acquisition process and increase their personal knowledge of functional specialties. The DAU catalog is published annually and is available in hard copy and on the Internet. It lists available courses, identifies course prerequisites, provides information on where, when, and how courses are taught, and includes course registration forms. The latest educational technologies, including distance learning options, are incorporated into the courses whenever possible. In addition, the consortium sponsors acquisition-related research, procurement case studies, professional publications, and symposia on defense acquisition policy issues.

The capstone course within the consortium program is the Senior Acquisition Course, conducted by the Industrial College of the Armed Forces.* It is designed to prepare selected military officers and civilians for senior leadership positions within the DoD acquisition system. Military officers are chosen competitively as part of their service's senior professional military education selection process and then designated for the senior course enrollment by their service's defense acquisition career manager. Civilians are normally selected by their service or agency career manager. All senior course students are concurrently enrolled full-time in ICAF's senior service college program. The additional Senior Acquisition Course curriculum includes two mandatory acquisition policy courses that focus students on strategic-level acquisition issues. Students meet in small groups with senior-level policy makers from the DoD, defense industry, and academia on a nonattribution basis. All students are required to research and write on topics of current interest to the defense acquisition community. In addition, students are given the opportunity to produce a major research paper for publication. Those senior course students who successfully complete ICAF's overall program are awarded a Master of Science degree in national resource strategy from the National Defense University* (ICAF's parent institution). Completion of the program also fulfills the Office of Personnel Management's education requirement for Senior Executive Service status.

The president of the DAU reports to the Under Secretary of Defense for Acquisition and Technology through the Deputy Under Secretary for acquisition reform. A board of visitors, selected for their personal distinction in academia, business, and public service, advises the undersecretary and the university president regarding institutional management, training technology, curriculum, facilities, and other areas of importance to the university.

The relationship between the Defense Acquisition University and its consortium members is defined by memoranda of agreement. Under the consortium concept, member schools continue to operate within their service or agency's normal command structures. In addition to their acquisition courses, most consortium members offer other education programs or training courses that support requirements of their parent organization. Current consortium members are Air Force Institute of Technology,* Army Logistics Management College, Defense Contract Audit Institute, Defense Logistics Agency Civilian Personnel Support Office, Defense Systems Management College, Industrial College of the Armed Forces,* Information Resources Management College, Lackland Training Facility, Naval Center for Acquisition Training, Naval Facilities Contracts Training Center, Naval Postgraduate School,* and Naval Warfare Assessment Division.

The acquisition university uses functional boards to ensure its curriculum is relevant and current. There is a functional board for each acquisition career field. Board members are senior-level acquisition officials from the Office of the Secretary of Defense and DoD components. They advise the university administration on overall education, training, and professional development requirements of the acquisition workforce. They identify core competencies required to perform at basic, intermediate, and advanced levels within the various acquisition career fields. These core competencies are the foundation for the consortium's curricula. The boards also help the DAU faculty review training modules to ensure that information being taught is factual, relevant, and current.

The consortium concept is based on teamwork. From the undersecretary down through the DAU president to the functional boards and faculty of the consortium member schools, the focus is on improving the acquisition workforce. The result is an accessible, high-quality education and training program that helps DoD acquisition professionals develop the skills they need to keep pace with a rapidly changing world.

Sources:

Defense Acquisition University Catalog for Fiscal Year 1997 (Washington, DC: Office of the Undersecretary of Defense [Acquisition and Technology], 1997).
Defense Acquisition Workforce Improvement Act (Public Law 101–501, Title XII, 10 U.S.C. 1701–1764, 1990).

Colonel David E. Price, USAF

DEFENSE REORGANIZATION ACT OF 1986. *See* GOLDWATER-NICHOLS ACT.

E

EARLY ARMY PROFESSIONAL MILITARY EDUCATION SYSTEM.
Military school and officer assignment structure established by Secretary of War
Elihu Root by 1903 and strengthened following World War I.

During the antebellum period the War Department established a number of
schools to provide practical training and theoretical grounding of commissioned
officers in their professional duties. As early as 1818, reform-minded officers
familiar with French Army schools of practice had recommended postgraduate
training for selected officers in mathematics, fortifications, topography, and artillery. In 1824 Secretary of War John C. Calhoun* established the Artillery
School at Fortress Monroe,* Virginia, while two years later his successor, James
Barbour, authorized an infantry school at Jefferson Barracks, Missouri. These
early efforts were in essence schools of practice for both officers and enlisted
men, with no clearly established curriculum, course of study, or faculty. By the
1830s both schools had faded from the scene as more pressing concerns, such
as the Black Hawk War, required the attention of the Army. In 1858 the War
Department revived Fortress Monroe as a school for "the theoretical and practical instruction of artillery." The Civil War, however, ended the school's development, and it did not reopen until 1867.

The Artillery School in the period after the Civil War gained some measure
of prestige when Colonel Emory Upton,* its most prominent faculty member,
became a close ally of the Commanding General of the Army, William T. Sherman,* in advancing military reform and professional development. Its course
was one year, eventually extended to two, with the purpose of teaching young
officers about the technical aspects of artillery, but also about "the general progress of military science." In 1881 Sherman established a School of Application
for Infantry and Cavalry* at Fort Leavenworth, Kansas,* initially to impart basic
military skills to undertrained lieutenants, but eventually with the intent to create
a more advanced institution for the study of military art. By the time of the

Spanish-American War this goal had been achieved with true military intellectuals on the faculty and an increasingly sophisticated curriculum of strategy, tactics, military engineering, and military history. The last decades of the 19th century also saw creation of the Cavalry and Light Artillery School* at Fort Riley, Kansas; the Engineer School of Application* at Washington Barracks; and the School of Submarine Defense at Fort Totten, New York. The purpose of each was to provide basic instruction in their branch specialties for junior officers. In 1891, to provide additional forums for professional discussion and study, the Commanding General, John M. Schofield, ordered creation of lyceums at all posts garrisoned by troops of the line.

In 1898, therefore, there were several U.S. Army schools, but not a system, devoted to the professional development of officers. There was no relationship among the courses of study at the several schools. Nor was there any means by which an officer could progress through increasingly challenging courses. Moreover, there were no entrance requirements, and attendance was largely voluntary.

Although the Army performed satisfactorily at the tactical level, the Spanish American War revealed significant shortcomings in military policy, planning, and strategy. Elihu Root,* appointed Secretary of War in August 1899, endeavored to improve the War Department performance in these areas and perceived a robust system of military education as central to the reforms he proposed to undertake. Root's closest advisor, Colonel William Harding Carter, an instructor at the Leavenworth school of application from 1894 to 1896, furnished the secretary with the details and a rationale for creating a system of military education: the "rapid advance of military science" had created a growing and continuing need for a "through and broad education for military officers."

The system that Carter proposed and Root adopted was progressive, competitive, and built around the schools already established. The objective was to provide appropriately changing educational opportunities as an officer progressed through his career. Each school would concentrate on a single level of military science—either branch specialties, basic tactics, combined arms and staff functions, or strategy and national policy. In his scheme, as the curriculum became more advanced professionally, the students would become more adept, because only the best graduates at one level would advance to the next highest school.

Carter began with the premise that the existing lyceum system was "most unsatisfactory" for educating junior officers because it lacked structure and rigor. To replace the lyceums, he proposed officers schools at each post to provide instruction in the tactical and administrative duties required of all lieutenants. These schools also would serve to qualify officers for admission to the basic branch schools. Carter incorporated existing schools, such as that for coast artillery at Fort Monroe and for cavalry and field artillery at Fort Riley, into the next level of this educational system. He added other branch schools, such as for signal corps, field engineering, and medical service. The infantry, interestingly, did not have a separate branch school until 1907 when the War Department opened the Infantry School of Musketry at the Presidio of Monterey. For training in combined arms, Carter utilized the existing school at Fort Leavenworth; in 1904 this became two schools, the Army School of the Line, concentrating on division operations, and the Staff College,* which emphasized general staff duties and field army operations. The Army War College,* at the apex of the system, was both an educational institution and an adjunct to the newly created War Department General Staff.*

The War Department launched the PME system Root and Carter created during the years 1901 to 1903 through the issuance of a series of general orders. From that period to World War I, however, the system suffered from several problems that served to limit its effectiveness. Initially the Army used a number of the schools, especially Leavenworth, to remedy professional deficiencies of the large number of junior officers commissioned in the Regular Army following the Spanish-American War and the Philippine Insurrection. At the higher end of the system, the immediate needs of the War Department General Staff for experienced field grade officers sometimes required appointment of officers not graduates of the Staff College or War College. These problems, therefore, somewhat mitigated the progressive and competitive elements Carter had tried to build into the system. Another shortcoming was that, except for the post schools, attendance still was essentially voluntary. The best officers did not always compete and progress through what was supposed to be an increasingly challenging succession of schools. Finally, most of the army schools in the decade before World War I had rather limited student capacity. The School of the Line and Staff College, for instance, respectively averaged only 21 and 36 graduates annually from 1905 to 1916.

In the wake of World War I a succession of reforms, initiated in the 1920 amendments to the National Defense Act and by measures instituted by General John J. Pershing as Chief of Staff of the Army, rationalized PME in the Army and rectified problems inherent in the pre–World War I system. Student capacity increased considerably, with Leavenworth, for one example, during the 1920s and 1930s, often graduating over 200 officers annually. The War Department also more clearly delineated the purpose of each school within the system by designating "special service schools" operated by the separate arms and services and "general service schools" for the combined arms. An effort to reduce overlap and duplication among all of the schools' courses of study further rationalized the system. Finally, the system became truly competitive and progressive when selection devolved to the War Department bureaucracy. At each level, whether for the branch schools, Leavenworth, or the War College, selection became a matter of performance, based on previous schooling and annual efficiency ratings. From a succession of unrelated educational institutions in the 19th century, through the skeletal outlines of a system created by Root and Carter, by the early 1920s the U.S. Army had created a truly integrated system of professional military education for its officers.

Sources:

Harry W. Ball, *Of Responsible Command: A History of the U.S. Army War College* (Carlisle Barracks, PA: Alumni Association of the Army War College, 1984).

Edward M. Coffman, *The Old Army: A Portrait of the American Army in Peacetime, 1784–1898* (New York: Oxford University Press, 1986).

Timothy K. Nenninger, *The Leavenworth Schools and the Old Army: Education Professionalism, and the Officer Corps of the United States Army, 1881–1918* (Westport, CT: Greenwood Press, 1978).

Timothy K. Nenninger

L'ÉCOLE D'APPLICATION DE L'ARTILLERIE ET DU GÉNIE. During the 19th century, France's most significant school of application for newly commissioned army officers, visited and examined closely by American educators and military officers.

In 1794, officials of France's revolutionary Convention closed the school of military engineering at Mézières (formerly the École du Corps Royal du Génie*), which had been allowed to deteriorate under the earlier revolutionary regimes. In its place, a provisional engineering school was set up at Metz, where it soon became a school of advanced military engineering for recent graduates of the École Polytechnique.* Graduates selecting corps of artillery commissions were sent to a similar provisional school at Châlons sur Marne. The two programs were united in a single institution at Metz in 1802.

The École d'Application de l'Artillerie et du Génie occupied the cloistered quadrangle of a Benedictine monastery that had been suppressed during the Revolution. The outer walls of one side, an old church with a lofty roof, were retained to provide a drill hall. Here were housed several mortars, fieldpieces, and siege guns, many of which were maneuvered during tactical exercises performed inside the building. The buildings of the remaining three sides of the quadrangle were converted into lecture rooms, galleries, halls of study, and staff offices. The lecture rooms, of which there were two, were large enough to accommodate 70 students. The halls of study, of similar capacity, were designed to seat an entire class. The galleries displayed models of ancient and modern artillery pieces, sets of small arms, models of different fortifications, bridges and canal locks, and various specimens of materiel and equipment used in the construction of weapons and structures.

The students, approximately 140 in number, were quartered in a separate, "modern" four-story building erected on the site. Almost all arrived from the École Polytechnique with a provisional commission in either the field artillery, naval artillery, or the engineers corps. All *sous-lieutenants* 21 to 23 years of age, they were required only to sleep and study in their rooms. After attending a reveille roll call at 6:00 A.M., the students were allowed access to and from the town until 10:00 P.M. except during scheduled lectures and study sessions. Organized into sections of approximately 15 students each, they took their meals in the town at restaurants engaged by the individual sections; the daily fare, however, was limited by a maximum value fixed by the school commandant. Apart from completing their assigned classroom and fieldwork by times specified in the approved course of study, the young sublieutenants were required only to avoid indebtedness and refrain from all games of chance.

Their course of study was normally two years in length and followed a rigid daily schedule. Lectures, nearly daily, were given at 10:00 A.M. and followed by work on drawings, designs, and other projects until 4:00 P.M. in the halls of study. When no lectures were scheduled, the workday began at 10.00 A.M., as always, but in the study halls. From 4 until 5:30 P.M. each day, a portion of the students were called to drills, riding, or field exercises. Although all students had a particular corps affiliation, their first year of study was common to all. It included military art and legislation, topography and geodesy, field fortification, permanent fortification, and the theory and practice of construction. The second year continued with several of these same subjects plus the "attack and defense of places" and also introduced new work unique to each corps specialty. Engineering aspirants received 85 additional days devoted to permanent fortifications and structures. Artillery students alone received 81 days of instruction in artillery and related machinery.

Unlike the Polytechnique, the genre at Metz was thoroughly military. The school was commanded by a general officer of either artillery or engineers, supported by an administrative staff of 16 officers divided evenly between the two services. Of a faculty of nine professors, four assistants, and a drawing master, only the latter and two professors were civilian. No examinations were given at the end of the first year, but an order of merit was established for the students in each arm of service based on oral interrogations by the professors after every eight or ten lectures. Formal examinations were given at the end of the entire course, however, and students were given approximately six weeks of free study to prepare for them. Regarded as leaving examinations qualifying the graduate for regimental duty in his service, these were administered by a special board of general and field-rank officers, not of the faculty, appointed annually by the minister of war. The final order of merit, which determined each graduate's seniority in his corps, was based on a weighted combination of the examination results, the quality of his drawings and memoirs produced during the two years of study, and his previous performance in the school.

L'École d'Application de l'Artillerie et du Génie continued at Metz, following essentially the same program until 1872, when it was relocated at Fontainebleau. At this latter location, the school gained notoriety for producing a number of outstanding military leaders, including the field marshals Maunoury and Foch. The school continued to educate French artillerists and engineers until 1942, including nearly two years at Nimes during the early years of the German Occupation.

Following the Allies' defeat of the Third Reich, the reconstituted French Army established a successor school of artillery. Immediately after the war, it was located for a time on occupied German territory near the vast gunnery range at Baumholder. In 1953, this school was relocated to France at Chalons-sur-Marne, site of its original artillery school of application in the 18th century.

Sources:

Frederick B. Artz, *The Development of Technical Education in France, 1500 to 1850* (Cambridge, MA: Society for the History of Technology and the M.I.T. Press, 1966).
Henry Barnard, *Military Schools and Courses of Instruction in the Science and Art of War* (rev. ed.) (New York: Reprinted by Greenwood Press, 1969).
La Grande Encyclopédie (Paris: Librairie Larousse, 1975).

L'ÉCOLE DU CORPS ROYAL DU GÉNIE. Prior to the American Revolution, France's premier school of military engineering and source of advanced technical education for French engineers advising the American Continental Army.

During the reign of the Bourbon kings prior to 1789, the most advanced engineering education in France, indeed in all of Europe, was conducted in a few military schools. Even after the formalization of civil engineering instruction, in 1775 at the École des Ponts et Chaussées, the systematic preparation of French military engineers exceeded that given their civilian counterparts. The École du Corps Royal du Génie, founded at Mézières in 1749 by Louis XV's foreign minister, the Comte d'Argenson, stood at the pinnacle.

Many features of the instructional program at Mézières established a tradition among French schools of technical education. Its course covered two years with theoretical instruction taking place in the mornings and practical exercises, involving the drawing of plans and the solution of real engineering problems, coming in the afternoons. Summers were devoted to fieldwork. Theoretical study was bolstered by work in well-equipped laboratories for physics and chemistry. With the exception of its first two years, students were admitted only after being examined severely in arithmetic, geometry, and drawing. Some of the students from the nobility arrived from the elementary *écoles militaires* and others from the Royal school of artillery at La Fère. Until 1777, some bourgeois youths were admitted as well. After admission, all were grouped according to their ability, and each was questioned by an instructor on the daily lecture and assigned reading. The more advanced students assisted with this aspect of the instruction, a forerunner to the system of *répétiteures* later installed at the École Polytechnique.* At the end of each year, students were required to pass a stiff examination in each element of their study programs in order to advance or graduate.

Several of the faculty members and students at the École du Génie became leaders in European scientific development. For many years, the professor of mathematics and physics was Gaspard Monge, who developed a system for teaching descriptive geometry that was, in the words of one distinguished historian, "perhaps the most significant contribution ever made by a single man to the teaching of engineering." His method created the foundation for all mechanical drawing and other graphic engineering processes. Noteworthy students included J. V. Poncelet, who built upon the mathematical concepts of Monge, and Charles-Augustine Coulomb, who contributed significantly to modern structural theory and later taught at the renowned École Polytechnique.

Between 1750 and the beginning of the French Revolution in 1789, the École du Génie produced about 300 graduate engineers. French military engineers were recognized as Europe's finest. Their competence was highly regarded in North America as well, since several engineers were recruited as advisors and construction project commanders for the Continental Army during the American fight for independence. For example, the Lt. Colonel Louis Dashaix de la Radière and Brig. General Louis LeBegue DuPortail, both products of the school at Mézièrre, were instrumental in the establishment of the American army post at West Point*; Radière laid out its initial fortifications and DuPortail, under General Washington's instructions, critiqued the early installation and recommended several modifications. Washington later appointed DuPortail his chief engineer.

Sources:

Frederick B. Artz, *The Development of Technical Education in France, 1500–1850* (Cambridge, MA: Society for the History of Technology and the M.I.T. Press, 1966).
Henry Barnard, *Military Schools and Courses of Instruction in the Science and Art of War* (rev. ed.) (New York: E. Steiger, 1972).
Elizabeth S. Kite, *Brigadier General Louis LeBegue Duportail, Commandant of Engineers in the Continental Army* (Baltimore, MD: Johns Hopkins Press, 1933).

L'ÉCOLE (IMPÉRIALE) POLYTECHNIQUE. France's national college of engineering which, in the early 19th century, provided models for the curriculum and academic practices adopted by the U.S. Military Academy at West Point.

At the height of the French Revolution, Talleyrand's proposal of 1791 to suppress all existing academies and schools and replace them with a new national system of education was implemented only in part. The revolutionists' zeal to eliminate the Church's domination of schooling at the secondary and higher levels resulted also in the deterioration of existing military schools, including the then-paramount college of engineering, l'École du Corps Royale du Génie,* and several specialized schools for the public works.

In late 1794, a commission of public works, created earlier that year by the Convention, founded a central school to serve the nation's engineering needs. In the following year, under the Directory, it was redesignated as l'École Polytechnique. Partly military and partly civilian, the school originally was intended to replace all the specialized schools of engineering created by the royal regime and furnish graduate engineers to the different military services and civil bureaucracies serving the state. One year after its founding, aspiring artillerymen also were admitted to the school, and it became the primary source of fundamental engineering studies. More advanced learning in the various technical fields of work nourished by Polytechnic graduates was provided by specialized schools of application. Napoleon, as emperor, imposed military discipline on the Polytechnique and made good use of its graduates—in his army and in his vast enterprises to improve the civil infrastructure and create an efficient network of public works throughout France. Its graduates populated all the scientific offices of the army and directed the building of fortresses and arsenals, the improvement of cities, and the development of canals, roads, mines, and shipyards.

With the restoration of the Bourbon monarchy in the early 19th century, l'École Polytechnique experienced occasional turmoil, as public displays of pro-republican sentiment by its students resulted in government action to close it temporarily. However, by the time of its reopening in 1816, during Sylvanus Thayer's* visit, the academic routine had become quite rigorous and set a high standard. Basic course information was presented in a daily lecture by France's leading scholars, like LaPlace (mathematics) and Fourcroy (chemistry), after which the students met in small groups with *répétiteurs*. In these sessions, the *répétiteur* reviewed the lecture, questioned the students individually, and clarified the key points. Students, all of whom were selected on the basis of demanding competitive examinations, arrived usually with the classical educational background provided by the *lycée*. In addition, many of them had received private tutoring to obtain advanced preparation in mathematics. That subject provided the basis for most of the highly theoretical two-year curriculum. Totally prescribed, its main components included descriptive geometry, differential and integral calculus, theoretical mechanics, physics, and chemistry. Evening classes were also held in figure and landscape drawing and French composition and literature. Staffed by outstanding teachers and scientists, the Polytechnic had become France's primary scientific body and would yield mathematics and engineering treatises that were to provide the theoretical basis for much of Europe's science

In time, the Polytechnic's early heavy emphasis on mathematics came under criticism and led to government initiatives during the 1850s that broadened its academic program and introduced some practical engineering content. Some of the pure mathematics was eliminated and the abstract nature of several of the courses was reduced to a level more directly applicable to engineering practice. However, the pedagogical methods appropriate to mathematics instruction that were so influential on Thayer and West Point* were still in evidence later in the century when l'École Polytechnique was reexamined by Henry Barnard* (1868). Students were graded on their performance daily, and competition among the students was encouraged. Its purpose was to establish an academic order of merit according to which graduates were permitted to enter a school of application and select their initial service assignments. That the higher-ranking students expressed a preference for the civil services was the subject of frequent complaints by the Empire's military authorities.

After establishment of the Third Republic (1875–1940), the military character of the Polytechnique became reinforced, and the school launched the careers of a large number of artillery and engineering officers who became instrumental in the rebuilding of the French army. These officers contributed mightily to the efficiency of the technical services during preparations for World War I and also, one must speculate, to construction of the ill-fated Maginot Line prior to World War II. A total of 915 graduates of the Polytechnic died in World War I. During the second World War in which 345 graduates perished, many while supporting the Résistance, the École Polytechnique functioned for three years outside Paris, moving to Toulouse in June 1940 and thence to Lyons. When all of France was finally occupied by the German army, in 1943, it resumed classes in Paris.

In the immediate postwar period, concern that the Polytechnic be equipped to meet the demands of the modern world encouraged a trend that served for a time to erode the rigor traditionally associated with the academic program. A national commission appointed in 1950 set out to adjust the traditional methods of instruction and prepare, by 1957, for an expanded student body organized into two year-groups of approximately 300 students each. In the process of providing more liberal working conditions in the school the resident program became less strict. The trend continued after 1961 when a new commission moved the Polytechnic even further toward becoming a major research center and relocated the school to new facilities outside of Paris.

More recently, much of the École Polytechnique's earlier rigor has returned, in keeping with a reaffirmed mission established by law in July 1970. That mission is to provide its students with the proper scientific and general grounding to occupy, after the necessary specialized training, highly qualified positions of scientific, technical, or economic responsibility in the national civil and military bodies and in other public service. During their two years of study, the students receive training as reserve officers and, after graduation, satisfy their obligation for national service through an additional seven months of military training. Since 1972, the school has admitted young women of the same 17-to-22 age group as the male entrants, all of whom are subject to the same regimen, participate in the same classes, and have access to the same employment opportunities.

Sources:

Frederick B. Artz, *The Development of Technical Education in France, 1500–1850* (Cambridge, MA: Society for the History of Technology and the M.I.T. Press, 1966).
Henry Barnard, *Military Schools and Courses of Instruction in the Science and Art of War* (rev. ed.) (New York: Reprinted by Greenwood Press, 1969).
Ernest R. Dupuy, *Where They Have Trod: The West Point Tradition in American Life* (New York: Frederick A. Stokes Co., 1940).
La Grande Encyclopédie (Paris: Librairie Larousse, 1975).

L'ÉCOLE ROYALE MILITAIRE D'ARTILLERIE. The preeminent school of artillery instruction in pre-Revolutionary France, which provided a precedent for that country's later establishment of schools of application in several civil and military technical fields.

Substantial improvements during the early 18th century in the accuracy and range of artillery fire and in the construction of fortifications created a demand for better preparation of artillery officers among all the armies of Europe. In France, theoretical classroom instruction had become a routine aspect of the training of artillery officers and enlisted artillerists preparing to become officers. Since the army reforms introduced in 1720, good basic artillery schools had developed in the garrisons at Grenoble, La Fére, Metz, Perpignan, and Strasbourg. At each of these schools, the weekly schedule alternated three days of theoretical work in mathematics, mechanics, fortification, and tactics of defense and attack with three days of practical exercises. The latter included tactical uses of artillery, fortification, bridge building, and mining. Prior to the reign of Louis XVI, the need to recruit sufficient numbers of officer candidates willing to undertake and educated well enough to absorb the theoretical studies led to the admission of an unusual proportion of bourgeois youths into the *corps d'artillerie*. After 1781, however, entry into the artillery schools and other pre-commissioning institutions was restricted to proven members of the nobility.

At the opening of the Seven Years' War (1756–1763), an advanced school of artillery instruction, the École Royale d'Artillerie, was established at La Fère. Louis XV's foreign minister, the Comte d'Argenson, who earlier had founded a central school for the corps of engineers (École du Corps Royal du Génie*), wanted to insure a comparable opportunity for advanced technical education for France's other *arme savant* (learned military arm). The school was assigned two resident professors of mathematics and two of drawing; one of these was Bernard Forest de Belidore, author of several outstanding manuals on the application of mathematics to the use of artillery and of engineering textbooks, including the four-volume *Architecture Hydraulique*. Belidore began his career at La Fère in 1720 by teaching in the regimental artillery school and stayed on as a distinguished member of the advanced school's faculty until his death in 1761. Like its forerunners in the five garrison schools, the program at the École d'Artillerie combined both theoretical study and practical exercises. The theoretical work was conducted in a classroom supplied with models but lacking in real laboratory equipment such as that required for the study of chemistry or physics.

The advanced school at La Fère benefited briefly from the reforms and reorganization of the *corps d'artillerie*, under the strong ministers of war, Claude Louis de Saint-Germain and Phillipe-Henri de Ségur. Its student body was comprised largely of the best officer-students from the garrison artillery schools which, after 1774, were collocated with the newly formed and officially recognized artillery regiments. Unlike officers in the cavalry and infantry, artillery officers were expected to pass both written and practical examinations. In 1781, however, the French nobility's hostility to the growing bourgeois influence within the officer corps—even blaming these officers for the embarrassing defeats suffered during the Seven Years' War—led Louis XVI to take action. He forced Minister Ségur to issue an edict that caused admission to all military schools to be restricted to persons with four generations of noble ancestry and who could present original documents to prove it. Such reactionary policies served to limit the effectiveness of the reformers' efforts and so widen the internal officer corps rifts as to contribute to a collapse of the French army from within.

Like its engineering counterpart, the École Royale d'Artillerie suffered from neglect in the early years of the Revolution. In 1791, the functions of all the artillery schools, including that at La Fére, were consolidated in a central school of artillery at Châtons-sur-Marne. In 1802, this institution was combined with the engineering school at Metz into the École d'Application de l'Artillerie et du Génie.* This school provided advanced technical education to those graduates of the École Polytechnique who were commissioned in the army's artillery and engineering corps.

Sources:

Frederick B. Artz, *The Development of Technical Education in France, 1500–1850* (Cambridge, MA: Society for the History of Technology and the M.I.T. Press, 1966).
Jean-Paul Bertraud (trans. R. R. Palmer), *The Army of the French Revolution: From Citizen-soldiers to Instrument of Power* (Princeton, NJ: Princeton University Press, 1988).
John R. Elting, *Swords Around a Throne: Napoleon's Grande Armée* (New York: Free Press, 1988).

L'ÉCOLE SPÉCIALE MILITAIRE DE SAINT-CYR. France's first (1803) precommissioning school for officer candidates preparing for careers in the infantry and cavalry, now serving all current branches of the army.

The history of France's national military academy, l'École Spéciale Militaire de Saint-Cyr, illustrates most of the key issues in the history of Western junior officer education: the appropriate social, educational, and military background for officer cadets, the relative importance of practical and academic education at the academy, the role of discipline in officer training, the balance between academy traditions and military innovation, and the very existence of elite officer academies in democratic societies.

Professional officer education was a by-product of the French Revolution's "career open to talent." European armies had long trained their artillery and engineer officers in technical schools, but the traditionally aristocratic infantry and cavalry had to wait for the foundation of Britain's Royal Military College at Sandhurst* in 1802 and Napoleon's École Spéciale Militaire in 1803. Established to teach young *lycée* graduates "the art of war," l'École Spéciale Militaire retained throughout several changes of name and location its essential characteristics—intellectual rigor, Spartan living conditions, strict discipline, and the intense pride that led some 30 cadets to swear on July 31, 1914, to go into battle wearing the distinctive white gloves and plumed shakos of the cadets dress uniform.

In general, admission to Saint-Cyr has gone to young civilians chosen for their educational attainment, demonstrated by completion of a demanding secondary-school education, rather than military experience. In the late 19th century, Saint-Cyr accepted some candidates from the ranks of the French army, and the reforms imposed upon the French Army in 1906 in the aftermath of the Dreyfus Affair included the provision that successful applicants to l'École Militaire Spéciale had to serve a year in the ranks before admission. This attempt to give future officers some contact with the conscripts they would eventually command was abolished, however, in 1913 on the grounds that the year's service interrupted intellectual growth without providing authentic military experience. Throughout the 20th century, academic standards have become more flexible, but noncommissioned officers have no longer been able to substitute military experience for the baccalaureate certificate now required of all applicants.

Throughout most of its history, Saint-Cyr has been famous for unequaled rigor and rigidity in the classroom, on the parade ground, and in the barracks. In the second half of the 19th century, the cadets were in constant motion daily from 0500 to 2100, with only short breaks for meager meals. The day's main lecture was followed by a lengthy study period during which the cadets were required to write up their lecture notes to the satisfaction of the professor. Independent study was impossible for lack of time, and personal books were forbidden.

The deaths of 1,131 Saint Cyriens in the Franco-Prussian War testified to their patriotism and courage, but the war's outcome aroused concerns about the soundness of the academy's program. Under the guidance of a new commandant, Brig. General Hanrion, Saint-Cyr's curriculum was revised and streamlined. Only over the course of almost 20 years was Hanrion's most important objective fulfilled, with the replacement of some parade ground training with practical field exercises. In this period the physical training of cadets was intensified through mandatory equitation, boxing, fencing, and dancing. Hanrion's tenure as commandant also saw both the cadet population begin to expand from 350 toward the 600 it would reach at the end of the century and the consequent expansion of the physical accommodations.

A second period of renovation occurred under General Tanant, who became commandant in 1919. Numbers of cadets dropped precipitously but returned to about 300 per class during the Great Depression. The addition of a reserve officer training platoon in 1920 provided salutary reduction in the traditional distance between regular and reserve officers. From 1932 to 1935, Saint-Cyr briefly took responsibility for training officers for the Air Force. More permanent was the tendency to call upon Saint-Cyr for artillery officers, as graduates of l'École Polytechnique* increasing abjured military service for more lucrative civil service careers.

The German invasion of France in May 1940 caused the permanent abandonment of the buildings of Saint-Cyr, but the academy's traditions survived translation into new facilities. The current class moved to Aix-en-Provence in Unoccupied France, which had to be abandoned in the face of the German advance six months later. On April 1, 1943, a new academy was opened at Cherchell in French North Africa. Cherchell took the name l'École Militaire Interarmes in December 1944, but several of its companies consisted of cadets from the Saint-Cyr classes of 1943 and 1944. Other wartime "saint-cyriens" were products of a new academy in French Indochina and of de Gaulle's École Militaire des Cadets de la France Libre in Worcestershire, England, which commissioned 211 officers for the Free French Forces. These officers were officially recognized as saint-cyriens by a law of March 17, 1954. All three of France's Second World War marshals, Le Clerc, Juin, and De Lattre de Tassigny, were graduates of Saint-Cyr.

After the Second World War, both l'École Militaire Interarmes at Cherchell and l'École Spéciale Militaire de Saint-Cyr moved to new grounds in Coëtquidan, in Brittainy, where ample space existed for practical military training, although the hastily constructed facilities were a far cry from the grandeur of Saint-Cyr l'École. At that time, l'École Spéciale Militaire took on the additional mission of producing the artillery, engineering, and other more technically oriented officers formerly educated at l'École Polytechnique.

The 25 years following the Second World War saw a constant flux as the army and government agonized over the proper relationship between l'École Spéciale Militaire de Saint-Cyr, which provided a two-year commissioning program for well-educated civilians, and l'École Militaire Interarmes (formerly Cherchell), most of whose cadets came from the noncommissioned officer branch schools at Saint-Maixent, Saumur, and Versailles. After a bewildering variety of experiments, temporary amalgamations, and changes both of program and of nomenclature, the government settled on September 13, 1961, on two separate schools. L'École Spéciale Militaire de Saint-Cyr was reestablished with its two-year course, Napoleonic uniforms, and ancient flag and traditions. L'École Militaire Interarmes continued to offer a one-year course for noncommissioned candidates. Graduation from either school is followed by a year's branch training at one of the six branch "écoles d'application."

Since 1983, when women were also first admitted to the academy, the program at Saint-Cyr has been modified to provide the equivalent of a four-year university degree. Candidates do two years of postsecondary study before taking the admissions examination, and the course itself has been extended to three.

In their third and final year, saint-cyriens, now members of the famous 1st Batallion of France, are sous-lieutenants rather than cadets. The year includes a grueling tropical warfare exercise in French Guiana, but the emphasis is on academic work in preparation for their final oral examinations. After graduation, the new officers undergo a further year's training at their respective branch schools.

Although l'École Spéciale Militaire continues to take great pride in its heroic traditions and stresses the importance of military discipline, the cadets now enjoy considerable personal freedoms. No longer, arguably, the harshest among the traditional military academies, Saint-Cyr instead offers a program that aims to be intellectually and physically rigorous without creating an excessive distance between future officers and French society.

Sources:

Georges Merz, *Saint-Cyr* (Paris: Office français de diffusion artistique et littéraire, 1962).
Captain Stephane, *Sous le Casoar: Vie et Tradition de l'École Spéciale Militaire* (Paris: Oberthur-Rennes, 1994).

Eugenia C. Kiesling

L'ÉCOLE SUPÉRIEURE DE GUERRE. The French army's premier school of professional military education, equivalent to the Marine Corps Command and Staff College. Before the Second World War, it was the only foreign professional military school attended by Marine Corps officers.

After the Franco-Prussian War and the collapse of France's Second Empire, the army underwent a major reorganization and a variety of reforms. Under the new Republic, beginning in 1873, the corps and divisions of the French army were brought together under central command for the first time during peacetime. Concurrent with this change plans were drawn up for a true general staff within the central headquarters; its actual establishment, however, awaited another seven years. The same law of March 20, 1880, that brought the General Staff into existence created France's premier school of higher military education, l'École Supérieure de Guerre.

Under its first commandant, the school provided a two-year course for students, mostly captains, selected on the basis of competitive admissions.* According to van Creveld, the course consisted of lectures and written exercises on "strategy, general tactics, the tactics of the various arms, fortifications, general staff work, administration, naval warfare, mobilization, railway transport, military health service, and German" and field exercises. The emphasis was on practical studies with the students being given the opportunity "to participate in the development of new weapons and tactics" and make extensive surveys of historic battlefields. The faculty was of highest quality and included some of France's most distinguished officers: men like Bonnal, Fayolle, Foch, Grandmaison, and Pétain. These were the French army's military intellectuals prior to World War I and a major source of French military doctrine of the late 19th and early 20th centuries.

On the eve of the First World War, at the height of the school's fame and productivity, it was eclipsed by creation of the Center for Higher Military Studies from within its own resources. Known popularly as "the School of the Marshals," the Center, under the influence of Foch, was to identify and create an elite group of officers certified to deal with all the complexities of managing military operations under the exclusive jurisdiction of the commander-in-chief. Both institutions survived the war, but the teaching of strategy was removed from the postwar program of the École Supérieure de Guerre and reserved to the Center. In van Creveld's judgment, the school never regained its prewar status as a stimulus of intellectual ferment within the French army.

A U.S. Marine presence at l'École Supérieure de Guerre commenced in 1926, largely on the initiative of Marine Commanding General Lejeune and stemming from respect gained for the French during World War I. At least one officer was in France every year until 1939. All total, 12 Marine officers had orders to this institution before World War II; of these, eight graduated from the two-year course, one finishing one year before the Second World War forced its suspension. Two other officers were preparing for the course when that war commenced in 1939; another died (Brig. General Robert Dunlap, who would have been an observer) before his class commenced in 1934. In the 1930s, by Marine Corps policy, graduates of l'École Supérieure de Guerre were assigned to the Marine Corps Schools at Quantico, Virginia,* as instructors in the Marine Corps Professional Military Education* system. The most significant prewar graduates were Maj. General Charles Barrett, "action officer" for the development of amphibious warfare doctrine in the 1930s, and General Oliver P. Smith, Commanding General, 1st Marine Division, during the Chosin Reservoir operation in 1950 during the Korean War.

Immediately after World War II, Marine officers returned to France to attend the French War College, but this soon terminated, not to be resumed until the 1980s.

Sources:

Donald F. Bittner, "Foreign Military Training in Reverse: U.S. Marine Corps Officers in the French Professional Military Education System, 1926–1939," *Journal of Military History* (Summer 1993).

Martin van Creveld, *The Training of Officers: From Military Professionalism to Irrelevance* (New York: Free Press, 1990).

"La Politique Militaire et les Armées de la III Republique," *La Grande Encyclopédie* (Paris: Librairie Larousse, 1975).

Donald F. Bittner

EDUCATIONAL WARGAMING. The use of hypothetical combat situations and simulated combat and support elements in a training exercise to illustrate the effects of different strategies and/or tactics on the outcome of a theater or battlefield engagement between opposing forces.

There have been four distinct eras of wargaming. The first, the "war chess" era, is considered by historians to predate written history and extend to the early 1800s. These games, which included chess but also encompassed games with more extensive sets of pieces and elaborate rules, were played on boards with varying number of squares. The Japanese game of Go originated in China about 3,000 B.C. as *Wei-Hai*, which in Chinese means encirclement. The Hindu game of Chaturanga used pieces representing foot soldiers, light cavalry, and elephants and is known by us today, in simplified form, as chess.

The second era, extending to about 1875, replaced the board with a map on which terrain was represented. Games of this era were characterized by voluminous rules that specified the movement rate of forces over different types of terrain; what maneuvers were permissible; and, when forces interacted, how attrition was calculated. These so-called "rigid" wargames, defined by the inflexible rule set, required considerable experience before play and ponderous manual record keeping and calculation. In 1811 Herr von Reisswitz invented a game in Prussia using a sand table representation of terrain and colored blocks of wood to represent troops. This game was improved on by von Reisswitz's son and called *Kriegsspiel*. The game spread to virtually every country with standing military forces, and handbooks were published to assist anyone interested in the play of the game.

In the third era, dissatisfaction with the complex and inflexible rules let to a freer form of gaming. While retaining much of the paraphernalia of second-era games, these games replaced most of the assessment rules governing movement and losses with the military judgment of an umpire. The "free play" games allowed faster progress and permitted a wider variety of considerations to enter into the games. Alfred Graf von Schlieffen made extensive use of wargame experimentation in the development of the Schlieffen Plans for the invasion of Belgium and France in World War I.

The fourth, and present, era began after World War I and included extensive use in Germany under Hitler. The smoothness of the initial phases of the German invasion of France is attributed to the wealth of detailed knowledge of the German unit commanders derived in large part from extensive wargame experience. German games revealed the tremendous difficulties associated with the proposed assault on Great Britain. The U.S. Navy is credited with considerable foresight due to wargaming of World War II operations in the Pacific years before at the Naval War College.* As Fleet Admiral Chester Nimitz told War College students in 1951: "The war with Japan has been re-enacted in the game room here by so many people and in so many different ways that nothing that happened during the war was a surprise—absolutely nothing except the Kamikaze tactics towards the end of the war; we had not visualized those."

Since World War II the biggest change in the technology of wargames has been the introduction of the digital computer. The computer can automatically keep track of the location and status of forces, equipment, and supplies; track force movement; provide situation display; and perform damage assessment. By computerizing the bookkeeping and by incorporating movement and attrition models in computer programs it is possible to circumvent the delays associated with rigid wargame play without making the game totally dependent upon the experience (or whim) of an umpire.

In 1975 the Clements Blue Ribbon Panel Report on Excellence in Professional Military Education called for intensive courses and innovative methods to instruct students at the joint and service war colleges in war fighting. In carrying out this mandate, the task was summarized as "put more war in the war colleges." The primary means to do this was wargaming, and many of these games made use of computers to automate the assessment of a player move and define the conditions described to the players for their next move. In the mid-1970s the Air University* at Maxwell Air Force Base developed a simulation called Theater Warfare Exercise (TWX), representing air and land combat on NATO's Central Front. In this model the ground war was stylized and automated, and the major model inputs controlled the air apportionment and allocation decisions. In the late 1970s Fred McClintic, at the U.S. Army War College, developed another theater model (MTM) that provided for the free play of ground forces— one of the first microcomputer-based combat simulation models.

The Army War College* and the Air War College* got together in the mid-1980s and developed an innovative joint game in which one seminar of students at the Air War College linked up with one seminar from the Army War College for a joint educational wargame. The so-called "CarMax" exercise initially made use of both the TWX and MTM models. Two years later, the Naval War College and the National Defense University* (NDU) joined the game, and it was renamed the Joint Land Aerospace Sea Simulation (JLASS). The role of NDU was as the opposing force, a role previously played by the control cell. In 1992 players from the Marine Corps University joined the game playing in their natural role. Student preparation is serious, with students at the colleges devoting one or two elective periods to campaign planning in preparation for the game. The JLASS game continues as the only joint senior service school wargame and is played annually.

Based on the recommendations of the Clements Blue Ribbon Panel the Air University embarked on an ambitious effort to modernize the wargames used at the Air War College, the Air Command and Staff College,* as well as at the Squadron Officer School. The program was called the Command Readiness Exercise System (CRES) and development coincided with the construction of a new wargaming facility at Maxwell Air Force Base. One of the goals of CRES was to take advantage of modern computer technology and create modern graph-based input screens and displays for player use. Using this new system, all the existing games have been fully modernized.

For years, the program of the Armed Forces Staff College* (AFSC) has included a wargame to allow students to experience some of the war-fighting command issues, such as decision making under uncertainty. The original scenario outlined a contingency for which no plans had been prepared, and the students were cast in the role of the Joint Task Force commander responsible for responding to a rapidly developing crisis. The students were required to play out the first four or five moves of their own plan. In 1982 the Joint AFSC Wargaming System (JAWS) model was conceived by Lt. Colonel Carl Jones, USA, to automate the bookkeeping for what had previously been a labor-intensive manual game. The model represented an advance over models like MTM in that greater emphasis was placed on allowing inputs and providing outputs in units more natural to the players. The computer was programmed to conform to player requirements rather than forcing the players to conform to the needs of the computer.

In the early 1980s the RAND Corporation developed the RAND Strategy Assessment system (RSAS), an ambitious program designed to investigate issues in nuclear escalation as well as conventional theater warfare. As analytical attention increasingly turned from nuclear to conventional warfare the RSAS evolved into a world model that encompassed strategic mobility and ground, air, and sea theater combat simulation. In the early 1990s, after the fall of the Berlin Wall, combat analysis shifted from the Central Front in Germany to worldwide contingencies. In response to these developments, the RSAS ground and air combat models were completely revised to reflect the wide variety of contingencies now of interest, and the simulation's name was changed to the Joint Integrated Contingency Model (JICM). The JICM is used to support a number of war college wargames, including the current JLASS series.

Sources:

Alfred Hausrath, *Venture Simulation in War, Business, and Politics* (New York: McGraw-Hill, 1971).

Francis J. McHugh, *Fundamentals of War Gaming* (3rd ed.) (Newport, RI: Naval War College, 1966).

Andrew Wilson, *The Bomb and the Computer* (New York: Delacorte Press, 1968).

John P. Young, *A Survey of Historical Developments in War Games* (Bethesda, MD: Operations Research Office, Johns Hopkins University Press, 1959).

Daniel B. Fox

ENGINEER SCHOOL. Official designation given to the school for army engineers when it reopened at Washington Barracks, D.C., in 1905. The school continued the history of professional education for military engineers in the U.S. Army and retains the name in its current location at Fort Leonard Wood, Missouri.

Training and education of Army engineers dates to the early days of the American Revolution. Following the war for independence, a school for engineers and artillerists began at West Point, New York.* It was the precursor of the U.S. Military Academy* that President Thomas Jefferson founded in 1802 as part of the Corps of Engineers. When West Point was transferred to the War Department in 1866, efforts began to establish an engineering school of application* at Willets Point, N.Y., the home of the Engineer Battalion. In 1885, this school received formal approval by the War Department and continued providing education and training to officers and enlisted men until the turn of the century, after which it was transferred to Washington Barracks.

The Engineer School, which admitted its first classes in 1906 because of instructor shortages and the demand for engineer officers, had three major departments. These focused on civil, military, and electrical and mechanical engineering. Specific courses ranged from surveying, military topography, masonry and carpentry, bridging, fortifications, and explosives. Students, after a year with an engineer unit or a district, went to the school for a thirteen-month course. A trades school for enlisted personnel taught courses in carpentry, blacksmithing, plumbing, photography, and masonry among other subjects. A major shortcoming of Washington Barracks, however, was a shortage of space for field problems. Accordingly, in 1910, the Army established a School of Field Engineering at the much larger Fort Leavenworth, Kansas,* as a part of the Army Service Schools. In a one-year course, the Field Engineering School focused on those aspects of military engineering dealing with the operations of maneuver forces in the field. However, in the 1916 expansion of active regular and national guard forces in anticipation of possible war with Mexico, the School of Field Engineering was closed, and responsibility for its curriculum passed back to the Engineer School.

America's entry into the war in Europe a year later caused a temporary closing of the school as the instructors and students were needed for service overseas. It also marked the end of Washington Barracks as the school's location. In 1912, the War Department had acquired a tract of land on the Potomac River known as Belvoir, for use as a rifle range and summer camp for Engineer School students. In time this tract of land in Virginia was designated Camp A. A. Humphreys in honor of that noted Chief of Engineers. Following the war, the Engineer School was moved to Camp Humphreys. In 1922, the installation was renamed Fort Humphreys and in 1935 renamed Fort Belvoir. The curriculum at the Engineer School continued to focus on military and civilian engineering, the latter being confined to instruction on rivers and harbors. Enlisted courses on both field and technical subjects continued as well. The school also functioned as a testing facility where new equipment was examined for the Engineer Board.

The advent of the Second World War caused the normal interruptions in the standard peacetime course of instruction. The school and Fort Belvoir offered countless specialist courses for newly inducted soldiers and orientation courses for those commissioned in the engineers but lacking in practical engineer training and troop leading. The evolution of military education in the post-Korean and post-Vietnam periods was reflected in the school's various programs of instruction. Faculty and staff created or revised professional development courses for officers, warrant officers, and noncommissioned officers to reflect the changing needs of the service and the evolution of warfare. Training for new soldiers focused on the constantly changing nature of enlisted military occupational specialties. This effort continued with the Engineer School's move to Fort Leonard Wood in 1988. By the end of this century, the Engineer School, along with the Chemical and Military Police Schools, will have formed the U.S. Army Maneuver Support Center. However, the nature and need for practical engineer education and training have remained relatively unchanged since the days of the first "engineer school" during the American Revolution.

Sources:

Col. David M. Dunne, "The Engineer School—Past and Present," *Military Engineer* 41, no. 284 (November–December 1949).

Capt. E. F. Gaebler and Capt. W. E. Duckering, "The Engineer School at Camp A. A. Humphreys, Va." *Engineering School Professional Memoirs* 11 (September–October 1919).

Capt. Ira L. Reeves, *Military Education in the United States* (Burlington, VT: Free Press, 1914).

Larry D. Roberts

ENGINEER SCHOOL OF APPLICATION. On February 28, 1885, after almost twenty years of development and effort, the War Department formally recognized the Engineer School of Application at Willets Point, New York.

The official recognition of the School of Application, however, constituted only a continuing evolution of professional military education and training for engineers. During the days of Valley Forge, General George Washington signed an order calling for volunteer officers to form a company of sappers. This company was also to constitute a "school of engineering" for the officers and men of a new corps of engineers. Transferred to West Point, New York,* shortly thereafter, the school continued through the end of the war. Although reestablished in 1794, the school burned two years later. The establishment of a Corps of Engineers, separate from the artillery, provided for an opportunity to once again establish some system of formal military engineering school. The resulting U.S. Military Academy* at West Point, the station of the new Corps of Engineers, became in fact the third school for engineers. However after the Civil War, the War Department decided to relieve the Chief of Engineers from the responsibility of managing the Military Academy. This reflected a desire to more broadly militarize the orientation of West Point beyond the purposes and technical details of military and civil engineering.

In 1866, the Chief of Engineers, Brig General Andrew A. Humphreys, decided that additional education and training was needed for both new commissioned engineer officers and those who had entered service during the Civil War. What was generally lacking was an understanding of those aspects of civil engineering which the Corps had applied to its civil works projects prior to the war. However, this was to be a school of application where officers could expand their understanding of engineering theory by reading and apply that understanding in practical experiments. The senior officers of the Battalion of Engineers would be the advising faculty of the school. This school of application would also serve to investigate scientific matters for the Chief of Engineers and conduct necessary experiments on new engineer equipment. Much of this effort would occur during the summer months and would supplement the normal military drills of the battalion. During the winter months, the officers of the battalion were encouraged to continue their reading through the vehicle of the Essayons Club, a volunteer association formed by the battalion commander, Major Henry

L. Abbot and the Post Commander, Major James C. Duane. Members of the club prepared professional studies and wrote papers that were ultimately published by the Engineer School of Application.

The school's resulting curriculum was divided into summer and winter phases. The first was seven months in duration and focused on torpedoes (submarine mines), practical astronomy, and hydrology. The winter phases examined torpedoes, photography, and meteorology. The plan of study spanned two years. This was in addition to general construction and field fortification training conducted within the Battalion of Engineers. There was a corresponding voluntary school for soldiers. Initially the school focused on general education subjects such as mathematics, English grammar, languages, history, and geography. Military subjects such as mining, explosives, bridging, masonry, and carpentry were either taught by the school or in the battalion as a normal part of training. The construction of countless fortifications allowed the practical application of lecture material.

In 1890, the name of the school was changed to the United States Engineer School. The restructured school had five departments: military engineering, submarine mining, civil engineering, practical astronomy, and military photography. Eleven years later the school was redesignated as the Engineer School of Application and was moved to Washington Barracks, D.C. The Enlisted Specialist School was reestablished with instruction in carpentry, masonry, blacksmithing, plumbing, drafting, and surveying. A shortage of Engineer officers prompted the closing of the school in 1903. However, two years later, instruction resumed and the name of the school changed for the final time to the Engineer School.*

Sources:

Col. Henry L. Abbot (Ret.), "Early Days of the Engineer School of Application," Occasional Papers No. 14, Engineer School of Application, Washington Barracks, D.C., 1904.

Col. David M. Dunne, "The Engineer School—Past and Present," *Military Engineer* 41, no. 284 (November–December 1949).

Capt. Ira L. Reeves, *Military Education in the United States* (Burlington, VT: Free Press, 1914).

Larry D. Roberts

F

FORT LEAVENWORTH, KANSAS. Longest continually active U.S. Army post west of the Mississippi River, which has become the site of the Command and General Staff School and the School of Advanced Military Studies and an important army center for other professional military education and training activities.

On April 19, 1827, Colonel Henry Leavenworth and four companies of officers and men from the 3rd Infantry Regiment traveled from their home garrison in St. Louis to the banks of the Missouri River to establish an advance post for overseeing and protecting the Santa Fe Trail. Initially directed to build the fort on the eastern shore of the Missouri, Leavenworth observed that the commanding bluffs on the west offered much more in terms of defensive position. So it was that Fort Leavenworth, the longest continually active military post west of the Mississippi, was founded.

The fort has been the site of many events of historical significance, including the establishment of four black regiments in 1866 who became known by the name given to them by the Kiowa Indians—Buffalo Soldiers. One year later, Fort Leavenworth was the site of the court-martial of brevet Maj. General George Armstrong Custer, for absence without leave and conduct to the prejudice of good order and discipline. In 1875, the United States Military Prison was established, forever marking Leavenworth as representing both the best and the worst of the military profession. In 1877, the last of the Nez Perce Indians, led by the legendary Chief Joseph, were brought to a resettlement camp at the fort after surrendering to General Nelson Miles following an 105-day, 1,800-mile running battle. Chief Joseph and remnants of the tribe were kept at the post until 1879. Today, one of the major roads at the fort still bears his name, as an honor to one of the finest fighting retreats in military history. Fort Leavenworth began its legacy as a stalwart of professional military education, in 1881, when Army commanding general William Tecumseh Sherman* founded the School of Application for Infantry and Cavalry,* the forerunner of the modern U.S. Army Command and the General Staff College.* The graduates of Fort Leavenworth's educational institutions have fought with valor in every conflict since the Spanish-American War.

Today, the post flourishes as the hub of corps- and division-level tactical education. It is home to the Combined Arms Command and is recognized as the U.S. Army's senior tactical institution. The Command and General Staff College is accredited to offer the master's degree in Military Arts and Sciences and is subdivided into five separate schools, the Command and General Staff School, the Combined Arms and Services Staff School, the School of Advanced Military Studies,* the School for Command Preparation, and the Directorate of Nonresident Studies. The U.S. Disciplinary Barracks remains active as the only maximum-security correctional institution for U.S. Army, Air Force, and Marine prisoners. The post also is home to a national cemetery and an outstanding museum.

In an era of military base closures, downsizing, and mission consolidation, the life span of a military installation can be relatively short. That makes the longevity of Fort Leavenworth all the more significant. It continues to provide not only a glimpse at the past, but with its mission of educating the officer elite of the Army (as well as sister services and foreign nationals), it clearly has a critical impact on the future. As the official post history states, "Fort Leavenworth is not, and never was, an ordinary frontier post. Her story is far from complete, and the epilogue will not be written for many years to come."

Sources:

Talbot Barnard, *The History of Fort Leavenworth, 1952–1963* (Fort Leavenworth, KS: U.S. Army Command and General Staff College, 1964).
Boyd L. Dastrup, *The U.S. Army Command and General Staff College: A Centennial History* (Manhattan, KS: Sunflower University Press, 1982).
Elvid Hunt, *History of Fort Leavenworth, 1829–1927* (New York: Arno Press, 1979).
George Walton, *Sentinel of the Plains: Fort Leavenworth and the American West* (Englewood Cliffs, NJ: Prentice-Hall, 1973).

Lt. Colonel Tony Kern, USAF

FORT LESLEY McNAIR. The second-oldest continually active U.S. military post, located in Washington, D.C., which in the 20th century became the site of several professional military schools for army officers. For the last half of the century, it has served as the principal educational center for the U.S. Department of Defense.

In 1791, the site now occupied by Fort McNair became part of Major Pierre L'Enfant's plan for the new national capital. In L'Enfant's plan, the site was identified as Military District #5, located in what is now the southern half of the present post. It soon acquired an earthen fortification to shield the site for an artillery battery. In 1797, the land was transferred to the commissioners of the federal city by President George Washington.

Very little construction took place on the area, originally known as Buzzard Point, until 1803. By 1814, the reservation included an arsenal and a battery of eight cannons. However, in August, when a detachment of 200 British troops marched in, the American soldiers occupying the post had retreated, partially destroying the arsenal and hiding in a well some of the powder kegs that had been stored there. While other British troops were burning the Capitol and the White House, this detachment finished burning the arsenal. In the process, the kegs in the well exploded, causing a number of British casualties.

Another arsenal was built in 1816 and became a hub of activity during the Civil War. It also became a powder keg for some of those who worked there, when sparks from accidentally ignited fireworks flew through an open window into the main assembly room. The resulting fire and explosion killed 21 women who were making rifle cartridges. The women were buried in Congressional Cemetery following a public ceremony attended by President Abraham Lincoln, who led the funeral procession.

After the war, when Lincoln was assassinated by John Wilkes Booth, the arsenal and the military reservation figured prominently in the subsequent public drama. The suspected co-conspirators were rounded up in a few weeks and locked up in a prison on the post. After a trial, conducted by a nine-man military commission on the third floor of the prison building, four conspirators were sentenced to death and hanged in the prison courtyard on July 7, 1865.

The arsenal was closed in 1881 and the post renamed Washington Barracks. In 1901, the army's Engineer School of Application* was relocated there, and a year later plans for renovating the post were approved. Meanwhile, the Spanish-American War had demonstrated the need for additional training of officers in assembling and employing large bodies of troops, and Secretary of War Elihu Root* proposed establishing an Army War College,* to be built at Washington Barracks. On February 21, 1903, President Theodore Roosevelt and Secretary Root laid the cornerstone for the Army War College building in the area of the original military reservation.

Classes at the Army War College were suspended during both World Wars I and II, as the post facilities were used for activities more directly tied to the respective war efforts. In 1917 the post became a basic training site and a processing center for troops being sent to France. In World War II, the principal tenant of the War College building was the Headquarters, Army Ground Forces, commanded by Lt. General Lesley J. McNair.

Following the war, in 1946, the National War College* was established in the building which had been built for the Army War College. The Army Industrial College* was also moved to the post in 1946 and renamed the Industrial College of the Armed Forces.* In 1948 the post itself was renamed in honor of General McNair, who was killed in Normandy in 1944 and awarded a fourth star posthumously. In 1960, President Eisenhower, a graduate of the Army Industrial College, dedicated the newer college's new building. Two years later, the opening of the Inter-American Defense College, a multinational institution of higher military studies under the Inter-American Defense Board, contributed even further to McNair's academic atmosphere.

In 1971, the Headquarters for the Military District of Washington moved to the post and has gained recognition as an organization furnishing personnel and equipment for such activities as inaugural parades, special White House functions, burial of the dead, guards at the Tomb of the Unknowns, and arrival and departure ceremonies for visiting heads of state. It also provides administrative, financial, and logistical support to many of the military personnel residing or working in the Washington, D.C., metropolitan area.

Fort McNair's most recent major tenant, the National Defense University* (NDU), was established in 1976. It provides administrative support and educational services for all the resident colleges plus other joint educational bodies. The NDU also conducts special studies of defense issues, as tasked by the Joint Chiefs of Staff.

Sources:

"Fort Lesley J. McNair: A Brief History of the Post," The National War College, Washington, DC (undated pamphlet).

Phyllis I. McClellan, *Silent Sentinal on the Potomac: Fort McNair, 1791–1991* (Bowie, MD: Heritage Books, 1993).

FRUNZE MILITARY ACADEMY. Since 1921, the most prestigious of the many official Soviet (Russian) military-educational institutions responsible for preparing officers for combined arms warfare, principally at the tactical level (army and below), and for the formulation and promulgation of tactical military thought. Roughly equivalent to the U.S. Army's Command and General Staff College, at Fort Leavenworth, Kansas, and the German Fuhrungsakademie.

The Frunze Academy's lineal ancestor was the Military Academy of the RKKA (Workers and Peasant Red Army), which was founded in August 1921 on the basis of the former RKKA Academy of the General Staff. Unlike its predecessor, which focused on the preparation of general staff officers, the new military academy was responsible for Tactical training and the preparation of politically reliable mid-level Red Army officers. In 1925 the RKKA Academy was named after M. V. Frunze, a distinguished Red Army leader during the Russian Civil War and Allied Intervention in Russia and briefly the Soviet commissar of war, who died earlier that year.

Between 1925 and 1936, while the academy's primary focus was tactical (regiment to corps), it conducted a variety of courses to prepare a higher-level command cadre, including the famous Course for the Perfection of Senior Officers (KUVNAS). From 1931 until the creation of a new Soviet General Staff Academy in 1936, the Frunze Academy also included a faculty for operational level instruction (army through *front* [army group] level) and separate faculties for motorization and mechanization, air force operations, and other new forms of warfare. After 1936, the Frunze Academy prepared "combined arms command and staff cadre at the operational-tactical level, while the General Staff Academy focused on education at the operational-strategic level." From the late 1930s, the Frunze was also responsible for collecting, analyzing, and exploiting combat experiences in the service of formulating new Red Army regulations and manuals, a responsibility which the purges of the late 1930s seriously disrupted.

On the outbreak of the Soviet-German War, the Frunze Academy taught short courses and played an instrumental role in the creation of the Moscow Defense Zone, while producing the bulk of the Red Army's tactical leadership. Among its many graduates who distinguished themselves throughout the war were at least 16 marshals of the Soviet Union, including G. K. Zhukov, P. Ia. Malinovsky, K. K. Rokossovsky, F. I. Tolbukhin, V. I. Chuikov, N. N. Voronov, and A. A. Novikov. Many of its graduates, such as M. P. Kirponos and N. F. Vatutin, perished while serving during the war.

After war's end, while continuing its education function for the Soviet Army and the armies of Soviet allies, the Frunze Academy played a leading role in the study of wartime operations and the formulation of new methods of warfare, a process that continues today. The academy's recent works include detailed analysis of the Afghan War, the Persian Gulf War, and recent hostilities in Chechnya. Since 1945 the Frunze Academy has educated thousands of Soviet and allied officers in operational-tactical disciplines and a variety of political subjects. The academy has also set new standards by its advanced theoretical work on the problems of contemporary warfare. Faculty members have produced a steady stream of noteworthy analytical and historical works, including A. A. Sidorenko's *Nastuplenie* (The offensive), V. E. Savkin's *Osnovnye printsiy operativnogo isskustva i taktiki* (The Basic Principles of Operational Art and Tactics), and Reznichenko's imposing series of books, each entitled *Taktika* (Tactics). During the 1970s and 1980s, the Frunze Academy's theoretical work provided the essential basis for subsequent U.S. and Western adoption of modern concepts for warfare at the operational level.

While the academy has dropped much of its ideological studies from its curriculum since 1991, it has succeeded in maintaining its prestige despite the debilitated condition of the current Russian Army, and it continues its sound theoretical analysis of the nature of future war. At the same time, pressured by the forces of reform, it is striving to determine its proper role in a fledgling democratic state.

Sources:

Harriet Fast Scott and William F. Scott, *The Armed Forces of the USSR* (London: Arms and Armour, 1984).

B. Sholokhov, ed., *Voennaia akademiia imeni M. V. Frunze: Istoriia Voennoi ordena Lenina i Oktiabr'skoi Revolutsii, Krasnoznamennoi, ordena Suvorova akademii*

[The Military Academy in the Name of M. V. Frunze, The History of the Military Order of Lenin and the October Revolution, the Red Banner, and the Order of Suvorov Academy] (Moscow: Voenizdat, 1988).

"Voennaia akademiia imeni M. V. Frunze" [The Military Academy in the Name of M. V. Frunze] in A. A. Grechko, ed., *Sovetskaia voennaia entsiklopediia T. 2* [Soviet Military Encyclopedia, vol. 2] (Moscow: Voenizdat, 1976).

David M. Glantz

G

GEROW BOARD. A War Department board of general officers appointed in late 1945 to prepare a plan for the education of U.S. Army officers in the years following World War II. Many of its recommendations are reflected in the current system of joint education administered by the National Defense University.

As Allied forces advanced eastward into Germany in early 1945, different staff elements of the U.S. Army began to plan for a demobilized, peacetime force, including the officers' needs for formal military education. Headquarters, U.S. Army Air Forces (USAAF), anticipating the eventual status of a separate service, had proposed to the War Department as early as September 1944 a separate, three-tiered system of military education designed primarily for air officers. Further, it had recommended that the War Department establish an even higher level of formal instruction consisting of several new schools focusing on the joint employment of all arms and services. With this recommendation in hand, the War Department tasked each of the major army commands and the Command and General Staff School* to submit its own recommended "Plan for Postwar Military Education" by November 1945.

On November 23, 1945, the War Department appointed a special board of general officers from each of the major commands, headed by Lt. General Leonard T. Gerow, to prepare "a plan for the postwar educational system of the Army." The board was asked specifically to outline "a plan of schools" for commissioned officers in each major command (Ground Forces, Air Forces, and Service Forces) and a separate plan for operation by the War Department to meet the requirements of officers serving at levels of command higher than branch-level. In this latter respect, the board was asked for recommendations on the advisability of reopening the Army War College,* where classes had been suspended since June of 1940. Provisions for "school training" for officers of the reserve components were also requested.

The four board members met at Fort Leavenworth, Kansas,* over a period of three weeks in December 1945, for about ten days at the Pentagon in early January 1946, and continuing at Fort Leavenworth until February 5. They and their support staff reviewed the plans submitted by each of the major commands and other relevant documents. They also interviewed 77 witnesses, all but five of whom were colonels or above from all major commands, the existing colleges (including the Army-Navy Staff College), the ROTC,* and the National Guard; and they explored relevant issues.

Assuming a postwar organization of the Army like that in effect on January 1, 1946 (i.e., before formation of the Department of Defense), but explicitly recognizing the possibility of such a development, the board recommended a school structure based on the "functional requirements" placed on serving officers. Names assigned to the different schools, however, reflected a unilateral Army cast. In its report, the board distinguished between "regular" (10 months in length), "basic" (5 months or less), and "associate" courses (3 months), the latter intended for Reserve and Guard officers on temporary active duty. Only enrollment in the "regular" courses were intended to involve a permanent change of duty assignment.

The Gerow Board recommended a three-tiered structure with both the top and bottom levels offering alternative school choices, depending on an officer's basic branch and subsequent career specialty. At the bottom tier, each of the three major commands would maintain its own hierarchy of schools, from "basic" courses for younger officers through a "regular" course at each command's college for experienced officers. Aware of the impact of rapidly emerging technology on each of different arms, the board provided for both entry and intermediate-level branch schools in the ground and service commands and endorsed the USAAF's earlier educational proposal for air officers.

At the next higher tier an Armed Forces College would be maintained by either the Joint Chiefs of Staff or the War Department, depending on whether or not the Navy participated "on an equal basis," as the board recommended. This "regular" course would be for officers of all three commands with at least ten years' commissioned service, to prepare them for command or staff duties associated with combined arms operations, to include coordinating army operations with the actions of naval forces. It would absorb that part of the Army War College program dealing with the coordination of field operations.

A "National Security University" comprised the uppermost tier of the Gerow Board's recommended educational system. Maintained and supervised by the Joint Chiefs, the "University" would embrace five different colleges and "regular" courses, each of which would maintain a joint-service focus in its curriculum. A "National War College" would aim to develop commanders and staff officers "for the highest echelons of the Armed Forces" and qualify them "for participation in the formulating of national policy." Its program would "include the political, civil, logistical and operational interests and responsibilities" of these echelons with respect to grand strategy and both domestic and international issues involved in the causes, prevention, and prosecution of war and the transition from war to peace. In this respect, the proposed "National War College" would "take over that part of the Army War College course which was devoted to . . . organization and employment of the national means for waging war."

Intended for equal status with the "National War College" and attendance by officers with the same level of experience were three other military colleges and a "State Department College." The latter was considered essential to a complete system of military requirements; but the proposal was labeled "tentative," with its structuring left to State Department officials. An "Industrial College" would address on a national scale the same kind of industrial mobilization issues examined for the War Department by the Army Industrial College* before the war. Looking at the problems faced by all services in mobilizing the industrial resources needed to expand their increased consumption of materiel in wartime, the college would produce a pool of trained senior officers qualified to advise on and make critical policy decisions. It would also examine the industrial capabilities of other nations for war. Reflecting military manpower mobilization problems encountered during World War II, an "Administrative College" would emphasize policy issues and procedures pertaining to the procurement, management, and utilization of military personnel and of civilians under military control. It would also study the potential effects of population trends and changing methods of warfare on personnel management considerations and the interaction of military manpower problems with those of government and industry. An "Intelligence College" would focus on the essential principles of intelligence and counterintelligence operations. It would endeavor to impart to specialists and users alike an appreciation for the importance of intelligence from the national to a theater operational level and a sensitivity to factors that can affect its value for the planning and conduct of military operations.

Even though the National Security Act of 1947 and that of 1949 subordinated the service departments, including a separate Air Force, under a cabinet-level Department of Defense, many of the educational system features recommended by the Gerow Board found direct applicability within the new structure. Principally, the new authority given the Joint Chiefs of Staff enabled them to set policy for and oversee the operation of most of the schools that the board had proposed above the level of the wartime Army's major commands. Thus, today's National Defense University* and its National War College,* Industrial College of the Armed Forces,* Armed Forces Staff College,* and Joint Military Intelligence College owe their germination to General Gerow and his fellow board members.

Sources:

John W. Masland and Laurence I. Radway, *Soldiers and Scholars: Military Education and National Policy* (Princeton, NJ: Princeton University Press, 1957).
"Report of the War Department Education Board on Educational System for Officers of the Army" (Gerow Board), Washington, DC, February 5, 1946.

GOLDWATER-NICHOLS ACT. The Department of Defense Reorganization Act of 1986 (Public Law 99–433) that made major changes to statutes grounded on the National Security Act of 1947.

In an early section of the Goldwater-Nichols Act, Congress listed eight items as its intent "in enacting this Act": to reorganize major parts of the Department of Defense (DoD) and thereby strengthen civilian control; to "improve the military advice" to civilian authorities; to place "clear responsibility" on field commanders; to ensure that field commanders' authority is "fully commensurate" with their responsibility to carry out assigned missions; to "improve strategy formulation and contingency planning"; to "provide for more efficient use of defense resources"; to "improve joint officer management policies"; and "otherwise to enhance" military operations, management, and administration of the Department of Defense.

Significantly, five of the eight congressional-intent items focus on correcting perceived inadequacies in the performance of the joint military components of the Department of Defense. The joint organizations, composed of multiservice forces and staffs, are the cutting edge of the nation's defense, the combat formations responsible for completing the missions assigned to the armed forces. To achieve improvements in military advice, authority and accountability of the field commanders, strategy formulation, and contingency planning required better performance from those organizations. Consequently, to realize congress's "intent," the Goldwater-Nichols Act makes fundamental changes in the structure of the joint organizations. The modifications include replacing the Joint Chiefs of Staff committee with the chairman of the Joint Chiefs of Staff (JCS) as the principal military advisor to the President, National Security Council, and Secretary of Defense; establishing the position of vice chairman of the JCS; giving the JCS chairman control of the Joint Staff; streamlining the chain of command to the field commanders; and vastly increasing the command authority of the field commanders.

These structural changes, Congress believed, would fail if not accompanied by improvements in the qualifications of the officer personnel serving the JCS chairman and the field commanders. The personnel in those joint positions are responsible for the most complex matters facing the armed forces, from strategy formulation and resource allocation to contingency planning to direction of military operations during conflicts. Nevertheless, despite their overarching importance, congressional hearings over a period of four years from 1982 to 1986 revealed that the services were not assigning their best officers, those who would be the future military leaders, to the joint positions. Consequently, Title IV of the Goldwater-Nichols Act, titled Joint Officer Personnel Policy, requires changes in officer career development, including professional military education (PME), intended to ensure that the joint positions are filled by outstanding officers qualified by dint of experience, education, and talent to deal with the most complex military issues.

The education-related provisions in Title IV mandate significant changes in the PME system. The most far-reaching provisions apply to the schools that educate intermediate (major, junior lieutenant colonel) and senior (lieutenant colonel, colonel) grade officers. Separate provisions distinguish between the "joint" schools, principally the schools of the National Defense University* (NDU), and all "other" schools that educate senior and intermediate grade officers. The effect of this distinction is to recognize three NDU schools as joint institutions: the National War College,* the Industrial College of the Armed Forces,* and the Armed Forces Staff College.* The "other professional military education schools" category encompasses the service staff and war colleges.

The act requires that the joint schools, whose faculties and student bodies are composed of roughly equal numbers from each military department and whose curricula are considered to be inherently multiservice, are to be reviewed by the Secretary of Defense assisted by the JCS chairman. The purpose of the review is to effect revisions in the curriculum "to enhance the education and training of officers in joint matters." The secretary is also required to "maintain rigorous standards" for the education of officers destined to specialize in joint duty assignments. Thus the requirement for the joint schools is to continue to do what they do but do it better.

A second provision related to joint PME is intended to ensure that officers who receive the rigorous education in joint matters are subsequently assigned to joint duty positions. It requires that each graduate of a joint school who has already been designated a specialist in joint matters (as a result of previous schooling and joint experience) "be assigned to a joint duty assignment for that officer's next duty assignment." Moreover, it requires that "a high proportion (. . . greater than 50 percent)" of the other joint school graduates "also receive assignments to a joint duty assignment as their next duty assignment." In addition to guaranteeing that personnel educated in joint matters fill the joint ranks, this provision is significant in that it directly links professional military education to a follow-on assignment in which the officer will use the knowledge gained in school; although logical, officer career progression patterns have seldom made this linkage.

The provision relating to the "other" schools is aimed primarily at the service staff and war colleges. Although the words are similar, the impact is different. The Secretary of Defense is mandated to require that each school concerned with PME "periodically review and revise its curriculum . . . to strengthen the focus on . . . joint matters and preparing officers for joint duty assignments." Implementing this provision would require major revisions to the curriculums of the service schools to incorporate joint military subjects into courses of study that heretofore placed most of their emphasis on service-related subjects.

Another provision addresses the education of officers recently promoted to general or flag rank. They are required to attend "a military education course designed specifically to prepare new general and flag officers to work with the other armed forces." In the paragraph lead-in, Congress names the course it has in mind the CAPSTONE course at the National Defense University that had been established earlier in the 1980s. Thus this provision transforms a recently formulated, less stringent DoD policy into a statutory requirement.

The act also addresses the career management of the reserves, albeit not with the same specificity as for active officers. The Secretary of Defense is required to "establish personnel policies emphasizing education and experience in joint matters for reserve officers. . . . Such policies shall, to the extent practicable for the reserve components, be similar to the policies provided" for active duty officers.

Despite the breadth and scope of the Goldwater-Nichols Act provisions related to PME, they initially failed to effect the changes sought by Congress. Unlike many of the other provisions of the act, the education provisions left the initiative in the hands of the Secretary of Defense, who was made responsible for reviewing and revising the PME schools curriculums. In the year following enactment of the legislation, in the view of the House Armed Services Committee leadership, DoD took few, if any, actions to implement the provisions.

Consequently, Congress took back the initiative in November 1987. Representative Les Aspin, the chairman of the House Armed Services Committee, appointed a Panel on Military Education to be chaired by Representative Ike Skelton. Using the provisions of the Goldwater-Nichols Act as its starting point, the panel conducted a comprehensive review of intermediate and senior PME. The Skelton Panel's* report contained numerous findings, conclusions, and recommendations that, coupled with vigorous congressional oversight, resulted in the full implementation of the Goldwater-Nichols joint education provisions as well as a great many additional changes to professional military education.

Sources:

U.S. Congress. Conference Report. *Goldwater-Nichols Department of Defense Reorganization Act of 1986*. House Report 99–824, 99th Congress, 2nd session, September 12, 1986. Washington, DC: Government Printing Office, 1986. Also available as Public Law 99–433, October 1, 1986.

U.S. Congress. House. Committee on Armed Services. *Report of the Panel on Military Education of the Hundredth Congress*. Committee Print no 4. 101st Congress, 1st session, April 21, 1989. Washington, DC: Government Printing Office, 1989.

U.S. Congress. House. Investigations Subcommittee of the Committee on Armed Services. Hearings. *Reorganization Proposals for the Joint Chiefs of Staff*. Committee Print 97–47. 97th Congress, 2nd session. Washington, DC: Government Printing Office, 1982.

U.S. Congress. Senate. Committee on Armed Services. Staff Report. *Defense Organization: The Need for Change*. Senate Committee Print 99–86. 99th Congress, 1st session, October 16, 1985. Washington, DC: Government Printing Office, 1985.

Archie D. Barrett

H

HAINES BOARD. Officially titled the Department of the Army Board to Review Army Officer Schools, its recommendations in February 1966 led to improved articulation of the respective objectives of different schools in the Army's professional military education system and important changes in student and faculty selection policies.

The Chief of Staff's order, June 23, 1965, directed the board, the fourth formal review of the Army school system since World War II, to (1) determine the adequacy and appropriateness of the system for education and training of Army officers at service schools; (2) review the current school curriculum; (3) review the operation of Army-operated Defense Department and joint-service schools; (4) review the requirements for and management of service school and college graduates; and (5) examine thirteen specific PME issues. The latter included civil schooling, faculty selection, student evaluation, and instructional provisions pertaining to command, management, operations research/systems analysis, automatic data processing, logistics, counterinsurgency, chemical and nuclear operations, foreign languages, intelligence, and Army aviation.

Noting the views of the Gerow,* Eddy, and Williams boards, which preceded it, the Haines Board was to determine whether the Army's system of officer education and training met its needs during a period of major change: Increasing consolidation and unification within the Department of Defense (DoD) included increased DoD-directed and DoD-conducted education and training. Integrated management of supply and service functions and the consolidation of the logistics system were under way. With an eye focused on the support of the North Atlantic Treaty-Organization (NATO), the field Army (under the Reorganization Objective Army Division) and the combat support system were undergoing major restructuring. Finally, the war in Vietnam was dominating Army operations and manpower administration.

The board had as voting members its president (Lt. General Ralph E. Haines,

Jr.), three other general officers representing the three major continental Army commands (Combat Developments; Continental Army; Materiel), six colonels/ lieutenant colonels representing the Department of the Army staff agencies responsible for officer training and education, and a civilian educator. A full-time consultant (a retired general officer with broad service-school experience) completed the board.

The full board commenced its research on July 6, 1965, by reviewing reports from the three previous boards and later received briefs on the operation of the Army school system and its problems. Board members interviewed appropriate staffs in the Office of the Secretary of Defense and the Organization of the Joint Chiefs of Staff, the heads of principal Army staff agencies, and distinguished retired officers with established training and education reputations. They conducted inquiries with the Department of Health, Education and Welfare; the Bureau of the Budget; the Civil Service Commission; and private organizations such as the American Council on Education and the American Management Association. The board received in-depth briefs on the Navy, Air Force, and Marine Corps school systems and visited several of their sites plus those of the Army, the Defense Department, the joint colleges, civilian universities, operations research agencies, and the major Army continental commands—more than 70 locations overall.

The board conceded the "general excellence" of the system. Nevertheless, the members agreed that some changes would make it more responsive to current needs and to the challenges of the next decade (Vietnam and reorganization, in particular). The board's recommendations were designed to encourage and accelerate self-analysis within the Army school system and reflected the practical field, command, and staff experience of its members

The board's work revealed that some of the problems under study could not be separated from broader issues such as branch functions and career patterns. Hence, its recommendations, published in February 1966—74 requiring decision by Headquarters, Department of the Army—dealt with all aspects of officer training and education and included topics such as officer procurement and retention, entry and career training, Command and General Staff College* schooling, senior service colleges, curriculum changes, extension/correspondence courses, prerequisites, and quotas.

The board recommended educational and training objectives for each level of Army officer schooling: Officer basic courses were to emphasize practical work and field instruction relevant to initial duty assignments. Career courses (advanced courses) were to prepare officers for command and staff duties at battalion through brigade, placing emphasis on command at battalion level, and for duty as assistant division staff officers. The Command and General Staff College was to prepare its students primarily for duty with the Army, and secondarily with Department of the Army (DA), combined and major command staffs. The Army War College* was to focus on the Army's role, doctrine, and operations in the context of national strategy and the joint and international environment.

The board also recommended the introduction of electives at the upper-level schools beginning in the 1967–68 academic year and that Headquarters, DA set quotas for service school and college attendance.

The board reexamined the relative importance of command, leadership, and management at the different levels of officer education and training. The members recommended that the basic course stress leadership training, that the advanced courses of branches with many command opportunities emphasize command responsibilities, and that management studies be provided for those branches with few command opportunities.

The board also recommended that the Army establish formal training programs for comptrollers, operations research/systems analysis, and automatic data processing. It presented very specific revisions to improve training in a number of operational and special weapons areas. Included in its findings were recommendations to consolidate existing schools and courses and, in some cases, to effect major reductions in enrollments. Specific recommendations for improvements in faculty selection, qualifications, and roles; educational innovations; and foreign officer schooling throughout the Army were also presented.

The majority of the Haines Board recommendations were eventually approved without significant revision. These included the recommendations that the Army War College establish an extension program, that it end the graduate degree study program with George Washington University, and that civilian college professors and four officers be added to its faculty. The Deputy Chief of Staff for Personnel recorded disapproval of only sixteen recommendations as late as 1970, including its rather aggressive recommendations to reorganize the Army school system so as to shift command responsibility for the major schools. A requirement that preparatory extension courses be required for branch advanced and the Command and General Staff College courses was also disapproved.

The recommendations that gained approval sought to improve the rigor and quality of officer education, facilitate school administration and operations, strengthen the faculties, and encourage programs to provide needed technical expertise. They included recommendations outlining a distinct and progressive focus for each level of officer schooling. Today's progressive and sequential system of army officer education, the establishment of extension courses, the presence of civilian faculty members, and the continuing need for graduates of the formal training programs suggested by the board indicate that it did accomplish its goal of providing a "blueprint for the Army school system for the next ten years."

Sources:

Harry P. Ball, *Of Responsible Command: A History of the U.S. Army War College*, rev. ed. (Dallas, TX: Taylor Publishing Company, 1994).
Department of the Army, "Report of the Department of the Army Board to Review Army Officer Schools (Haines Board), Record of Completed Actions," Office of the Adjutant General, December 9, 1970.

Department of the Army, "Report of the Department of the Army Board to Review Army
Officer Schools, Volume I—Summary and Recommendations," February 1966.
Thomas L. Hendrix

HARMON, HUBERT R. Hubert Reilly Harmon, Lt. General, U.S. Air Force
(born 1892, died 1957), graduated from U.S. Military Academy, Air Service
Engineering School, Air Corps Tactical School, Command and General Staff
School, and Army War College. He was the foremost planner for, and the first
superintendent of, the U.S. Air Force Academy, Colorado, founded in 1955. His
roles were central in establishing the academy's concepts and organization, in
obtaining its legislative authorization, in choosing its permanent site, and in
providing its early leadership.

Harmon attended the Army Flying School at San Diego, graduating as junior
military aviator in June 1917. He went to France in September 1918 for advanced pursuit training and then to Germany for postwar staff responsibilities.
After duties in the office of Chief of Air Service in Washington and as aide in
the White House, he was assistant military attaché for air in London 1927–29,
and later instructor at U.S. Military Academy.* He commanded Thirteenth Air
Force in the South Pacific during 1944.

In late 1949, while serving with the U.S. delegation at the United Nations,
Harmon assumed an additional duty as Special Assistant for Air Academy Matters at U.S. Air Force headquarters. There, he led a small group of officers
engaged in advancing the idea of an Air Force Academy,* developing concepts
for its future, talking with civilian and military educators throughout the United
States and Europe, and working with high civilian officials in seeking legislation
to create the academy. Harmon and the recent Air Force chief of staff, General
Carl Spaatz, served on a site selection board that in 1951 reached the recommendation, never announced, that the academy should be situated in Colorado
Springs. Harmon himself favored that location but was willing to go elsewhere—to San Antonio, for example—if necessary to achieve the needed legislation. After the 1952 election of President Dwight D. Eisenhower (a classmate
of Harmon's at West Point), Harmon worked closely with the new Secretary of
the Air Force, Harold C. Talbott, in pushing forward the Academy idea and
presenting it before Congress, resulting in the legislation of April 1, 1954, that
created the Air Force Academy. To avoid alienating congressmen from states
other than Colorado, the report of the earlier site selection board remained sealed
in Harmon's safe. Harmon and Spaatz then joined Charles Lindbergh and two
other civilian members in a new site selection committee, which recommended
three possible sites, of which Talbott chose Colorado Springs.

Harmon, who had been twice retired in 1953 but twice returned to active
duty, was appointed superintendent on August 14, 1954. He believed that the
academy should provide motivation and preparation for a full career in the Air
Force, including matters of character—i.e., integrity, patriotism, and leadership.
He strongly felt that the academy's role was to prepare future generals, not just

provide an annual flow of second lieutenants. He generally held to the West Point* model, including a robust mix of academics, military training, and competitive sports, and he was responsible for imposition of a cadet honor code. In an interesting forerunner of the academy's later departure from the prescribed curriculum traditional at West Point and Annapolis,* Harmon in 1955 called for the department heads to examine the idea of three alternative majors.

Although the Air Force was perhaps the most scientifically and technically oriented of the American services, Harmon insisted on a broad emphasis on humanistic studies, reflecting his own experiences in working with British officers in London and his service at the United Nations. Harmon in 1955 explained that "officers of the armed services serving in all parts of the world become in effect a quasi-diplomatic corps."

West Point graduates were prominent at the Air Force Academy's outset in all three areas—military, athletic, and academic. During the first academic year, criticisms welled from several directions on matters of curriculum, admissions policies, and the place of athletics, all intensified by pressure to obtain full accreditation for the academy in time for graduation of the initial class, a matter already of wide concern. Obliged to search for a replacement dean, Harmon himself temporarily took the position, assisted by then-Colonel Robert McDermott,* who was appointed by Harmon as Head of the Department of Economics and Vice Dean.

In guiding the academy during its founding days, Harmon was admired for his tact, humaneness, and sensitivity to the views of both seniors and subordinates. He gave attention to a vast array of matters—from faculty and student recruiting policies, to construction of facilities at the permanent site, to erstwhile curriculum planning. He pushed himself in giving countless outside talks, realizing that it was important that the Air Force Academy become known and understood by the public.

Seriously ill, and with regret that he would not see the initial class graduate, Harmon turned the academy over to his successor, James E. Briggs, in a rainsoaked ceremony on July 31, 1956. Harmon died on February 22, 1957. His name has been given to the academy's administration building and to a lecture in military history given annually to the cadets by an outside scholar.

Sources:

Edgar Holt, M. H. Cannon, C. R. Allen, Jr., *History, U.S. Air Force Academy, 27 July 1954–12 June 1956*, microfilm copy, Office of Air Force History, Washington, DC.

John P. Lovell, *Neither Athens Nor Sparta? The American Service Academies in Transition* (Bloomington: Indiana University Press, 1979).

Edward A. Miller, Jr., "The Founding of the Air Force Academy: An Administrative and Legislative History," Ph.D. dissertation, University of Denver, 1969.

R.P.C., "Hubert Reilly Harmon," in *Assembly* 16–17, Association of Graduates, U.S. Military Academy, April 1957–Winter 1959.

Ray L. Bowers

INDUSTRIAL COLLEGE OF THE ARMED FORCES. Direct descendent of the Army Industrial College that was converted to a joint institution following World War II and admitted its first class in January 1946. It moved to Fort Lesley J. McNair while this first postwar course was under way.

On December 28, 1943, the War Department reopened the Army Industrial College,* not to educate officers on how to mobilize for war, but rather to teach how to demobilize smoothly by focusing almost entirely on contract renegotiations and termination. The course was only three weeks long, whereas most of the classes during the 1920s and 1930s had been ten months long. The first class entered the three-week school in January 1944.

Before the war ended in August 1945, senior army officers began to lobby for the recreation of the Army Industrial College as a joint (all-service) institution at the war-college or seniormost level. A key proponent was Brig. General Donald Armstrong, who had served in mobilization position during World War II in the assistant secretary of war office. Armstrong received support from other military and government civilian leaders and also from some industrialists. Two War Department boards (the [Maj. General Oliver P.] Echols Board and the [John M.] Hancock Board) also recommended the recreation of an institution of learning that would focus on mobilization planning for war.

The Hancock Board was created through an agreement between the Secretary of the Navy and the Secretary of War. The former, James Forrestal, in late 1944 wrote to Secretary Henry Stimson that he believed the two cabinet departments "should set up at this time adequate courses of instruction in Logistics" for both the Army and Navy that "fully meet both the common needs of all services and the peculiar needs of each service." He called for a board of senior officers and civilians to develop a program that considered "logistic training." General Armstrong, by then commandant of the Army Industrial College, was tasked with drafting a concept that would transform the school into an "Army and Navy Industrial College."

General Dwight D. Eisenhower, Army Chief of Staff—former faculty member of the Army Industrial College and a member of the college's class of 1933— was a proponent of the concept to create a joint senior-level school that focused on logistics. He testified before the Hancock Board that the United States "must be preeminent in technical research and industrial mobilization" to prevail in future wars. He believed that establishing an industrial college would save time mobilizing the nation's power.

The first Hancock Board recommendation was to change the institution's name to Industrial College of the Armed Forces. Other key recommendations focused on the perceived lack of prestige of the Army Industrial College—thus a proposal that the distinction and importance of the school must be heightened in order to recruit officers of "professional competence" for the student body. The board also proposed that a flag officer—general or admiral—be the commandant.

The short contract-termination course ended with the conclusion of World War II, and on January 4, 1946, the new concept was put into place with a six-month course and a student body of 81 officers representing all services. During this first postwar course, on May 3, 1946, the name of the institution changed from Army Industrial College to Industrial College of the Armed Forces, as it has been called ever since (as of August 1999). The first ten-month course began on September 3, 1946. The faculty totaled 66 military officers and civilians, and the student body numbered 81 officers selected from the Army (including Army Air Forces), Navy, and Marines. There were no civilian students in the first several classes. The Industrial College moved to Fort McNair,* its present campus, in March 1946 to place it close to the newly founded National War College.* In August 1948, in a memorandum signed by now Secretary of Defense James Forrestal, the Industrial College was removed from army jurisdiction and formally "reconstituted as a joint educational institution operating under the direction of the Joint Chiefs of Staff." Forrestal's directive elevated the Industrial College to the same level as the National War College, Air War College,* Army War College,* and Naval War College.*

The mission of the Industrial College has been for some time to prepare highly selected military officers and civilian officials "for senior leadership positions by conducting postgraduate, executive-level courses of study and associated research dealing with the resources component of national power with special emphasis on material acquisition and joint logistics and their integration into national security strategy for peace and war." Its curriculum and organization have changed often in the more than half-century of its existence; however, the emphasis consistently has been on the resources component of national security strategy. While defense-related industry has been central to the program since the mid-1920s, the nucleus of the academic effort has been resources—human and material—or, put in military terms, logistics.

Instead of trying to summarize the curriculum and organizational changes over the past 50 years, the remainder of this article will focus on the program as it existed in 1998, which has been formally sanctioned by the Chairman of the Joint Chiefs of Staff.

The Industrial College of the Armed Forces has a student body of about 300 military and civilian officials. The military students are lieutenant colonel/commanders and colonel/captains from all five services (Army, Navy, Marine Corps, Coast Guard and Air Force); the civilian component, one-third of the total, is of equivalent grade. There are 20 officers from foreign countries in the program and also three executives from the defense industry. The average age of the students is about 41. There are about 84 faculty members, 35 military (from all five services) and 49 civilian. Most of the civilian professors are professional educators with doctoral degrees, and some represent various agencies in government, such as the State Department, Central Intelligence Agency, Federal Emergency Management Agency, etc. The college program is ten months long, and students earn a diploma that is the equivalent of other war college graduation certificates and, since 1995, an accredited graduate degree—master of Science in resource strategy.

The program is divided into two semesters. The first deals with national security strategy and the second with organizing the resources to support a strategy. In the first semester the students take five core (or mandatory) courses: Military Strategy and Warfare, Strategic Decision Making, Political Science, Economics, and Historical Studies in Grand Strategy. Each student also participates in a regional security study, examining a world region of his or her choice. In addition, students choose two elective courses from a selection of more than 70 offered at the Industrial College and other institutions at the National Defense University.* In the second semester students are organized into 20 industry studies in which they will focus on a specific industry from a defense point of view. Some examples: aircraft, shipbuilding, land combat systems, advanced manufacturing, construction, electronics, financial services, etc. In addition to focusing on a specific defense industry (and the students brief one another on the findings of their semester-long study), the students take two more electives and five core courses: Elements of National Power, Acquisition, Strategic Logistics, Mobilization, and Economics.

In the fifty-plus years of the Industrial College's existence, while the focus has remained the same—logistics—the curriculum has changed many times, and so has its organization. The four most significant changes have been the following: In 1976 the college became a constituent part of the National Defense University, an institution commanded by a three-star general or admiral that also supervises the National War College and the Armed Forces Staff College,* among other programs.

After the Goldwater-Nichols* legislation was passed in the 1980s an acquisition course was added to the curriculum for all students, and in 1991 the Industrial College was given responsibility by the chairman of the Joint Chiefs of Staff to educate the Senior Acquisition Corps (military and civilian) of all services and the Department of Defense at the war-college level of professional military education. That is, the Industrial College was given that task instead of the Defense Acquisition University,* becoming another war-college-level school. The major reason for this decision was the fact that the Industrial College devotes an entire semester to grounding the students in national security strategy.

Devoting a semester to the study of strategy was another major change over the 50-year history. Prior to this change the college focused on logistics without solidly grounding the students in the strategic concepts that provided meaning to logistics. That changed in the late 1980s.

The fourth major change was adding international travel to the student curriculum. Prior to the mid-1980s Industrial College students examined industries only in the United States. The change in the nature of the world of business from national firms to international firms made this program unacceptable. Since the late 1980s students and faculty from the Industrial College have researched industries in the United States over an entire semester, traveling widely for one week inside the United States, but they have also explored industries overseas for two weeks. The Industrial College has found this to be a more meaningful approach.

The mission of the Industrial College is unique, and the college continuously reviews and adjusts its curriculum and course content to ensure that its graduates are prepared for the national security demands of the future.

Alan L. Gropman

J

JOINTNESS. A term in vogue following the Department of Defense Reorganization (Goldwater-Nichols) Act of 1986 characterizing unity of effort among the armed services (and, as appropriate, other executive agencies and nations), a topic increasingly pervading U.S. professional military education (PME).

Joint operations (military efforts by two or more services) and combined operations (two or more allied nations) are an American military heritage, in large part dictated by U.S. geography and strategic circumstances. Examples include the 1781 American and French army and naval collaboration at Yorktown; Civil War riverine operations of the U.S. Army and Navy; joint or combined efforts at Saipan (1944), Normandy (1944), Okinawa (1945), and Inchon (1950); amphibious/airborne collaboration at Beirut (1958), the Dominican Republic (1965), and Granada (1983); and the Vietnam and Gulf Wars.

To understand the role of PME in fostering jointness, one must begin by inventorying the tools for unifying action. The first of these necessarily is a rational division among the armed services of military operational competencies—combatant functions—which are fundamental both for developing military capabilities and employing them. Service functions have been broadly defined in the National Security Act of 1947 and are amplified by Department of Defense directive.

This system of service combatant primary and collateral functions allows the nation to develop a broad range of military capabilities with which to cope with the uncertainties of the future. The United States has initial forces and doctrine covering each of the possible categories of need (land warfare, naval warfare, strategic air warfare, amphibious warfare, airborne operations, etc.) that may emerge. While a single service may not have enough peacetime strength in any one primary function to meet a full-blown challenge in that category, all appropriate primary and complementary capabilities—depending on what actually unfolds—may be concentrated on the specific requirement. Marines may reinforce

Army land warfare requirements; soldiers may land administratively behind marines to expand an amphibious lodgment or vice versa for an airborne lodgment; naval aviation and missiles may reinforce the Air Force in a strategic air campaign or vice versa for a maritime campaign. This system of complements provides the flexibility to respond to a far broader range of strategic problems than we could otherwise afford in peacetime.

The second tool is the body of joint doctrine developed to link together the various service capabilities into patterns of unified military action for a wide range of requirements. The most venerable of these, Unified Action Armed Forces (UNAAF), derives from a 1927 joint Army-Navy board agreement that established the first service combatant functions. It serves as the foundation for all joint doctrine, provides choices available to a joint force commander for structuring his force, and defines what those choices and associated authorities mean. Building on the principles of UNAAF, other joint doctrines have been developed to focus on the functions of joint command (intelligence, operations, logistics, planning, command and control) and a variety of joint operations (air, amphibious, counterdrug, anti-terrorism, riverine, etc.).

The third tool—and the one essential for synthesis of the others for tomorrow's commanders and staff officers—is a joint military educational establishment comprising an Industrial College of the Armed Forces,* a National War College,* the Armed Forces Staff College* (all three established in 1946), and a National Defense University* (established in 1975) drawing these three colleges into a coordinated whole.

The fourth tool is the historical record of past joint and combined military operations for study and analysis. Other than civilian writings, most of this is the result of individual service military history efforts and naturally emphasizes the role of the authoring service. However, in 1993, the Chairman of the Joint Chiefs of Staff (CJCS) moved the Joint History Office under his direct authority and rechartered it to develop histories of U.S. military operations from the joint perspective.

These tools, used in concert, can advance military unity of effort, and the 1980s witnessed increasing political pressures for just that. Following the Iran hostage rescue attempt, the Beirut Marine barracks bombing, and the Grenada expedition, there existed in Congress and elsewhere in Washington some vocal concern—primarily from the self-styled Military Reform Caucus—over the U.S. approach to national defense. This touched on training, organization, and doctrine but focused heavily on the issue of higher direction of military forces. Those favoring a strong CJCS/Joint Staff and weak JCS won the day in Congress with the passage of the Defense Reorganization Act of 1986 (Goldwater-Nichols).* Among other provisions, that act established the CJCS as principal military advisor to the President and Secretary of Defense, and placed the Joint Staff exclusively in support of CJCS.

While these events unfolded, the National Defense University (NDU) undertook some initiatives of its own. During the summer of 1985, the President of

NDU (Lt. General Richard Lawrence) initiated a new program to resurrect military study at the theater and subtheater levels, with emphasis on the joint and combined aspects of planning and conducting large-scale campaigns. While the U.S. historical experience—both in joint and combined operations and in the planning and conduct of campaigns—was extensive, the course, together with its instructional materiel and faculty expertise, had to be developed from the ground up.

Passage of Goldwater-Nichols brought a great rush of interest in joint professional military education, and by virtue of General Lawrence's foresight, NDU was ahead of the requirement. Through a series of semiannual meetings originally conceived by NDU and rotated among the senior service schools and NDU, joint and combined warfare faculty from all colleges shared approaches and concepts for teaching joint operations and campaign planning. These efforts laid the foundation for theater-level instruction in all PME colleges and subsequent theater-level learning objectives in the CJCS's PME guidance.

In November 1987, the House Armed Services Committee established the Panel on Military Education (chaired by Ike Skelton) to evaluate the Defense Department's ability to develop joint specialty officers through its different PME systems. After hearings, visits, and analyses, the Skelton Panel* found the DoD's military education system to be sound and fully comparable to even the most prestigious foreign schools but made a number of suggestions for improvement. Responding to several of the panel's recommendations, the department took action to:

- Establish a PME framework specifying the primary educational objectives at each PME level (this is done by CJCS);
- Establish a two-phase Joint Specialist Officer education process with Phase I taught in service colleges and Phase II at the Armed Forces Staff College (also managed by CJCS);
- Implement a capstone course for all newly selected general and flag officers (conducted at NDU under CJCS supervision).

Given the CJCS's new Goldwater-Nichols authority for joint doctrine development, joint military education policy formulation, and triennial service combatant functions assessment, the chairman has been given directive authority over two of the aforementioned tools, influence over a third, and has taken steps to expand the utility of the fourth (joint history). While the adequacy of jointness in PME may become an issue from time to time in the years ahead, there can be no issue as to the responsibility for it: that lies firmly in the hands of the Chairman of the Joint Chiefs of Staff.

Sources:

U.S. Department of Defense, "Functions of the Department of Defense and Its Major Components," DoD Directive 5100.1, September 25, 1987.

U.S. Department of Defense, *Unified Action Armed Forces*, Joint Pub 0–2 (Washington, DC: Government Printing Office, 1995).

The Joint Board, *Joint Action of the Army and the Navy* (Washington, DC: Government Printing Office, 1927).

James E. Toth

K

KNOX, HENRY. Henry Knox (born 1750, died 1806), Maj. General, Continental Army, and U.S. Secretary of War (1785–94), was an early voice on behalf of a professional American officer corps, one which might provide leadership for the nation's citizen-soldiery in time of war. Professional military education was a critical part of his vision, and he long championed the idea of an American military academy.

Prior to the Revolution, young Henry Knox was proprietor of a bookstore in Boston, a member of a local militia unit, and an avid student of books on artillery, engineering, and other military matters. He knew some of the British officers stationed in Boston, and on the streets of the town on March 5, 1770, he tried to head off the so-called Boston Massacre. He joined the patriot army after Lexington in 1775 and personally led the difficult wintertime transport of ordnance captured at Fort Ticonderoga for use by General George Washington's forces outside Boston. As the youthful chief of artillery under Washington from the siege of Boston through Yorktown, Knox proved a superb organizer and combat leader. Knox's artillery was unquestionably the Continental Army's strongest feature, and it contributed decisively in all of Washington's battlefield victories.

Knox regularly gave thoughts and information to the wartime Congress, often in letters to Massachusetts delegate John Adams. Consulted by a congressional committee in September 1776, Knox wrote out his "Hints for the Improvement of Artillery in the United States." His proposals included the founding of "an Academy established on a liberal plan, where the whole theory and practice of fortification and gunnery should be taught, to be nearly on the same plan as that at Woolwich [the military academy for youths in Britain]." These ideas are usually taken as the earliest to envision an American military academy. Congress in 1777 instead authorized a Corps of Invalids (i.e., disabled personnel), which would garrison certain forts and provide training for "young gentlemen" destined to become officers in field regiments. Meanwhile in 1778–79, at the winter bivouac at Pluckemin, New Jersey, Knox organized a school for his artillerymen. The school building was solidly made, had a good-sized classroom, and stood at the center of an orderly layout of huts and ordnance pieces. Instruction covered tactics, gunnery, and like subjects. Knox called it the "academy"; he himself was one of the instructors in this early example of organized professional training in the American army.

Washington's army spent much of the war in the region around New York City, which included the fortifications at West Point,* whose guns commanded navigation of the Hudson River. The small Corps of Invalids was stationed at West Point, and it operated a small training program resembling the one envisioned in the initial legislation. As commander of the forces at West Point in 1783, Knox addressed the nation's Secretary at War, proposing the idea of a military academy, to be located at West Point where, he noted, the technical services of artillery and engineers were already concentrated. In his "Plan for a Military System," dated April 17, 1783, Knox called for "a complete system of military education which would embrace the whole theory of the art of war." The paper advocated that Congress create two academies, one each for the army and navy, each to admit about 40 students annually.

In early 1785 Knox became Secretary at War under the Articles of Confederation, and in 1789 he became the nation's first Secretary of War under the Constitution. It was a difficult role, as the states and the new nation were scarcely inclined to provide resources for, indeed even to tolerate, a national army. Within the cabinet Thomas Jefferson typically disagreed with Knox on such matters, and in November 1793 a heated argument between the two ensued, described by Jefferson. The subject was a national military academy, strongly favored by Knox and Hamilton. Washington cut off the discussion, commenting that he thought an academy would be advantageous and, the next month, the president so recommended in his annual message to Congress.

By legislation of May 7, 1794—Knox's final year in the cabinet—Congress established the rank of cadet and provided that a total of 32 cadets should be attached to units of a newly organized Corps of Artillerists and Engineers,* to be stationed at West Point. The law provided for the purchase of books and instructional equipment; cadets and junior officers were to attend classes. The corps was duly founded, but only a few cadets actually served. Neither instruction nor instructors were of high order; and the school's main building was destroyed in a 1796 fire, possibly set by dissatisfied officers. The cadet program at West Point was somewhat revitalized later in the Adams and early in the Jefferson administrations, and the U.S. Military Academy* was permanently established by legislation of March 16, 1802.

Henry Knox remains an intriguing figure in the building of the new nation, a man of remarkable ideas and energy. His career oddly contradicts his own vision, as he—a self-educated individual without professional military background, a true citizen-soldier—became an outstanding army officer in the most technical branch of his times and a foremost voice in the founding of American professional military education.

Sources:

Capt. Edward C. Boynton, *History of West Point and Its Military Importance during the American Revolution and the Origin and Progress of the United States Military Academy* (New York: D. Van Nostrand, 1863).

North Callahan, *Henry Knox. General Washington's General* (New York. Rinehart & Co., 1958).

James Ripley Jacobs, *The Beginning of the U.S. Army, 1783–1812* (Princeton, NJ: Princeton University Press, 1947).

Edward S. Holden, "Origins of the United States Military Academy, 1777–1802," in *Centennial of the U.S.M.A.*, vol. 1 (Washington, DC: Government Printing Office, 1904).

Ray L. Bowers

KNOX-KING-PYE BOARD. Navy board of inquiry (1919–20), named for its members, that studied the line officers' need for career education and training and whose recommendations led to several important innovations in the Naval War College program and in officer assignment policies. Its most important contribution was its insistence that the "instruction and training" of officers (the board's report does not use the word "education") needed to be considered in the context of an officer's entire career.

Following the First World War all the U.S. military services entered a period of important transition. The Navy had greatly expanded during the war but was then contracting; prewar patterns of education and career progression were unlikely to suffice. The chief of the Navy's Bureau of Navigation (later to be renamed, more accurately, the Bureau of Naval Personnel) created a board of inquiry to survey the Navy's requirements for the training and education of its officer corps, particularly its line officers.

The board consisted of three members: Captain (later Commodore) Dudley Knox, member of the faculty of the Naval War College*; Captain (later Fleet Admiral) Ernest J. King, head of the Naval Postgraduate School,* then a department at the U.S. Naval Academy*; and Commander (later Vice Admiral) William Pye, previously on the Naval War College faculty, then on the staff of the Chief of Naval Operations. The three board members were well acquainted with each other. King and Pye had been classmates at the Naval Academy, and later they had together applied for a patent on a "range machine." King had served with both Knox and Pye on the staff of the Commander-in-Chief, U.S. Atlantic Fleet. All three had previously been prizewinners in the U.S. Naval Institute's* annual essay contest.

The report of the Knox-King-Pye Board, which met from August 1919 to April 1920, makes little reference to its own purpose and powers; but the board at least examined "existing arrangements" because it found that they "provide only for the special instruction of younger officers in matters relating to the design and production of material." The board reported that it reached its conclusions only after considering the entire career of a naval officer (of the line) "from midshipman to admiral."

The board first examined the successive functions performed during a naval officer's career and derived from that examination the requirements for periodic education. The board found that the career of a naval line officer could be divided into four phases of increasing responsibility and authority and concluded that prior to the start of each new phase, officers should receive some formal education as preparation. It believed that this alternation between formal instruction and practical experience was "the best means to develop judgment."

Preparation of officers for their first phase—to become division officers aboard ship—was provided for by the Naval Academy, but the board felt that an academy education could *not* be expected "to prepare the naval officer thoroughly for other than the duties . . . [of] a junior officer." When officers were about to become heads of department aboard ship, more education in the functions of a "superior subordinate" was deemed to be in order; the board thus recommended the establishment of a year-long General Line School (between the fifth and tenth year of commissioned service).

Later, when officers became prospective commanding officers of ships, additional education was required; so the board recommended establishment of a junior course at the Naval War College (for officers between their tenth and twentieth years of commissioned service, but preferably as lieutenant commanders). Although couched in terms of preparation for command, this recommendation incorporated the views of Rear Admiral William S. Sims*—then President of the Naval War College—who favored a new second course as the counterpart to the Army's Command and Staff College,* as well as the views of King and Pye: that naval officers needed to learn how to be staff officers *before* being ordered to staff duty. (Officers in the junior course at the Naval War College are attached to what is still called the College of *Command and Staff.*)

Finally, as an officer approached flag rank and the command of fleets, further education "in the advanced elements of the profession" would be needed, and the board felt that this would be provided by the senior course at the Naval War College (at some time after the twentieth year of commissioned service, preferably while officers were in the grade of captain). Convinced that commanding officers and unit commanders (as well as their staffs) should share common conceptions of the cooperation and coordination needed to achieve "unity in action," board members felt that preparation for the duties of *command* was best conducted during two periods—at a junior war college course and a senior course.

The report of the board was drafted by one of the members, Captain Ernest J. King. In August 1920, the board's report was published in the U.S. Naval Institute *Proceedings*, where a footnote informed readers that the report had been "published by permission of the Navy Department for the information of the service" and that the report had "been approved, but the shortage of officers will not permit the recommendations to be carried into effect at present." Achieving publication was also the work of Captain King, then a member of the Institute's board of control.

In January 1923, a board of flag officers agreed with the proposal for a junior war college course and drafted for the Secretary of the Navy a general order, entitled "Training for Higher Command," which specifically provided for two separate courses at the Naval War College. The general order was issued on March 6, 1923; students for the first junior course arrived at Newport, Rhode Island, during the summer of the same year. In a July 1923 talk at the Naval War College, the Assistant Secretary of the Navy distinguished between the two courses by saying that the senior course was to assist in the preparation of naval officers for high command in war; and the junior course was to assist in the training of officers for duty on the staffs of flag officers afloat, and for command of small units in war.

In 1928 and as late as 1944 and 1948, subsequent boards reviewed the Knox-King-Pye Board Report and found its conclusions to be basically sound.

Sources:

Thomas B. Buell, *Master of Sea Power: A Biography of Fleet Admiral Ernest J. King* (Boston: Little, Brown & Co., 1980).

John B. Hattendorf, B. Mitchell Simpson III, and John R. Wadleigh, *Sailors and Scholars: The Centennial History of the U.S. Naval War College* (Newport, RI: Naval War College Press, 1984).

"Report and Recommendations of a Board Appointed by the Bureau of Navigation Regarding the Instruction and Training of Line Officers," U.S. Naval Institute *Proceedings*, August 1920.

U.S. Naval War College, *Outline History of the United States Naval War College, 1884 to Date [1937]* (Newport, RI: Naval War College, 1937).

Frank M. Snyder

KRIEGSSCHULE. Established during the era of Prussian military reform (1808–10) and later known as the Kriegsakademie, this institution of professional military education provided the intellectual foundation for the Prussian and German officer corps in the 19th and 20th centuries.

In the late 18th and early 19th centuries, General Gerhard von Scharnhorst* witnessed the rise of Republican France and the success of its new, national army. He recognized that the concept of a nation-in-arms was revolutionary and would completely change the way in which states conducted warfare. Beginning with his control over the Berlin Institute for Young Officers in 1801 and continuing after the disasters of 1806, Scharnhorst began to reorganize the educational structure of the Prussian military. His ideal system was a change from the emphasis on tradition and formality that had driven the Prussian officer corps since the time of Frederick the Great. Scharnhorst believed that only an educated leader could understand the complexities of modern war making and successfully utilize both socioeconomic and technological-tactical advancements to achieve victory.

The first step came with the *Reglement* (Regulations) of 1808, which dismantled the existing system of military schools, none of which had formal curricula, and established a three-tiered hierarchy in their place. The first level was a network of cadet schools, accepting young boys at an average age of twelve years. These cadets would spend four years receiving a general education and preparing for examinations that would allow them to advance to the next level of instruction. That level consisted of three schools, located at Berlin, Breslau, and Königsberg, which offered students a nine-month course in basic military instruction. Graduates of this school could be commissioned, but only a select few advanced to the third, and highest, level of schooling in Berlin. Here they participated in an intense program of instruction under which they studied general topics such as mathematics, French, German, physics, and chemistry as well as military subjects such as strategy, tactics, artillery, military geography, and mess administration. It was this school in Berlin that eventually grew to a three-year program, later becoming the Prussian Kriegsakademie, and provided the bulk of the officers for Scharnhorst's other great contribution, the General Staff.* The key elements in Scharnhorst's program were advancement solely through successful completion of examinations, state funding for all students, and focus on preparing students for duty as general staff officers and adjutants rather than officers of the line.

Unfortunately, in the years following the Wars of Liberation, Prussia's military education system did not sustain Scharnhorst's vision. General von Hake, War Minister from 1819 to 1833, did not share Scharnhorst's faith in educational reform and, as historian Gordon A. Craig notes, "believed that an officer was competent if he could read, write, and figure." The Kriesgsschule drifted from the enlightened ideals of Scharnhorst's era as its leaders allowed the vague, idealistic notions of romanticism and nationalism to override both professional training and personal cultivation. The "science of war," as perceived by Scharnhorst, was replaced by a mixture of literature, philosophy of history, and a predominance of mathematics. The student would even develop his own schedule and program of instruction—a far cry from the Age of Reason and its systems. Only in the 1850s, under General von Peucker, were the first steps taken toward formalization and the name of the Kriegsschule officially changed to the Kriegsakademie.

Peucker reorganized the program by shifting the focus to administration and planning and requiring that certain military courses be taken by all students. His concepts were solidified in 1872, when the Kriegsakademie became the special training ground for the general staff, and was transferred to the direction of the Chief of the General Staff of the army (at the time, Field Marshal Helmuth von

Moltke the Elder). Moltke wanted to emphasize the importance of the new changes in warfare, such as railways and the telegraph, and to teach students to adapt their leadership style to these new conditions. During the period between the Wars of Unification and the First World War, Moltke and his successors succeeded in shifting the bulk of instruction away from courses in mathematics, science, and history, focusing instead on the specific components of modern warfare. The revised curriculum saw an increased number of courses on the conduct of war at the expense of the liberal arts and physical sciences, which were reduced to *Nebenfacher* (minor subjects). A look at the curriculum of 1890 reveals that first-year classes were split equally between military and scientific studies, while in the last two years the number of military courses gradually increased, with special courses focusing on military law, military hygiene, and general staff service.

The greatest problem with the system at this time, as historian Manfred Messerschmidt notes, was that no classes addressed the contemporary socioeconomic or political issues in this age of industrialism. By refusing to consider these new questions and the political debates they generated, the army saw national mobilization and war making from a one-dimensional, purely military perspective. These shortcomings were apparent in 1918, when the army found itself unable to understand how the First World War had been lost and how modern ideologies and movements such as socialism, liberalism, and democracy had influenced the outcome.

The Treaty of Versailles abolished both the General Staff and the Kriegsakademie. Colonel-General Hans von Seeckt, the organizer of the postwar army, sought to overcome this by establishing a system of *Wehrkreis-Kommandos* (military district commands) in order to train new staff officers. Similar to the Kriegsakademie in curricula, to include examinations to gain advancement, it provided very little progress in a student's all-around educational development.

In 1932, the *Wehrkreis* evolved into the *Offizierslehrgange* (Training Courses for Officers) *Berlin*. This new institution sought to establish a curriculum that offered a better "all around" education and succeeded to a degree in formulating a broader program, with the addition in the third year of courses on foreign policy and economics. As in the Kriegsakademie, an examination was required to receive commission. In October, 1933, the Kriegsakademie reopened its gates, only operating, however, as a two-year program. The curriculum continued along the lines of the *Offizierslehrgange Berlin*. In 1936, the Kriegsakademie and all other institutes of military education were ordered to incorporate instruction of the National Socialist *Weltanschauung* into their program. Following the Second World War, the Kriegsakademie was closed again, only to reopen in 1957. Although changing social, political, and economic factors have influenced its development along democratic lines, the institution continues to maintain its role in a system providing an advanced education balanced between military instruction and arts and sciences.

Sources:

Gordon A. Craig, *The Politics of the Prussian Army, 1640–1945* (London: Oxford University Press, 1964).

Manfred Messerschmidt, "German Staff Officers' Education since the Beginning of the 19th Century. Innovations and Tradition," *Militarhistorisk Tidskrift* 187 (1983).

Hans Eberhard Radbruch, "From Scharnhorst to Schmidt: The System of Education and Training in the German Bundeswehr," *Armed Forces and Society* 5, no. 4 (1979).

Charles E. White, *The Enlightened Soldier: Scharnhorst and the Militärische Gesellschaft in Berlin, 1801–1805* (New York: Praeger, 1989).

Major Michael A. Boden, USA

L

LOWRY AIR FORCE BASE. Large U.S. Air Force training base in Denver, Colorado, and temporarily (1954–58) the initial location of the Air Force Academy.

On June 24, 1954, Secretary of the Air Force Harold E. Talbott announced that Denver would be the interim location of the U.S. Air Force Academy* while workers constructed the permanent facilities north of Colorado Springs. Lt. General Hubert R. Harmon* went to the Denver area and examined Fort Logan, in west Denver, and the University of Denver as sites for the academy. General Harmon also studied Lowry Air Force Base in east Denver. He concluded that the Air Force could easily rehabilitate the Lowry's World War II wooden barracks and other buildings and landscape the surrounding areas to present a creditable appearance and a suitable academic environment. On July 19, General Harmon recommended to Secretary Talbott that the government designate Lowry AFB as the interim location. The rehabilitation of the buildings and facilities got under way immediately.

Logistical and financial problems plagued the academy during the early months of its existence. The Air Force directed Air Training Command, through its USAF training center at Lowry, to furnish logistical support. Although Lowry's base commander, Maj. General T. John Sprague, directed his troops to aid the academy, his support officers felt a primary responsibility to the base and the Air Force technical schools located there. Also, there was a long delay in transferring academy funds to the base; space and equipment were difficult to obtain. Until January 1955, all of the academy personnel had to work out of two rooms in Building 905. Even after more office space became available to the growing staff of military and civilian personnel, equipment like typewriters, desks, and chairs were in short supply. Logistical support arrangements were not formalized until after the joint tenancy agreement was signed on August 15,

1955, fully fourteen months after the first class of cadets arrived for their summer indoctrination.

In spite of the financial problems, base officials constructed six standard football fields, seven tennis courts, five softball fields, and a large cadet parade ground. The Air Force converted 24 buildings from two-story, open bay barracks to buildings containing 28 two-man rooms. The academy administration modernized other buildings to serve as academic buildings, a dining hall, chapel, theater, library, dispensary, gym, cadet club, cadet store, and other miscellaneous functions. Academy officials promptly attached the names of famous airmen to the buildings serving major cadet functions. For instance, the dining hall became General Billy Mitchell Hall; the cadet social center was called General H. H. Arnold Hall. These names were transferred to buildings with the same functions at the permanent site in 1958.

Since all of the incoming cadets would be freshmen, some provision had to be made for upperclassmen who could serve as role models and help to indoctrinate the neophytes to the cadet way of life. Early in January 1954, the Air Staff decided to use young USAF second lieutenants, right out of pilot training, as surrogate upperclassmen. These officers became known as air training officers (ATOs). The ATOs had a strong influence on the early classes of cadets.

Among the new faculty there was much skepticism about how all the academy's goals could be accomplished in such a short time as four years. Collectively, the department heads agreed that they and their staffs had to concentrate first on constructing the academic and professional military courses in the previously prescribed syllabus. The first semester, however, soon made apparent a glaring problem in curriculum planning that had become endemic in U.S. service academy education. The department heads and their staffs had overplanned the courses; the demands on the cadets were too great; and practically every minute of the cadet's day had a scheduled activity. Consequently, there was intense competition for the cadet's time by all elements of the academy. This dilemma, in varying degrees, was to cause much agony and discontent for the academy, even at its permanent site, over the next quarter of a century.

Sources:

M. Hamlin Cannon and Henry S. Fellerman, *Quest for an Air Force Academy* (Colorado Springs, CO: U.S. Air Force Academy, 1974).
George V. Fagan, *The Air Force Academy: An Illustrated History* (Boulder, CO: Johnson Books, 1988).

Major Timothy J. Matson, USAF

LUCE, STEPHEN B. Stephen Bleecker Luce (born 1827, died 1917), Rear Admiral, U.S. Navy, was the key figure in the development of professional military education in the U.S. Navy during the latter half of the 19th century. He was the first American naval officer to make successive contributions at all three principal levels of instruction: training for naval and merchant marine apprentices, preparation of newly commissioned officers, and midcareer education in preparation for high command at flag rank.

Stephen Luce, born in Albany, New York, obtained an appointment as midshipman in the Navy from President Martin Van Buren in 1841 through his father's connections as a clerk, since 1835, in the Treasury Department. Ordered immediately to the receiving ship *North Carolina* at New York City, he was soon assigned to the 50-gun frigate USS *Congress* for his initial sea training. In 1845, he was ordered to the ship of the line USS *Columbus* just before her eventful round the world cruise in 1845–47, including among other missions taking the ratification for the first U.S. treaty with China to Canton.

Upon the decommissioning of *Columbus* in the spring of 1848, Luce was ordered to the three-year-old U.S. Naval Academy* at Annapolis, Maryland,* where he spent one year of residence before returning to sea, warranted as a passed midshipman in 1849. There began a typical pattern of junior officer assignments, serving in the Caribbean, on the East Coast of the United States, and in the Eastern Pacific.

In March 1860, Luce was ordered to the Naval Academy as head of the seamanship department. Observing the weaknesses of professional education at that point, he wrote to the Commandant of Midshipmen: "Compared to the Army with their wealth of professional literature, we may be likened to the nomadic tribes of the East, who are content with the vague traditions of the past." Gaining approval to remedy the situation by preparing an appropriate textbook, Luce published *Seamanship* at Newport, Rhode Island,* in 1862, and it remained the leading textbook in the field for forty years.

Immediately upon his return to the Naval Academy in January 1862, after a temporary assignment with the South Atlantic Blockading Force, Luce used his recent experience to revise the academy's textbook on *Instructions for Light Artillery, Afloat and Ashore*, originally by William H. Parker. In the summer of 1863, he received his first command, the Naval Academy practice ship *Macedonian*. In the midst of war, Luce was ordered to train midshipmen during a cruise to England and France. During these visits, he compiled a report on European naval training, submitting it to the Navy Department. Luce also used his observations for his first published articles, a series of five on "Training Ships" which appeared in 1863 in the *Army and Navy Journal*.

After more duty with the South Atlantic Blockading Squadron, the end of the war brought Luce a series of assignments yielding personal contact with individuals who would become instrumental in Luce's later PME accomplishments. At first, he was promoted to commander and ordered to Annapolis as the Commandant of Midshipmen, serving directly under Superintendent David D. Porter.* In 1873, as Equipment Officer at the Boston Navy Yard, Luce found himself advising the City of New York Board of Education on the establishment of a nautical school. In that same year, Luce delivered a lecture on "The Manning of the Navy and the Mercantile Marine," which was published in the first issue of the journal of the newly established U.S. Naval Institute.* From 1875

to 1877, while in command of USS *Hartford*, he met Colonel Emory Upton,*
then in command of the Artillery School at Fort Monroe, Virginia.* Through
this contact, Luce formulated his first thoughts on establishing an advanced
school for naval officers.

Before his ideas on this subject matured, however, Luce was assigned to
command an apprentice and gunnery training ship, USS *Minnesota*, based at
New York. Devoting his full energies to the Navy's only shipboard enlisted
training program, Luce introduced a number of innovations but began also to
work toward establishing a permanent naval apprentice training system with its
own head and a permanent location. In February 1881, a promotion to commodore and command of the Apprentice Training Squadron provided Luce with
a flagship, the ship-of-the-line USS *New Hampshire*, moored permanently in
Coasters Harbor at Newport, Rhode Island. An advocate of a permanent operating base in Narragansett Bay since his Civil War faculty days at the Naval
Academy, Luce now planted the idea of the City of Newport donating Coasters
Harbor Island for the Navy's training needs, in this case for apprentice drills
and recreation. Even though the shipboard sea training promoted by Luce would
eventually be replaced by training ashore, the Naval Apprentice Training system
he established and the continuing, long-term connection with Newport were two
of Luce's important legacies.

In 1883, Luce turned his attention to the highest level of professional military
education, what he conceived as "a 'War School' for officers—the prime object
being to teach officers the science of their own profession—the Science of War."
Revitalizing the thoughts he developed in 1877, Luce delivered a lecture to the
Naval Institute on the subject of "War Schools" and wrote to the Secretary of
the Navy to promote his general plan. Through the intervention of two of Luce's
friends, Admiral David Dixon Porter and Commodore John G. Walker, Chief
of the Bureau of Navigation, Luce was ordered to Washington for further discussions of his proposal. In March 1884, to examine the proposal, Secretary
William E. Chandler appointed a board of officers headed by Luce, then temporarily commanding the North Atlantic Squadron, that submitted its report in
June. Chandler signed the general order creating the Naval War College* four
months later, establishing on Coasters Harbor Island the first bona fide war
college in the United States. As the college's first president, Luce was promoted
to rear admiral and began to lay out the course of instruction, appointing staff
members whose initial work inaugurated a century-long tradition of professional
education and research in key areas of the college's interest: Lieutenant William
McCarty Little to elevate naval wargaming to where it could be used as means
of analysis; Army Lieutenant Tasker Bliss,* as the first instructor in military
affairs; Professor James R. Soley* as the first civilian professor and lecturer in
international law; and Captain Alfred Thayer Mahan* as lecturer in naval history. Passing the presidency of the college to Mahan in June 1885, Luce returned
to command the North Atlantic Squadron, testing in the fleet the operational and
tactical ideas being developed in Newport.

Retiring from active duty in February 1889, Luce turned to becoming a prolific writer on a variety of professional subjects, much of which focused on establishing a professional uniformed advisor and staff under the Secretary of the Navy. In August 1901, as a retired rear admiral, he was ordered to active duty on the faculty of the Naval War College and remained in that role until November 1910, when at the age of 83, he was retired. A year later, Luce suffered a severe stroke which ended his productive writing career.

Sources:

Alfred Gleaves, *Life and Letters of Stephen B. Luce, U.S. Navy: Founder of the Naval War College* (New York and London: G. P. Putnam, 1925).

John B. Hattendorf, B. Mitchell Simpson III, and John R. Wadleigh, *Sailors and Scholars: The Centennial History of the Naval War College* (Newport, RI: Naval War College Press, 1984).

John D. Hayes and John B. Hattendorf, *The Writings of Stephen B. Luce* (Newport, RI: Naval War College Press, 1975).

John B. Hattendorf

M

MacARTHUR, DOUGLAS. General Douglas MacArthur (born 1880, died 1964), graduate of the U.S. Military Academy and the Army War College, returned to West Point as Superintendent (1919–22). He later served as Army Chief of Staff (1930–35) and, after retiring in 1937, was recalled to active duty in 1941 to command U.S. Army forces in the Far East and, later, United Nations forces in Korea.

The son of a Congressional Medal of Honor winner in the Civil War, the younger MacArthur entered West Point* as a cadet in 1899 and graduated with honors four years later. MacArthur had a distinguished record as commander of the 42d Rainbow Division in World War I and returned from France to become West Point's 31st superintendent. Convinced by his experiences in France that modern wars requiring national mobilization demanded a new kind of leadership, he was determined to foster a cadet program of academic, military, and physical training equal to the demand. As he explained in his first annual superintendent's report (1920), "Such changed conditions will require a modification in type of the officer, a type . . . possessing an intimate understanding of the mechanics of human feelings, a comprehensive grasp of world and national affairs, and a liberalization of conception which amounts to a change in his psychology of command."

For the academic program, MacArthur's perception of leadership was felt most strongly in the social sciences and humanities. Semester-long courses in economics and in government were introduced to the prescribed curriculum; the time devoted to English literature was significantly increased, as was the course in European history. To make room for this shift in emphasis, mathematics lost 169 classroom hours; drawing lost 188; military art (largely civil engineering) lost 85—producing more than a little consternation among the Academic Board members representing the slighted departments.

A related MacArthur initiative was to encourage deviation from the traditional

West Point reliance on the classroom recitation method of teaching. Traditionally, lecturing was minimal, with the bulk of each class session absorbed in
quizzing each cadet orally or through his demonstration of selected elements of
the daily lesson at the blackboard. In some departments, such as Mathematics,
the so-called Thayer* method had become a rigid ritual, prescribing how the
cadet should announce his assigned problem, where and how (at attention) he
should stand at different phases of his recitation, and so forth. For his performance he received a daily grade, limiting the instructor's impact largely to that
of a scorekeeper.

MacArthur regarded such classroom routine as one factor that rendered a
cadet's West Point experience "abnormally confining," and he set out to change
it. Seeing it as helping to create an observed "habit of just going along by rote"
among cadets, he made it policy in his first year as superintendent that the formal
blackboard recitation was not to be regarded as binding "in subjects which do
not lend themselves readily to it." He went on to encourage more use of lectures,
laboratory work in the physical sciences, and oral drills in foreign languages as
examples of supplementary methods that had been proven effective elsewhere.
Moreover, he required all academic department heads to spend one month each
year observing the methods practiced in civilian universities.

This encouraged loosening of classroom routine was regarded by some professors as a dangerous innovation that threatened the "West Point system," and
it added to the core of hostility toward MacArthur within the Academic Board.
Indeed, one of his biographers, William Ganoe, alleges that some members were
critical of MacArthur's appointment from the beginning: (paraphrased) "Seems
only yesterday he was reciting to me." More fundamentally, this innovation and
some he introduced in nonacademic areas of the program were seen by some
as an assault on West Point's traditional "democracy of the Corps."

Before World War I, this concept had been based on a set of traditional
practices designed to ensure that no cadet received privileges or advantages not
shared by all: a totally prescribed curriculum; daily grading of students; a competitive merit roll; a common, rigorous novitiate strictly within the confines of
West Point. One of its program elements was the Summer Encampment, an
annual event that saw the entire Corps of Cadets bivouacked for training on the
Plain, an experience one alumnus characterized as an occasion "where the Corps
became a single family, a period filled with exciting and romantic memories."
In fact, the concept was so dominant that, until the 20th century, it prevented
the introduction of intercollegiate sports as authorized cadet activities. As articulated by the academy's director of physical education until 1923, Herman
Koehler, competitive athletics provided opportunities only for the talented few
and were not compatible with West Point's goal of "mass excellence."

Hence, MacArthur's innovations apart from the academic program also added
to the resentment of his forward-looking changes, both inside the academy and
among the alumni. Deploring the cadets' isolation from the outside world, he
introduced weekend-pass privileges for upperclassmen, authorized cash allow-

ances for cadets, and promoted intercollegiate—as well as intramural—sports competition. Believing modern warfare required more realistic practical military training, he canceled the Summer Encampment, instead sending the Corps of Cadets to train under regular army sergeants at Camp Dix, New Jersey.

Even though many of his innovations were undone by the Academic Board following his replacement as superintendent in 1922, Douglas MacArthur's contributions to the Military Academy were major and, in time, lasting. Several of the younger officers who served under him at West Point or in France saw real merit in his ideas and implemented many of them when they returned to academy duty in influential positions in later years. Through his subsequent career as well as his accomplishments as superintendent, MacArthur left many permanent marks on West Point and set a standard for future innovators, some within the Academic Board, to emulate.

Sources:

Stephen E. Ambrose, *Duty, Honor, Country: A History of West Point* (Baltimore, MD: Johns Hopkins Press, 1966).
William A. Ganoe, *MacArthur Close-Up* (New York: Vantage Press, 1962).
William E. Simons, *Liberal Education in the Service Academies* (New York: Bureau of Publications, Teachers College, Columbia University, 1965).

MAHAN, ALFRED T. Captain Alfred Thayer Mahan, U.S. Navy (born 1840, died 1914), graduate of the U.S. Naval Academy and professor at the Naval War College, was a world-famous author of books and articles on sea power.

Alfred Thayer Mahan was the son of Dennis Hart Mahan,* a professor of military and civil engineering and of the science of war at the United States Military Academy,* and was raised at West Point.* In 1856, the younger Mahan entered the United States Naval Academy* as a cadet, graduating second in his class in 1859. Mahan served at sea during the Civil War on the Union side but saw virtually no action. From 1865 to 1885, his career involved routine assignments to ships and shore establishments. In 1885, Mahan was granted leave to prepare lectures for his forthcoming duty as a professor at the newly founded Naval War College* at Newport, Rhode Island.* Mahan joined the school as a faculty member and became its president in 1886. Mahan's fame as an author was established in 1890 with publication of *The Influence of Sea Power upon History, 1660–1783.* In 1893, he left the Naval War College with the rank of captain to command a cruiser. Mahan retired from active duty in 1896 in order to devote all his attention to writing about history and current political and military events, which occupied him until his death.

Mahan was intelligent and literary, and his father was a distinguished pedagogue, circumstances that favored an interest in education. The younger Mahan's specific views on the importance of command in war, the role of military education in promoting improved command, and the function of historical study in a properly constituted curriculum, strongly resembled those of his father, who no doubt influenced his outlook. The younger man's first publication was an essay entitled "Naval Education for Officers and Men," which won third prize in a contest at the Naval Academy while Mahan headed the academy's Ordnance Department. In this piece, published in 1879 in the *United States Naval Institute Proceedings,** Mahan argued that effective executive command depended upon the possession of the moral strength to assert judgment in the face of great uncertainty and danger. The development of character that embodied moral strength, he maintained, was best served by courses in the liberal arts. The materialism that Mahan believed was a property of scientific endeavor, on the other hand, was criticized as detrimental to the encouragement of the idealism necessary for war leadership. He thus called for a shift in emphasis for the Naval Academy curriculum toward literature, tactics, and languages.

Mahan's first book, *The Gulf and Inland Waters*, an account of naval operations in the Civil War, was published in 1882. One of the major themes of this work was the nature of executive command in war. Mahan criticized failures of leadership that were attributable to poor discipline, lack of initiative, and inadequate forethought. He praised willingness to assume responsibility, and action based upon a carefully calculated risk combined with bold spirit. In an address to the War College in 1888, he maintained that the study of past warfare was capable of inspiring correct executive conduct and advocated separating study of the art of war from that of science and technology arguing that the latter undermined the development of martial spirit.

Mahan's work at the Naval War College resulted in a grand strategic conception of sea power as an important force in international politics past, present, and future and largely defined his work in his own time and afterwards. Through the analytically rigorous study of naval operations during the age of sail, however, this work was also intended to provide an approach to teaching the art of naval command. These two issues were the major themes of *The Influence of Sea Power upon History, 1660–1783*, and its three two-volume sequels: *The Influence of Sea Power upon the French Revolution and Empire, 1792–1812* (1892); *The Life of Nelson: The Embodiment of the Sea Power of Great Britain* (1897); and *Sea Power in Its Relations to the War of 1812* (1905). A pedagogy of command in war that would enhance naval professionalism was also the main subject of his later *Naval Strategy* (1911) and discussed in a number of his essays.

Mahan recognized that contingency in war precluded mechanistic prescription as the basis of operational decision making. He also knew that in war, the difficulties posed by incompleteness of information would be compounded by fear of dire consequences in the event of decision-making error. The faculty of judgment, therefore, had to be paired with will in order to overcome timidity. The synthesis of judgment and will was intelligent emotion—or, in a word, intuition. When the degrees of uncertainty and danger were extremely high, as they were likely to be during a battle or campaign, extraordinary intuition was required to promote rapid and decisive command. Such intuition about matters naval was optimally the product of war experience. Mahan believed that in peacetime, the ability to improve intuition from war experience could be developed by education based upon the study of history.

Mahan's concern with the enhancement of the ability to learn, as opposed to the formulation of doctrine, meant that theory was an auxilliary—it served as a means rather than an end. As Mahan read history in preparation for lecturing at the Naval War College, he was particularly impressed by the works of Antoine Henri Jomini, from whom he adopted the conception of the decisive battle, particular principles of strategy such as "concentration of force," and the model of presenting analysis in narrative form accompanied by critical commentary. But while Mahan posited the existence of immutable principles of strategy, these were few, platitudinous, and drawn from the works of others. What really mattered to him was not the principles as such, but their practical application. Application could only be described through the examination of many case studies, with principles used as a point of departure or guide. The main analytical subjects of these narratives were the difficulties posed by contingency and the insufficiency of information; also the rational and emotional instruments of command that were required, if not to overcome them, to mitigate their negative effects.

In sum, Mahan regarded war as a complex and contingent phenomenon whose nature could not be encompassed by any system of theory. He believed that the purpose of instruction about decision making was to produce a mind-set that was better prepared to learn from actual operational experience and that the resulting synthesis of peacetime preparation and wartime learning would be an invaluable and possibly decisively important asset. Mahan regarded the engagement with a portion of practical reality to be more important than construction of a system necessarily requiring a simplification that compromised the veracious representation of war operations. The incompleteness of his writing from a theoretical standpoint can thus be seen as inherent, not an oversight. The common identification of Mahan with the mechanistic and theoretically comprehensive approach of Jomini is thus mistaken. Mahan's thinking much more closely resembled that of Carl von Clausewitz,* whose work, however, was probably unknown to Mahan until the mid-1890s, and his influence, therefore, actually negligible.

The critical and popular success of Mahan's writing legitimized the study of naval history by naval officers. Although Mahan's own work was widely regarded as obsolete for instructional purposes by the Second World War, the analysis of past naval operations as an important part of naval officer education continues to this day. The existence and survival of nontechnical study for naval professionals have proved so far to be Mahan's most important contribution to military education. The substance of his approach to the pedagogy of command prompts useful discussion of a subject that rightfully still engages the strong interest of military leaders in the United States and elsewhere.

Sources:

W. D. Puleston, *Mahan: The Life and Work of Captain Alfred Thayer Mahan* (New Haven, CT: Yale University Press, 1939).

Robert Seager II, *Alfred Thayer Mahan: The Man and His Letters* (Annapolis, MD: Naval Institute Press, 1977).

Jon Tetsuro Sumida, *Inventing Grand Strategy and Teaching Command: The Classic Works of Alfred Thayer Mahan Reconsidered* (Washington, DC: Woodrow Wilson Center Press/Johns Hopkins University Press, 1997).

Jon T. Sumida

MAHAN, DENNIS H. Dennis Hart Mahan (born 1802, died 1871), graduate of U.S. Military Academy, later its distinguished professor of engineering and the science of war, and father of Alfred Thayer Mahan.

Dennis Hart Mahan entered the U.S. Military Academy* in 1820. He emerged as the top student in his class by the end of his first year, a position he maintained through graduation in 1824. Mahan's excellence in mathematics in particular resulted in his appointment as acting assistant professor in mathematics in November 1821, though still a second-year cadet. In the fall of 1824, after a short term in the Corps of Engineers, he returned to West Point* to take up the position of Assistant Professor of Mathematics. In August 1825, he became the principal assistant professor in engineering. In the summer of 1826, Mahan left the academy for France to study European military engineering. Several extensions of his leave enabled him to pursue his studies through the spring of 1830. In October 1830, Mahan was appointed acting Professor of Engineering. In January 1832, he became Professor of Military and Civil Engineering, and of the Science of War and, in 1838, became Dean of the Faculty, positions he held until his death.

Dennis Hart Mahan was intelligent, a hard worker, and religious, qualities that attracted the favor of superiors, such as Sylvanus Thayer,* West Point's dynamic superintendent, and that explain his rapid professional advance. His great success and formidable reputation in the classroom are explained by several factors: Mahan's knowledge of military engineering was second to none; his rigorous and systematic intellect enabled him to convey this knowledge clearly in oral exposition and in written texts; and he possessed both the will and capacity to subject students to searching examination in pursuit of both intellectual excellence and moral virtue. He believed that effective practice was a matter of imaginative application of theory, not the inflexible following of rules. Mahan was convinced that mathematics and engineering should be the basis of military education because they required mental discipline as well as being directly applicable to the attack or defense of fortifications. He held as an article of faith that the study of a few subjects thoroughly was preferable to superficial surveys of a wide range of material.

In addition to courses in civil and military engineering, Mahan was responsible for the course in the science of war. He had a thorough command of the military historical and theoretical literature, argued that the science of war did not receive enough attention in the curriculum, and in particular made frequent recommendations that more time should be devoted to instruction in history. Mahan was opposed, however, to military history taught as chronology and, in 1844, reversed his 1838 support of the addition of history to the formal teaching program after witnessing its degeneration into an exercise in rote memorization. As an alternative, Mahan played a leading role in the formation and deliberations of the Napoleon Club, a group of officers who met regularly during the 1850s to discuss papers on the campaigns of Frederick the Great and Napoleon researched and written by members. Participants in this activity included many who were to become generals during the Civil War.

Mahan recognized that West Point could not provide a complete military education, at best only a sound foundation for further learning—basic military technique, an understanding and acceptance of the value of scientific logic, and an appetite for the further study of military history. In partial support of these goals, he wrote books: In addition to a highly regarded textbook of civil engineering, these included *A Complete Treatise on Field Fortification with the General Outlines of the Principles Regulating the Arrangement, the Attack, and the Defence of Permanent Works* (1836); *Summary of the Course of Permanent Fortification and of the Attack and Defense of Permanent Works, for the Use of the Cadets of the U.S. Military Academy* (1850); and *Advanced-Guard, Out-Post, and Detachment Service of Troops with the Essential Principles of Strategy and Grand Tactics for the Use of Officers of the Militia and Volunteers* (1863). While largely technical, Mahan repeatedly noted in these works that war was highly contingent and that decision-making thus could not be based upon the following of rules. In his appreciation of the artistic character of the military executive function, Mahan resembled Carl von Clausewitz* rather than Antoine-Henri Jomini, which would explain his preference for military history over military theory, an attitude that grew stronger over the course of his teaching career.

Sources:

Thomas E. Griess, "Dennis Hart Mahan: West Point Professor and Advocate of Military Professionalism, 1830–1871," unpublished Ph.D. dissertation, Duke University, 1969.

W. D. Puleston, *Mahan: The Life and Work of Captain Alfred Thayer Mahan* (New Haven, CT: Yale University Press, 1939).

Jon Tetsuro Sumida, *Inventing Grand Strategy and Teaching Command: The Classic Works of Alfred Thayer Mahan Reconsidered* (Washington, DC: Woodrow Wilson Center Press/Johns Hopkins University Press, 1997).

Jon T. Sumida

MARINE CORPS COMMAND AND STAFF COLLEGE. Since 1920, an institution at Quantico, Virginia, offering a professional military education course of one academic year in length to selected field grade officers primarily of the Marine Corps. Founded in 1920 as the Field Officers Course of the Marine Corps Schools, the college assumed its current name in 1964; between 1920 and 1990, it was the senior Marine Corps PME school.

The college traces its origins to the Marine Officers Infantry School. Founded on January 12, 1920, and disestablished on August 31, 1920, its sole class was comprised of senior company grade officers and field grade officers. The Field Officers Course was formed on September 1, 1920, with the establishment of the Marine Corps Schools on that date, and it welcomed its first students for a one-year course of study in October of that year. From 1934–36, the course was renamed the "second year class" and between 1936 and 1941 the "senior course." From 1934, the staff organization was structured and patterned after that of the Fleet Marine Force, formed in 1933: i.e., personnel, intelligence, operations, and logistics. The curriculum then focused on what the Fleet Marine Force deemed would be its primary mission: amphibious warfare—with the amphibious assault being emphasized in lieu of defense of an advanced naval base or raid, demonstration, and withdrawal. By 1941, "small wars" instruction had dwindled to only three days in the academic year.

The initial courses of instruction in 1920s were modeled after those of the U.S. Army schools at Forts Benning and Leavenworth,* both with an infantry orientation in support of continental ground campaigns. By the 1930–31 academic year, however, the students were receiving 216 hours of instruction in "landing operations." By then, a struggle was occurring for the "heart and soul" of the Marine Corps. Much of this was waged within its educational system at Quantico*—specifically within the Field Officers Course. This focused on the development of an *offensive* amphibious mission for the Marine Corps, leading to the seizure, not just the defense, of advanced naval bases as part of a naval campaign.

This ferment led to the writing of the "Tentative Manual for Landing Operations" during the 1933–34 academic year and a complete curriculum shift toward amphibious operations. Associated with this process, in the late 1920s and early 1930s, a close relationship developed between the Marine Corps Schools (primarily the course for field officers) and the Naval War College.* The latter annually provided the Marine Corps Schools with an advanced base (i.e., amphibious warfare) problem, usually in the Central and Western Pacific, for which the students and staff at Quantico developed a solution. This was then presented at the Naval War College, the Department of the Navy, and the Marine Barracks, Quantico.

Class size was small between 1920 and 1941, ranging from 13 to 29 in number and from captain to brigadier general in rank; however, the students were normally senior captains or majors. The first U.S. Army student appeared in the 1921–22 academic year, and the initial U.S. Navy officer in 1928–29. By 1941, 431 officers had attended: Marine Corps—385; Navy—40; Army—6. Almost all marine regimental commanders early in World War II and brigade, division, and amphibious corps commanders in that conflict were graduates of this course and/or served on its faculty.

World War II forced an expanding Marine Corps to prioritize several competing needs. The immediate ones were to screen officer candidates and train company grade officers. Hence, in January 1941, the senior course suspended classes, and its staff and students assumed other duties associated with these tasks. In 1943, with continued expansion, the need for trained commanders and staff officers at battalion, regimental, and division levels became apparent. Hence, the Command and Staff Course, in 1944 renamed the Command and Staff School, was founded. Its twelve-week, tactically focused curriculum covered staff functioning, general tactics, offensive combat, defensive combat, special operations, defense of an advanced naval base, and amphibious operations. To keep current, members of the faculty observed amphibious operations in the Pacific. With its students primarily Marine captains and majors, 523 officers had completed this course by the end of the war. By the end of the war students from six allied countries also had graduated: Australia, Canada, France, New Zealand, The Netherlands, and the United Kingdom. This practice was resumed following the war as well.

With the reestablishment of the three-tiered professional military education system in the autumn of 1946, the first postwar course for field grade officers convened. It was now called the Senior School, the name it retained until 1964. The course of study ran from August to June, and the focus of the curriculum remained amphibious operations. However, instruction reflected further changes in warfare, especially due to the advent of nuclear weapons and the use of helicopters in ship-to-shore movement. In the late 1940s and early 1950s, the course culminated in a final exercise called Operation Packard. This combined an amphibious planning exercise in Quantico, with the students (along with those of the Junior School) then embarking aboard amphibious vessels and sailing to Camp Lejeune, North Carolina, then moving ashore and implementing their plans in an exercise supported by the 2nd Marine Division.

From the 1960s to the 1980s, the amphibious role of the Marine Corps remained central to the curriculum. However, the college, in 1964 now officially named the Command and Staff College, took cognizance of other events in a rapidly changing world. Counter-insurgency and computer instruction became part of the course of study. Then, in the 1982–83 academic year, further reforms occurred. These included the return of military history to the core curriculum, adding an execution phase to all operational problems, and additional instruction in ground combat, aviation, and combat service support areas for officers with those respective specialties.

By the 1989–90 academic year, further changes had occurred in the curriculum, the most significant since the 1930s. It now rests on four foundations: military history and theory, operational techniques, operational and tactical doctrine, and the integration of joint professional military education throughout the course of instruction. The courses now include Theory and Nature of War,

Strategic Level of War, Operational Level of War, and Warfighting from the Sea, with a primary focus on amphibious and expeditionary operations (to include military operations other than war) all taught within a joint and multinational orientation. As its name implies, command is also an inherent part of the curriculum; an art of command course is taught throughout the academic year.

The Marine Corps Command and Staff College was founded for Marine Corps officers, but there has always been strong sister service and international presence. In the 1990s, in a class of approximately 200 students, there typically will be 24 U.S. Navy, 12 U.S. Army, 12 U.S. Air Force, and 24 international officers, with an occasional U.S. Coast Guard and a small but increasing civilian presence; the rest of the student body is composed of marines. These students are then divided into 12 permanent conference groups, each led by a military-civilian faculty team. With a focus on peer interaction in a seminar mode (the educational philosophy since 1920), every conference group will have at least four sister service, two international, and eleven or twelve Marine officers. Students generally are of the grade of major/lieutenant commander. The faculty has also increased in size. From 10 officers as instructors, with a nonteaching staff of five, as recently as 1979, the college's staff numbered over 60 by the late 1990s; this figure includes sister service and international officers and civilians with Ph.D.s in their respective fields of study.

The evolutionary process continues. With the 1990–91 academic year, two new schools were established: A second-year course, the School of Advanced Warfighting,* and a senior-level school, the Marine Corps War College.* The latter became a separate school in 1992, thus adding a fourth tier to the Marine Corps professional military education* system. Then the college was authorized by Congress and the Department of Education to confer a graduate degree, the Master of Military Studies (MMS), the first awarded in 1994. Not all graduates receive this, for an officer must apply for admission, be accepted into the program, and do additional work beyond that required in the core curriculum. Graduation diplomas and the MMS degree for those who complete the requirements are conferred at graduation each June.

Sources:

Donald F. Bittner, "Creation of a P.M.E. Institution: The Field Officers Course, 1920–1941," 1945, unpublished manuscript in the Marine Corps University Archives, Quantico, Virginia.

Lt. Colonel Donald F. Bittner, USMCR, *Curriculum Evolution: Marine Corps Command and Staff College, 1920–1988* (Washington, DC: Marine Corps Historical Center, 1989).

1st Lt. Anthony Frances, USMCR, "History of the Marine Corps Schools," 1945, unpublished manuscript in the Archives Branch, Marine Corps Research Center, Quantico, Virginia.

Lt. General Victor Krulak, USMC (Ret.), *Fight to Fight: An Inside View of the U.S. Marine Corps* (Annapolis, MD: Naval Institute Press, 1984).

Donald F. Bittner

MARINE CORPS PROFESSIONAL MILITARY EDUCATION. A service system of career education for U.S. Marines, both officers and enlisted, encompassing both resident and nonresident programs. It is progressively broadening in scope and is distinguished from On-the-Job Training (OJT) or Military Occupational Specialty (MOS) training. The first element of the system, the School of Application (now called the Basic School), was founded in 1891.

The establishment of a complete system for officers occurred in September 1920, with the formation of the Marine Corps Schools at the Marine Barracks, Quantico, Virginia.* This formalized on a permanent basis the temporary officer schools of World War I. In concept, the Corps created a three-tiered system of professional military education: The Basic School* for newly commissioned second lieutenants; a company officers course for senior 1st lieutenants and captains; and a field officers course for senior captains to colonels. Although the names, curriculum focus, and grades of students have changed in the ensuing decades, this system has remained intact into the contemporary era. However, during World War II the company and field grade officers' courses were suspended. After the Second World War, the three-tiered structure for career officers was reestablished, with the schools eventually titled under their current names: The Basic School, the Amphibious Warfare School,* and the Command and Staff College.* In the post–World War II era, responsibility for PME passed to a renamed subordinate organization at Quantico, the Education Center. In 1989, this organization was renamed the Marine Corps University.

This three-tiered system remained intact from 1920 to 1989. Then two new schools were established in 1990: the School of Advanced Warfighting* and the Marine Corps War College.* Both initially were within the Command and Staff College, but in 1992 the Marine Corps War College became an independent institution, with its director reporting to the president, Marine Corps University. Thus, since 1990, the Marine Corps has had a four-tiered professional military education system. Excluding Officers Candidates School (called OCS), which screens candidates for a commission entering the Corps through various accession programs, the schools are: The Basic School for newly commissioned second lieutenants; the Amphibious Warfare School for captains; the Command and Staff College, an intermediate-level college for majors; and the Marine Corps War College, a top-level college for lieutenant colonels. In addition, another school is indirectly part of this system. The Command and Control Systems School (formerly titled Communications Officers School) has an advanced course for captains already in the communications field or transferring to it, which for them is the career equivalent of Amphibious Warfare School;* this school also has a basic communications officer's course for lieutenants who will have that MOS.

The schools of the Marine Corps professional military education are now guided in curriculum development by three orders: MCO 1553.1, Marine Corps Training and Education System; MCO 1553.2, Management for Marine Corps

Formal Schools and Training Centers; and MCOP1553.4, Marine Corps Professional Military Education. These provide service guidance for each school. The objectives and curriculum of each focus on both the military skills needed by the Marine Corps officer commensurate with his or her grade and the military specialty by law associated with the Corps, amphibious warfare. For joint curriculum matters, all professional military education schools receive joint guidance on curriculum matters; this is provided in Chairman Joints Chiefs of Staff Instruction 1800.01. However, only the Command and Staff College and Marine Corps War College are evaluated by an outside team reporting to the Joint Chiefs of Staff: The Process for Accreditation of Joint Education (PAJE) visit. This occurs every five years. The resident curriculum of each school (and nonresident program of the Command and Staff College) must pass evaluation on joint matters for the institution to be accredited, which in turn certifies its graduates for assignment to joint billets.

In theory, the Marine Corps would send all of its officers to the appropriate resident school at the appropriate time in their careers. In reality, other than The Basic School (and there have been exceptions here), this has proved to be an impossible goal. Also, officers generally would not receive duplicate schooling: Attendance at a sister service or foreign military school would count as having attended the equivalent Marine Corps school. Hence, the Marine Corps has recognized that its resident professional military education system was pyramidal, with fewer positions available in the resident schools above The Basic School in relation to the number of officers available to attend them.

To address the needs of those officers not attending the resident schools, the Corps established various nonresident programs that conceptually have paralleled the resident courses. Initially, in the 1930s, these were administered by the Correspondence School, which later became the Extension School; both were part of the Marine Corps Schools and Education Center. In 1979, this function was assumed by the Marine Corps Institute, based at the Marine Barracks, Washington, D.C. In May 1997, the Marine Corps University created the College of Continuing Education. This, in conjunction with the resident schools and the Marine Corps Institute, coordinates and administers the nonresident courses and students.

There is one last element to the professional military education system of the Marine Corps: that for enlisted marines. By previous tradition, although troops, noncommissioned officers, and staff noncommissioned officers received MOS training, the establishment of a career sequential professional education system occurred only recently. The Staff Noncommissioned Officers Academy was founded at Quantico in 1971, and by the 1980s a complete PME system had been established throughout the Marine Corps providing appropriate education for enlisted marines from the ranks of corporal/sergeant to sergeant major/master gunnery sergeant. This system is staffed and headed by staff noncommissioned officers, with the Staff Noncommissioned Officers Academy at Quantico having cognizance in curriculum matters over all the other academies in the Corps. Its director, a sergeant major, has co-equal status with the directors and commanding officers of the other schools within the Marine Corps University.

Sources:

Lt. Colonel Donald F. Bittner, USMCR, *Curriculum Evolution: The Marine Corps Command and Staff College, 1920–1988* (Washington, DC: Marine Corps Historical Center, 1989).

Colonel Kenneth Clifford, USMCR, *Progress and Purpose: A Development History of the United States Marine Corps* (Washington, DC: Marine Corps Historical Center, 1974).

1st Lieutenant Anthony Frances, USMCR, "History of the Marine Corps Schools," 1945, unpublished manuscript retained at the Archives Branch, Marine Corps Research Center, Quantico, VA.

Allan R. Millett, *Semper Fidelis: The History of the United States Marine Corps* (New York: Macmillan, 1993).

Donald F. Bittner

MARINE CORPS WAR COLLEGE. Since 1990, the senior Marine Corps professional military education school, providing PME for selected lieutenant colonels and commanders of the Armed Forces of the United States.

The Marine Corps War College, (MCWAR) has become the fourth tier in the corps's professional military education* system, which from 1920 to 1989 consisted of only three. MCWAR's director is a colonel reporting directly to the president of the Marine Corps University, a component organization of the Marine Corps Combat Development Command, Quantico, Virginia.* Its faculty is composed of Marine Corps and sister service officers, as well as civilian academics. The mission of the Marine Corps War College is to educate its officer students in the nature of, preparation for, and conduct of war. Its graduates will be prepared to assume senior positions of increasingly complex responsibility associated with the application of maritime expeditionary warfare, Marine Air-Ground Task Force operations, joint and combined warfare concepts, and other elements of national power in support of national military strategy, and national security strategy.

The students are of the grade of lieutenant colonel and commander. They are selected by formal boards of each of the four services, and the graduates receive top-level school (i.e., war college) certification. A generic class is generally composed as follows: USMC—6; USN—2; USA—2; USAF—2. There are no international officers enrolled in MCWAR. After graduation, by Marine Corps general policy (there are exceptions on a case-by-case basis), Marine officers will join the faculty of the Marine Corps Command and Staff College* for a follow-on two-year tour; sister service graduates, on an every-other-year planning sequence, also generally join the faculty of the Command and Staff

College. All of this emphasizes the truly joint aspect of the Marine Corps professional military education system, which is reflected in curriculum matters, students, and faculty.

The method of instruction at MCWAR is that of the case study within a seminar mode. The heart of the curriculum is reading, research, analysis, writing, and the seminar dialogue. As appropriate, historical and contemporary site visits, coupled with internships within U.S. government organizations, are also used. Historical studies, contemporary national security affairs, and operational problems compose the curriculum; the course is divided into three areas: war, policy, and strategy; Marine air-ground task force operations; and national security and joint warfare. The academic year is approximately ten months in length.

Donald F. Bittner

MAURY, MATTHEW F. Matthew Fontaine Maury (born 1806, died 1873), naval officer, world-renowned oceanographer, and man of letters who brought the methods of science to the art of navigation, charted the waters of the planet's seaways, and was an early advocate of broad education for naval officers.

Born near Fredericksburg, Virginia, January 14, 1806, Matthew Fontaine Maury entered the U.S. Navy as a midshipman in 1825. His naval service commenced on board the frigate *Brandywine* at the time she was ordered to convey our national guest, General Lafayette, back to France and then to cruise in the Mediterranean. Two years later Maury joined the sloop-of-war *Vincennes* aboard which he was destined to circumnavigate the globe. . . .

It was during this long and useful cruise—an absence of four years—that young Maury arranged the material for his valuable work [*New Theoretical and Practical Treatise on Navigation* (1836)], "a volume of the greatest usefulness to the young men of our Navy and of the highest order of merit," wrote an officer of our Navy in 1841. . . .

In June 1836 Maury was commissioned a lieutenant in the U.S. Navy, [*sic*] in September of the following year he was appointed "Astronomer" for the Exploring Expedition to the South Seas; and in 1839 he was selected as assistant to the "Hydrographer" in carrying on the work of examining and surveying Southern harbors with the view of establishing a Navy yard in the South.

It was while returning from a month of leave to visit his family in the fall of 1839 that Matthew Fontaine Maury's leg was broken in a stagecoach accident, and he was relieved temporarily from active duty. During his enforced leisure he turned to the pen to expound the needs of the Navy and in a series of articles published in the *Southern Literary Messenger* under the *nom de plume* Harry Bluff, USN, he offered his "Scraps from the Lucky Bag."

"Every man-of-war, you know, has her lucky *bag* containing a little of everything, and something belonging to every body . . . ," wrote Maury in 1840. "The bag which I am about to overhaul, has been open for fifteen to twenty years. . . .

"Nearly a half century gone by, Congress passed an act for the building of six small frigates; and without any settled policy or fixed principles as to a Navy, the government upon the most simple and economical plan, organized a mere handful of officers for those ships. . . .

"Times have changed since then. The maintenance of a Navy is no longer a matter of doubtful expediency. . . . But many of its laws are wrong—many of the principles engrafted upon it, have, by the changes of time, become defective. Experience points out many amendments and improvements which should be made; and necessity *calls loudly* for reorganization." . . .

"Harry Bluff" wrote at length and the arguments which he employed were forcible and convincing. He clearly revealed that the immediate and pressing demands of American commerce, the interest of American citizens, and the dignity and honor of the American nation, all required that a larger naval force than was then (1840) maintained, [*sic*] should be kept in commission.

In another offering under the caption "Scraps from the Lucky Bag," Maury raised the question as to whether, for the true interests of the service, the officers should be adept and proficient in *one particular* branch of science that had a bearing on their profession—[*sic*] or whether each officer should understand something of all—a man of real solid parts, well grounded in mathematics and sufficiently indoctrinated in the elements and principles of the other branches of science to . . . enable him to put into practice, whenever the exigencies of the service should require it of him, the principles of any other branch of science which may have formed a part of his studies. . . . Examples of occasions that he knew vividly emphasized his recommendation that the foundation of a school for the Navy officer be on the most substantial basis—broad, solid and comprehensive—not too deep, lest the means defeat the end. . . .

For a long time nobody knew who the author of "Scraps from the Lucky Bag" was and the criticisms of the Navy, though severe, were so wisely constructive that naval officers welcomed them and set about embodying them in a new and better organization. Out of the reforms inaugurated there can be little doubt that the Naval Academy,* founded at Annapolis* in 1845, is the product of the suggestions made by Maury in his articles. At first, he had proposed merely a school-ship for the instruction of midshipmen but after his articles were so well received he let it be known that he would welcome the establishment of a naval school ashore, a parallel to the Army's Military Academy* at West Point.*

Matthew Fontaine Maury was sent to Washington in 1842 and placed in charge of the Depot of Charts and Instruments which some years later became officially known as the United States Naval Observatory and Hydrographical Office. He was destined to make this office or bureau the observed of all observatories, and he was to prove to all scientists and to the masters of vessels at sea that the ocean is as law-abiding as the land. . . .

The effect on navigation was immediate and dramatic. From the thousands of [ships'] logbooks returned to him, Maury studied, arranged, and charted the data; and he soon began to issue his "Wind and Current Charts and Sailing Directions," pointing out to mariners the natural paths of sea travel. . . . His research in oceanography led him to publish the first depth-map of the North Atlantic and to point out the pathway for the laying of the first Atlantic telegraph cable in 1858. . . .

Maury was 55 years of age when in 1861 a tragic call sounded throughout the country—the War Between the States. All was changed and, like Robert E. Lee and other loyal Virginians, he resigned his commission in the Federal Service and offered his sword to his beloved State. . . . Later he was sent on a diplomatic mission to England and he did not return to his native land until 1868. In that year he declined the directorship of the French Imperial Observatory and accepted the call to head the department of physics at the Virginia Military Institute* at Lexington, preferring to give himself to the service of his impoverished State.[4]

MAXWELL AIR FORCE BASE. *See* AIR UNIVERSITY.

McDERMOTT, ROBERT F. Robert Francis McDermott (born 1920), attended Norwich University, graduate of the U.S. Military Academy, MBA, Harvard University, was Dean of Faculty of the U.S. Air Force Academy during its formative years where he pioneered curriculum developments that were a marked change from American service academy tradition.

Robert F. McDermott was born in Boston in 1920 and attended the Boston Latin School. After two years at Norwich University he entered the U.S. Military Academy* at West Point, New York.* Upon graduation, in 1943, he was commissioned in what at the time was the U.S. Army Air Corps. Following completion of pilot training, McDermott flew a number of combat missions in Europe during the later stages of World War II.

Subsequent assignments in the postwar period included duty as a faculty member in the social sciences department of the U.S. Military Academy and then duty as a member of the faculty as Professor of Economics and Vice Dean at the brand new U.S. Air Force Academy,* established by act of Congress in 1954. He became Dean of Faculty at the same institution in 1956, was promoted to brigadier general in 1959, and served as Dean until 1968, when he retired to become head of the United Services Automobile Association, an automobile insurance company for officers of the uniformed services.

McDermott served the Air Force Academy in a variety of roles. In the school's first years, acting as faculty secretary, he and the officer who would become the academy's second superintendent, Lt. General James E. Briggs, met frequently with officials of the North Central Association of Colleges and Secondary Schools regarding the essential steps required for the academy before it could receive that agency's full accreditation. Later, as Dean, he reorganized the faculty to provide each major subject matter area its own department with direct representation on a faculty council with authority to approve all curricular decisions, thus assuring that the faculty's five representatives on the Academy Board would present a "united front" regarding curricular matters. McDermott also played a major role in helping to resolve the academy's later crisis resulting from flagrant cheating on major examinations and related violations of the cadet honor code.

As Dean of the new Air Force Academy, McDermott soon brought important changes to the type of curriculum that had become traditional among service academies in the United States. While the academic programs at the older academies had altered gradually throughout the years, they had remained fairly rigid,

[4]Excerpted, with permission, from Ruby R. Duval, "Matthew Fontaine Maury—Man of Genius," *Shipmate*, February 1959, Copyright 1959 by the United States Naval Academy Alumni Association. (Asterisks added.)

and all cadets, regardless of their academic backgrounds or abilities, were required to pursue a common program. In explaining his concept of academic program enrichment, McDermott often cited the analogy with varsity athletics in which especially talented students were encouraged to move up to a more challenging level of performance.

Under McDermott, academic enrichment began at the Air Force Academy with course offerings that were primarily meant to be taken on an overload basis; they were disparate in content, according to the preferences of individual academic departments. In the autumn of 1957, it was determined to channel elements of this program into cohesive subject areas with useful goals in terms of the academy's mission. At first, two such areas of the Enrichment Program were selected: the engineering area, totaling 17 credit hours, leading to a "major in missile technology"; and the social sciences area, also totaling 17 credit hours, leading to a "major in public affairs." It was felt that cadets who completed either of these programs would benefit from obvious self-improvement but would also be more fully prepared for graduate study in fields appropriate to Air Force career specialties.

These two majors were by no means the exclusive feature of the Enrichment Program, however. A variety of other elective courses were offered in response to specific cadet interest, and any cadet was permitted to take any course or combination of courses provided his work in the required academic program was not impaired. In addition to the method of taking these courses as an overload, a cadet might participate in the Enrichment Program in two other ways: (1) accelerated coverage of required courses in less than assigned class time followed by advanced material in the same field or other courses; and (2) validation of required courses by demonstrating proficiency in them, through examinations, and taking enrichment courses in their place.

Under McDermott's guidance, the Enrichment Program had thus become a significant part of the curriculum during the first two years of the Air Force Academy's operation. Further, its general objectives influenced development of new curriculum patterns at the other service academies as well, notably at West Point and Annapolis.* By the time the Air Force Academy came up for accreditation by the North Central Association in 1958 (and in 1959 was accredited before its first class graduated), almost half of its cadets were participating in the Enrichment Program to some degree. Ultimately, additional majors were added.

Throughout his tenure as Dean of Faculty at the Air Force Academy, General McDermott enthusiastically promoted the expansion of the Enrichment Program, which developed ultimately into planned provisions for the award of master's degrees in selected areas. However, opposition from the other service academies, made more significant by a timely suggestion from then-President Dwight Eisenhower that the proposal for graduate coursework be evaluated "with a view to taking uniform action among all three [academies] . . . ," effectively squelched the Air Force's initiative.

Still, General McDermott's leadership in developing the Enrichment Program brought about significant changes in the evolution of professional military education at the service academy level, and it played an important part in the preparation of career officers for service in the nuclear age. The advent of ICBMs and missiles of a shorter range, the challenges of the cold war and its aftermath, and the changes brought about in warfare by jet propulsion and almost-instant communication substantially altered the professional functions of a military officer. In preparing for these changes, enriched service academy curricula, in the development of which General McDermott had so vital a part, became a major component in the growth of modern professional military education.

Sources:

John P. Lovell, *Neither Athens Nor Sparta?: The American Service Academies in Transition* (Bloomington: Indiana University Press, 1979).

———. "The USAF Academy Academic Program," *Air University Review* 20, no. 1 (November/December 1968).

Robert F. McDermott, "Educating Officers in the Twentieth Century: A Fresh Start," *Assembly* (November/December 1996).

Harold L. Hitchens

MILITARY ACADEMY (VOROSHILOV) OF THE GENERAL STAFF.

Since 1936, the premier Soviet (Russian) military-educational institution responsible for educating and training the Soviet Army's senior command cadre and for solving the military scientific problems of contemporary and future war at the operational-strategic (army-*front* [army group]) level.

The current General Staff Academy is the lineal descendent of the tsarist Nikolaev Academy of the General Staff, which in December 1918 the new Bolshevik government renamed the Workers and Peasants Red Army (RKKA) Academy of the General Staff. During the Civil War and Allied Intervention in Russia, the RKKA Academy trained the senior leadership of the fledgling Red Army. After war's end, however, disastrous economic conditions in the new Soviet state required a sharp reduction in the Red Army's size. This, plus a critical shortage of ideologically pure midlevel army command cadre, prompted a change in the academy's focus and name.

Consequently, in August 1921 the Soviets converted the Academy of the General Staff into the Military Academy of the RKKA and assigned the new academy the responsibility for tactical training and preparing midlevel officers for the Red Army. In 1925 the RKKA Academy was formally renamed the Frunze Academy.* Thus, between 1925 and 1936, no General Staff academy existed. However, to fill the vacuum in the preparation of senior command cadre, the Soviet government created several separate "higher academy courses," including in particular, the Course for the Perfection of Senior Officers (KUVNAS), many of whom were associated with or taught at the Frunze

Academy. In 1931 the Frunze Academy established an operational faculty to help fill the void.

Despite these stopgap measures, by the mid-1930s, it was clear that the growing Soviet military establishment and worsening international security situation required formation of a new academy to prepare a larger number of senior officers for higher command at *front* level and above. This was particularly true since the Soviets created a new General Staff in 1935 and clearly required an academy to educate General Staff officers. Consequently, on April 2, 1936, the government created a new Academy of the General Staff and assigned the pre-eminent military theorist, B. M. Shaposhnikov, as its first chief. The academy's first class, which began its studies in November 1936, also became its most notorious class. During the ensuing year, about half of the 137-man class was purged during Joseph Stalin's bloodletting in the military well before the men completed their 18-month course. Many others graduated early to fill vacancies produced by the purges. The survivors, however, would earn everlasting fame and establish a high reputation for the new academy. Two graduates (A. M. Vasilevsky and A. I. Antonov) would become chiefs of the General Staff, four would command *fronts*, eleven would become *front* chiefs of staff, and at least eight would become commanders at the army level.

Despite the purges, the Academy of the General Staff continued its work and during World War II prepared senior officers in shortened courses. During 1941 the academy was renamed for K. E. Voroshilov, and in 1958 it was assigned its current mission of "preparing cadres for working in the central apparatus of the Ministry of Defense and the General Staff, in large formations and all formations of all services of the armed forces." In addition to preparing high-level commanders and staff officers from the Soviet Union (Russia) and abroad, since 1945 the academy has played a key role in the formulation of military doctrine, military strategy, and operational techniques for both conventional and nuclear war. The academy's theoretical work on the nature of operational art was critical in the formulation of Western views concerning warfare at the operational level.

This senior Russian military educational institution has no equivalent in the West, although each former Warsaw Pact nation created academies modeled after it. The Voroshilov Academy's two-year course graduates 100–150 colonels and generals each year after a rigorous course of instruction at the operational-strategic level. Most graduates also prepare dissertations (generally classified) and earn doctoral degrees in military science. Since the collapse of the Soviet Union, the academy, other Russian educational institutions, and its counterparts in other former Warsaw Pact countries, with some justification, have been criticized for excessive rigidity and educational atrophy. All therefore are now amid varying degrees of reform.

Sources:

M. M. Kozlov, chief ed., *Akademiia general'nogo shtaba: Istoriia Voennoi ordena Lenina i Suvorova I stepeni akademii General'nogo shtaba Vooruzhennykh Sil SSSR imeni K. E. Voroshilova* [The Academy of the General Staff: The History of the Military Order of Lenin and Suvorov 1st degree Academy of the General Staff of the Armed Forces of the USSR named after K. E. Voroshilov] (Moscow: Voenizdat, 1987).

Harriet Fast Scott and William F. Scott, *The Armed Forces of the USSR* (London: Arms and Armour, 1984).

Harold Shukman, ed., *Stalin's Generals* (London: Weidenfeld & Nicolson, 1993).

David M. Glantz

MILITARY REVIEW. The official journal of the U.S. Army since 1965, although having been published under a variety of titles at the Army's Command and General Staff School, Fort Leavenworth, Kansas, for several decades.

Military Review and its predecessors have provided a forum for the open exchange of ideas on military affairs since 1922. The publication focuses on concepts, doctrine, and warfighting at the tactical and operational levels of war and supports the education, training, doctrine development, and integration missions of the Combined Arms Center and U.S. Army Command and General Staff College* (CGSC) at Fort Leavenworth, Kansas.* Today the professional journal of the U.S. Army, *Military Review*, has supported the U.S. Army over the years in its professional development and educational needs and has earned widespread respect as one of the world's preeminent professional journals for students of military affairs.

In February 1922, the General Services Schools (GSS), which later became the CGSC, published the first issue of a pamphlet, the *Instructor's Summary of Military Articles*. The GSS then held, as the CGSC does today, a key position in the overall Army plan for officer education. The *Summary* furnished the GSS instructors digests of selected articles from foreign military literature, reviews of new military books, summaries of new documents and magazines, and an index of selected magazine articles, documents, and books available for instructor use.

During the next twelve years the *Summary* went through three name changes—*Review of Current Military Writings* (1925), *Quarterly Review of Military Literature* (1932), and *Review of Military Literature* (1933). The content, however, remained essentially intact. A substantial portion of the books and articles were by European authors and publishers. Instructors in the GSS prepared the reviews and digests, while the reprinted articles came primarily from Europe.

In December 1933, a major milestone was reached when the *Review* published its first original article. This article, "Conduct of a Holding Attack," by Major J. Lawton Collins, was significant as a precedent in two areas. It initiated the very important function of serving as a forum for the exchange of ideas on contemporary topics and also opened the door for practitioners of the profession to use the journal as their microphone. Collins later distinguished himself as the VII Corps commander at Normandy, as chief of staff of the Army during Korea, and as ambassador to South Vietnam. Collins heads a long list of key leaders and famous persons who have contributed original writings to *Military Review*.

In the mid- and late 1930s, as world tensions increased, the writings and content of the *Review* quickly changed from those recounting experiences and lessons from the first World War to the anticipated applications of military force in future conflict. European authors continued to be prominent, but the frequency of articles written by American authors increased as well.

Between 1936 and 1939, three more name changes occurred, before it finally became *Military Review* in 1942 (*Command and General Staff School Quarterly Review of Military Literature, Command and General Staff School Quarterly*, and [in 1939] *Command and General Staff School Military Review*). In September 1938, the *Quarterly* published its revised mission statement, which advised, "The opinions expressed by authors are not necessarily official." This 1938 statement provided the first disclaimer, which in effect opened the door for more original and controversial articles, not only those in line with accepted Army positions or doctrine. In the years immediately preceding and throughout World War II, original articles became the dominant part of *Military Review*. By 1942, numerous articles were published in each issue using the wartime experiences as the foundation for discussions on current tactical and logistic concepts and applications.

These articles made *Military Review* the most valued source of thinking and discussion on the most important military issues. To better satisfy the demand from the military community, *Military Review* became a monthly publication in April 1943.

Military Review's efforts during World War II further exemplify its flexible character in adapting to the needs of the profession. By late 1944, *Military Review*'s respected position as an esteemed journal of military concepts prompted its consideration by the War Department as a tool in its cooperation and defense initiatives in the hemisphere. The concept of publishing *Military Review* in Spanish and Portuguese for distribution to Latin American nations was quickly endorsed by all senior military leaders and in October 1944 was approved by the State Department. In April 1945 the Latin American issues began publication and *Military Review* thus vastly expanded its reach and impact as a professional journal.

Following the Soviet Union's collapse in the late 1980s and the success of the U.S.-led coalition in Operation *Desert Storm*, significant changes have taken place within the U.S. Army. Most notable are the budget cuts that have reduced personnel, equipment, and support for soldiers. These cuts affected *Military Review* as they did every area of military life. Beginning with the publication of 1994's last issue. *Military Review* became a bimonthly journal. However, some losses can be made up by innovative new technologies. For example, the decision to go on-line in 1996 opened opportunities to reach an even wider audience using the Internet and World Wide Web. The web site now attracts over 250,000 visits annually.

The subtitle "The Professional Journal of the US Army" appeared on the journal's title page in January 1965. In 1999, *Military Review* continues professionally to serve the military profession with its balanced approach, maintaining considerable flexibility in direction and content. It is printed bimonthly in English and Spanish and quarterly in Portuguese. Distributed to readers in more than 100 countries, *Military Review* is widely quoted and reprinted in other publications throughout the world and is readily available for reference at most military and civilian university libraries and research agencies. In addition, *Military Review* is available on-line at: *<http://www-cgsc.army.mil/milrev/>*.

Military Review *staff*

MITCHELL, WILLIAM. William (Billy) Mitchell, Brig. General, Air Service, U.S. Army (born 1879, died 1936), a graduate of the U.S. Army's School of the Line (1908) and General Staff College (1909), is best known for his strenuous advocacy in the years after World War I on behalf of air power and the need for an independent air force. Mitchell influenced professional military education in two principal ways: (1) he was the leading figure in initiating the postwar system of professional education for air officers, including the founding in 1920 of the Air Service Field Officers' School, later renamed the Air Corps Tactical School, and (2) his visionary ideas on future warfare influenced doctrines developed at the school during the 1920s and '30s.

As an official observer in France in early 1917 and then as commander of America's air combat units under Chief of Air Service, AEF, Mitchell grasped the vast promise inherent in the air weapon. He was convinced that air units should be centrally controlled, not apportioned among commanders of ground units for their local needs. The concept was demonstrated in Mitchell's operational control of some 1,400 Allied aircraft during the September 1918 St. Mihiel campaign. To Mitchell, the air weapon could hugely affect the land campaign by (1) defeating the enemy's air power, (2) attacking military targets behind the enemy's lines, and (3) providing reconnaissance and close firepower support. Air forces also could conduct strategic campaigns deep in the enemy's interior against his vital centers, and Mitchell urged that America build a force of multi-engined bombers to join the Royal Air Force in such operations.

Mitchell returned to Washington in early 1919, the second-ranking officer of the staff of the Army's Air Service. As Chief, Operations and Training Group, Mitchell and his assistants turned to the day-to-day affairs of the Air Service, including the shaping of a system of professional education for officers of the air arm. Believing that the future air officer corps needed an educational structure parallel to but distinct from those of the Army and Navy, Mitchell listed his recommendations in a paper of April 11, 1919, envisioning two or more air staff colleges and, for more-senior students, an air war college. Soon afterwards, Mitchell and his staff sent recommendations to his superior, the Director, Air Service, that air staff colleges should be founded on the East and West Coasts and that schools be organized to train squadron-level officers. Students would obtain education "in the proper duties of command, in order that they might fill higher positions later on." Studies would be organized into administrative, tactical, and technical (engineering) areas. Soon afterwards, Mitchell's staff's planning documents were revised to show that an air academy was to be established, "to bear the same relation to the Air Service that West Point* formerly bore to the Army as a whole."

Although the air staff college and the undergraduate air academy ideas were not immediately realized, the 1919 planning yielded a memo to the War Department signed by Director, Air Service, requesting authorization to establish an Air Service field officers' school at Langley Field, Virginia. Authorization was given by War Department order of February 25, 1920. The idea was that classes would consist of officers having about two years of squadron service; some individuals, selected for a technical education, would go first to an engineering school, also established in 1920, at Dayton, Ohio. More-senior air officers would attend the Army's School of the Line and its General Staff College.* Mitchell wrote that after about five years, "a splendid body of aeronautical officers will be the result."

Instruction at the Field Officers' School began in fall 1920. Colonel Thomas DeW. Milling, who had been Mitchell's chief of staff in France, left Mitchell's staff in Washington to become the school's first officer-in-charge, and soon afterwards Lt. Colonel. W. C. Sherman, who had been Mitchell's chief of training in Washington, became Milling's deputy. Late in the first academic year, all instructors and students served in the First Provisional Air Brigade at Langley, led by Mitchell in conducting the test bombings of the captured German battleship *Ostfriesland* (1921). Participants later deemed that the experience, including their association with Mitchell, was invaluable.

The idea of an undergraduate academy continued to appeal to Mitchell. During a 1921–22 trip to Europe, Mitchell visited the young Royal Air Force College-Cranwell,* which he deemed "a splendid institution." Youths studied aerodynamics, maintenance, and flying. Mitchell liked the emphasis on sports, and he noted that each cadet was issued a motorcycle, which the cadet maintained and repaired, thereby learning about gasoline engines.

The influence of Mitchell's thinking at the Tactical School was direct through the mid-1920s, when Sherman wrote many of the school's doctrinal texts and when nearly all instructors knew and thoroughly agreed with Mitchell's ideas. Laurence Kuter, a graduate and a later faculty member of the Tactical School, recalled that a 1922 paper of Mitchell's on bombardment became the basis of instruction at the school. Mitchell left the Army after his court-martial in 1925, but younger officers who had served under him, including Kenneth Walker, Harold L. George, and Robert Olds, continued to work with and extend his ideas. Mitchell's writings on strategic air operations against an enemy's vulnerable points, along with the more extreme theories of the Italian Giulio Douhet, were variously reflected in the bomber offensive doctrines emerging at the school prior to World War II, doctrines which strongly colored how the United States waged that conflict.

Sources:

Robert Finney, *History of the Air Corps Tactical School, 1920–1940*, USAF Historical Study 100 (Maxwell Air Force Base, AL: Air University, 1995; reprinted Washington, DC: Center for Air Force History, 1992).

Raymond Flugel, *United States Air Power Doctrine: A Study of the Influence of William Mitchell and Guilio Doubet at the Air Corps Tactical School, 1921–1935*, Ph.D. dissertation, University of Oklahoma, 1965.

R. F. Futtrell, *Ideas, Concepts, Doctrine: A History of Basic Thinking in the United States Air Force 1907–1964* (Maxwell Air Force Base, AL: Air University, 1971).

Alfred F. Hurley, *Billy Mitchell: Crusader for Air Power* (Bloomington: Indiana University Press, 1964, 1975).

Ray L. Bowers

MORRILL, JUSTIN S. Vermont Congressman Justin Smith Morrill (born 1810, died 1898), formally educated for one term in each of the academies at Thetford and Randolph, Vermont, sponsored the landmark 1862 land-grant college legislation that included a provision for mandatory military training and thus prompted the first in a long series of congressional initiatives that culminated in the 1916 legislation establishing the Reserve Officers' Training Corps (ROTC).*

The Morrill Act of 1862 can be seen as a partial realization of the 1841 proposal submitted to the U.S. Congress by Alden Partridge* calling for federal land grants to support educational institutions offering curricular options that would include military science. According to the 1862 enactment, framed by Representative Morrill, federal assistance could be made available to endow and support in each state at least one college in which the leading objective would be education focusing on "agriculture and the mechanic arts." However, the curriculum of these land-grant colleges was not to exclude "other scientific and classical studies." It was further mandated that instruction in "military tactics" also be offered. As prescriptive as the Morrill Land Grant Act was, much latitude was left to the various states in the implementation of the various curricular requirements.

In an 1862 speech given on the floor of the House in support of his proposal for land-grant colleges Congressman Morrill offered a rationale for requiring instruction in military tactics. Had similar legislation passed a quarter of a century earlier, Morrill opined, the United States would have been in a much better state of military preparedness to suppress the rebellion of the Confederacy. While the United States Military Academy* might be adequate to supply officers for the U.S. Army in times of peace, it could not meet the officer needs for a large army in time of war. If the United States was to rely on a citizen-soldiery for its defense in the future, each state would need the means to "organize and officer" its militia forces. With the establishment of colleges such as those proposed by Morrill, the states would have sufficient and properly trained forces "to support the cause of the nation." In an 1883 address in which he further clarified the purpose of the land-grant act, Morrill explained that it was intended to educate men who would not only understand agriculture and the mechanical arts, but who would also "be perfectly trained for service in time of invasion or rebellion to organize armies, and lead them on the battle-field."

In 1890, then U.S. Senator Justin Morrill sponsored a legislative proposal that increased annual support of land-grant colleges and enlarged the scope of eligible institutions to include colleges for African Americans. By the end of the century, every state in the Union had at least one land-grant institution under the terms of the legislation crafted by Justin Morrill, but there was little agreement about compliance with the requirement for offering instruction in "military tactics."

Each land-grant institution interpreted the laconic and vaguely worded imperative for military tactics somewhat differently. Some institutions made military instruction mandatory for four years and others for three years or shorter lengths of time. Often instruction did not go beyond basic drill while in other instances military science was taught in its broadest and most comprehensive sense. Most of the teaching, however, consisted of military drill that was seen as effective in fostering discipline as well as providing a healthful exercise. Students engaged in military training in a wide array of military attire, and many institutions made no arrangements for uniform apparel whatsoever. At first, there were no federal provisions for military instructional staff, equipment, or curriculum guidelines.

The passage by Congress of the Detail of Army Officers Act in 1866 authorized the assignment of active or retired officers as professors of military science and tactics to land-grant institutions but also made it possible to make similar assignments to other qualified colleges and universities. In 1870, Congress took another important initiative to promote military education by authorizing the War Department to issue arms, supplies, and equipment to schools involved in military education. Although the number of officers who could be detailed to schools was increased through subsequent congressional action, there was widespread dissatisfaction with the War Department for its indifference and neglect in connection with supporting military education in institutions of higher learning. In 1889 the War Department proposed that professors of military science and tactics be accorded full faculty status by host institutions and that students train in military uniforms when receiving military instruction. These objectives would not be fully realized until the creation of ROTC in 1916.

The implementation of Justin Morrill's 1862 proposal for making military education an integral part of the curriculum of land-grant colleges was an important first step in broadening national government's role in officer education beyond the limits of the existing military and naval academies. The resulting collaboration between the War Department and institutions of higher education in development of a program of officer education would slowly reach maturity in the form of a comprehensive national program of military education for reserve officers in 1916.

Sources:

Edward D. Eddy, *Colleges for Our Land and Time: The Land-Grant Idea in American Education* (New York: Harper and Brothers, 1956).

Gene M. Lyons and John W. Masland, *Education and Military Leadership: A Study of the R.O.T.C.* (Princeton, NJ: Princeton University Press, 1959).

William B. Parker, *The Life and Public Services of Justin Smith Morrill* (Boston: Houghton Mifflin Company, 1924).

Earle D. Ross, *Democracy's College: The Land-Grant Movement in the Formative State* (reprint of 1942 edition) (New York: Arno Press, 1969).

Gary T. Lord

N

NATIONAL DEFENSE UNIVERSITY. Parent organization for all joint-service postgraduate schools operated by the Department of Defense, established in 1976 to set broad policy and provide administrative support. Its headquarters is located at Fort Lesley J. McNair,* in the heart of Washington, D.C.

The National Defense University (NDU) is tasked to prepare selected commissioned officers and civilian officials from the Department of Defense, Department of State, and other agencies of the government for command, management, and staff responsibilities in a multinational, intergovernmental, or joint national security setting. It was formally established on January 16, 1976, to oversee the National War College* (NWC) and the Industrial College of the Armed Forces* (ICAF) and allow their commandants to devote full attention to education and academic leadership rather that to administrative and logistical concerns. By bringing the two schools together into one university, economies were realized and redundancies eliminated by streamlining overlapping functions. A more efficient organization was fine-tuned by combining functionally similar activities such as libraries; computer and simulation programs; external programs (i.e., correspondence, seminars, reserve components); administration and budget; printing, graphics, and visual arts; logistics and supply; military and civilian personnel; and public affairs. In 1981, NWC and ICAF were joined by the Armed Forces Staff College* (AFSC) and a year later by the Department of Defense Computer Institute, now the Information Resources Management College (IRMC).

Although these four colleges make up the university's primary educational effort, the last two decades have seen marked growth in the NDU's support and research functions. Through research it aims to create a national repository of expertise on mobilization, military strategy, and joint or combined policy and plans. On January 7, 1982, the deputy secretary of defense announced the formation of the Strategic Concepts Development Center, the Mobilization Concepts Development Center, and the Wargaming and Simulation Center. These were later consolidated into a single research organization, the Institute for National Strategic Studies (INSS). Also in 1982, the Joint Chiefs of Staff approved a CAPSTONE course* for recently selected general and flag officers. Development of the course was later mandated by the Department of Defense Reorganization Act of 1986, and it is designed to continue the professional development of senior officers with the objective of increasing understanding between the services.

The president of the National Defense University is a lieutenant general or vice admiral chosen on a rotating basis from one of the military services. The vice president is a Foreign Service officer of ambassadorial rank appointed by the Department of State. A chief of staff reports directly to the president and provides a range of support functions to the university and colleges. The directors of the Institute for National Strategic Studies and Academic Affairs also report directly to the president. The president's staff includes professionals with a combination of educational and military experience that enables them to assess ongoing academic programs, to interact with key Joint Staff and DoD officials, to maintain liaison with the service headquarters and other government agencies' staffs, and to work closely with civilian academic institutions.

The college commandants and Dean, IRMC, report directly to the university president, who provides them with policy guidance and direction. The commandants have principal responsibility for curriculum development, student activities, faculty development, and matters of internal college administration.

Since its formation, the university has been asked to research and organize a number of relatively short courses to serve specific training needs. In 1986, NDU was tasked by the Joint Staff to study a concern of the Supreme Allied Commander, Europe, relating to the preparation of U.S. officers serving in NATO. The result was the implementation of an intensive two-week course on NATO policy, organization, roles, and missions. Similarly, the Reserve Component's National Security Course is a unique two-week program offered two times each year at various installations for officers of the Reserve components and selected civilians who work in the field of mobilization preparedness. The course is presented by NWC and ICAF faculty members and by distinguished guest speakers. In July 1996 the Deputy Assistant Secretary of Defense for civilian personnel policy invited NDU to assist in development and implementation of a new Defense leadership and management program for departmental civilians. One of the university's contributions has been the development and implementation of a three-month course in national security decision making for program participants. Occasionally, NDU has also been asked to conduct short-range and long-range studies of national security policy, military strategy, the allocation and management of resources for national security, and civil-military affairs.

NDU's Information Resources Management College evolved from recognition of the growing financial and strategic significance of information resources management. Its predecessor, the Department of Defense Computer Institute, was founded in 1963 to provide management training in computer technology. In 1990, the resources from the institute were absorbed when the Information Resources Management College was established to provide executive-level information management education. In 1993, the NDU president encouraged the college to take on an additional responsibility in the form of a senior service college curriculum that emphasizes information warfare and strategy. The first information warfare class began its course of study in August 1994, and a year later the new School of Information Warfare and Strategy (SIWS) moved to INSS for the second year of its pilot program. Beginning in academic year 1996–97, the SIWS program, offering advanced studies to all ICAF and NWC students, continued to evolve.

In 1993, elements of ICAF and the information management college were combined in a consortium to facilitate creation of the Defense Acquisition University.* In response to an Under Secretary of Defense for Acquisition tasking, the two colleges took on an enhanced educational mission for senior members of the Department of Defense acquisition workforce. Although ICAF remains part of NDU, it has also become a cooperating college in the DoD acquisition consortium.

At the direction of Secretary of Defense William Perry, the National Defense University announced the establishment of the Center for Hemispheric Defense Studies (CHDS) on September 19, 1997. The center's mission is to develop and provide graduate-level academic programs for civilians with defense-related duties in the executive and legislative branches of government and in the private sector. CHDS will collaborate with U.S. civilian academic programs, the Inter-American Defense College, and interested military and civilian counterpart institutions from all of the hemisphere's democratic countries.

Following the congressional legislation known as the Goldwater-Nicholas Act (1986)* and the House Armed Services Committee's Skelton Panel Report* (1989), the university decided to seek authority to grant master's degrees. On November 30, 1993, President Bill Clinton signed legislation giving the president of NDU provisional authority to confer the degree of Master of Science in National Resource Strategy upon graduates of the Industrial College and the Master of Science in National Security Strategy upon graduates of the National War College. From 1994 through 1996, the university worked with the Commission on Higher Education of the Middle States Association to obtain accreditation and was visited by a seven-member team representing colleges and universities throughout the region. Following a vote of the commission in March 1997, the university was accredited for five years (the highest possible award for an initial accreditation). On June 11, 1997, graduates of ICAF and NWC were awarded accredited master's degrees. Degrees granted to members of the classes of 1995 and 1996 have been updated to reflect their accredited status as well.

Sources:

Susan K. Lemke, "National Defense University Genesis and Evolution," unpublished manuscript in the NDU Library, June 1997.
National Defense University Catalogue, 1996–1998 (Washington, DC: NDU Press, 1996).

James R. Graham

NATIONAL WAR COLLEGE. Original senior school for joint professional military education within the educational system under the direct purview of the Chairman, Joint Chiefs of Staff, established in 1946.

The National War College, a component of the National Defense University* located at Theodore Roosevelt Hall, Fort Lesley J. McNair,* Washington, D.C. conducts a senior-level course of study in national security strategy to prepare future leaders of the armed forces and some civilian agencies for service in high-level policy, command, and staff responsibilities. The student body for the 10-month course includes military officers from each U.S. military service, the Department of State and other federal departments and agencies, as well as military officers from other countries. The college graduated its fiftieth class in 1997, still retaining the joint and interagency focus existing since the school's inception following World War II.

During World War II, shortcomings of U.S. officers engaged in joint and combined planning with their British counterparts led to the creation of the Army and Navy Staff College, an immediate predecessor of both the National War College and the Armed Forces Staff College.* Then Lt. General Henry Arnold,* a member of the wartime Joint Chiefs of Staff (JCS), cited these short-comings in a memorandum and proposed a course to educate officers in the essence of joint actions and high-level coordination between the military services. Sparked by the memorandum, the Army and Navy Staff College began its first four-month course in July 1943 for 30 Army, Navy and Marine Corps officers, one-third of whom were air officers. Shortly thereafter, Foreign Service officers from the State Department began participation in the course. British, Canadian, and Australian officers also took part in several classes. The first commandant of the Staff College, Lt. General John L. DeWitt, USA, served in that position throughout the war, graduating twelve classes. At the direction of the JCS, he also oversaw the planning for postwar military education, including a college to complete the formal joint education of senior officers of the armed forces and the Department of State.

Vice Admiral Harry W. Hill, USN, replaced General DeWitt in the fall of 1945, with the task of establishing the new college. He was joined shortly thereafter on the planning team by Maj. General Alfred M. Gruenther, USA, and Brig. General Truman H. Landon, Army Air Forces, who had been serving as an instructor at the Staff College. These three officers along with George F.

Kennan from the State Department became the initial leadership team of the National War College (NWC), reflecting the joint sponsorship of the school by secretaries of the War, Navy, and State departments. The mission of the school as advocated in the report of the Gerow Board,* one of the groups established to formulate military education policy, was "to be concerned with grand strategy and the utilization of the National resources necessary to implement that strategy." The college formally came into existence on July 1, 1946, occupying Roosevelt Hall, its present location, the building occupied by the Army War College* prior to World War II. Classes for the 10-month curriculum began in September 1946 with a student body of 100 Americans, including members from each military service and 10 from the State Department, along with several British and Canadian observers.

Since 1946, the student body has changed in both size and composition, growing from 100 students to nearly 200 in 1997. Military officers in equal parts from Army, Air Force, and sea services (Navy, Marine Corps, and Coast Guard) have comprised approximately 75 percent of the American students, with the remaining 25 percent being government civilians. In addition to State Department officers, civilian students also come from the Defense Department, the intelligence agencies, Commerce, Treasury, and other U.S. government organizations. After several years of initially including foreign observers in the class, the school accepted only U.S. students until 1984, when military officers from countries allied with or friendly to the United States, called "international fellows" again became participants in the academic program. In 1997, 14 military officers from different countries were taking part in the college's program.

When founded, the National War College was to be the highest-level military education institution, and the rank of the students reflected that status; all military students were at least colonels/Navy captains, with several officers of more senior rank. In the years since, NWC has come to share senior college status with each of the service colleges and the joint Industrial College of the Armed Forces.* While the founders intended for the top-qualified officers from each service to attend NWC, that intent has had to contend with the services' sending their best officers to their own war colleges. Reflecting this change NCW's military students now are primarily of lt. colonel/Navy commander rank, with fewer numbers of colonels/Navy captains. Civilian students have corresponding levels of experience. Institutionally, too, the college saw a change in status in 1975 with the creation of the National Defense University (NDU). NDU became the parent organization for National War College, the Industrial College of the Armed Forces, and other schools and institutes. No change in the college's focus or curriculum took place, but NDU took over many of the college's administrative and associated support responsibilities.

Faculty recruitment and composition saw several changes during the history of the school. Initially, 18 military officers comprised the entire faculty, along with fewer than five nationally known civilian professors on loan from their universities. At the time, the curriculum included international political and economic affairs in the fall semester and military strategy and operations in the spring. The civilian professors served at the school only for the first four months, teaching courses in international affairs. This system continued into the 1950s, when visiting professors began serving during the entire academic year. During this same time, first the State Department, then agencies such as the Central Intelligence Agency and the United States Information Agency, began sending personnel to serve on the faculty, a practice that still continues. By the 1970s, the college had moved from a policy of using visiting professors to one of direct hire of civilian faculty members. Hearings held in 1989 by Representative Ike Skelton, chairman of the House Armed Services Committee's Professional Military Education Panel,* led to further changes to increase the size and qualifications of the faculty, now numbering approximately 50, with civilians comprising approximately 60 percent of the total.

The school's academic program has always centered on a core curriculum taken by all students, with national security strategy provided the organizing principle. Soon added were study of U.S. domestic politics and area studies of regions important to U.S. security, including travel to those regions. Military strategy courses changed from an emphasis on current capabilities and planning to broader strategic concepts. The core curriculum at the college remains a series of interconnected courses with a focus on national security strategy in general and military strategy in particular.

The relative emphasis on military subjects in the curriculum has varied over the years, a subject addressed by several defense and congressional panels, most often in the context of five senior military colleges having similar and overlapping missions. In 1975, the Department of Defense Committee on Excellence in Education (Clements Committee) took note of the convergence of their curricula and attempted a correction. The committee directed the National War College to concentrate on national security policy formulation, while each of the service colleges were to have a sharper service mission focus, and it recommended that students be selected for the various colleges based on projected follow-on assignments. Those recommendations received no teeth for implementation until the Goldwater-Nichols legislation* of 1986. Changes embodied in this legislation included the raising of qualifications and promotion rates for those officers in joint duty assignments and the requirement for more than one-half of the military graduates of each National War College class to be assigned immediately to a joint assignment. With the emphasis on joint education came an increased attention in the curriculum to joint warfare and operational level-of-war topics.

In means of presentation, the academic program has changed considerably over the years. Lectures by visitors, followed by question-and-answer periods, once served as the primary teaching method. Since 1950, the number of lectures has declined by half, and college faculty members now give a far larger number of lectures. Correspondingly, the number and length of seminar sessions have expanded, so that the small seminar with approximately a dozen students is now the prime means of instruction. Elective courses taught by the resident college faculty also became a part of the curriculum in the late 1960s, coincident with the direct hiring of civilian faculty. Over 100 elective courses are now offered by the faculty. The rigor and extent of the core and elective courses provide the students with the means for dealing with the highest levels of national security policy and strategy. Since 1994, National War College graduates have been granted a master's degree in national security strategy.

Sources:

"History of the National War College, 1946–1956," 1982, National Defense University Library, Special Collections, Washington, DC.
James Keagle, "National War College: A Summary of Major Activities and Their Evolution, Academic Year 1946–47 through Academic Year 1989–90," 1990, National Defense University Library, Special Collections, Washington, DC.
George Stansfield, "Establishment of the National War College," undated, National Defense University Library, Special Collections, Washington, DC.

Thomas A. Keaney

NAVAL ASYLUM, PHILADELPHIA. The U.S. Navy's first central shore-based educational institution, provided specifically to help prepare midshipmen of the early 19th century for their promotion examinations to lieutenant.

Since 1813, schoolmasters had been appointed to conduct the formal education of midshipmen aboard the larger ships of the U.S. Navy—by congressional directive, ships having a complement of at least 12 midshipmen. On the smaller ships, providing instruction in theoretical subjects was an added duty for the ship's chaplain, who frequently was not well schooled in math and navigation. Even on ships with schoolmasters aboard, theoretical learning was minimal; classes held on the gun deck or in the dimly lit berth deck were frequently interrupted by the bustle of a man-of-war's routine, and individual midshipmen constantly were being called away by the precedence of their regular ship's duties. By the mid-1820s, however, even the midshipmen assigned to smaller vessels were required, like officers of most ranks, to pass qualifying examinations for promotion. After two years at sea, midshipmen were examined in theoretical subjects like mathematics and navigation as well as practical astronomy, seamanship, and naval gunnery.

Given the obstacles aboard ship to the absorption of theoretical studies and each captain's authority to vary the instruction according to his own biases, the need for midshipmen to study while ashore became apparent. By the 1830s, government facilities and one or two instructors had been provided at three different navy yards—Boston, New York, and Norfolk. But their programs varied, and attendance by the midshipmen was neither required nor encouraged through the availability of traveling funds. During the latter part of this decade, both naval officers and civilian supporters were petitioning the government for a permanent institution for the education of aspiring young naval officers.

In a political era when West Point* was being attacked in Congress as "the retreat for the pampered sons of the rich," legislators resisted the creation of another permanent academy for the preparation of career officers. Accordingly, the Navy acted without specific authorization. Beginning in 1838, midshipmen preparing for examinations leading to the rank of lieutenant were ordered to the Naval Asylum at Philadelphia to undertake a newly organized course of study. Taught initially only by one of the naval schoolmasters, the course ran for eight months and included algebra, geometry, trigonometry, navigation, seamanship, and French.

By 1842, when schoolmaster William Chauvenet* was placed in charge, the school program also included Spanish and mental and moral philosophy. Chauvenet, now having the rank of professor of mathematics, worked diligently to improve the quality of the instruction and upgrade the course in mathematics. He also laid plans for a two-year program that would include additional subjects of value to the naval officer. Although the plan had backing from within the Navy, President John Tyler's newly appointed Secretary of the Navy was not persuaded that the fleet could be spared the services of midshipmen for two years at a time. However, the attempts to expand the program resulted in the appointment of two more civilian professors to the faculty and the Navy's first detailing of active officers to teaching duties ashore.

When George Bancroft* was appointed Secretary of the Navy in March 1845, Chauvenet urged the establishment of a permanent academy and again presented his plan for a two-year program. Bancroft, who had himself been an educator, solicited the views of the other faculty members at the Naval Asylum School. He also sent one of the members, Passed Midshipman Samuel Marcy, who also happened to be the son of the then Secretary of War, to the U.S. Military Academy* at West Point to observe its program. Marcy's report "praised Professor Chauvenet's work and stressed the need for a naval academy comparable to West Point."

When Marcy's father agreed to transfer Fort Severn, at Annapolis, Maryland,* to the Navy later that year for its conversion to the Naval School, Chauvenet and three of the Asylum's instructors, including Marcy, were also transferred there as original members of the faculty.

Sources:

Park Benjamin, *The United States Naval Academy* (New York: G. P. Putnam's Sons, 1900).

Jack Sweetman, revised by Thomas J. Cutler, *The U.S. Naval Academy: An Illustrated History, 2nd Ed.* (Annapolis, MD: Naval Institute Press, 1995).

John A. Tierney, "William Chauvenet—Father of the Naval Academy," *Shipmate* (September/October 1969).

NAVAL POSTGRADUATE SCHOOL, ANNAPOLIS. Graduate education in the U.S. Navy had its origins in different programs that existed at various times about the turn of the century. For almost 50 years, the institution that fostered the development of this education to its maturity was the Naval Postgraduate School, co-located with the Naval Academy at Annapolis, Maryland.

During the late 19th century, the U.S. Navy was technologically adept and active. However, in matters of personnel policy, including officer technical education, the situation was not so bright. In the operating Navy, debates were rife over the relative status of line officers and engineers and the "evils of technicism." This classic generalist-versus-specialist argument was resolved by the Naval Personnel Act of 1899; among its many provisions setting the stage for modern officer personnel management, it mandated that all operating engineers would henceforth be line officers rather than a separate corps. This act facilitated the development of formal graduate education in the Navy.

The Navy had conducted what it called "postgraduate courses" at a number of locations, both Navy and civilian, during the 1880s; these were short and in the nature of functional technical training. Also, for twenty years small numbers of U.S. naval officers were sent to study naval construction at the Royal Naval College at Greenwich.* This ended in 1897 when the British Board of the Admiralty decided to exclude foreign students. In the first decade of the 20th century some of the navy's technical bureaus set up "graduate" courses, which were mostly self-study programs. These types of experiments eventually led to another basic issue: Should the Navy develop its own "in-house" postgraduate program or rely on the nation's already extensive civilian educational establishment?

Rear Admiral George W. Melville, of earlier Arctic exploration fame, was Chief of the Bureau of Steam Engineering from 1887 through 1903. His responsibilities placed him in the middle of both controversies. His 1901 report to the secretary of the navy recommended that (1) a postgraduate course in marine engineering and design be established at the U.S. Naval Academy* at Annapolis Maryland,* and (2) an engineering laboratory be established, also at Annapolis. Congress authorized appropriations for the Engineering Experimental Station at Annapolis in 1903. Navy Department General Order 27 of June, 1909, established the School of Marine Engineering at Annapolis, under the control of the Naval Academy superintendent.

The 1909 general order enabled the true beginning of graduate schooling in the Navy, albeit a humble one. The first class, which convened in October 1909, consisted of 10 officers. The school was allocated two Naval Academy classrooms. No faculty, either military or civilian, were assigned; academy department heads guided the program. The activities were mostly "discretionary reading," tours of engineering facilities, and guest lecturers (including one Rudolph Diesel, who spoke, appropriately, of diesel engines).

In October 1912, the school was redesignated the Postgraduate Department of the Naval Academy. This allowed for a number of substantive changes. Studies were expanded to include six basic fields of technical study instead of only marine engineering. The first steps were taken to establish a resident faculty, which numbered six by 1916. Also, courses became more rigorous and more theoretical, and formal evaluations of the program were instituted. One hundred and fifty officer students were ordered to study in the department from 1912 through 1916, although some did not complete their studies because of "the Mexican trouble." The operation of the department was suspended in March 1917 for the duration of World War I.

In June 1919 the program, now renamed the Postgraduate School, reopened under the leadership of Captain Ernest J. King, who would later lead the U.S. Navy through World War II. The name change was essentially cosmetic; institutional arrangements at the academy were the same. However, the formalization of the Postgraduate School and its sponsors (the technical bureaus) in Navy Regulations of 1920 was significant. The regulations specified that the school was to "conduct and direct" all postgraduate education, including "general professional subjects." This meant the programs no longer had to be strictly technical. Also established was the provision that a mix of Navy and civilian institutions would be used for the programs. The school at Annapolis was often used as a basic groundwork course, with officer students being sent to civilian schools after the first year.

Discord developed during the 1920s. Rear Admiral Henry B. Wilson,* superintendent of the Naval Academy, was a strong advocate of the prevailing view that naval officers learned their profession at sea, not in classrooms, and he pressed that debate. In addition, as the Postgraduate School continued to grow, it made greater demands on the academy's resources.

In 1931, initiatives were taken by the Postgraduate School leadership to move to the University of California at Berkeley. Conspirators in this drama included the university president, Robert G. Sproul; Rear Admiral Thomas C. Hart, academy superintendent, who would later be involved in the traumatic opening stages of World War II in the Pacific; and some of the technical bureau chiefs. At the behest of the Annapolis Chamber of Commerce, advanced plans for the move were killed by the House Naval Affairs Committee under the leadership of Chairman Carl Vinson.

As a result, the school stayed at the Naval Academy. From 1931 to the opening of the World War II, 2,130 officers attended the program at Annapolis, and 943 attended civilian institutions. During the depression years the General Line Course, more professional than technical in nature, was the entry program for most officer students. It later evolved into the undergraduate program at Monterey, California.* Programs during World War II focused on officers' technical skills, mostly in communications and electronics. In 1944, Captain (later Rear Admiral) Herman A. Spanagel came from two years of continuous combat duty in the Pacific to assume duties as head of the Postgraduate School. In this position, he was instrumental in initiating and guiding the developments in the postwar period which made the Postgraduate School a viable institution of higher education.

There were three seminal events which took place following World War II.

Public Law 250 of December 1945 authorized the Postgraduate School to confer advanced degrees "in engineering and related fields." In June 1947, the position of Academic Dean was established by Public Law 402 to provide for attracting a "top-notch civilian faculty" to the school. Finally, in October 1949, the Engineer's Council for Professional Development gave initial accreditation to three of the school's curricula. Accreditation of others followed over the years.

Moreover, the search for a new location to escape the constraining (and sometimes hostile) conditions at Annapolis was started in 1945. Under Public Law 302 of July 1947, it culminated in the acquisition of the school's current site at Monterey: the old Del Monte Hotel on 600 acres that had been used by the Navy as a preflight and electronic training school during the war. The Postgraduate School moved to Monterey during 1951.

With these four actions in the relatively short period of five years, four decades after its modest beginnings, the Naval Postgraduate School was ready for continuing growth and diversification.

Source:

Alexander W. Rilling, "The First Fifty Years of Graduate Education in the United States Navy, 1909–1959," Ph.D. dissertation, University of Southern California, September 1972.

Alexander W. Rilling

NAVAL POSTGRADUATE SCHOOL, MONTEREY. Since 1951, the U.S. Navy's resident college offering a variety of technical and management educational programs at the graduate level, with emphasis on the application of these areas of knowledge to the Navy's special needs.

The impact of new military technologies as a determinant of victory in World War II reaffirmed the importance of the Navy's advanced technical education program. A series of postwar Secretary of the Navy instructions and congressional acts redefined the scope and authority of the Naval Postgraduate School (NPS) and laid the foundation for the present-day institution.

The cross-country move from Annapolis, Maryland,* to Monterey, California, in late 1951 and the construction of a new academic campus marked a key turning point in the school's history. The actions were taken, in part, to enhance faculty recruiting and address critical needs identified in the 1947 Heald Board study of the school, which had been conducted under the auspices of the American Council on Education. The engineering educators on this committee had noted that "the essential ingredients of a good graduate school are students, qualified by training and intelligence for graduate work; a competent faculty, well trained and active in research and professional activities; and a proper environment and facilities for instruction and research." While they found that the Postgraduate School at Annapolis was "properly conceived, well organized, and presented curricula of a quality deserving academic degrees," they also noted deficiencies: the lack of opportunity for research, excessive teaching loads, a poor library, overcrowded facilities, and a sometimes unstable budget. The needed facilities were built around the old Del Monte Hotel, requisitioned by the Navy during World War II and used to train thousands of electronic technicians.

The decades of the 1950s and 1960s were marked by refinements in the philosophy and operating principles of the school and by continued experimentation in program administration. The NPS organization of the early 1950s included an engineering school, the General Line School, and an administrative command. In addition, NPS provided a one-year, nondegree program for line officers, had responsibility for a subordinate Naval Intelligence School in Anacostia, D.C., and administered contracts with civilian universities. The school earned provisional accreditation to award degrees and initiated its first funded research programs in 1955 and, in 1956, conducted a detailed study of postgraduate education and added a management school at the direction of the Navy Department. In a summary letter to the Secretary of the Navy, Vice Admiral James L. Holloway, Jr., Chief of Naval Personnel, stated that the study "reaffirmed our long-held desire that Line officers, as a matter of policy, should hold baccalaureate degrees, and averred the value of professional postgraduate education for the maximum number of Line officers. Considerable increases in technical postgraduate education were recommended; this in recognition of a need to stay with, and ahead of, technological developments."

In a 1959 commencement address, marking the 50th anniversary of NPS, Admiral Arleigh Burke, Chief of Naval Operations, commented on the return-on-investment for the Navy's long-term commitment to postgraduate education:

Rapid technological advance . . . did not come by accident, nor did it come overnight. It has been the result of educating carefully selected officers in each succeeding generation of officers. . . . The naval leaders of 50 years ago . . . recognized that ships and naval weapons were becoming more complex, that their proper employment at sea would require officers who were familiar not only with the age-old profession of the sea, but who could understand and could use effectively the complex weapons of the years to come.

The Naval Postgraduate School was reorganized in 1962, merging the Engineering School, Management School, General Line and Naval Science School (formerly the General Line School), and the administrative command into one unit with unified policies and procedures. The school also received full accreditation from the Western Association of Schools and Colleges in 1962. Although execution-year budgets often fell short of projections, funding for the Postgraduate School was generally stable. In subsequent years, as war in Southeast Asia escalated and noncombat programs were cut back, the Navy would eliminate the nondegree program and the General Line and Naval Science School and make drastic cuts in the officer-student population at NPS.

Austere defense budgets in the 1970s prompted a series of studies on the role and value of postgraduate education for military officers. Three major studies, completed in 1975, illustrate the nature of the debate: A Department of Defense

Select Committee on Excellence in Education, chaired by Deputy Secretary of Defense W. P. Clements, Jr., noted that officers with postbaccalaureate education were "absolutely vital to defense programs" and outlined several initiatives for the management of DoD's fully funded graduate education programs. A study by a panel representing the National Academy of Public Administration stated: "Throughout this inquiry, no serious question has been raised about the value of graduate education or the need for it among military officers. The problem is how much is needed, and how, and at whose expense, should it be acquired?" A Navy Graduate Education Program Select Committee, chaired by the University of California Provost George Maslach, looked specifically at the Naval Postgraduate School and Air Force Institute of Technology.* The Navy Select Committee, which included future Secretary of Defense William Perry, then president of Electromagnetic Systems Laboratory, and future Secretary of the Air Force Donald Rice, then president of the RAND Corporation, examined key issues such as costs, curriculum content, utilization, faculty qualifications, and research relevance. This committee reported that programs relevant to the Navy at the Naval Postgraduate School could not be developed or offered at civilian institutions at equal or lower costs. But the controversy over fully funded advanced education would continue into the first term of Ronald Reagan's presidency.

Earlier studies, even those which were critical of fully funded postgraduate education, had consistently commended the Postgraduate School for its ability to develop programs to meet emerging Navy needs. The school leadership had become skilled in the integration of courses from traditional academic tracks with specialized courses focused on warfare issues, including classified lectures, laboratory work, and thesis research.

The Naval Postgraduate School expanded this capability in the latter part of the 20th century and accelerated the development of warfare-oriented interdisciplinary studies. Programs in anti-submarine warfare and electronic warfare were in place when the Navy Select Committee conducted its study. Programs that emerged after the study included command, control, and communications (later expanded to become command, control, communications, computers, and intelligence); space systems operations and engineering; combat systems; total ship systems engineering; special operations and low-intensity conflict; undersea warfare (replacing anti-submarine warfare); and information warfare. Faculty research and associated student thesis research provided several striking examples of direct benefit to combat forces, and several groups of researchers provided real-time operational support during the brief *Desert Storm* campaign in 1991.

From World War II through the 1990s, the Naval Postgraduate School strengthened its scientific and technological foundation and bolstered its ties to the operating forces. At the same time, the school diversified with the addition of management and national security affairs programs and built a reputation for a unique ability to address emerging and over-the-horizon military issues.

Sources:

"Military Officer Graduate Education: Achieving Excellence with Economy," National Academy of Public Administration, Washington, DC, May 1975.
"Post-baccalaureate Education: Conclusions and Initiatives," Office of the Deputy Secretary of Defense, Washington, DC, November 1975.
"Report of Navy Graduate Education Program Select Study Committee," Office of the Secretary of the Navy, Washington, DC, September 1975.
"Report on the Educational Program of the Naval Postgraduate School," American Council on Education, Washington, DC, June 1947.

John Sanders

NAVAL RESERVE OFFICERS' TRAINING CORPS (NROTC). The U.S. Navy's principal annual source of newly commissioned junior officers who, since 1996, compete with Naval Academy graduates for Regular officer commissions following their obligated period of active service. The NROTC admitted its first class of students at six college campuses in 1926.

Following World War I, Japanese designs on China and the Western Pacific islands had become increasingly clear, and the Navy Department was convinced that Japan would be its most likely opponent in any future naval conflict. Accordingly, it shifted the U.S. battle fleet to the Pacific and won approval to convert two battle-cruiser hulls, already under construction, to aircraft carriers as permitted under special concession by the Washington Naval Limitation Treaty of 1922. It also prevailed upon the Congress to authorize expansion of its reserve officer ranks in anticipation of a possible future need for emergency enlargement of the fleet.

In March 1925, Congress authorized establishment of a Naval Reserve Officers' Training Corps and, in July of the following year, voted to appropriate funds for the program. NROTC units of 50 to 60 young men each opened at the University of California (Berkeley), Georgia Institute of Technology, University of Washington, and the Harvard, Northwestern, and Yale universities during academic year 1926–27. In staffing these units, the Navy's Bureau of Navigation advised:

An officer with the rank of captain or commander [one of whom was future Fleet Admiral Chester W. Nimitz] will be ordered to each of these universities and will be known as the professor of naval science and tactics. He will be in charge of the instruction of the students in the naval unit. One commissioned assistant [and several non-commissioned officers] will be detailed to each university.

The original NROTC program enabled selected college students to add the naval science courses to their regular undergraduate degree programs and qualify for a commission in the Volunteer Naval Reserve. The naval science curriculum, which afforded the naval professor some leeway in accommodating to local college practices, included "seamanship, navigation, gunnery, military and international law, strategy and tactics, electricity, and engineering." Apart from furnishing naval science textbooks and materials and a uniform, the Navy did not subsidize the early students. In return, no active duty was required of the graduates unless they were called up in a national emergency, as occurred in the run-up to World War II. As the war drew nearer, a small number of graduates with Supply Corps commissions were permitted to apply for active service. By 1941, the number of campuses with NROTC units had grown to 27.

In the midst of World War II, the Navy explored various ways to furnish competent junior officers for a much larger peacetime fleet than the one with which it had entered the war. For example, in March 1943, a Navy board headed by Rear Admiral William Pye was charged with exploring, among other matters, "the question of carrying on preliminary education in established colleges rather than at the Naval Academy."* Even though the Pye Board rejected the notion, a similar concept—the Jacobs-Barker plan—was still alive and contending with other alternatives when the war ended in August 1945. This plan called for two years of NROTC for all officer candidates, followed by three years at the Naval Academy.

The latter plan was one of several alternatives considered and rejected by the special board of officers and civilian educators appointed in August 1945 and headed by Rear Admiral James L. Holloway, Jr. Another of the rejected concepts was the option to build a second naval academy, rejected in part because of the delays necessarily incurred in building a totally new campus and enlarging the facilities at Annapolis.* The board's preferred alternative was to continue the four-year pattern at both the existing Naval Academy and the NROTC, taking full advantage of the methods and traditions for preparing and motivating career naval officers already proven at the academy and similarly generated in the NROTC. Also, as Admiral Holloway later explained, maintaining a separate NROTC source whose annual input of career officers could be varied in response to changing officer requirements provided the Navy with added flexibility in its personnel administration.

The Holloway Board's recommendation, approved by Secretary of the Navy James Forrestal on October 30, 1945, proposed a new form of subsidized NROTC within a broader scheme of postwar officer procurement, known as the Holloway Plan. The plan called for meeting the Navy and Marine Corp's requirements for career officers by supplementing the Naval Academy's output with NROTC graduates selected following two-years of required active duty (changed to three years in 1952). The portion of the Holloway Plan pertaining to the new NROTC was fully authorized in Public Law 729, 79th Congress, on August 13, 1946, providing for four years of subsidized undergraduate education in return for a period of obligated active and reserve service. The new law also reestablished the older NROTC program, enabling "contract" students to participate, unsubsidized, in the same naval science classes in return for use of the necessary textbooks and a subsistence allowance during the last two years. The obligated service requirement for a "contract" student was governed only by current Selective Service regulations, from which he was shielded while in college.

The new, so-called "regular" NROTC provided under the Holloway Plan was activated at 52 college and university campuses in the 1947–48 academic year. The selection of candidates eligible for subsidization was done by state boards appointed for the purpose from a national list of 10,000 young men determined by examination; approximately 3,000 were selected. The selectees were required to apply for admission to the colleges (from among the 52) of their choice, and they were accepted (or not) according to the standards of each institution. Application for selection for the "regular" NROTC program was made available to qualified enlisted men serving active duty tours as well as interested civilians. The "regular" Reserve midshipmen received a small monthly cash allowance, plus their books, tuition, and lab fees, but were not subsidized for board and lodging. Under the plan's original conception of line officer preparation, the subsidized students could select any major field of study but were required to satisfy Navy course requirements in mathematics, physics, and English and complete 24 semester hours of naval science courses.

The "regular" NROTC program, known by the 1990s as the NROTC Scholarship Program, has retained most of these same features over the ensuing years. However, the student population and the participating institutions have changed with the evolution of American society. In 1968, the NROTC opened its first unit at a historically Negro college, Prairie View A&M in Texas; the number increased to seven by 1998. In the early 1970s, the increasing unpopularity of the Vietnam War contributed to the closing of six units at Ivy League colleges, as well as at Stanford and Tufts universities. However, in 1972, enrollment in the scholarship program was opened to women at four units: Jacksonville, Purdue, and Southern universities and the University of Washington. Sixteen women were permitted to enroll in each during that first year, but by the late 1990s, women were able to enroll in any NROTC unit. In 1998, units were operative at 69 colleges and universities.

Other changes have included the introduction of new programs and the potential for four-year "contract" students to switch into the Scholarship Program for their last two years of training. In the 1990s, participants in a four-year NROTC program have spent four to six weeks each summer training aboard naval ships or submarines, with naval aviation squadrons, or with Marine Corps units in the field. A two-year scholarship opportunity is another of the new program features. This is available only during a student's last two years of college, usually beginning in the junior year but also available to five-year degree enrollees following completion of their third year of study. Another new program is the Nurse NROTC Scholarship Program, preparing students for commissioned service in the Navy Nurse Corps. Persons selected for a scholarship may enroll in this program if they major in a nursing program leading to a bachelor of science degree in nursing.

Incorporating these changes, the NROTC has become the largest single source of young men and women serving as officers in the U.S. Navy and U.S. Marine Corps.

Sources:

Rear Admiral James L. Holloway, Jr., "The Holloway Plan—A Summary View and Comment," *United States Naval Institute Proceedings* 73, no. 11 (November 1947).

John W. Masland and Laurence I. Radway, *Soldiers and Scholars: Military Education and National Policy* (Princeton, NJ: Princeton University Press, 1957).

"Navy Marine Corps ROTC—College Scholarships Bulletin," (NAVCRUIT 1131/6 [Rev 7–95]), Navy Recruiting Command, Washington, DC, 1997.

E. B. Potter, *Nimitz* (Annapolis, MD: Naval Institute Press, 1976).

THE NAVAL SCHOOL. *See* U.S. NAVAL ACADEMY.

NAVAL WAR COLLEGE. The United States Navy's senior educational institution and the first war college in this country whose curriculum and organization served as a model for naval war colleges in other nations.

The Naval War College was founded by Commodore Stephen B. Luce,* naval reformer, who saw the need for the professional education of officers in the art and science of naval warfare. The college, formally established on October 10, 1884 although no students attended until 1885, emphasized the theoretical aspects of naval warfare and, in Luce's words, was to be "a place of research on all questions relating to war." He believed that naval officers needed a thorough grounding in naval history, international law, strategy and tactics to understand the higher aspects of their profession and to hold command positions.

As president (1884–86), Luce brought together an outstanding faculty who helped the college gain prestige and acceptance by its opponents, who stressed technical training over political-military education. Captain Alfred Thayer Mahan's 1886 lectures on naval history were published in 1890 as *The Influence of Seapower Upon History, 1660–1783* and as such had a far-reaching impact. Captain William McCarty Little gave his first lectures on wargaming in 1886. By 1894, war gaming of battle situations was a permanent part of the curriculum and has continued so up to the present day.

The few naval officers who were assigned to the college for several weeks in the early years read books and heard lectures on naval history, strategy, tactics, and international law. By 1894, Captain Henry C. Taylor, Naval War College president, had expanded the course to four months and the new curriculum, which demonstrated the need for a Navy general staff, remained in place until 1919, with minor modifications. In this period, the college also took the lead in campaigning for a Chief of Naval Operations.

By 1909, the Navy had fully accepted the college; efforts to either close the institution or move it elsewhere abated. It now received the necessary appropriations and student body to continue its mission. In 1912, the applicatory system, a rational three-step process for solving a military problem—the estimate of the situation, the formulation of orders, and the execution of orders—was adapted from a method developed at Fort Leavenworth, Kansas.* The applicatory system provided a common doctrine understood by all officers and remained an essential part of the curriculum for the next fifty years. By 1914 the college had settled into a 12-month session and ceased preparing war plans for the Navy's General Board in order to focus on the main curriculum.

The Sims and Pratt post–World War I presidencies were a time of both change and continuity for the college. Rear Admiral William S. Sims,* president from 1919–22, attended the course in 1911 and became a firm advocate of the institution. He and his fellow officers took the lessons learned there into the fleet, where they developed naval doctrine for destroyers. Sims focused on the practical benefits of a Naval War College education for officers who, with a thorough understanding of the general principles of naval warfare, could then formulate and execute plans in wartime. It was on Sims's watch that a junior course was established. Though similar in content to its senior predecessor, it was pitched toward lt. commanders and commanders preparing for their first ship-commands, as recommended by the Knox-King-Pye Board* in 1919.

The regime of lectures, readings, and war games continued as before, but with the focus of gaming now on the rising threat of Japan the aircraft carrier was introduced as a new element in the game. Fleet Admiral Chester W. Nimitz, in a letter to War College President Charles L. Melson in 1965, averred that nothing that happened in World War II was unanticipated at the college, with the exception of the kamikaze attacks. Rear Admiral William Veazie Pratt headed the college from 1925–27 and introduced several innovations, some of which remain in place today. A Logistics Department was created; a course in international relations instituted; and, finally, joint military exercises were held with the Army.

In the dozen years before the beginning of World War II, the Naval War College continued its mission of preparing officers for positions of command in war and peacetime. The vast majority of WW II flag officers in sea commands were educated at the college. An important contribution of the college to professional military education during this period was Rear Admiral Edward C. Kalbfus's revision, by 1942, of the pamphlet that contained the principles of the applicatory system. Renamed *Sound Military Decision*, it provided an update of a practical, step-by-step method of thinking about and solving a military problem—a legacy of the college to future military leaders.

During the two decades after World War II, the college continued to give officers a sound education in naval warfare and seapower, despite the Navy's failure to plan sequentially for officer education and to send enough officers of high intellectual caliber to Newport. Admiral Raymond A. Spruance, college president, hoped to stimulate creative thinking on naval warfare issues that would incorporate the new technologies and realities of the postwar world. A logistics course was reestablished in 1947 and the college replaced *Sound Military Decision* with *The Naval Manual of Operational Planning*, still in use Navy-wide.

Throughout this period, new courses and programs were introduced to improve and enrich officer education. In 1950, the Junior Course was changed to the Command and Staff Course, which focused on "the operational functions of command and the organization, functions, and procedures of operational staffs." Three years later, Vice Admiral Richard L. Conolly instituted a three-year course entitled Advanced Study in Seapower and Strategy, tailored to develop creative thinking, research, and scholarly works on naval strategy. The course revived the notions that Luce had for the college but unfortunately lasted only three years. The '50s saw the college reach out to extend the benefits of a Naval War College education to senior foreign officers in the newly created Naval Command Course. Student contacts with the civilian world were enhanced by global strategy discussions, begun in 1948 and still held today as the Current Strategy Forum, and by the Military Media Conference, which brought together students and representatives of the press, television, and radio.

By 1966, the first of two major innovations in the curriculum occurred, stimulated by PME critics. Vice Admiral John T. Hayward, president from 1966–68, established a building program and added depth and breadth to the curriculum. A basic course, entitled Fundamentals of Strategy, provided an overview of strategic thought, economics, international law, and international relations. Military management and systems analysis were included in the economics segment, and elective courses were added. Hayward was not able to improve the quality of the student body nor make a war college education more career enhancing; however, the college was well positioned for the next decade.

In 1972, Vice Admiral Stansfield Turner* became president of the college and initiated radical changes to revitalize the curriculum, challenge the student body, and hone their analytical and problem solving skills. Three courses— Strategy, focusing on historical case studies of warfare; Management, treating national policy problems and allocation of scarce resources; and Tactics, stressing the art of naval operations—were implemented. Under Turner seminar discussions, team teaching, fewer lectures, a heavy reading load, papers, examinations, and grades added rigor to a curriculum requiring more individual effort. An advanced research department to support original student/faculty research and a new and permanent faculty completed the reform program. By 1997, the names of the courses had changed, but the curricular approach was similar.

The Naval War College offers the best in military professional education to officers of all services, who since 1992 have received a Master of Arts degree in National Security and Strategic Studies. With a thorough grounding in naval warfare, including joint operations, graduates of the late twentieth century are well prepared to serve on joint staffs worldwide and to assume leadership roles in the Armed Forces.

Sources:

John B. Hattendorf, "Luce's Idea of the Naval War College." *Naval War College Review* (September-October 1984).
John B. Hattendorf, B. Mitchell Simpson III, and John Wadleigh, *Sailors and Scholars: The Centennial History of the Naval War College* (Newport, RI: Naval War College Press, 1984).
Gerald J. Kennedy, "Naval Commands," unpublished manuscript, ca. 1978.
John H. Maurer, "The Giants of the Naval War College," *Naval War College Review* 37 (September-October 1984).

Evelyn M. Cherpak

NAVAL WAR COLLEGE REVIEW. Official journal of the Naval War College, dedicated to the advancement and exchange of thought about the range of strategic, tactical, and foreign policy issues of interest to the college community.

Implicitly recognizing that an officer's professional education is rooted in more places than just the classroom, early in 1948 Vice Admiral Thomas L. Sprague, Chief of Naval Personnel, proposed to Admiral Raymond A. Spruance, president of the Naval War College,* that he publish "for the majority of officers who . . . are not able to attend the college" the text of some of the lectures delivered there. Spruance agreed to this proposal.

The result, beginning in September 1948, shortly after Spruance had retired, was a series of pamphlets, usually 10 a year, each some 40 or 50 pages in length, and, in most cases, consisting entirely of the text of two or three recent lectures to the assembled student body. Most of the lecturers were prominent people of the day—flag and general officers, diplomats, academics, journalists, clerics, and businessmen. Occasionally the lecturer was a member of the college's staff or faculty. The pamphlets, entitled *Information Service to Officers*, were classified at a low level, first "Restricted" and, from December 1953, fifteen months after they had been renamed *Naval War College Review*, "For Official Use Only." Originally mailed only to individual officers of the grade of commander or above, later the periodical was also sent to major commands, for distribution as the command saw fit.

In 1958, Admiral Arleigh Burke, the Chief of Naval Operations, noted that while the Air Force and Army's comparable publications were unclassified, and thus could be distributed to civilians, the *Naval War College Review*'s classified status denied it influence upon the thought of interested people outside the armed forces. It took six more years, however, before the *Review* achieved the unclassified status it has since held.

By the late '60s, after nearly twenty years of publication, the *Review* had taken on the main characteristics a current reader would recognize. Short book reviews had become a regular part of the contents, and article-length papers by students were also published on occasion. The first issue to have a recognized editorial staff was that for Summer 1967. Colonel T. C. Dutton, USMC, director of the Naval War College's correspondence school, was listed as editor, and

Commander David Oleson, USN, was managing editor. The following issue, that for September 1967, introduced the illustrated cover on glossy paper that ever since has helped identify the *Review*. Indeed, by 1968, it was a handy-sized periodical (6 inches by 9 inches) of 100 or more pages printed on good stock. Its contents consisted chiefly of several main articles on subjects of interest to people concerned with foreign policy, the military and naval aspects of strategy (and what later would be called the "operational level of war"), as well as substantive reviews of books published recently in those fields.

In 1970, Commander R. M. Laske, USN, who for two years had been managing editor, became the first full-time editor. Commander Laske's principal contribution was to open the pages of the journal widely to all officers and scholars interested in taking part in discussions in the fields of the War College's interest. By so doing he made the *Naval War College Review* an important instrument for the advancement of thought in those fields. In the May–June 1975 issue, Commander Laske published for the first time ever in an unclassified publication the text of the basic document on which postwar U.S. strategy rested, NSC-68. Since then the editorship has been held by Lieutenant Commander B. Mitchell Simpson, USN (1975–77), Commander William R. Pettyjohn, USN (1977–81), Frank Uhlig, Jr. (1981–93), and Thomas B. Grassey.

Since 1948 the trends have been: from a large number of thin issues (nine issues in 1948, averaging 44 pages each and carrying collectively 24 articles, all but three of which originated as lectures) to a small number of large issues (four issues annually, each of about 160 pages); from an almost total dependence on lectures delivered to the student body (of the 24 articles published in the first year, all but three originated as lectures) to a variety of carefully prepared, selected, and edited articles (of the 26 published in 1996, only three originated as lectures). The four issues published that year also included substantive reviews of 84 new books in the fields of interest to the readers. From the beginning the contributors have included both officers and civilians. Eleven of the first year's 24 articles were by officers, the other 13 by a variety of civilians. Of the 26 articles published in 1996, 15 were by officers and 11 by scholars. All but a handful of the articles published in 1996 were written by people not then assigned to, or employed by, the Naval War College, though many had had a connection to the college in the not-far-distant past.

Using essentially the same staff members and facilities as it employs to publish the journal, the Naval War College Press (established as such in 1980) has, since 1975, also produced several series of books on subjects of interest chiefly to scholars and members of the naval community. The first of these was *The Writings of Stephen B. Luce* (the naval officer responsible for the founding of the Naval War College in 1884), edited by John B. Hattendorf and John D. Hayes. The more recent titles have included *Foundations of Moral Obligation*, by Joseph Gerard Brennan (1992), *Chaos Theory: The Essentials for Military Application*, by Glenn E. James (1996), and *The Queenstown Patrol, 1917: The*

Diary of Commander Joseph Knefler Taussig, U.S. Navy, edited by William N. Still, Jr. (1997).

For the use of distant readers anxious for the latest material carried in the journal, the editor established a web site early in 1997. Most of the other 10,000 readers, including about one thousand in the Naval War College's resident student body and faculty, get the quarterly journal by mail. The books published by the press can be obtained through the Naval War College Foundation, which supports their publication.

The chief constant in the life of the *Naval War College Review*, made clear by the fact that most readers of (and most contributors to) the journal are outside the college's classrooms, is the *Review*'s steady adherence to serving those for whom Vice Admiral Sprague was concerned half a century ago, those not able to attend the college. But now this number includes not only naval officers but also officers of the other services, many civilians, and those from other lands. The only requirement is that they be interested in the subject matter with which the *Naval War College Review* deals, and it is they who will best know that.

Frank Uhlig, Jr.

NEW LONDON, CONNECTICUT. Manufacturing center and port-of-entry, located at the mouth of the Thames River just inland from Long Island Sound, and site of the U.S. Coast Guard Academy.

New London was originally founded by John Winthrop, Jr., son of Massachusetts Bay Colony's governor, as Faire Harbour, in 1646. He gained chartered access to the disputed territory under authority from the proprietors of both the Bay Colony and Connecticut but was thwarted in his ambition to be appointed Connecticut's governor. Renamed New London in 1658, the town gained early recognition as a ship-building center and steadily growing port. As residents of a county seat, the families of New London benefited from the colony's encouragement of education; the town was granted an additional 600 acres of land by Connecticut's General Assembly with which to support a grammar school, required of such towns under penalty of fines for noncompliance.

By the mid-18th century, New London had developed into a prosperous port, shipping lumber, flour, and food supplies to the West Indies, Gibraltar, and the Barbary Coast. In recognition of the strategic value of its harbor, as tensions with Britain increased, two protective fortifications—Forts Trumbull and Griswold—had been erected on the west and east banks, respectively, of the Thames. In 1776, New London's harbor became the assembly point for the first naval expedition authorized by the Continental Congress; and during the next three years, 20 privateers were fitted out there.

New London became a focal point of Connecticut Colony's opposition to British rule. In 1765, its Sons of Liberty arranged a meeting at a local tavern with their New York counterparts that marked the first concrete step toward intercolonial cooperation in the movement toward independence. The *New Lon-*

don Gazette, one of Connecticut's first newspapers, was a vociferous critic of Britain's taxes and trade policies. It did much to mobilize opinion behind the independence cause and drew the ire of British officials and Tories alike. During the Revolution, the town became a virtual storehouse of foodstuffs, cannon, and other war supplies and, in 1781, the target of a British and Tory military campaign. In this last northern engagement of the war, New London and neighboring Groton were burned, the two forts overrun, and 84 of the Griswold garrison put to death despite its surrender.

Following the war, New London was rebuilt and, for three decades, resumed its lucrative shipping trade. But this trade declined beginning with the War of 1812, during which the British blockaded the harbor. In the meantime, a whaling industry had taken root which continued to thrive, along with shipbuilding, throughout most of the 19th century. In more recent times, the city has become a vibrant manufacturing center, producing pharmaceuticals, diesel engines, radio and television equipment, paper products, textiles, and tools.

But it is the harbor and ready access to the sea that have largely defined New London's character. Besides shipping many of its manufactured goods, the city and harbor have invited and welcomed the presence of the U.S. seagoing services. Proposals for a naval operating and training base at New London first surfaced in the 1870s but fell victim to political maneuvering in both the Navy Department and the Congress. Around the turn of the century, however, the Treasury Department determined its need for a shore-based "school of instruction"* to train young officers for the Revenue-Cutter Service; and it purchased some land near the Maryland winter-quarters docking facility for its school ship, *Chase*, to serve temporarily. In 1910, the War Department transferred the now obsolete Fort Trumbull to the Revenue-Cutter Service, and the School of Instruction and its training ship moved to New London. Five years later it became the U.S. Coast Guard Academy.* By the time of American entry into World War I, the U.S. Navy also had established a permanent presence in New London, an operating base for minelayers, submarines, and submarine chasers. By the second world war, New London had become virtually synonymous with submarines, becoming a principal manufacturer and lending its name to the U.S. Submarine Base across the river in Groton.

Sources:

Collier's Encyclopedia, vol. 17 (New York: Macmillan Educational Co., 1983).
Encyclopaedia Britannica, Eleventh Edition, vol. 19 (New York: Encyclopaedia Britannica, 1911).
Encyclopedia Americana, International Edition, vol. 20 (Danbury, CT: Grolier, 1997).
Robert J. Taylor, *Colonial Connecticut: A History* (Millwood, NY: Kto Press, 1979).

NEWPORT, RHODE ISLAND. Thriving seaport and commercial center during colonial America, approximately 70 miles south of Boston, that served along with Providence as Rhode Island's joint state capital until 1900. Since the mid-

19th century, it has had a special relationship with the U.S. Navy as the location of a training center and operating base and the site, beginning in 1884, of the Naval War College.

In 1638, a small band of religious dissenters left the repressive Massachusetts Bay Colony and settled on an island purchased from local Indians along the eastern shore of Narragansett Bay. Recognizing a fine natural harbor, the group settled at the island's lower end. A year later plans were set for the layout of houses and streets for the new harborside town. Newport's early settlers, a group of experienced farmers and merchants, soon put the island's fertile soil to work raising sufficient surplus crops to trade for manufactured goods. During the rest of the 17th century, "agriculture, the sheep and cattle industry, and commerce grew hand-in-hand," and Newport's entrepreneurs and ship builders began to cultivate firm commercial markets in the other colonies and overseas.

Overlooked by British administrators who concentrated on the larger ports, Newport merchants ignored Britain's navigation laws and practiced free trade through much of the 18th century. As a result, by 1760, the town prospered, "collecting cargoes from all who would sell, and redirecting them to whoever [sic] would buy." Uniquely among the colonies' more active ports, however, Newport was heavily involved in the "triangular trade"; it imported molasses and distilled rum and shipped most of it to other American colonies and Africa, then used the African shipments to purchase slaves who were the shipped to the West Indies—from whence came the molasses. As Rhode Island's colonial governor, Stephen Hopkins, once commented, "This distillery [Newport] is the main hinge upon which the trade of the colony turns."

Newport's laissez-faire attitudes toward trade had their counterpart in social matters, as diverse groups of people were attracted to and welcomed by the town. As a result, Newport's liberal attitudes and prosperity encouraged development of a cultural life that persisted long after its economic vitality had waned. Baptists, Friends, and Jews, all groups unwelcomed in several of the American colonies, thrived in Newport. A philosophical society was formed early in the 18th century, and one of the colonies' first private circulating libraries was established not long after. Rhode Island's first newspaper and a weekly journal, the Newport *Mercury*, were started there by Benjamin Franklin's brother and nephew.

Beginning with stiffer enforcement of Britain's mercantile laws in the 1760s and its military occupation of Newport during the American Revolution, the port's commercial importance readily declined. Its economic life did not begin to recover until the mid-19th century, when wealthy New York families built luxurious summer "cottages" there and began an annual round of lavish parties. Then, at the beginning of the Civil War, the U.S. Navy enhanced its modest presence in Newport by temporarily relocating the Naval Academy* in the downtown Atlantic House hotel and mooring the academy's training ship, *Constitution*, alongside a Goat Island dock. The academy remained in Newport until the summer of 1865.

This began a special Navy relationship that has remained until the present day. A few years after the academy returned to Annapolis, Maryland,* the Navy selected Newport Harbor as the location for permanently mooring the flagship of its Apprentice Training Squadron and established the Narragansett Bay Naval Station and Torpedo School on Goat Island. In 1884, it obtained Newport's Coasters Harbor Island as the site for the new Naval War College.* In later years, Newport became the home port for destroyer squadrons which exercised regularly with submarines stationed at New London, Connecticut.*

Sources:

Elaine Forman Crane, *A Dependent People: Newport, Rhode Island, in the Revolutionary Era* (New York: Fordham University Press, 1985).
Encyclopedia Americana, International Edition, vol. 20 (Danbury, CT: Grolier, 1997).

NORWICH UNIVERSITY. Founded in Norwich, Vermont, by Captain Alden Partridge in 1819 as the American Literary Scientific and Military Academy, Norwich is the nation's oldest private military college and is recognized by the Department of Defense as the birthplace of the nation's Reserve Officers' Training Corps (ROTC) concept. Norwich is regarded as one of the nation's leading military-educational institutions.

Alden Partridge* attended Dartmouth College and was an early graduate, professor, and former superintendent of the United States Military Academy* at West Point, New York.* Unable to implement his far-reaching plans for reforming West Point and developing a national system of citizen-soldier academies while an active duty army officer, Partridge resigned and established the American Literary, Scientific, and Military Academy in his native state. The academy's name was carefully selected to identify the factors of a liberal education that Partridge deemed most important. Following his departure from West Point, philosophical disagreements between Alden Partridge and Sylvanus Thayer,* the erstwhile Father of Military Academy, were the subject of vitriolic disputes between these two military-educational pioneers and their followers for many years. Recent scholarship suggests that Partridge probably did more than any other individual to promote military education on civilian campuses in the United States prior to the Civil War.

For more than thirty years after founding Norwich, Partridge strove to promote what he termed the "American System of Education." The system's basic premise, as stated in academy catalogues of the period, was that the country's contemporary educational system needed reform in order to properly prepare American youth "to discharge, in the best possible manner, the duties they owe to themselves, to their fellow-men, and to their country." Interfaced with this concept was Partridge's belief that the defense of the nation was more properly vested in the mass of its citizenry rather than in a regular army and professional officers such as those trained at West Point. Therefore, his American System of Education would be conducted in an atmosphere where military studies were an important appendage to a liberal education; Norwich University and its Corps of Cadets were the principal medium to accomplish these objectives. Partridge linked military science and training with a pragmatic "civil" curriculum so broad and innovative that it gained national attention at the time. The Vermont institution served as a model for nearly twenty other private academies and colleges founded by Partridge or his students throughout the United States prior to his death in 1854. The influence and impact of Partridge and his American System of Education upon the establishment of the Virginia Military Institute* in 1839 and The Citadel* in 1842, though possibly substantial, remain to be fully identified.

Among the "firsts" achieved on the Norwich campus was the presentation of the first courses in civil engineering offered in the United States. It also pioneered the implementation of a physical education regimen, the offering of some of the first courses in agriculture, the adoption of an ambitious field training program to augment classroom instruction, and, in 1820, Partridge's academy fielded the nation's first collegiate band. Field training featured far-ranging "hikes" for the cadet corps that took them as far afield as Washington, Niagara Falls, and Boston. The guiding philosophy behind the organization of Partridge's academy and his curriculum reform heavily influenced Senator Justin Morrill's* College Land Grant Act of 1862 and the legislation which created the Reserve Officers' Training Corps* in 1916. A "risk taker" in the modern sense of the word, Partridge encouraged creative thinking in his cadets. The words "I Will Try," spoken by a citizen-soldier officer in the 1814 Battle of Chippewa when asked to assault a particularly dangerous battery, were selected as the academy's motto. To this day, the words "I Will Try," symbolizing perseverance in the face of adversity, are prominently displayed on the university seal, the cadet class ring, and on the regimental colors of the Norwich University Corps of Cadets.

In 1825, the academy relocated to Middletown, Connecticut, partially to facilitate instruction in naval affairs as Partridge's cadets were prepared for service on land or sea. Prior to the establishment of the United States Naval Academy,* a number of future prominent naval officers, including Hiram Paulding, Josiah Tatnall, and James H. Ward, attended the academy for training. While in Middletown, the school's popularity and reputation was such that, for a time, its cadet crops was larger than that of West Point. In 1829, however, the academy returned to Norwich, Vermont, following the State of Connecticut's refusal to grant Partridge a charter. In 1834 the academy finally received its charter when the State of Vermont officially recognized the institution as Norwich University. Following a disastrous fire which destroyed Norwich's principal buildings in March 1866, the university relocated to its current central Vermont site in Northfield.

Norwich received its first federal commandant of cadets and professor of military science and tactics in 1887, and in 1898 the university was designated as the Military College of the State of Vermont by legislative act. In 1916, the first African-American cadet matriculated, and Norwich was designated as the first site for a senior ROTC cavalry unit. For more than fifty years, this "cavalry connection" resulted in Norwich men playing prominent roles in the final decades of the United State's Army's horse cavalry branch and, later, in the emergence of its tank and armored cavalry units. Military flight training was instituted for selected cadets in 1939, and as the wartime need for officers became critical, an early graduation took place in March 1943. The remaining three lower classes of cadets entered the armed forces at the same time. For the next three years, the university's facilities were under military control and were dedicated to the Army Air Corps Air Crew Training Program, the Army Specialized Training Program, and the Army Specialized Training Reserve Program. In 1945, the first veterans returned to finish their degrees, and in 1947 the United States Army initiated a unique ROTC program in mountain and cold weather warfare at the school. This program was recently used by the Department of Defense to prepare forces for the peacekeeping mission in Bosnia.

In the 1950s, Norwich entered a period of unprecedented growth and prosperity that continued into the Vietnam Era. In 1972 Norwich University merged with Vermont Junior College, a two-year college for women located in Montpelier, Vermont. The Montpelier campus became a site for traditional civilian student programs and has since evolved into the center of the university's adult education and nursing programs. In 1974 women joined the Corps of Cadets as Norwich became the first senior military college in the nation to admit women, preceding admission of females to the national service academies by two years. Concurrently, the Department of Defense's policy of sending nearly all its Norwich commissioned graduates into the United States Army, particularly the armored corps, evolved to where cadets can now be commissioned in any of the armed services. Lastly, in 1987, the nation's first Peace Corps Preparatory Program was instituted at Northfield.

The ongoing preparation of Norwich cadets as "citizen-soldiers" and leaders has repeatedly demonstrated its value to the nation. Starting with the Blackhawk War of 1832, many thousands of Norwich alumni have served with distinction in all the nation's wars in all ranks from private (seaman) to four-star general (admiral). More than 25 alumni served in the Black Hawk War, at least 80 served in the Mexican War, and hundreds fought in the Civil War. In that greatest of American conflicts, more than 600 served the Union and 60 the Confederacy. The impact of Norwich officers and their contribution to the Union was second only to those of West Point. Following the end of that war, Norwich cavalrymen helped to open up the West, fighting in hundreds of engagements, including the famed Battle of the Little Big Horn, June 25, 1876. Alumni also served in the Spanish-American War, where Admiral George Dewey (Class of 1855) became a national hero, and in the Philippine Insurrection. Thousands of other Norwich men and women served in all of America's 20th-century wars. Sixteen died in World War I, 87 in World War II, three in Korea, 22 in Vietnam, and one in Operation *Desert Storm*. Seven alumni have earned the Congressional Medal of Honor while countless others have earned valor and service awards.

Included in a long and distinguished list of Norwich alumni are Grenville M. Dodge, Civil War hero and chief engineer of the Union Pacific Railroad; Gideon Welles, Abraham Lincoln's Secretary of the Navy; Admiral George Dewey, the "Hero of Manila Bay"; Edward D. Adams, the engineer who harnessed the water power of Niagara Falls; Harry B. Thayer, an early president and chairman of the board of the American Telephone and Telegraph Company; William G. Wilson, a co-founder of Alcoholics Anonymous; and prominent modern military leaders such as Generals Ira D. White, Edward H. Brooks, and Ernest N. Harmon, legendary World War II tank unit commanders, and, most recently, General Gordon R. Sullivan, former Chief of Staff of the United States Army.

At the close of the 20th century, Norwich University maintains its Corps of Cadets, traditional civilian student programs, and unique adult education initiatives while remaining faithful to the principles of its founding father to prepare leaders for an educated citizenry, fully capable of serving the nation in peace or war.

Sources:

William Arba Ellis, *Norwich University, 1819–1911, Her History, Her Graduates, Her Roll of Honor*, 3 vols. (Montpelier, Vermont: Capital City Press, 1911).

Gary Thomas Lord, "Alden Partridge: Promoter of an 'American System' of Education," Annual Meeting of the American Military Institute, The Virginia Military Institute, Lexington, Virginia, April 14, 1989.

Robert G. Poirier, *By the Blood of Our Alumni: Norwich University Citizen-Soldiers in the Army of the Potomac* (Campbell, CA: Savas Publishing, 1998).

Brian Smith and Gary T. Lord, *Norwich University, 1819* (Louisville, KY: Harmony House Publishers, 1995).

Robert G. Poirier

O

OFFICER/CADET EXCHANGES. The practice of sending American officers abroad for duty in foreign military schools or international staffs and inviting other countries to select officers for enrollment in U.S. military schools in the interest of furthering mutual understanding among allies who might be serving together in future politico-military coalitions. Similar exchanges take place among the different U.S. military services in pursuit of more effective cooperation in joint operations and staff work.

World War II and its economic and political aftermath left the United States as the strongest and most capable nation in the Free World. Its undeniably higher standard of living and a military-industrial complex built on the shoulders of its wartime production capacity placed it in a position of leadership in the cold war to thwart the commonly perceived threat of communism. Other nations, some of which were organized into regional alliances or less-binding mutual security arrangements, looked to the United States for help in developing their own institutions for national defense.

Accordingly, in the postwar period, the U.S. military establishment expanded the practice of detailing American officers for temporary tours of duty with allied military organizations and inviting reciprocal practice on the part of allied services. In 1947, for example, when the Joint Forces Staff College was established at Latimer House, Buckinghamshire, to train British officers from all services for joint command and staff positions, a number of American officers were also admitted to the classes. Arrangements like these were complemented by encouraging foreign allies regularly to send selected officers to study in U.S. military schools.

Beginning in the late 1940s, foreign officers began appearing in U.S. service school classes. Officer-students from six of the wartime allies had already begun attending the Marine Corps Command and Staff School* before the Pacific war ended. In 1946, the first class of the new Air War College* included one officer each from Britain's Royal Air Force and the Royal Canadian Air Force, a relationship that continued (with different numbers) through the mid-1950s, after which classes were opened also to officers from other NATO countries. Meanwhile, the Marine Corps extended its admission of allied officers to the Amphibious Warfare School.* The following year, the newly opened Air Command and Staff School* followed suit and began long-standing curriculum exchanges with the Royal Canadian Staff College; similar exchanges with the RAF Staff College (Bracknell) began in May 1950.

The other services began the practice in the 1950s, but only at the command and staff level. By 1956, classes at the Army Command and General Staff School* included "international officers" (as they came to be called) from 40 different countries. In that same year the Naval War College* established a new Naval Command Course that was designed especially for allied officers, but it was presented separately from its regular command and staff course and thus afforded little opportunity for student interaction with allies. The mid-1950s also saw British, Canadian, and French officers admitted annually to classes at the Armed Forces Staff College.* Unlike the Air War College, however, neither the Army nor the Navy began admitting international officers to its war colleges until the next decade.

Meanwhile, the United States had begun sending a few officers annually to Britain's Imperial Defence College, the Royal Canadian Staff College, France's l'École Superieure de Guerre,* and the NATO Defense College.

One of the main benefits from the practice of sending officers to foreign schools and admitting international officers to PME institutions in the United States is the opportunity to mingle socially and work with foreign counterparts and learn of their attitudes, work habits, and concerns firsthand. Similar learning opportunities were extended to many U.S. officers after World War II through the establishment of international mutual defense organizations, associated combined military commands, and military assistance advisory groups (MAAGs) throughout the planet. U.S. military officers had served abroad as attachés in American embassies since the 19th century, and a select few had been official observers on different sides of foreign military conflicts since the Crimean War. But with the forming of the NATO alliance in 1949, opportunities for peacetime duty with non-American military organizations increased manyfold. Officers were needed in the international staffs at Brussels, at Supreme Headquarters Allied Powers Europe (SHAPE), and at NATO's three regional military headquarters in Norway, West Germany, and Italy. Moreover, U.S. officers serving in U.S. units throughout Western Europe found themselves planning and exercising frequently with allied counterpart units in the field and at sea. These experiences both created new demands for better interallied understanding and training and provided unique educational benefits in themselves.

Similar demands and benefits accrued also from duty in the many MAAGs established in relation to other regional mutual security commitments. U.S. officers found themselves working elbow-to-elbow with foreign counterparts in an attempt to improve, and in some cases initiate, their own military and technical training programs and combat support services. According to John Masland and Laurence Radway, by 1955 American officers were serving in MAAGs and other military missions in 35 different countries. Moreover, other missions were established in support of United Nations commitments: "A United States delegation served the UN military staff committee. Military observers were sent with UN commissions in Pakistan, Indonesia, the Balkans, and Palestine. Air Force officers operated bases in North Africa, the Middle East, the Near East, and the Far East." And these demands for U.S. officer participation (and eyeball-to-eyeball international cooperation) expanded as the cold war evolved.

In similar fashion, in recognition of the frequent wartime demonstration of the importance of interservice cooperation in joint operations, senior officers sought ways of reducing service rivalries that many thought were spawned in the service academies. Accordingly, the still-current practice of exchanging several-day visits by junior-year cadets and midshipmen with students from a different academy was initiated, beginning in 1946 between West Point* and Annapolis.* At least once, for a three- or four-day period, each cadet and midshipman takes the place of his or her exchange counterpart—marching in the student formations, attending classes and special lectures, taking meals with the host student body, joining in recreation activities, etc. Getting to appreciate, at first hand, the demands and concerns confronted by the peer in a different uniform and sometimes establishing lasting friendships are the frequently reported outcomes of this experience. As Army Chief-of-Staff, General Dwight D. Eisenhower even advocated whole classes spending a year at a counterpart academy, but the closest the interacademy exchanges have come to this standard has been a swapping of military staff and faculty members for a like or even longer period.

Sources:

John W. Masland and Laurence I. Radway, *Soldiers and Scholars: Military Education and National Policy* (Princeton, NJ: Princeton University Press, 1957).
"Report from the Social Science Panel . . . ," *A Report and Recommendation to the Secretary of Defense from the Service Academy Board*, Appendix E, January 1950.

OPERATIONAL ART. A term denoting the employment of military forces in activities above the level of tactics but below that of strategy which has, since the 1980s, occupied increasing importance in United States military education curricula.

Current U.S. joint doctrine describes operational art as "The employment of military forces to attain strategic and/or operational objectives through the design, organization, integration, and conduct of strategies, campaigns, major operations, and battles. Operational art translates the joint force commander's strategy into operational design, and, ultimately, tactical action, by integrating the key activities of all levels of war." The scope of activities represented in the definition gives some indication of the term's importance in teaching military strategy and operations.

One can better grasp an understanding of operational art and its related term, the operational level of war, by tracing the emergence of these terms in the development of military thought. Theorists such as Clausewitz* and Jomini had discussed differences between strategy and tactics, with no intervening field of study in between. Jomini had, however, introduced the level of "grand tactics," which pertained to many of the concepts now thought of as operational matters. Later in the 19th century the growth of mass armies and the increasing complexity of warfare required further study in the art of maneuvering and sustaining a large, distributed military force over great distances and for prolonged periods of time. While not called operational art, the focus of Helmut von Moltke the Elder and the Prussian General Staff* was clearly directed at what is now termed the operational level of war: employment of several independent field armies operating in the same theater, complete with the logistics and command and control necessary to attain common objectives.

General-Major Alexander A. Svechin of the Soviet Union, a professor at the General Staff Academy,* introduced the term "operational art" through his books and lectures in the 1920s. He had studied the ideas of Moltke and the history of World War I but gained his first appreciation of the problems of directing military forces as a junior staff officer in the Russo-Japanese War. Significantly, he was particularly struck by the Russian failure to integrate the maritime and continental aspects of the strategy employed. In Svechin's view, "tactics and administration are the material of operational art," while strategy "subordinates the actual kinds of operations undertaken, their scale and intensity, their sequence and relative importance," based on the nature of the war. He also emphasized the close relationship of air forces, land armies, and navies necessary in operational art. In addition to Svechin, Soviet theorists of the time, such as Frunze, Tukhachevsky, and Triandafillov, were developing related theories of maneuver and massing, deep operations, and consecutive operations.

The United States military began using the term "operational art" in the 1980s, but study of the relevant concepts dated to much earlier. The Army War College* in the 1930s had studied the planning and execution of historic military campaigns, and board games during the same period at the Naval War College* exercised War Plan Orange against the Japanese Navy. It was not until 1982, however, that U.S. Army Field Manual 100-5 introduced the term "operational level of war" and then, in the 1986 version of the manual, discussed the nature of operational art. Subsequently, U.S. Air Force and U.S. Marine Corps doctrinal publications have begun discussing operation-level matters, and the term's inclusion in joint publications has made study of operational art a routine part of military education. The Army initiated and popularized study of operational art in reaction to what was perceived as too much of a service-specific orientation in tactical training on the one hand and high-level strategic studies on the other. The attention to operational art also coincided with the Army's increasing focus on NATO strategy and the problem of coordinating the employment of large air and land forces to meet a Soviet attack.

Education in operational art gained an added impetus with the Goldwater-Nichols Legislation* of 1986. That legislation had many ramifications, including an increased emphasis on interservice coordination and joint education. Teaching joint doctrine and planning brought increased attention to theater operations and campaign planning, both subjects dealing with the operational level of war and operational art. In specific guidance to each of the U.S. Armed Forces military schools, a Chairman of the Joint Chiefs of Staff policy document directs operational-level attention in two ways: first, it specifies that all officer education be concerned with the operational level of war; second, it focuses intermediate-level education (major and lt. commander ranks) "on large-unit warfighting within the context of operational art."

Education in operational art brings its own set of difficulties. First, there are few effective simulations that can support instruction in campaign planning and execution, unlike the many tactical-level aids available. Second, unlike tactics, operational art considerations vary much more between theaters of operations and over time based on social, geographical, and political contexts. As a result, the education in operational art has relied a great deal on the study of military history and theory in general and on past military campaigns in particular. Useful too have been exercise scenarios that mirror the ones used by the U.S. unified commands in their training programs. And, finally, military education has had to struggle with the application of operational art to the concepts that govern the conduct of what are now termed in U.S. doctrine "operations other than war."

Sources:

L. D. Holder, "Educating and Training for Theater Warfare," *Parameters* (September 1990).

Vasiliy Y. Savkin. *The Basic Principles of Operational Art and Tactics (a Soviet View)*, Translated by the U.S. Air Force (Washington, DC: Government Printing Office, 1975).

James J. Schneider, "The Loose Marble and the Origins of Operational Art," *Parameters* (March 1989).

Alexander A. Svechin, *Strategy*, edited by Kent D. Lee (translation of the original work, *Strategiia*, Moscow: 1927) (Minneapolis, MN: East View Publications, 1991).

Thomas A. Keaney

P

PARAMETERS. The quarterly journal of the U.S. Army War College located at Carlisle Barracks, Pennsylvania.

Parameters is a refereed journal of ideas and issues, providing a forum for the expression of mature professional thought on the art and science of land warfare, joint and combined matters, national and international security affairs, military strategy, military leadership and management, military history, military ethics, and other topics of significant and current interest to the U.S. Army and Department of Defense. It serves as a vehicle for continuing the education and professional development of USAWC graduates and other senior military officers, as well as members of government and academia concerned with national security affairs.

The impulse to publish an Army War College* journal traces back at least into the early 1950s, when the college was relocated at Carlisle Barracks.* It was not until the mid-1960s, however, that the off-and-on efforts to create a journal resulted in a tangible product. The predecessor to *Parameters*, called *U.S. Army War College Commentary*, was first published in April 1966. The editor was Colonel John B. McKinney; the war college commandant who directed and supported the venture was Maj. General Eugene A. Salet. The first issue was a modest start, containing four student essays and not intended for distribution outside the Army. Several subsequent issues of *Commentary* were published irregularly over the next four years.

In 1970, under commandant Maj. General George S. Eckhardt, the college applied to the Department of the Army to have its publication classified as an official U.S. Army periodical. The print run would increase to 5,000 copies, distribution would be expanded, and the title would change to *Parameters: Journal of the U.S. Army War College*. The first issue of *Parameters* appeared in the spring of 1971. The editor during this important transitional period was Colonel Keith L. Monroe. In 1977, under the editorship of Colonel Paul R.

Hilty, Jr., the journal began publishing on a regular quarterly cycle. The Army War College commandant at that time, Maj. General DeWitt C. Smith, Jr., was both an eloquent contributor to the journal and a strong supporter of the concept of a war college quarterly.

The editors of *Parameters* and its predecessor have each worked to make the journal increasingly professional in scope and structure and to extend its depth and its reach. Prominent among them was Colonel Lloyd J. Matthews, who served as editor for nine years over two separate tenures between 1979 and 1993. Matthews sought to elevate the journal's prose and to attract as contributors the nation's most prominent military writers and thinkers. He brought to the pages of *Parameters* his belief that military professionals should be the expositors of their own craft. He also focused the content of the journal more precisely and more productively on land warfare and national strategy. That effort was continued by his successor, Colonel John J. Madigan III, who further developed the journal's contribution in helping to shape the Army of the 21st century. Madigan dramatically increased the number of pages printed each quarter and added such innovations as expanded review essays and thematic "features" consisting of three or four articles on closely related and timely topics.

Over the years, *Parameters* has survived fluctuations in budget and staff; it has endured times of varying degrees of scrutiny, oversight, control, and neglect; it has seen its share of bureaucratic pushing and pulling; and it has enjoyed widespread institutional and public support. Historian Martin Blumenson has referred to *Parameters* as being among "the best military journal[s] in existence." Edward Luttwak has applauded it as "one of the causes of the intellectual renaissance of the U.S. Army since Vietnam." Alistair Cooke called it "one of the small but odd mixture of magazines I would not want to be without." Daniel Bell said, "I find *Parameters* [to be] one of the more interesting and useful journals I read, largely because issues and questions discussed [in it] rarely are found in *Foreign Affairs* or *Foreign Policy*," and then may have given the journal the bit of praise that the editors have enjoyed hearing the most: "What I like . . . is the sense of honest and candid opinions and assessments of policy issues, and my feeling that I can trust the 'disinterest,' so to speak, of the magazine."

"Disinterest" is a flattering term to an editor's ear, particularly when the intention is to publish a journal that seeks to treat all sides of contentious issues in military and national security affairs. The editors of *Parameters* have worked from the premise that it is essential for diverse views on important issues to have a fair hearing in our country, in the Army, and in *Parameters*. That premise is one of the elements that distinguishes professional military education from military training.

The U.S. Army War College is among the world's premier institutions for education and research in military strategy, national and international security affairs, military history, military leadership, and military ethics. The emphasis is on land warfare and on joint and combined force issues. And these are the platforms on which are built the pages of *Parameters*. As the journal has increased in substance and acceptance, its mission has developed a stronger focus as well. The journal's predecessor, *U.S. Army War College Commentary*, began as an outlet for "occasional papers." In the late 1990s, the mission of *Parameters* is threefold. First, the journal is published to assist in the *education* of Army War College students and graduates, to help them continue their professional development after they leave Carlisle, and to educate as well other military officers, Department of Defense officials, and civilians who come in contact with the journal's articles and reviews. Second, *Parameters* exists to encourage *research* by military officers and civilians working the fields it surveys, to help disseminate their ideas, and to provide a forum for the broad exchange of views within the United States and among our allies and friends in other countries. Finally, the journal plays an important role in the *outreach* of the Army War College to government, to the greater defense community, to other nations and their military forces, and to the American public.

Parameters has a quarterly circulation of about 13,500. The journal reaches Army War College alumni from more than 80 nations; defense-minded members of government, academe, think tanks, business, and the news media; other U.S. and foreign service schools; U.S. military groups, attachés, and embassies; and ROTC* detachments. More than 500 federal, state, public, and college libraries receive *Parameters* through the Depository Library Program of the Superintendent of Documents; another 250 civilian and military libraries receive *Parameters* apart from that program. The journal is available on microfilm and microfiche through University Microfilms and about a thousand copies are purchased by members of the general public through subscriptions. Military and political policymakers in Poland, the Czech Republic, Slovakia, Hungary, Slovenia, and Albania receive copies of the journal, as do international students and faculty at the Marshall Center in Garmisch, Germany. That is but a glimpse of the journal's international distribution. More than 500 copies of each issue are distributed to foreign recipients in Asia, in Africa, and to U.S. allies worldwide.

The journal is indexed in, among other indexes, *ABC Pol Sci, Air University Library Index to Military Periodicals, American Foreign Policy Index, Lancaster Index to Defence & International Security Literature* (UK), and *PAIS Bulletin*; its reviews are indexed in Gale's *Book Review Index*. To this measure of acceptance, add an even greater one: the journal's articles are reprinted widely and often for use in military and civilian classrooms around the country and the world. In 1996, *Parameters* received 282 article reprint requests, resulting in the reproduction of more than 150,000 copies of its articles. In 1997, there were 334 requests and more than 120,000 copies. Yet even those figures don't capture the entire reprint story; since most of the journal's articles are not copyrighted, many reprints undoubtedly are not reported to the editors. The journal in essence sustains a wide and growing readership as a source of teaching materials. The missions of *education, research*, and *outreach* are certainly served, and the influence of the Army War College, the Army, and its most insightful members is extended.

The journal's latest contribution to the college's missions and to the broader realm of professional military education is its adaptation to the technology of the Internet. *Parameters* is now available on-line (at http//carlisle-www.army.mil/usawc/Parameters/). This electronic edition of the journal offers complete articles, review essays, and book reviews from recent issues; scores of past articles; a comprehensive, searchable index of articles and essays; links to other on-line research sources; and much more of interest to military professionals and educators worldwide. The on-line version of *Parameters* exemplifies the journal's continued development and hints at its bright prospects for the future.

Gregory N. Todd

PARTRIDGE, ALDEN. Alden Partidge (born 1785, died 1854), educated at Dartmouth College and the United States Military Academy, conceived a highly innovative plan of national education that encouraged growth of the private military school movement in the United States and served as model for the 1916 legislation creating the Reserve Officers' Training Corps (ROTC).

Alden Partridge's interest in educational reform first emerged when he was superintendent of the U.S. Military Academy.* After studying at Dartmouth College for three years, Partridge entered the recently founded academy at West Point,* New York, where, in 1806, he was commissioned a first lieutenant in the U.S. Army. Partridge's assignment was to teach at West Point, first mathematics and later engineering. He concurrently served in an administrative capacity, becoming superintendent in 1815 at age 29.

That same year the then Captain Partridge submitted to Congress, through his superiors, a detailed plan to correct deficiencies in the curriculum at West Point along with a proposal for a comprehensive national system of military education. He saw the conclusion of hostilities with Great Britain as an opportune time for an enlargement of the curriculum. Partridge, whose own education was a blend of technical study and the liberal arts, sought authorization to add teaching staff who could offer instruction in natural history, chemistry, mineralogy, literature, ethics, and history. Despite its many virtues, the plan died in committee—a victim of pressures to reduce military spending and sectional jealousies over the location of two proposed new academies.

Captain Partridge's replacement as superintendent by Major Sylvanus Thayer,* in 1817, further vexed him and prompted protests and obstructionism on Partridge's part that ultimately led to his resignation from the Army. Before resigning, Partridge had begun to develop plans for a private institution, the American Literary, Scientific and Military Academy, in his hometown of Norwich, Vermont. Formally established in 1819, Partridge's academy, recognized as Norwich University* in 1834, was the first private institution for military education in the United States.

Alden Partridge shared the widely held notion of his contemporaries that standing armies are potential threats to civil liberties and republican institutions. Since a well-trained citizen-soldiery was seen as the best protection for a republic, the militia had to be trained in at least the rudiments of military science and tactics. Accordingly, Partridge devised a novel "American System of Education" that was designed to meet the needs of a democratic republic. He sought to make the traditional curriculum more practical, scientific, and modern, an integral part of which was its distinctive provision for military instruction. However, even though his students lived under a military regimen Partridge did not recommend a strictly military education for them, favoring one in which military instruction would only be an "appendage" to civil education. Thus, Partridge worked to prepare his students for useful and responsible roles as civilians, but, when necessary, they could assume military responsibilities as officers in a citizen army. For this reason Partridge is generally regarded as the "spiritual" father of the Reserve Officers' Training Corps.*

The American System of Education, including the provision for military education, was replicated numerous times throughout the United States. Schools following the Partridge plan were organized in most states of the Northeast. A few schools were started in the West and many more were started in the South, some calling themselves "Literary, Scientific and Military" academies. But fire, economic depression, war, and the deaths of key administrators cut short the lives of many of these schools. Among the more successful that followed the Partridge pattern prior to the Civil War was the Virginia Literary, Scientific and Military Academy at Portsmouth; Mt. Pleasant Military Academy, Sing Sing, New York; and Highland Military Academy, Worcester, Massachusetts.

After obtaining a charter from the Vermont Legislature in 1834 for Norwich University, Partridge helped cultivate state legislative support for the creation of the Virginia Military Institute* (1839) and The Citadel* in South Carolina (1842). Although Partridge was unsuccessful in persuading the legislature to fund a military professorship for the University of Virginia, he joined the growing chorus of support for converting the state arsenal at Lexington into a school that would offer "literary, scientific, and military instruction." Partridge also delivered a series of military lectures in South Carolina with the encouragement of its governor. Significantly, the plan of education assembled by the board of visitors* of The Citadel reads very much like a Partridge text.

Partridge also encouraged state sponsorship of military colleges through a military convention at Norwich attended by several hundred interested citizens in 1838. The proceedings of the convention, heavily influenced by Alden Partridge, reached publication as a memorial to Congress in 1839. The memorial, focusing on militia reorganization and reform, characterized West Point as a costly nursery of military elitism that fostered values antithetical to republican principles. The proposal called for its replacement by a network of state-sponsored institutions that would combine civilian and military education.

The fullest and most highly developed exposition of Alden Partridge's American System of Education appeared as a memorial to Congress in 1841. This was the first proposal submitted to Congress requesting land grants to support colleges offering to combine civilian studies, like agriculture and engineering, with military science. Congress was asked to apply 40 million dollars derived from the proceeds of land sales to endow as many as 80 institutions of higher learning. And, foreshadowing what was to finally occur in the National Defense Act of 1916, the plan called for the federal government to provide funding to support courses of instruction in military science.

In 1862, Congress enacted a very similar land-grant proposal introduced by Justin Morrill,* a Vermont representative. Although Morrill never acknowledged borrowing any of the ideas contained in the land-grant act bearing his name, the similarities of the Morrill Act to the deceased Partridge's 1841 memorial are striking and suggest that Partridge influenced the Vermont congressman to a significant extent.

After Partridge resigned from the presidency of Norwich University in 1843, he continued vigorously to promote his American System of Education. A skillful and effective lecturer, Partridge was a great success in public forums throughout the country and probably did more than any other individual to promote military education in American civilian institutions prior to the Civil War. His concept of combining civilian and military studies in order to produce enlightened and effective citizen-soldiers continues to have currency today.

Sources:

Henry Barnard, *Military Schools and Courses of Instruction in the Science and Art of War* (rev. ed.) (New York: E. Steiger, 1872).

Marcus Cunliffe, *Soldiers & Civilians: The Martial Spirit in America, 1775–1865* (2nd ed.) (New York: Free Press, 1973).

William A. Ellis, ed., *Norwich University, 1819–1911, Her History, Her Graduates, Her Role of Honor*, 3 vols. (Montpelier, VT: Grenville M. Dodge, 1911).

Lester A. Webb, *Captain Alden Partridge and the United States Military Academy, 1806–1833* (Northport, AL: American Southern, 1965).

Gary T. Lord

PITCHER, THOMAS G. Thomas Gamble Pitcher (born 1824, died 1895), Brevet Brig. General, U.S. Army, graduate of the U.S. Military Academy, served as its superintendent, 1866–71. His influence guided the slow academic reform of the curriculum as the first non–Corps of Engineer superintendent.

Pitcher graduated as an "immortal," next to the last in his graduating class (1845). He started his military career with an appointment as a second lieutenant of the 5th U.S. Infantry Regiment on July 1, 1845. His leadership skills emerged during the Mexican War. He earned a first lieutenant brevet, on August 20, 1847, for "gallantry and meritorious conduct in the battles of Contrearas and Churubusco, Mexico." He led troops during eight other Mexican War battles and was one of the West Point* graduates cited later by General Winfield Scott as the reason for the rapid success of the American campaign. Between this war and that between the states, Pitcher served as a regimental adjutant and company officer in the 8th U.S. Infantry Regiment.

Pitcher's remarkable military leadership developed through the test of 29 Civil War battles, skirmishes, and sieges. He ably commanded parts of the defenses of both Washington, D.C., and Fort Pickens, Florida. His appointment as a brigadier general of volunteers in November 1862 led to a series of combat commands: 8th U.S. Infantry Regiment, 2d Brigade of Horse Artillery, 4th New York Volunteer Artillery, and the artillery of the 2d Corps, Army of the Potomac. Although severely wounded in his right knee joint during the Battle of Cedar Mountain, Virginia, he continued his war service after his recuperation. Pitcher gained a brevet major honor for gallantry at Cedar Mountain. Additional awards included a colonel brevet and brigadier general brevet in 1865 for gallantry and meritorious services.

Pitcher's successful war experiences led to his appointment as the Commandant of Cadets and Instructor of Artillery, Infantry and Cavalry Tactics at the U.S. Military Academy* from July 10, 1864, to September 22, 1864. His tour resulted in a favorable impression that led to his appointment as colonel of the 44th U.S. Infantry in July 1866. Shortly thereafter, in an effort to make the Military Academy more of a professional military institution, the War Department removed it from the Corps of Engineers and selected Pitcher to become its 17th superintendent. Pitcher was named the first nonengineer superintendent on August 28, 1866, a responsibility he held until September 1, 1871.

In the ensuing years, the academy became more sensitive to the political mood of the country as Pitcher and his successors reported directly to the Secretary of War. But during Pitcher's tenure, even a nonengineer as superintendent and closer scrutiny from the War Department did little to reduce the power of the school's Academic Board. Even though a new curriculum went into effect in 1867, it differed little from that of the early 1850s; new lessons in penmanship and signaling supplemented the courses in drawing and tactics. Between 1866 and 1871, however, a substantive change in the rate of academic failures did take place. As a result of stiffer entrance requirements the rate, which had been 48.7 percent during the war, declined to 30.35 percent. Mathematics still produced the largest number of casualties, just as it always had.

After leaving the academy, the kindly gentleman served as governor of the Washington, D.C., Soldiers' Home from 1870 to 1877. He retired in 1878 because of war wounds and lived at Fort Bayard, New Mexico, until his death.

Sources:

Association of Graduates, alumni file, Special Collections and Archives Division, U.S. Military Academy Library, West Point, New York.

George W. Cullum, ed., *Biographical Register of the Officers and Graduates of the U.S. Military Academy At West Point* (New York: Riverside Press, 1891).

Walter Scott Dillard, "The United States Military Academy, 1865–1900: The Uncertain Years," Ph.D. thesis, University of Washington, 1972.

James L. Morrison, Jr., *"The Best School in the World": West Point, the Pre–Civil War Years, 1833–1866*, (Kent OH: Kent State University Press, 1986).

                                                                    Alan C. Aimone

PORTER, DAVID D. David Dixon Porter (born 1813, died 1891) Admiral, U.S. Navy, shaped the post–Civil War Naval Academy by restructuring the faculty, curriculum, and physical plant during his tour as its superintendent (1865–1869). During his tenure as Admiral of the Navy (1870–91), he influenced and wholeheartedly supported the establishment and conceptual development of the Naval War College.

Born in Chester, Pennsylvania, Porter was the son of Commodore David Porter. In his youth Porter served under his father, who held the successive posts of commander-in-chief of the West India Squadron and commander-in-chief of the Mexican navy. Beginning his naval career as a midshipman in 1829, Porter rose to the rank of commander by late 1861. In 1862, during the American Civil War, he was placed in command of the mortar flotilla of the Union forces, joined the fleet of his adopted brother, Captain David Glasgow Farragut, and bombarded the New Orleans forts held by the Confederates. In command of the Mississippi Squadron, he helped to bring about the fall of Vicksburg in 1863. In 1865, Porter, now a rear admiral, took command of the North Atlantic Blockading Squadron and, in operations with the Army, captured the blockade-running port of Wilmington, North Carolina.

In 1862, following the dismissal of his son Carlisle from the U.S. Naval Academy,* Porter had written to Assistant Secretary of the Navy Gustavus Fox and declared: "I would ask nothing better after this war than to have command of the Naval Academy, and get the right sort of officers into the Navy. A new era should be instituted." Following the war, Porter was granted his request and served as superintendent of the U.S. Naval Academy from 1865 to 1869.

Admiral Porter's vision of the Naval Academy went far beyond mere renovation and revival; it encompassed the creation of a home for professional military education that would rival West Point in the development of officers of the highest character and ability. During his administration, many important changes and improvements were made. A new gymnasium, chapel, midshipmen's quarters, and mess hall were built; and the old Maryland governor's mansion, acquired in 1866, was converted into the academy's library. Academically, Porter restructured the faculty and curriculum in drastic fashion.

His guiding idea in this respect was the modernization and optimization of the professional side of the academy's curriculum. He decreased the number of civilian faculty, reorganized the system in favor of the military faculty members, and assembled an outstanding staff of officer-instructors (including Lt. Commander Stephen B. Luce,* Lt. Commander Winfield S. Schley, Lieutenant W. T. Sampson, and Lieutenant George Dewey). A new department of steam engineering was instituted in 1865, teaching its courses in a dedicated facility with a modern steam engine.

Nor did Admiral Porter neglect the physical side of the midshipmen's education. His high standards on smartness and precision in drill and exercise contrasted starkly with those of previous superintendents. For the first time in the history of the academy, athletics were encouraged, shooting galleries and bowling alleys were constructed, and a swordmaster and physical education instructor were added in 1865 and 1867, respectively. Discipline was restored, not through capricious punishment, but through the institution of an honor concept. Midshipmen were informed by Porter that their statements would be accepted as the truth. To Secretary Gideon Welles he explained: "I loosen or tighten the reins according as they conduct themselves."

Admiral Porter left the office of superintendent in 1869 but continued to foster the growth of naval professionalism by helping found the U.S. Naval Institute* in 1873, along with Luce and Foxhall Parker. In his newly appointed position of Admiral of the Navy, Porter served as the president of that body from its inception until his death in 1891.

During the establishment and precarious early years of the Naval War College,* Admiral Porter exerted political pressure by virtue of his position as Admiral of the Navy to ensure the school's continued existence. His support provided the vital link between the Naval War College staff, including Rear Admiral Luce and Captain Alfred Thayer Mahan,* and the power structure in Washington. This relationship continued until Porter's deteriorating health forced his retreat from Washington political circles late in the winter of 1889–90.

Sources:

Kenneth J. Hagan, "Admiral David Dixon Porter: Strategist for a Navy in Transition," *U.S. Naval Institute Proceedings* 63 (July 1968).

Chester G. Hearn, *Admiral David Dixon Porter* (Annapolis, MD: Naval Institute Press, 1996).

Walter J. Herrick, Jr., *The American Naval Revolution* (Baton Rouge: Louisiana State University Press, 1966).

Jack Sweetman, *The U.S. Naval Academy: An Illustrated History* (Annapolis, MD: Naval Institute Press, 1979).

Lieutenant Michael A. Steen, USN

PRINCIPLES OF WAR. Usually presented as lists of seven to thirteen maxims that express unchanging or immutable rules, regardless of major changes in the conduct and conditions of warfare, these summary ideas have long guided the planning and conduct of war, and they played an important role in the curricula of American military schools in the late-19th and early-20th centuries.

Being men of quick decisions and even swifter actions, military leaders have long relied on maxims or principles—summary ideas stripped of their justifications and qualifications—to guide the planning and conduct of war. Their use of principles reduces the intellectual tasks of analyzing long-term and intermediate goals; identifying tactical and operational options; relating means to ends as mediated by factors such as weather, terrain, and morale; computing appropriate actions; and choosing the best option. As a consequence, the decision problem becomes much simpler by allowing military leaders to ignore some, or emphasize other, factors.

Some principles of war have a long history. For instance, surprise, deception, and pursuit are described in the Book of Joshua (c. 1,200–600 B.C.E.), wherein Joshua instructs his warriors to "lie in ambush against the city" of Ai (Joshua 8:4) and to "pursue after your enemies, and smite the hindmost of them; suffer them not to enter into their cities" (10:19). The earliest-known book dedicated to strategy and military theory, Sun Tzu's *The Art of War* (c. 500 B.C.E.), emphasized surprise, mobility, flexibility, and deception. In the West, many philosophers, historians, and military leaders have tried to distill guidelines for action, including: Thucydides, *History of the Peloponnesian War* (c. 400 B.C.E.), Vegetius, *The Military Institutions of the Romans* (390), Niccolò Machiavelli, *The Art of War* (c. 1520), Count Hermann Maurice de Saxe, *My Reveries on the Art of War* (1757), Frederick the Great, *The Instruction of Frederick the Great for His Generals* (1747), Napoleon, *Napoleon's Maxims* (1827), and Carl von Clausewitz, *On War* (1832).

At the beginning of the nineteenth century, few nations had a truly professional officer corps as understood today. Yet, within one hundred years, the United States and all the European powers had developed such a corps. Changes in the nature and conduct of warfare and emergence of the centralized state served to instigate the professionalization of the military. The increasing size of armies created new managerial and administrative tasks, as well as the need to develop and practice new tactics. In addition, two innovations complemented professionalization of the officer corps: the creation of military schools and the production of a literature to guide the study of military affairs. These two innovations played a key role in the modern articulation of maxims or principles of war.

Attention to specific principles of war first affected American professional military education in the mid-19th century, as military schools became aware of Baron Henri de Jomini's *Summary of the Art of War* (1838), derived primarily from the study of Napoleonic warfare. Dennis Hart Mahan,* who lectured on the art of war to two generations of West Point* cadets, made use of Jomini and emphasized the importance of principles in laying out fortifications and planning campaigns; but he stressed the inadvisability of applying them rigidly. One of his star pupils, however, Maj. General-to-be Henry W. Halleck, who wrote the first American book on military policy, was a devotee of Jomini's principles. Another European work familiar to American military scholars, Sir Edward Hamley's *The Operations of War* (1866), explicitly criticized reliance on so-called principles or rules of war but itself offered a number of "deductions which seem to be of particularly wide application" following his strategic analyses of several Napoleonic campaigns. Later in the century, Jomini's *Summary* and Hamley's *Operations* became standard textbooks at the Artillery School of Application,* Fortress Monroe, Virginia, and the School of Application for Infantry and Cavalry,* Fort Leavenworth, Kansas.

Writers have inferred principles of war from their own experience and from the experiences of the great military leaders. Sun Tzu proposed only 13 principles, but Napoleon ended up with a list of 115 maxims. Depending upon the interpretation of his words, Clausewitz proposed three, seven, or more. Foch proposed four and added a significant "et cetera," suggesting that other principles could be added. J.F.C. Fuller at various times proposed six, eight, eleven, and nine.

Despite their role in 19th-century PME, the "principles" did not gain official recognition until after the experience of World War I. The U.S. Army's *Field Service Regulations* of 1904 did not contain a list of principles of war. The first American explicit use of principles of war to guide planning and operations was in the *Training Regulations No. 10-5* (December 1921). The nine principles listed were: objective (the attainment of a goal); offensive (the only means by which a decision is reached); mass (the employment of combat power at the proper time and place to accomplish a goal); economy of force (the judicious application of force); movement (maneuver); surprise; security (all measures to guard against observation and surprise); simplicity (preference for simplicity over complexity); and cooperation (coordination of separate actions to achieve the common mission).

Training Regulations No. 10-5 noted that principles of war:

Are basic and immutable. They are not subject to exception. Their application varies with the situation, the factors of which are the mission, time, space, terrain, weather, and relative strength. . . . These nine principles comprise the whole art of war. Their application to the preparation for war and the direction of war is called strategy. Their application to specific battles and operations is called tactics. These principles are few and may be learned in a short time, but a whole lifetime can be spent in the study of their application in war without exhausting the possibilities of the art.

The American principles of war listed in *Training Regulations No. 10-5* have their origin in Jomini's *Summary of the Art of War* and owe a more recent debt to the work of British Maj. Gen. J.F.C. Fuller, who attempted to distill lessons from the failed British campaigns of 1914–15. In 1923 the British printed a service manual containing a discussion of principles that remained mostly unchanged until after WW II. The U.S. Army's *Field Service Regulations* in 1923 discussed the principles of war but did not refer to them by name. The official U.S. Army list of principles of war was rescinded in 1928. Doctrinal documents succeeding the *Field Service Regulations—Field Manual 100-5* continued the approach of discussing principles without naming them. After twenty years, the 1949 edition of *Field Manual 100-5* named and discussed principles of war. In the 1990s the American principles of war are: objective; offensive; mass; economy of force; maneuver; security; surprise; and simplicity.

In fact, principles of war are common-sense statements that may be applied to activities other than war. But the common-sense nature of principles of war and their applicability to activities other than war suggest that the principles may be too general to be very useful to guide the conduct of combat. As Bernard Brodie noted, in the world of ideas, such immutability is characterized either by divine revelation or a level of generality too broad to be operationally interesting. This view is reflected by the caveat accompanying most discussions of principles of war: the principles do not apply in every situation or at all times, and their use does not necessarily assure military victory.

Sources:

John L. Alger, *The Quest for Victory: The History of the Principles of War* (Westport, CT: Greenwood Press, 1982).

Bernard Brodie, *Strategy in the Missile Age* (Princeton, NJ: Princeton University Press, 1959).

Carl von Clausewitz, *On War*, Trans. Michael Howard and Peter Paret (Princeton, NJ: Princeton University Press, 1976).

Marshall L. Fallwell, "The Principles of War and the Solution of Military Problems," *Military Review* 35, no. 2 (May 1955)

Mark D. Mandeles

PROCEEDINGS (U.S. NAVAL INSTITUTE). *See* UNITED STATES NAVAL INSTITUTE.

PROGRAMS FOR CADET-ENGINEERS. Special curricula established at the U.S. Naval Academy between the years 1866 and 1899 to prepare cadet-engineers for the operational and maintenance demands of shipboard steam propulsion technology.

The Civil War witnessed the first extensive use of steam-powered warships in operations against an enemy in this hemisphere. Freedom from dependence on prevailing winds and reduced concern with tidal currents proved to be real advantages in riverine warfare, in blockade station keeping, and in operating with ground forces ashore. The potential of steam-powered naval vessels for use in future warfare had been demonstrated.

Even before the war's end, in July 1864, Congress had authorized a course at the U.S. Naval Academy* for assistant engineers. The students were to be selected by competitive examination from young men 18 to 22 years of age with some previous scientific training and with experience in the fabrication of steam machinery. The winding down of the naval war together with the return of the academy to Annapolis, Maryland,* served to help delay implementation of the act, but a class of two acting third assistant engineers was ordered to the academy for instruction beginning in 1866. Their two-year course included steam engineering, mechanisms, chemistry, mechanics, and practical exercises with steam engines and in the machine shop. Two more students arrived in

1867, but only one of the four was able to complete the work, prompting the Navy to halt the project at the end of that academic year. The two-year program was revived four years later with classes beginning in 1871, '72, '73, and '74. French and mathematics through early calculus were added to the curriculum; but these students remained apart from the academy's regular student battalion, living outside the academy grounds.

Meanwhile, pressure was building within the Navy Department to include instruction in steam engineering for the regular cadet-midshipmen. According to Park Benjamin, the Navy "had had such a dismal experience with the engineers (chiefly volunteers) during the war, that it was ready to have the midshipmen educated in the handling of steam engines to any extent which would prevent a repetition of it." By an act of February 24, 1874, Congress authorized the appointment of 25 "cadet-engineers" annually to begin a four-year course, terminating the earlier two-year program. Integrated into the battalion for the first time, the engineers took the same courses as the cadet-midshipmen during the first two years. But as juniors and seniors, they studied engineering drawing, marine engines, engine fabrication, and strength of materials whereas the midshipmen were learning navigation, seamanship, and gunnery. The engineers made their summer cruises separately as well, traveling on small steamers to navy yards and shipbuilding facilities. As a final examination, Sweetman tells us, "they were required to design and build a steam engine, from raw materials to finished product."

The special four-year cadet-engineers curriculum continued until 1882, when Congress eliminated the formal distinction between these students and the cadet-midshipmen in an attempt to quell the intensifying dispute between the Navy's line and engineering corps. Thereafter, all appointees to the Naval Academy were designated as "naval cadets," and several classes then followed a common four-year curriculum. To make this possible within the allotted time, elements of both previously dedicated programs were either eliminated or reduced; those cadets interested in pursuing an engineering career could no longer study engine fabrication, physical measurements, or strength of materials and devoted less classroom attention to marine engines. The special, four-year cadet-engineer program had left a lasting legacy, however: two of the 1879 engineering graduates had gotten permission to take the advanced shipbuilding course at the Royal Naval College* at Greenwich, England. This initiated a decades-long Navy Department assignment practice for two or more academy graduates annually that, in the early 20th century, led to a decision to establish its own postgraduate institution.

But specialized precommissioning education for engineers was to receive one more shot—this time lasting ten years. In 1889, under the encouragement of Superintendent (Commander) William T. Sampson, who had headed the Department of Physics and Chemistry during much of the four-year cadet-engineers program, Congress approved a separation of the academy's senior class into two sections. After completing a common three-year curriculum, the cadets were permitted to follow separate sets of courses preparing them for service in either the Line Corps or Engineering Corps, a practice that ended with the latter's abolishment in 1899.

Sources:

Annual Register, United States Naval Academy, 1900–1901 (Washington, DC: Government Printing Office, 1901).

Park Benjamin, *The United States Naval Academy* (New York: G. P. Putnam's Sons, 1900).

William E. Simons, *Liberal Education in the Service Academies* (New York: Bureau of Publications, Teachers College, Columbia University, 1965).

Jack Sweetman, revised by Thomas J. Cutler, *The U.S. Naval Academy: An Illustrated History, 2nd ed.* (Annapolis, MD: Naval Institute Press, 1995).

PRUSSIAN GENERAL STAFF. The primary institution in Prussia and the German Empire for studying the history and nature of war and applying this knowledge to prepare for future conflicts. Since the turn of the 20th century it has frequently been held up as a model for emulation in the United States because of its purported efficiency in developing war plans and its effectiveness in implementing them.

The Prussian General Staff, like its counterparts elsewhere in Europe, began as a body of technicians, giving advice on specific issues and only when consulted. During the Napoleonic wars its functions expanded to include future-oriented study and planning. A war academy, established in 1808 to provide advanced general and professional education for selected officers, provided a pool of qualified candidates with a common intellectual experience for a general staff that by mid-century was establishing itself as "the brain of the army." The General Staff was also the army's nervous system. Its officers were regularly rotated between staff and field assignments and between appointments to division and corps staffs and duty in Berlin. This encouraged commanders to view their chiefs-of-staff in particular as colleagues rather than subordinates or rivals. The relationship between a commander and his chief was frequently described in terms of a marriage, and great care was taken to secure personal compatibility as well as to match professional skills.

Outside of Prussia the General Staff was widely credited with orchestrating the Wars of Unification between 1864 and 1871. The General Staff, however, also played an increasing role in the militarization of German policy making, successfully asserting its independence from any supervision either within the army or from outside. As a consequence the system was not widely copied. France, Germany, even Russia and Austria-Hungary, preferred to restrict their general staffs to military affairs, and to limit their positions within the armed forces.

The appeal of the German model in the United States was less a product of study and reflection than a manifestation of desire to overcome the decentralization and confusion that had characterized the planning and conduct of the Spanish-American War. Supporters of a general staff on German lines described an institution that would coordinate and control the army's overpowerful branches and departments. It would provide a central management agency. It would advise the War Department and the President on military matters. It would foster a climate of modern professionalism in place of the Indian-fighting legacies of a now-vanished frontier.

As created and developed, the General Staff of the U.S. Army* became neither the brain, the nervous system, nor the soul of its parent institution. Its limited impact is generally ascribed to some combination of internal resistance to the interloper and public suspicion of excessive professionalism—particularly when linked to "Prussian militarism." Two other factors contribute as well to the transplant's failure. One involved focus. Germany's geographic location and foreign policy created a situation in which winning the next war's first battle became essential to the only perceived alternative: war of attrition in which Germany was inevitably doomed. As a consequence, its General Staff focused on operational and tactical concerns to the eclipse, then the virtual exclusion, of strategic questions.

This tunnel vision created an increasing dissonance between the German General Staff's policy role and its military planning. More significantly, it had no congruence with objective American circumstances that made strategy and logistics of primary importance. Germany's potential major threats were next door; America's were an ocean away. In two world wars and afterwards, projection and sustainability—getting somewhere and staying there—have been the core issues of U.S. policy, and the U.S. military handles them well. What happens on arrival has been a secondary consideration. What the German General Staff did best is correspondingly placed in the "nice-to-have" category. In sharp contrast to the Germans, operational effectiveness and tactical proficiency are seldom cited as American strong points—because neither has been essential.

A second overlooked factor limiting the applicability of the German General Staff model has been the equal roles played by army and navy in the U.S. military system. This contrasts to the situation in every other major modern power, where (with the possible exception of Japan) the dominance of one service over the other is generally acknowledged and accepted. The American situation correspondingly favors a committee system, with the service chiefs of the Army, the Navy, and eventually the Air Force and the Marines, have participated on a collegial basis in which none concedes absolute primacy to any other. Often criticized as cumbersome, fostering interservice rivalry, and favoring a low common denominator in decision making, the American system also fosters flexibility and cooperation to degrees unachievable in a Germany where the General Staff was the beginning and the end of military wisdom. The United States has arguably been fortunate that periodic admiration for particular aspects of the German way of war has never been translated into institutional emulation.

Sources:

Arden Bucholz, *Moltke, Schlieffen and Prussian War Planning* (New York/Oxford: Berg, 1991).
Peter D. Skirbunt, "Prologue to Reform: The 'Germanization' of the United States Army, 1865–1898," Ph.D. dissertation, Ohio State University, 1983.

                                                          Dennis E. Showalter

PRUSSIAN WAR ACADEMY. *See* KRIEGSSCHULE.

Q

QUALIFYING EXAMINATIONS. Tests, written and sometimes oral, for admission to an educational program or to the next higher military rank, where qualification is indicated by reaching or exceeding a recognized minimum standard.

Since early in their existence, the precommissioning academies of American military departments have screened candidates for admission with qualifying examinations. At various points in their history, similar instruments have also been used by the Army and Navy to establish eligibility for officer promotions. Ironically for a democracy, the military services have been unable to acquire the authority to use competitive examinations to aid in their personnel selection processes. Internally, however, the academies have used test results and overall grades to establish class orders of merit, on the basis of which initial military assignments including branch selection have been based.

The reasons are historic and clearly reflect the gradual evolution of the American democratic society. In the early days of this republic, only the wealthy and privileged had access to an education beyond the elementary grades. And even as public education was extended, this did not occur throughout the nation simultaneously. For decades public education in the newer states beyond the Appalachians and, later, beyond the Mississippi lagged behind that along the eastern seaboard. Members of Congress representing these states and territories were determined that their constituents not be denied military career opportunities through selection devices that set standards beyond their grasp.

So it was, for example, that candidates for West Point* in the pre–Civil War era had only to demonstrate that they were "well-versed in reading, writing, and arithmetic." When formal entrance examinations were employed following the war, knowledge of English grammar, U.S. history, and geography were added. Even as late as 1919, the U.S. Naval Academy* entrance examinations were still so rudimentary as to prompt the third board of visitors* in succession to urge that *future* candidates be required to demonstrate "at least a high school equivalency." Among the service academies, only the U.S. Coast Guard Academy*—from its inception as the School of Instruction of the Revenue-Marine*—was permitted to screen candidates through use of competitive instruments.

Use of examinations that require a candidate to demonstrate only some minimum level of specified knowledge conveys the obvious advantage of permitting determined use of other, quite different criteria in personnel selection procedures, e.g., types of experience, demonstrated character, athletic ability, leadership potential, physical appearance, etc. The use made of qualifying examinations by other nations in the 19th century illustrates some of their potential strengths and shortcomings.

Unlike 19th-century France, where commitment to competitive selection was reflected in the admissions and graduate assignment procedures associated with every professional military school, both England and Prussia relied primarily on qualifying examinations. However, use was made by each government in sharply different fashion. Prussia, whose military performance in the field following the Scharnhorst* reforms was admirable, generally maintained higher standards in its use of examinations than the lackluster British Army of the post-Napoleonic period. Observers of British performance in both the Crimea and South Africa remarked critically on the lack of professional military knowledge evident among the British officers.

Britain's use of commissioning examinations was generally constrained by its perpetuation of the traditional myth that only the privileged and wealthy classes were qualified to lead. Whereas Prussia, since 1816, required two lengthy, very comprehensive tests—the first of general knowledge and later of professional military knowledge—before any young man could obtain a commission, Britain required no examinations for five-sixths of its annual infantry and cavalry officer input until 1849; the remaining sixth entered from the Royal Military College Sandhurst,* where the leaving examination was entirely oral and not very demanding on professional subjects. After 1849, qualifying examinations were required even of the large number who purchased commissions, but the only military knowledge tested was familiarity with one or two well-known works on fortification. Prussia's commissioning examination, on the other hand, included theory of arms and ammunition, rules and regulations, fortifications, tactics, and surveying, all written; candidates were questioned orally on all these subjects as well.

These differences reflected different motivations for the use of testing. Britain's introduction and, later, its modification of examinations for the nonscientific arms came in reaction to criticism from parliamentary sources and investigative commissions, and they were designed to show change but not enough to loosen the hold of the gentry on the nation's military institutions. Britain's examination procedures impressed several observers as rather perfunctory ceremonies primarily fulfilling a legal requirement. Commissioning examination reforms, beginning in 1858, resulted largely in an emphasis on the general knowledge more familiar to the sons of gentry being educated in the English "public" schools. Prussia's examinations were designed to complement its larger system of inspections and reports whereby it could form a general estimate of the "abilities, character, and military capacity" of each officer in its service. Observations by a board of examiners of his "character and military capacity" were a prime purpose of examining orally what had already been tested at great length in writing.

This difference in purpose was reflected in the character of the examinations themselves. While the essay questions in the Prussian tests were designed to evoke thought and evaluate the candidate's ability to apply his knowledge to a specific problem, those in the English tests tended to be technical and evaluate his powers of recall on specific facts. The distinctions were evident not only in the examinations required for commissioning but also in those taken for admission to precommissioning education. After 1829, Prussia's general knowledge examination, called the "Swordknot examination," became a requirement for admission to officer-training status in an active regiment, a year-long experience required of all officer candidates except those thirty cadets chosen annually for the coveted year-long *Selecta* class in Berlin. Comprehensive in character, the level of knowledge evoked by the "Swordknot" was comparable to the classical preparation for entry in the universities accomplished in the *Gymnasium* except that the "Swordknot" required more mathematics. By contrast, even though the entrance examinations for Sandhurst increased somewhat in difficulty and became competitive after 1858, when the minimum age for entrance was raised to sixteen, their knowledge requirements remained comparatively rudimentary.

It is perhaps no coincidence that in 1871, following Prussia's decisive defeat of France, Royal Warrants from Queen Victoria abolished all army commissions by purchase and directed changes in Britain's commissioning procedures that borrowed from Prussian practice. In particular, they insisted that each candidate acquire a year's experience in a regiment followed by a professional examination before fully qualifying for a lieutenancy.

Sources:

Henry Barnard, *Military Schools and Courses of Instruction in the Science and Art of War*, rev. ed. (New York: Reprinted by Greenwood Press, 1969).

Richard A. Preston, "Perspectives in the History of Military Education and Professionalism," The Harmon Memorial Lectures in Military History, Number 22, in Harry R. Borowski (ed.), *The Harmon Memorial Lectures in Military History, 1959–1987* (Washington, DC: Office of Air Force History, 1988).

QUANTICO, VIRGINIA. Location of the Marine Corps Combat Development Command and home of the Marine Corps professional military education system.* The Marine Corps Combat Development Command is a base now encompassing over 55,000 acres. The civilian town of Quantico, established before the arrival of the Marines in 1917, is unique in that it is surrounded on three sides by the Marine base and on the fourth by the Potomac River.

Situated on the Potomac River, Quantico is 35 miles south of Washington, D.C. and 23 miles north of Fredericksburg, Virginia. The Marine base was originally established there in 1917 for its location on the north-south railway line and proximity to water and movement by ship. It served as a training base and then a transhipment point for Marine units destined for France during World War I (and later for units deploying to Central America and the Caribbean). Operational units have also been based at Quantico. In the interwar years, the East Coast Expeditionary Force and later the Fleet Marine Force were stationed there; the latter included the 1st Marine Division and the 1st Marine Aircraft Wing. Today, HMX-1, the helicopter squadron providing rotary wing support to the President of the United States, is based at Quantico; there is also the Marine Security Guard Battalion, which trains all the Marine security guards stationed at American embassies abroad. Since 1940, the base has also been home to the FBI Academy.

In 1920, Quantico became the home of the professional military education system of the officer corps of the Marine Corps and has remained so ever since. Over the years, this system has had three names: the Marine Corps Schools (1920–48), the Education Center (1948–89), and, since 1989, the Marine Corps University. The base itself has had four names: Marine Barracks, Quantico (1917–48); the Marine Corps Schools (1948–68); the Marine Corps Development and Education Command (1968–87); and, from 1987 to the present, the Marine Corps Combat Development Command.

Officer training and education at Quantico span the spectrum from precommissioning screening at the Officers Candidate School, to newly commissioned officer professional education and training at The Basic School,* to specialist training (e.g., the Communications Officers School, established in 1944, and since 1996 called the Command and Control Systems School; and the Computer Sciences School for both officers and enlisted personnel), to the career officer professional military education system. The latter encompasses the Amphibious Warfare School* for company grade officers; and the Command and Staff College,* the School of Advanced Warfighting,* and the Marine Corps War College* for field grade officers. The Marine Corps University also includes professional military education for noncommissioned and staff noncommissioned officers; this Marine Corps–wide program comes under the cognizance of the Staff Noncommissioned Officers Academy, founded in 1971.

In addition to this organization, Quantico has been the home of the Marine Corps equipment and weapons procurement system, originally called the Marine Corps Equipment Board and now, after many reorganizations and name changes, the Marine Corps Systems Command. Also, the Marine Corps Combat Development Command now hosts the agencies responsible for doctrine and studies on the character of contemporary and future warfare; among these is the future-oriented Commandant's War Fighting Lab. Two major warfighting doctrines have been produced at the base: the amphibious doctrine used in World War II was written in the 1930s and that for the helicopter vertical ship-to-shore movement was developed in the early post–World War II era.

Sources:

Colonel Kenneth Clifford, USMC, *Progress and Purpose: A Development History of the United States Marine Corps* (Washington, DC: Marine Corps Historical Center, 1974).

Lt. Colonel Charles A. Fleming, USMC, Captain Robin L. Austin, USMC, and Captain Charles A. Braley III, USMC, *Quantico: Crossroads of the Corps* (Washington, DC: Marine Corps Historical Center, 1978).

Allan R. Millett, *Semper Fidelis: The History of the United States Marine Corps*, 2nd ed. (New York: Macmillan, 1993).

Donald F. Bittner

R

RESERVE OFFICERS' TRAINING CORPS (ROTC). *See* ARMY RE-SERVE OFFICERS' TRAINING CORPS.

REVENUE-CUTTER ACADEMY. *See* SCHOOL OF INSTRUCTION OF THE REVENUE-MARINE.

REVIEW OF MILITARY LITERATURE. See MILITARY REVIEW.

RODGERS, CHRISTOPHER R. P. Christopher Raymond Perry Rodgers (born 1819, died 1892), Rear Admiral, U.S. Navy, Commandant of Midshipman (1860–61) and twice Superintendent (1874–78, 1881) of the U.S. Naval Academy.

As commandant of midshipmen on the outbreak of the Civil War, then Lieutenant Rodgers acted quickly to relocate the academy's training ship, the school staff, and those midshipmen remaining loyal to the Union to Newport, Rhode Island.* His decisive leadership was directly responsible for the continued existence of the U.S. Naval Academy* and its contribution of trained naval officers throughout the war. Also as commandant, he introduced the first system of differentiating the responsibilities and privileges between junior and senior classes of midshipmen as an incentive for encouraging the development of their sense of duty.

But his greatest contributions to education in the Navy occurred during his first tour as the academy's superintendent. A Rodgers biographer, Stephen B. Brown, writes:

By upgrading and rationalizing the academy's curriculum, especially in regard to the new four year course for engineers, introducing the first mechanical engineering course in the country, "concentrating professional subjects in the first and second class [senior and junior] years, and adding upper level electives in mathematics, mechanics, physics, and chemistry," Rodgers laid the ground work for an American naval renaissance in the 1880s. The improved quality of academy graduates resulted in Congress and the public soon deferring to them on the issue of ship design for a modern navy.

His major contribution in curriculum design was a deft blend of theory and practice—against the opposition of many senior officers who believed that practice was sufficient in itself. He put his stamp on the teaching of theory by emphasizing the central role of mathematics and the scientific method. In the realm of practice he emphasized the hands-on instruction of engineering subjects (e.g., all "cadet-engineers" were required to build a functioning steam engine from basic stock, making their own drawings, patterns, and forgings, machined parts, etc.). By the end of his first tour as superintendent in 1878 the Naval Academy had won the prestigious Gold Medal of the Paris Exposition for the "best system of education in the United States."

After finishing his academy tour in 1878 he returned to the superintendency in 1881, as he neared retirement. The Navy at large had suffered the effects of congressional neglect, and discipline at the Naval Academy had become slack. Rodgers made a start in removing slack from the system by enforcing the academy's heretofore rarely enforced rules against hazing and by imposing strict punishment for related offenses. After a period of neglect or opposition by an academy leadership not comfortable with a collegial style of governance, he also re-instituted the Academic Board, the academy's instrument for designing the curriculum and passing on midshipman academic performance. Rodgers retired from the service in November 1881.

Rear Admiral Rodgers was a courteous and quiet leader whom some referred to as "the Chesterfield of the Navy." Stephen Brown has noted that Rodgers "has been overlooked as a naval reformer because he worked for change as an understated professional rather than as an active publicist."

Sources:

Stephen D. Brown, "Christopher Raymond Perry Rodgers: Mentor of the New Navy," in Daniel M. Masterson (ed.), *Naval History: The Sixth Symposium of the U.S. Naval Academy* [1983] (Wilmington, DE: Scholarly Re-sources, 1987).
William B. Cogar, *Dictionary of Admirals of the U.S. Navy, Vol. I, 1862–1900* (Annapolis, MD: Naval Institute Press, 1989).
"C.R.P. Rodgers Vertical File" U.S. Naval Academy, Nimitz Library special collections.

James A. Winnefeld

ROOT, ELIHU. Elihu Root (born 1842, died 1937), Secretary of War from 1899–1903, established the basic structure of 20th-century U.S. Army professional military education.

Root, the son of a mathematics professor at Hamilton College in New York State, never served as a soldier and made his career and reputation in the law. A graduate of Hamilton College and the New York University Law School,

Root was admitted to the New York bar in 1867 and two years later started his own firm. He rose rapidly in the legal profession, as counsel for wealthy corporate and business clients. His success rested on his capacity for hard work, mastery of detail, and the logic, clarity, and wit of his courtroom argument. Root also was active in New York Republican politics. He became a friend and advisor of Theodore Roosevelt during Roosevelt's term as New York City police commissioner and candidacy for governor of New York. Remarkably, Root managed to keep aloof from the seamier side of city and state Republican affairs; he acquired a reputation for integrity and statesmanship.

That reputation, plus his legal expertise, brought Root to the post of Secretary of War. President William McKinley appointed him to the job in July 1899 to improve the image of a department hard hit by Spanish-American War scandals and to work out the legal and constitutional details of governing Cuba, Puerto Rico, and the Philippines, newly taken from Spain. Root fulfilled McKinley's expectations in both areas, and he also successfully directed Army operations in the Philippine-American War and the China Relief Expedition. Unexpectedly in the light of his total lack of military experience, he also brought about organizational reforms that laid the institutional foundation for the modern United States Army.

Soon after he took office, Root came into contact with army officer reformers, disciples of the deceased Colonel Emory Upton.* Root adopted the essentials of the reformers' agenda: staff and command reform, an expansible Regular Army, and a trained national reserve. Reflecting Upton's influence, Root arranged for government publication of that officer's unfinished manuscript, *The Military Policy of the United States*. He brought his formidable legal, political, and public relations talents to the enactment of three far-reaching pieces of legislation—the Army reorganization act of 1901, the Dick Militia Act of 1903, and the act creating the Chief of Staff and General Staff, also passed in 1903—which embodied the major elements of the Uptonian program.

Professional military education early drew Root's attention as an area in which he could act on his own executive authority. The issue was important for both short- and long-range reasons. In the expanded postwar army, more than half the officers, commissioned from the 1898 Volunteers or from civilian life, had received no formal military education, a lack the service had to remedy. From a broader perspective, Root recognized that the new command and staff system he was creating must have educated officers to operate it and that efficient mobilization of wartime citizen armies would require a large number of trained commanders and staff officers. Fortunately, Root had in place the prewar system of branch schools and the rudimentary staff college at Fort Leavenworth,* all of which had been shut down during the conflict with Spain. Building on this foundation, he set out to create a system of professional education for both Regular and potential Volunteer officers, to ensure that "the nation may have at all times at its disposal a highly trained body of officers and may know who they are" and that the soldiers so trained would be prepared "to command men in war."

During his first two years in office, Root took a number of preliminary steps. He launched an ultimately successful campaign to expand the West Point* cadet corps, modernize the academy's entrance examination and curriculum, and enlarge and improve its physical plant. He secured funds from Congress to reopen the existing branch schools. Most important, in February 1900, he constituted a board of officers, headed by Brigadier General William Ludlow, to develop a plan for an Army War College.* As Root envisioned it, the college was to function as the capstone and controlling agency of the Army school system. It also would perform the study and planning functions of a general staff until Root could obtain legislation to create one.

Based on the Ludlow board's report and additional planning, Root on November 27, 1901, in War Department General Order 155, established for the first time in the Army's history a comprehensive hierarchical system of officer professional education.* At the lowest level, post schools were to instruct all officers in basic tactics and military administration. Next came the specialized branch schools for the artillery, the engineers, mine defense, the cavalry and field artillery, and the Army Medical School. Above them in the hierarchy, the General Service and Staff College* at Fort Leavenworth, an expansion of the pre–Spanish-American War Infantry and Cavalry School,* was to prepare selected lieutenants for higher command and staff duties.

At the top of the system was the Army War College,* to be located at Washington Barracks in Washington, D.C. (now Fort Lesley McNair*). A board of five officers detailed from the Army at large, with the chiefs of artillery and engineers, the superintendent of the U.S. Military Academy* and the commander of the General Service and Staff College as ex officio members, was to govern the War College and also supervise and coordinate the work of the lower schools. The war college classes, made up of distinguished graduates of the General Service and Staff College, as well as captains and field grade officers specially designated by the War Department, would take "an advanced course of professional study" aimed at preparing them for military attaché and general staff assignments.

To ensure intellectual rigor, Root's order required that at all the schools, the officer students were to be examined on their work with the results made part of their records. All schools but the War College would admit, in addition to Regulars, selected National Guard officers and civilian graduates of college military training programs, who would be earmarked for future Volunteer commissions on the basis of their work.

During the two remaining years of his stewardship as Secretary of War, Root put his educational system into operation. He secured congressional funding for the War College and the General Service and Staff College, including money for the War College building at Washington Barracks. By late 1902, the post and branch schools and the Leavenworth staff college were in at least limited operation. The War College Board, headed by Major General Samuel B. M. Young, oversaw the other schools and made plans for the college. As Root had intended, the board also acted as an interim general staff, making studies on various subjects for Root's guidance. On February 21, 1903, at a ceremony attended by President Theodore Roosevelt and other dignitaries, Root laid the cornerstone for the War College building (now used by the National Defense University*). In his address, he made his memorable and often quoted statement of the college's mission: "Not to promote war, but to preserve peace by intelligent and adequate preparation to repel aggression."

After establishment of the General Staff* by law in 1903, the War College Board was replaced by a president and two directors under "direct control" of the new Chief of Staff. The college continued for some time to serve more as a study and planning arm of the General Staff than as an educational institution. Only gradually, under Brigadier General Tasker H. Bliss* and subsequent presidents, did the War College fully take up its educational mission.

Elihu Root left the War Department late in 1903 and thereafter had little direct contact with Army affairs. He devoted the rest of his long, distinguished career to law and international relations. Yet his influence on the Army was profound. His organizational reforms, notably his creation of the General Staff, were instrumental in transforming the Army from a frontier and colonial constabulary to the fighting force of a world power. In professional military education, his role was equally significant. The school system he established, although much modified and expanded over the years, produced the great American commanders of World Wars I and II and continues to shape the Army's leaders to this very day.

Sources:

Harry P. Ball, *Of Responsible Command: A History of the U.S. Army War College* (Carlisle, PA: Alumni Association of the U.S. Army War College, 1984).
Philip C. Jessup, *Elihu Root*, 2 vols. (New York: Dodd, Mead, 1938).
Elihu Root, *Five Years of the War Department* (Washington, DC: Government Printing Office, 1904).

Graham A. Cosmas

ROYAL AIR FORCE COLLEGE-CRANWELL. Established as a Royal Navy flying training school during the First World War, Cranwell later became a precommissioning educational institution for Royal Air Force officer candidates.

The history of Cranwell does not begin with the Royal Air Force, but with the Royal Naval Air Service. Established in July 1914, the naval aviators initially shared flying training facilities with the air arm of the British Army, the Royal Flying Corps. By 1915 the Admiralty felt the need to establish its own flying training establishment and chose a site at Cranwell, Lincolnshire, for its Central

Depot and Flying School. By late 1916 Cranwell was a fully operational naval air station.

In April 1918, the Royal Air Force (RAF) became the world's first independent air arm and absorbed units from both the Royal Flying Corps and Royal Naval Air Service. Cranwell remained open as an RAF training base. After the close of First World War, the RAF succeeded in its efforts to remain a separate service and, in October 1919, received permission from the Cabinet to convert RAF Cranwell to an air force college. The new Royal Air Force College (RAFC), which opened in February 1920, was to combine flying training with higher education in a two-year program.

In order to gain entrance to the college, candidates had to pass a written examination in a variety of subjects, face an interview board, and pass a full aircrew medical examination. The initial curriculum for the first year included practical mathematics, history, literature, army and navy organization, and a series of practical courses in map reading, wood and metal work, gunnery, and Morse code. Second-year studies concentrated on the practical requirements of future pilots with courses in engines, principles of flight, aircraft rigging, wireless telegraphy, gunnery, and, finally, approximately fifty hours of flight instruction. Cadets who successfully completed the two-year program would be commissioned as RAF officers and proceed to follow-on flying training.

It was not until 1928 that the Treasury gave the RAF permission to proceed with plans to construct a new college building at RAFC Cranwell. The new College Hall included dormitories, lecture halls, classrooms, dining and recreation facilities, laboratories, and a library and officially opened in 1934. When World War II began in 1939, RAFC Cranwell ceased to function as a college and became a vast training center. In addition to intermediate and advanced flying training, it became the home to a variety of RAF technical and ground training schools during the war years.

RAFC Cranwell reopened in October 1946. The course was extended to two and a half years. By the mid-1950s, cadets received training in jet aircraft on longer, hard-surfaced runways constructed in 1954. By 1958, the curriculum was three years long, with the first year concentrating on academics and the last two years stressing flying training. In 1966 RAFC Cranwell merged with RAF Technical College Henlow, a science and engineering university that produced officers for the RAF's technical branches. Now RAFC Cranwell would train cadets aspiring to both aircrew and engineering positions in a new, two-and-a-half-year syllabus.

By the 1970s, RAFC Cranwell shortened its curriculum by eliminating most academic requirements and becoming the RAF's central initial officer training establishment. It was considered impracticable to offer intensive professional training (such as flying training) at the same time as a university academic degree. The RAF therefore decided to sponsor "cadetships" at the nation's universities through the University Air Squadron Scheme—similar to the U.S. Air Force's Reserve Officers' Training Corps* program. After completing an undergraduate degree, qualified cadets would attend Cranwell for their principal officer and professional training. By 1979, initial officer training lasted approximately three months. For many graduates, basic flying training followed at Cranwell, while advanced flying training moved to other airfields.

Today RAFC Cranwell continues as the initial training establishment for RAF officers. The current course is 24 weeks long, with five to six classes entering each year.

Sources:

Fifty Years at Cranwell: A History of the Royal Air Force College, 1920–1970 (Cranwell: Royal Air Force College, 1970).
E. B. Haslam, *The History of Royal Air Force Cranwell* (London: HMSO, 1982).
                                                    Major John J. Abbatiello, USAF

ROYAL MILITARY ACADEMY-SANDHURST. Officer training establishment in Britain, originally founded for schooling junior officers for the infantry and cavalry arms during the Napoleonic Wars, that currently trains officer candidates for all of the branches of the British Army.

Military schools in Britain originally took responsibility for training officers in the technical services. In 1741, King George II (also the last British monarch to lead an army in the field) signed a Royal Warrant to establish a school for training artillery and engineer officers in mathematics and the sciences. Thus the Army founded its first Royal Military Academy at Woolwich* to replace the former system of sending young men to artillery and engineering units in the field—many times in foreign armies—to learn their trade. At this time, cavalry and infantry junior officers also gained experience with units in the field and advanced in rank through the purchase of commissions. In these less technical branches, little effort was made to pursue academic training, and none was required of them.

The Wars of Revolutionary France and Napoleon posed a tremendous challenge to the British Army, which required a rapid expansion to meet this serious threat. Pressured by William Pitt the Younger and senior officers in the Army, including its commander-in-chief, the Duke of York, King George III signed a royal warrant in 1801 to establish educational institutions to improve the professional preparation of both junior and senior officers. These leaders felt that formal, consistent training would be required to lead and staff the growing British Army. The basic concept for a junior school was to reward the service of meritorious officers by educating those sons intending to follow in their fathers' footsteps.

The Junior Department of the Royal Military College, as the new school became known, received its first group of "gentlemen cadets" in 1802 at a temporary site in a large house in Great Marlow, Buckinghamshire. Within a few years, all but a dozen or so, who were sons of officers killed in service, were required to pay for their schooling. Still, the school soon enrolled nearly

300 cadets between the ages of 13 and 16 at entrance. Growing numbers of trainees required a larger institution, and in 1812 the college moved to Sandhurst—a site purchased from the Prime Minister, William Pitt the Younger.

Unlike the technical services, attendance at Sandhurst was not initially required to obtain a commission in the infantry or cavalry. However, gentlemen cadets from Royal Military College (RMC) Sandhurst could gain their first commission in these branches without purchase as long as they successfully completed their studies. This was a considerable award since an ensign's commission in the mid-19th century, for example, required a nomination and a payment of £450.

The course of study and cadet organization at Sandhurst has endured almost continuous evolution since 1812. Early coursework included a variety of subjects that included mathematics, languages, history, military fortification and drawing, geography, and English literature. Military drill was part of the daily routine. In the 1860s, military training, including fencing and gunnery, gained more emphasis, and the length of the course was fixed at one year. The absorption of the Indian Army in 1862 required an expansion of the establishment from 180 to 336 cadets.

By 1911 Sandhurst was graduating over 400 newly commissioned officers per year. It remained open during the First World War, in which over 3,000 of its graduates lost their lives. The course of study, however, was limited to strictly military training during the war. The course at RMC-Sandhurst was shortened to six months for most of the war; an officer shortage in 1918 forced a reduction in course time to two months.

During the interwar years, academic subjects gradually returned to the syllabus at Sandhurst. By 1939, over 600 cadets were enrolled. When World War II began, the British Army again converted RMC-Sandhurst into a six-month officer training unit for infantry and armor junior officers. Fifteen thousand cadets passed through Sandhurst during the five and a half years of the war, in which over 1,200 graduates died.

The postwar reorganization of the British Army had a significant impact on its officer-training establishment. In January 1947 the Royal Military College-Sandhurst and the Royal Military Academy-Woolwich amalgamated to form the Royal Military Academy-Sandhurst. This new eighteen-month course would produce all regular officers for the peacetime army. As Field Marshal the Viscount Montgomery of Alamein wrote that year, "This is the task of the Royal Military Academy Sandhurst: to produce officers who will be fit, morally, mentally and physically, to lead the British soldier." This belief was evident in Sandhurst's motto: "Serve to Lead." A balance of military training and academic subjects, such as languages, mathematics, international affairs, and war studies, provided a well-rounded curriculum.

Since 1947, RMA-Sandhurst has again evolved to meet the requirements of the British Army. Today it produces commissioned officers for all branches (with the exceptions of the nursing corps and direct commissioning of senior noncommissioned officers) of the regular, short-service, and territorial forces of the British Army.

Sandhurst has produced some of Britain's greatest wartime leaders including Generals Roberts, Haig, Allenby, Wavell, Alexander, and Montgomery, and, of course, Winston Churchill. Other famous graduates include the late King Hussein of Jordan, actor David Niven, and Ayub Khan, former president of Pakistan. From 1947 to 1990, almost 24,000 graduates—from 74 different countries—completed their studies at RMA-Sandhurst.

Sources:

David G. Chandler, (ed.), *Great Battles of the British Army: As Commemorated in the Sandhurst Companies* (London: Arms and Armour Press, 1991).
Brigadier Sir John Smyth, *Sandhurst: The History of the Royal Military Academy, Woolwich, the Royal Military College, Sandhurst, and the Royal Military Academy Sandhurst, 1741–1961* (London: Weidenfeld and Nicolson, 1961).
Hugh Thomas, *The Story of Sandhurst* (London: Hutchinson, 1961).
Patrick Ward with David G. Chandler, *Sandhurst: The Royal Military Academy* (Shrewsbury, U.K.: Harmony House, 1991).

Major John J. Abbatiello, USAF

ROYAL MILITARY ACADEMY-WOOLWICH. Britain's first precommissioning school, which served since the mid-18th century as a primary source of artillery and engineer officers for the United Kingdom until World War II.

A Royal Warrant, signed on April 30, 1741, directed George II's Master General of Ordnance (MGO) to establish a technical academy to include military cadets of the artillery and engineers. It was to be at the Warren, in Woolwich Arsenal. At the time, the Royal Regiment of Artillery consisted of seven companies with five cadets in each. A regularly officered Corps of Royal Engineers was not established until 1757, but engineer cadets joined the artillery for training before being commissioned. Not until 1761 were cadets, whose ages varied from 30 to 12, commissioned directly into the engineers.

In 1764, the MGO appointed James Pattison as Lieutenant Governor of the "Shop," as the academy was known. The cadets having been moved into a common barracks a decade earlier, their accommodation—in two or three classrooms, with up to seven cadets in a bedroom, no recreation rooms, and three plain meals a day—while adequate according to the standards of the day, was not luxurious. Bullying was common and corporal punishment not unusual. Pattison corrected, to some extent, the low academic standards and lax discipline and enabled the Shop to supply efficient officers for the growing Royal Artillery, Corps of Royal Engineers, and also the East India Company.

In the Napoleonic expansion the currently existing buildings on Woolwich Common, above the arsenal, opened in 1806. Only a few Shop cadets remained at the Warren.

The Shop was renowned for its rebels of which Orde Wingate is a recent example. "Chinese Gordon" entered in 1833. An eccentric, given to criticizing orders in a soto voce lisp, he was bad at mathematics but excellent at fortifications and surveying. Relegated a term for bullying in a "snooker" brawl, he was enabled to pass high enough in the order of merit to be commissioned as a sapper and go on to fame, if not fortune.

When the amalgamation of the Shop and the Royal Military College-Sandhurst,* was suggested in 1875, opponents argued that the Shop entrance examination and syllabus—mathematics, practical geometry, fortifications, artillery, military topography, military history, tactics, French and German languages, landscape drawing, natural philosophy, chemistry, and electricity—were beyond the capacity of Sandhurst cadets.

After South Africa, the British Army was prepared for a Continental war by Lord Haldane's Reforms of 1906. A two-year Shop course introduced indirect fire by long-range quick-firing guns, signaling and field telephones, musketry, interior economy, and military law. Khaki, first used in the Sudan war, 1896–98, became peacetime dress. From 1909 to 1912 the course was reduced to three terms, and entry numbers increased before the First World War.

In 1914 the course was reduced to six months, fees were abolished, four entrance exams a year were held, and there was no passing-out exam. Only military subjects were taught, and all civilian instructors departed. Sappers and gunners had separate syllabi. The age of wartime cadets ran from 16.5 to 25 years. By 1917 it was a struggle to maintain standards, even anachronistic ones. Swords were still carried on some parades. Dinner jackets were worn until 1918. But explosives, optics, wireless, hygiene, the slide rule, and mechanical transport were crammed into the syllabus. Yet the caliber of entrants from Britain's "public schools," still the main officer source, had declined. Young officers (YOs) attended artillery and engineering courses after graduation to ensure that field units were properly served. The custom continued after the war to allow more space in the Shop syllabus for academic subjects.

The sappers gave rise to the Royal Flying Corps before 1914 and in 1920 to the Royal Signals, to which 12 to 14 cadets were commissioned in 1924. A few entered the new Royal Tank Corps. Beginning in 1928 one or two cadets entered from the ranks without fee or examination. Foreign cadets, limited to four a class, came mainly from the Middle and Far East. The syllabus between the wars suffered from the financial axe hanging over the army itself. The Keogh and Haldane committees, in 1921 and 1922, considered amalgamating the cadet colleges to save money. The three technical arms were opposed; the dirty buildings by Woolwich Common, which generations of cadets had mapped, inspired loyalty. But when two terms of cadets left for their YO's courses in July 1939, on the eve of the Second World War, the Shop's time was nearly over. On September 1, 1939, the gates closed behind the remaining cadets. They never reopened.

In 1946, the staff of the new Royal Military Academy gathered at Sandhurst to plan the joint institution. The civilian staff were nearly all from the Shop, having served in the forces in the meanwhile, and the syllabus of Sandhurst was to be more academic than before. The chief military instructor and one of the two college adjutants had been at the Shop in 1939. They and the company instructors, fresh from campaigns in several theaters of war, ensured that the soul of the old Shop lived on.

Sources:

Sir Frederick Guggisberg, *The Shop: The Story of the Royal Military Academy* (London: Cassell & Company, 1900).

Colonel K. W. Maurice Jones, *The Shop Story, 1900–1939* (Woolwich: Royal Artillery Institution, 1955).

Richard A. Preston, "Perspectives in the History of Military Education and Professionalism," Harmon Memorial Lecture in Military History Number Twenty-Two, United States Air Force Academy, Colorado, 1980.

Dominick S. Graham

ROYAL MILITARY COLLEGE-SANDHURST. *See* ROYAL MILITARY ACADEMY-SANDHURST.

ROYAL NAVAL COLLEGE-PORTSMOUTH/GREENWICH. Britain's first institution of advanced professional education for experienced naval officers, to which a few selected American officers were sent annually before establishment of the U.S. Naval Postgraduate School.

The Puritan Revolution and Dutch Wars of 17th-century England led to the need for a permanent national navy and a professional officer corps to lead it. A royal proclamation in 1677 actually outlined the minimum qualifying factors for a commission in the Royal Navy—the kind of standards that, until fairly recently, have been absent in the British Army. At that time, requirements for a lieutenancy included three years of sea service, a minimum age of 20 years, letters of recommendation from former commanders, and most importantly, the successful completion of an examination demonstrating knowledge of seamanship and navigation.

In 1729 the Admiralty decided to establish the Royal Navy's first officer training school ashore. Naval leaders wanted to increase the general education of its officers and, perhaps more importantly, better control the quality of officer candidates. Until that time, young men could become naval officers in peacetime only through the personal patronage of a ship's captain (usually after having first come aboard as his personal servant) or by rising from the enlisted ranks and petty officer status. In wartime, an experienced merchant sailor could sometimes gain a commission in the Royal Navy where the opportunity for prize money, through participation in enemy ship capture, served as a tempting lure.

The new academy opened in a single building at Portsmouth dockyard in the summer of 1733. The Admiralty required "some progress in the Latin tongue," which excluded the lower classes from gaining entrance. Entering cadets were from 13 to 16 years of age; in the 19th century the required age was reduced to 12 to 14. Required courses included arithmetic, writing, drawing, gunnery, fortification, French, and dancing. During their second year, cadets also studied practical applications including boatwork, rigging, dockyard work, and ship-wrighting.

The academy's maximum capacity was 40 cadets; hence, graduates accounted for only a small proportion of naval officers. The Royal Academy produced only a handful of distinguished officers. Graduates had a reputation for poor discipline and vice, and few families who knew the Navy sent their sons there. The academy was temporarily closed in 1806, reformed and reopened as the Royal Naval College in 1808, and closed again in 1837. For the next 20 years, the Royal Navy sent its officer candidates straight to sea until establishing a series of floating but stationary training ships at various locations. In 1863, the school ship HMS *Britannia* settled in Dartmouth, where its shore-based descendant still exists as a precommissioning school today.

Meanwhile, in 1839, the Royal Naval College had reopened at Portsmouth—but, as James Soley* writes, "on an entirely different basis." Created to offer experienced officers and mates "further means of scientific education," the college soon expanded to serve officers in the higher ranks of the Royal Navy and Marines—"officers qualifying for the marine artillery, masters, naval instructors, and engineers." This institution continued to operate until 1873 when the Admiralty, acknowledging the program limitations imposed by Portsmouth's meager facilities, finally overcame its reluctance to move a naval school away from a dockside location. In February of that year, the Royal Naval College was relocated to Greenwich, where its larger physical plant and proximity to the resources of London enhanced its potential for meeting the Admiralty's objectives.

The result, as the Admiralty had intended, was an institution more complex and rigorous and less governed by military discipline than the precommissioning schools that preceded it. As stated in the government's circular just prior to the Greenwich opening, the Royal Naval College was intended "to provide for the education of naval officers of all ranks above that of midshipman in all branches of theoretical and scientific study bearing on their profession." Accordingly, courses were provided in many aspects of theoretical and applied mathematics, experimental science, applied mechanics, marine engineering and architecture, naval tactics, international and maritime law, and modern languages as appropriate for several different branches of naval service. Moreover, programs of study of different duration were made available, depending on a student's rank and experience and duty status. More experienced officers (lieutenant through captain) were permitted to volunteer for one academic year of study, at half-pay, and given free choice of courses. Engineers and assistant engineers who were assigned to ships could volunteer for three years of study with some choice of courses, at full pay. Other students, including chaplains aspiring to become naval instructors, line officers qualifying as gunnery or torpedo officers, civilians wishing to study naval architecture or marine engineering, and younger, acting sublieutenants or acting assistant engineers, were given totally prescribed curricula, each of different duration.

By the turn of the century, the Royal Naval College had achieved a world-class reputation, partly because of its outstanding faculty and also to its original contributions to naval technology. Until 1897, it had admitted a number of foreign students whose governments had sought benefit from the expertise assembled there. From shortly after its move to Greenwich, these had included small numbers of U.S. naval officers who were detailed there to study naval construction. Although the college's strength was based primarily upon its work in science and technology, it had since 1876 also included regular lectures on naval history and tactics. Under scholars like Sir John Laughton, Vice Admiral Philip Colomb, and in the pre–World War I era, Sir Julian Corbett, the study of naval history advanced in acceptance as an academic pursuit and was instrumental in bolstering the position of the Royal Navy in Britain's search for an effective defense strategy. In this field and others, the Royal Naval College came to fulfill the Admiralty's hope that the school's bringing together of naval officers with the nation's outstanding scholars would prove advantageous.

Sources:

Eric Grove (ed.), *Great Battles of the Royal Navy: As Commemorated in the Gunroom, Britannia Royal Naval College, Dartmouth* (London: Arms and Armour, 1994).
N.A.M. Rodger, *The Wooden World: An Anatomy of the Georgian Navy* (Glasgow: William Collins, 1986).
James R. Soley, *Report on Foreign Systems of Naval Education* (Washington, DC: Government Printing Office, 1880).
F. B. Sullivan, "The Royal Academy at Portsmouth," *Mariner's Mirror* 63 (1977).

Major John J. Abbatiello, USAF

ROYAL UNITED SERVICES INSTITUTE FOR DEFENCE STUDIES. *See* ROYAL UNITED SERVICES INSTITUTION.

ROYAL UNITED SERVICES INSTITUTION (RUSI). British scientific and literary organization, dedicated to advancing the study of military affairs and formed under royal patronage in 1831, whose *Journal* later achieved international acclaim. RUSI helped inspire the creation of several late-19th-century American military journals and provided a model for the U.S. Army's Military Service Institution of the United States.

A reader calling himself "an old Egyptian Campaigner" started the RUSI ball rolling in 1829 with a letter to *Colbourn's United Service Journal*. His letter pled a case for establishing a United Services Museum, to be managed by British officers of both the army and navy to signify that both professions were worthy of scientific study. The idea was seized upon by a small core of *Colbourn's*

Journal subscribers who were eager to study the military lessons of the Napoleonic wars and who formed an organizing committee.

The Duke of Clarence, encouraged by the Duke of Wellington, agreed to become a patron, and a formal proposal for assembling the organization was submitted to the recently crowned William IV. Assured that it could "proceed under His Majesty's gracious auspices," the committee, chaired by Maj. General Sir Howard Douglas, completed its work. From the beginning, the founders' intent was to create a "scientific and professional society," and pains were taken to encourage the free expression of ideas from its membership. Particular attention was given to attracting participation from a large number of serving junior officers, and the membership subscriptions for them were set at only 10 shillings annually. A regular series of scholarly lectures and member meetings was begun, and a library and museum were assembled from gifts which, according to former RUSI vice president Shelford Bidwell, "flowed in."

The organization grew steadily and acquired what it intended as a permanent facility in London's Whitehall area. By the early 1840s, its membership had risen to more than 4,000, and it had developed an active program of lectures and member discussions of original papers. In 1857, it began publishing its journal; and three years later it received its Royal Charter as the Royal United Services Institution, with "The promotion and advancement of Naval and Military science and Literature" as its official mission. In 1871, when faced with the prospect of having to abandon its Whitehall location in response to a Treasury order, RUSI was invited by Queen Victoria to move its museum holdings into the Royal Banqueting House. And, aided by fund donations raised by the RUSI Council, it was able to purchase adjacent land and build new office and program facilities that it occupied in 1895.

The *Journal of the Royal United Services Institution*, aided by an annual essay contest it initiated in 1878 (the same year in which the U.S. Naval Institute* began its contest), gained international acclaim. Many of its articles were written by Great Britain's finest officers and outstanding military authors—J.F.C. Fuller, General Sir Archibald P. Wavell, H. de Watteville, and General Sir William Slim among others. "Generalship" and the personal qualities that contribute to its effectiveness, relating directly to the purposes of professional military education, was one of the *Journal*'s themes on which articles occasionally appeared. Essays on that subject were awarded RUSI's Gold Medal in 1914 and 1919, and other articles carried forward a spirited dialogue on the theme throughout the interwar period.

During the period of the cold war, RUSI underwent a significant transition. Whereas the interwar years had seen RUSI's tiny in-house staff concerned mainly with administrative and financial matters and the intellectual effort handled largely by a core of active members, the staff took on new responsibilities and expanded accordingly beginning in the 1960s. This change came in response to member urging that RUSI develop the capabilities to serve as an independent "think tank" to study problems of national defense and the strong support of

Lord Louis Mountbatten for this idea. The change came slowly: As Shelford Bidwell captures it, "it was to be twenty years before sufficient staff of the right calibre could be afforded and assembled to carry out the essential in-house research and compose and edit an adequate range of publications." Beginning in 1968, under the leadership of Air Vice Marshal S.W.B. Menaul, RUSI gradually added publication of defense-related monographs and the reports of its seminars and joined with Brassey's Publications to produce a "defence" yearbook. By the late 1990s, the in-house staff had grown from Menaul's original staff of three to 23 administrators, editors, study and program directors, and area specialists assisted by seven research fellows. The transition has also brought about a name change—the Royal United Services Institute for Defence Studies.

Sources:

Shelford Bidwell, "The Royal United Services Institute for Defence Studies, 1831–1991," *RUSI Journal* 136, no. 2 (Summer 1991).
Lt. Colonel Russell W. Glenn, "Earning the Thanks of Harry and Jack: The Journal of the Royal United Services Institution and World War Generalship," *RUSI Journal* 142, no. 1 (February 1997).

S

SCHARNHORST, GERHARD VON. General Gerhard Johann David von Scharnhorst (born 1755, died of wounds suffered at the Battle of Grossgörschen, July 28, 1813) initiated and developed the first system of formal military education in Prussia. His reforms provided the groundwork for the professionalism of the Prussian and German officer corps.

Scharnhorst spent the first two decades of his military service in Hanover and became famous throughout the German states as a teacher, a military critic, and an advocate of formal technical instruction combined with *Bildung*, the cultivation of individual character and understanding. During his time in Hanoverian service, Scharnhorst edited three journals and published a number of books, the most famous being the *Militärisches Taschenbuch* (1792). In 1801 he left the service of Hanover for that of Prussia, where he served the remainder of his life in a variety of positions, finally rising to Minister of War and Chief of the General Staff (1813). The great German historian Friedrich Meinecke wrote that Scharnhorst was "the quiet hero . . . the tenacious, inflexible, secretive armorer, whose work alone made the Wars of Liberation possible."

A critical part of Scharnhorst's agenda upon entering Prussian service was the reform of the military. Among the numerous changes he advocated were the integration of infantry, artillery, and cavalry in combined arms operations; the creation of a general staff; and the reorganization of the services into standard corps and divisions. Central to all of these changes was the transformation of the tradition-bound Prussian standing army into a modern force of citizen-soldiers. Such an army, Scharnhorst believed, needed a professional officer corps based on the ideas of the Enlightenment. To create such a body, Scharnhorst initiated a transformation of the educational program of the Prussian military.

This new system of education served a number of purposes. First, it provided a foundation for advancement by merit, rather than the nepotism and formalism that dictated promotion in the past. Second, it provided soldiers with the necessary abilities both to use the technical equipment required in such branches as artillery and engineers on the battlefield, and to integrate those assets with the other forces on the ground. Third, it provided learned leaders who would, as Scharnhorst said, "know how to take the necessary measures in uncertain circumstances. In all circumstances he [the leader] must understand how to choose the best means appropriate to the situation."

At the center of Scharnhorst's program was his *Bildungsprinzip*—his attempt to instill in soldiers and officers alike the spirit and intellect that were necessary in order to win on the battlefield against the armies of Republican and Napoleonic France and its *levée en masse*. Only by altering its own military structure could Prussia hope to remain viable against such forces. The key to such change was individual *Bildung*. Only through study, reflection, and discussion, Scharnhorst believed, would leaders be able to develop ideas and formulate plans that would facilitate victory in war. Between 1801 and 1813 he established a system of military schools that encouraged these attributes. These academic schools, from the institutes for new cadets to the *Kriegsschule*,* brought together a synthesis of military training and general education that would, as Charles E. White writes, "develop leadership and promote realism and intellectual independence, avoiding the tendency of most earlier military schools of solely conveying facts and drilling officers in a particular theory of war." This was the core of what Scharnhorst wanted to achieve through *Bildung*. Although his ideas were not fully realized during his lifetime, he was the first to develop a system of military education that at its best produced liberal, intellectual, and ethically accountable individuals in Prussian army uniforms.

Sources:

Friedrich Meinecke, *The Age of German Liberation, 1795–1815*, ed. Peter Paret (Berkeley: University of California Press, 1977).
Peter Paret, *Yorck and the Era of Prussian Reform, 1807–1815* (Princeton, NJ: Princeton University Press, 1966).
Herbert Rosinski, "Scharnhorst to Schlieffen: The Rise and Decline of German Military Thought," *Naval War College Review* 29, no. 1 (1976).
Charles E. White, *The Enlightened Soldier: Scharnhorst and the Militärische Gesellschaft in Berlin, 1801–1805* (New York: Praeger, 1989).

Major Michael A. Boden, USA

SCHOOL OF ADVANCED AIRPOWER STUDIES. The United States Air Force's newest graduate-level program of professional military education conducted at Air University, Maxwell Air Force Base, Alabama.

Stemming in part from frustrations associated with the Vietnam War, the Air Force decided in 1988, to establish a new graduate-level institution for selected officers to explore more deeply the theory and doctrine of air power and the planning and execution of air campaigns. Accordingly the School of Advanced Airpower Studies was created to encourage the development of the air strategists of the future. The curriculum planning, organization, and staffing to achieve this purpose were done between 1988 and June 1991, when the first class entered. The goal has been pursued by an educational process blending operational expertise and scholarship in an environment cultivating the creation, evaluation, and refinement of ideas. The U.S. Congress authorized the award of a master's degree to all graduates of the school in 1994.

The School of Advanced Airpower Studies (SAAS) is one of the directorates of the Air Command and Staff College* located at the Air University,* Maxwell AFB, Alabama. It is administered by a dean, a USAF colonel, and an associate dean, a civilian. As of academic year 1996–97, its faculty included eight professors: four civilians and, the rest, field grade officers. All eight professors possessed the Ph.D.; most have published books, and many have had some sort of operational experience. Disciplines usually represented are political science, mathematics, history, economics, and public policy. In addition to teaching, the faculty is obligated to pursue an active program of research and publication on air power and national security topics. Since the founding, at least four new faculty books have appeared in print, and several other books and chapters have been accepted for publication.

To keep the quality high, only volunteers are assigned as students. Most of them are recruited and chosen from among the resident Air Force students at the various intermediate-level PME schools. In theory, that means they are chosen from the top 20 percent of the majors in the Air Force. A continual effort is made to acquire students from the other U.S. services. It has succeeded in the last four classes. Though the preponderance of the students are chosen from the operational career fields, there is a leavening from other specialties as well—public affairs and acquisition, for example. A board of general officers from the Military Personnel Center, Air University, and Air Force headquarters makes the final selections from the volunteers.

A vital factor in attracting highly competent officers for future classes is to assure that the postgraduation placements are suitable for quality officers with their special expertise. The assignments for the graduating classes have been consistent with their goal. More than half have been assigned to the staffs of the major commands, the unified commands, the Joint Staff, or Headquarters USAF. One graduate each year has been sent to a civilian university to obtain a Ph.D. with the intent that he will ultimately return to serve on the faculty.

The School of Advanced Airpower Studies achieves its mission through methods that are in part traditional for graduate schools, and in part unique. Many of the military professional education schools have been criticized as being too reliant on a parade of outside visitors delivering sleepy lectures inevitably more connected to their own work than to a coherent curriculum at the school. By keeping its enrollment small, SAAS can provide the students and the faculty with an atmosphere ideal for seminar work—a minimum of lecturing and a maximum opportunity for active student learning. Distinguished guests are plentiful, but they almost always meet with students outside the scheduled seminars and thereby do not disrupt the flow of regular instruction. Even there, the question and answer format is favored over lectures and briefings. As the reputation of the school has grown, it is becoming increasingly feasible to bring in important military, political, and technical leaders for intimate sessions with the students—one authority and only the 27 students in a seminar room. Among them have been the Chairman of the Joint Chiefs of Staff, General John Shalikashvili, as well as the USAF Chief of Staff, two former Air Force Chiefs of Staff, and a serving geographic theater commander-in-chief.

At the core of this eleven-month learning experience is an integrated set of courses organized in a way resembling scientific research. There are four courses at the beginning that are described as "theory," a loose equivalent of the laboratory research hypothesis. Two long courses described as "evidence" follow—basically, the history of air power. The curriculum is concluded by five courses described as Synthesis/Application. The last of these courses is Formulating Airpower Theory, presented by the associate dean. Periodically through the year, he has met with the students between courses to help them relate the course just finished and the one in the offing to the developing theme. During the last course, the student is charged to articulate his own personal theory of air power—comparable in purpose to drawing conclusions about an initial research hypothesis.

Seminar discussions are augmented by two field trips. One is to the Army Aviation Center at Fort Rucker, Air Force Armament Museum at Eglin AFB, and the National Museum of Naval Aviation at Pensacola NAS. That is followed by a visit to the Air Force Special Operations Command. The second field trip is the capstone to the technology course and it is usually conducted to Wright-Patterson AFB in the spring. It features a tour of the Air Force Museum plus visits and briefings at the Armstrong and the Wright Laboratories.

The technology course and both field trips are in the "conclusions" end of the curriculum, and another major element there is the annual war game. Recently, members of the Army's School of Advanced Military Studies* and of the Marines' School of Advanced Warfighting Studies* have traveled to Maxwell AFB to participate. In 1996, members of the Naval War College* attended for the first time.

A major innovation in the curriculum since Class V has been a series of trips to Air Operations Centers at the numbered air forces. Each is made by a different small group of students led by a faculty member and supplements the short course on campaign planning. Ideally each student participates in one of them during his year at SAAS. Three outcomes are anticipated: first, the SAAS students can supplement their academic work with some real-world experience. Second, the numbered air force staffs benefit from some external inputs from the SAAS students and faculty. Last, the interest of students in assignments to the numbered air force staffs is stimulated.

Finally, the curriculum's keystone remains the master's thesis. Each professor mentors up to three students for that work, depending on the students' choices of topic and the available faculty expertise. The criteria include a thesis of 40–60 pages, on a significant air power subject, fully documented and of high scholarly quality. The budget includes funds for student research elsewhere, and SAAS researchers have available in their building the leading air power library and air power archives in the world. Faculty and student computers are tied directly to the library's catalog yielding instant access to bibliographical information. They are also netted with those at the Air Command and Staff College as well as the rest of the Air University. Many of these theses have been published; one has already been expanded into a book, and several others have served as the bases for articles later published in professional journals by former students.

David R. Mets

SCHOOL OF ADVANCED MILITARY STUDIES. The U.S. Army's program of advanced PME for selected midcareer officers in preparation for operational planning staff assignments at division and corps levels.

The School of Advanced Military Studies (SAMS) was formed at Fort Leavenworth, Kansas,* in 1983 as an integral part of the U.S. Army's Command and General Staff College (CGSC).* Its purpose was to provide an additional year of advanced education focused at the tactical and operational levels of war to a carefully selected group of midcareer officers (most in the grade of major) who had recently completed the one-year course of instruction at CGSC. Additionally, SAMS conducted a senior service college-level fellowship for a small group of somewhat more senior officers (most in the grade of lieutenant colonel) that was focused at the strategic and operational levels of war. The former was referred to as the Advanced Military Studies Program, the latter as the Advanced Operational Studies Fellowship.

SAMS grew out of the perception of several senior officers that one year of intermediate military education was insufficient to provide professional soldiers with a detailed understanding of both higher-echelon tactics and the evolving subdiscipline of military art and science that was coming to be known as operational art. Most notable of the senior officers of this persuasion was General William R. Richardson, a former CGSC Commandant who went on to command the Army's Training and Doctrine Command. Richardson selected Colonel Huba Wass de Czege as the architect and general contractor who would design and build the school. Wass de Czege was ably assisted in the effort by Colonel Richard H. Sinnreich, who served as his deputy and subsequently succeeded him as the school's second director, and Colonel L. D. Holder, who was with Wass de Czege a principal author of the Army's 1982 edition of *Field Manual 100-5, Operations* and in turn succeeded Sinnreich. Although these four men had slightly varying qualities of temperament and intellect, they shared a common vision. That vision was the creation of a critical mass of officers who would provide the Army informed and analytical, yet also creative, thought about the manifold complexities of modern warfare. SAMS was the institution that was to help the Army create that critical mass. Additionally, each was aware of the tradition of army education that hearkened back to the period between World Wars I and II when at various times and in various forms, the Command and General Staff School had offered a two-year educational experience to midcareer officers.

The school began modestly in the summer of 1983 with 14 second-year students and five advanced operational studies fellows; within two years, it had expanded to its steady-state size of roughly 50 second-year students and eight fellows. The former were selected by senior members of the CGSC faculty based on the results of an entrance examination and a personal interview with the SAMS director or his deputy. The fellows were selected by a Department of the Army panel that slated senior service school selectees to various programs. The faculty consisted of army officers with advanced degrees in disciplines related to military art and science who had previous teaching experience in other venues, as well as several civilians with similar qualifications.

The second-year curriculum offered a rigorous and comprehensive approach to tactics and operational art that was generally divided into three portions. The first part of the course examined the classical works of military theory in order to establish a propositional inventory for further investigation. The second portion of the curriculum confronted a wide range of historical evidence with which to subject the theoretical constructs to empirical analysis. The third segment consisted of numerous war games and exercises designed to explore the implications of the theoretical and historical insights in conditions of contemporary and anticipated future reality. In addition to mastering each discrete portion of the curriculum, the student was required to produce two research monographs and pass an oral comprehensive examination. In recognition of the intellectual content of this program, graduates were awarded the Master of Military Art and Science degree, which was accredited by the North Central Association of Colleges and Schools.

The fellows curriculum consisted of courses that generally paralleled those of the Advanced Military Studies Program, with a substantial amount of time devoted to visiting American and allied commands to examine firsthand the strategic and operational challenges of war fighting at the theater level. Upon graduation, while the second-year officers were assigned to key planning billets at division and corps level, fellows were assigned to similar positions at theater and service component headquarters.

The general structure of SAMS has remained relatively consistent over its first decade and a half of existence. There have, however, been periodic modifications in response to new realities. The focus of the curriculum has broadened considerably since the end of the cold war to embrace several types of military operations. The organization has expanded to include an operational analysis group, which studies contemporary military issues and becomes intimately involved in the evolution of army doctrine. The source of military faculty has varied from fellows who remain at SAMS for a second year to returning advanced program graduates. The student body has also broadened to include officers from other services.

The influence of SAMS is difficult to measure. In the early years, there was significant anecdotal evidence from division and corps commanders that contributions from advanced program graduates were enhancing the quality of exercises, war games, and war planning. During the Gulf War, one fellow and several advanced program graduates were sent to the U.S. Central Command staff on an ad hoc basis to develop the ground portion of the theater campaign plan. Additionally, advanced program graduates occupied virtually all the key planning billets at corps and division levels. Furthermore, SAMS itself was directly involved in producing the initial drafts of the 1993 edition of *Field Manual 100-5* and its follow-on, which is still in draft as of this writing. SAMS was also clearly the model for formation of the Marine Corps' School of Advanced Warfighting* in 1989 and the Air Force's School of Advanced Airpower Studies* in 1990. Possibly the most judicious conclusion is that SAMS appears in some ways to have begun to realize the vision of its founders and perhaps to have had somewhat more far-reaching consequences than even they anticipated. However, one must also remember that the very concept of advanced military education is always in tension with strong military tendencies toward the purely pragmatic and that in a democratic society the mere whiff of elitism may generate countervailing tendencies. Thus, SAMS represents hope for an enlightened approach toward true military professionalism, but it also represents an experiment whose results are not yet fully comprehended.

Sources:

Rick Atkinson, *Crusade: The Untold Story of the Gulf War* (Boston: Houghton Mifflin, 1993).
Richard M. Swain, *"Lucky War": Third Army in Desert Storm* (Fort Leavenworth, KS: U.S. Army Command and General Staff College Press, 1994).

Harold R. Winton

SCHOOL OF ADVANCED WARFIGHTING. The second-year course of the Marine Corps Command and Staff College, established in 1990.

Affectionately known as SAW, the School of Advanced Warfighting has an academic year that starts in July and ends the following June. With its student body composed of field grade officers, most of its students are selected from the previous year's graduates of the one-year course at the Command and Staff College.* However, graduates of the U.S. Army's Command and General Staff College,* the U.S. Air Force's Air Command and Staff College,* and the Naval War College's* Naval Command and Staff course can and do compete for places.

Depending upon the needs of the Marine Corps and the sister services, the size of each class can vary. Generally, each course is comprised of up to 24 majors and lieutenant commanders, with recently promoted lieutenant colonels and commanders also occasionally in a class. A generic student body would be 12 to 15 Marine officers, three or four sister service officers (ideally, at least one each from the Army, Navy, and Air Force), and two or three foreign officers. Each course usually has at least one graduate from another service's intermediate-level professional military education school. International officer-students have come from Australia, Canada, Chile, New Zealand, Norway, Senegal, and the United Kingdom. The quality of graduates of this course creates pressure for increased class size, not reduced ones.

The course of study is divided into three areas: foundations of warfighting; contemporary institutions and the preparation for war; and future warfare, with the officers confronting challenging intellectual, planning, and exercise problems throughout the entire academic year. The case study method of instruction is used within a seminar method, with the curriculum focused on military history, theory, and contemporary national security issues. The school emphasizes seminar deliberations based on extensive reading, research, and writing. As appropriate, staff rides and appropriate site visits are made; these trips have included visits to Civil War, Franco-Prussian War, World War I, World War II, and Middle Eastern battlefields.

Graduates are generally assigned to Fleet Marine Force staffs or joint or combined staffs. Their two consecutive years of professional military education and the special focus of the SAW curriculum enables them to function in highly selective assignments in which they can use their enhanced analytical skills. In comparing the education and skills of the graduates of the first- and second-year courses of the Command and Staff College, directors of the Marine Corps Command and Staff College have commented as follows: "The graduate of the first-year course knows what questions to ask, the graduate of SAW knows how to answer them."

The School of Advanced Warfighting is within the Marine Corps Command and Staff College, and its head (by the Table of Organization a lieutenant colonel) reports to the director of the Command and Staff College. This course is the Marine Corps equivalent of the U.S. Army's School of Advanced Military Studies* of the Command and General Staff College, Fort Leavenworth, Kansas,* and that of the U.S. Air Force's School of Advanced Airpower Studies* of the Air University,* Maxwell Air Force Base, Alabama.

Donald F. Bittner

SCHOOL OF AEROSPACE MEDICINE. Institution, currently located at Brooks Medical Center, San Antonio, Texas, that serves the U.S. Air Force, like its predecessors, by preparing certified physicians for the responsibilities of fully qualified flight surgeons and conducting related research.

The School of Aerospace Medicine (SAM) has functioned as an institution of professional military education since its inception in 1918 as the Medical Research Laboratory, Aviation Section, U.S. Army Signal Corps, at Hazelhurst

Field, Mineola, Long Island. Historically, other military medical institutions have necessarily incorporated teaching functions to provide military physicians with the diagnostic and therapeutic skills to heal sick or wounded service personnel and return them to duty. By contrast, SAM trains physicians who have already been trained in normal healing skills to impart to healthy aircrew personnel that knowledge which is absolutely essential to their ability to operate physically and mentally in abnormal environments within which their combat duties must be performed.

The bodies of aircrew members cannot function normally in these environments if unprotected from hostile effects that range from a mild impairment of motor skills and thinking processes to quick death from the lack of oxygen. Additionally, potentially high levels of stress with resultant inability to function can be induced by the inherent risks of routinely operating in these environments even when not associated with combat missions. For these reasons, flight surgeons generally maintain close proximity to the flying personnel of the units to which they are assigned. The flight surgeons both educate the flyers continuously on the environmental perils associated with flying and observe them, particularly in combat situations, for signs of deteriorating performance rooted in either physical factors or mental stress. All flight surgeons routinely participate in flying activities and have historically also flown on combat missions in order to maintain close observation of aircrew personnel and the conditions within which they operate. Such a direct contribution to mission accomplishment by a military unit is quite different from the traditional military doctors' indirect support of the mission.

SAM's origins lie in the U.S. entry into World War I in April 1917. Seeing the role aviation had come to play during the first three years of war, the War Department established large flying training programs to provide combat aviators for what in 1918 became the U.S. Army Air Service. The British had initially experienced appallingly high fatalities among flying cadets in expanding the Royal Flying Corps (RFC). However, the RFC's training fatality rate had been successfully reduced after creation of a special aviation medical service. In September 1917, Lt. Colonel Theodore C. Lyster, the first Chief Surgeon, Aviation Section, U.S. Army Signal Corps, recommended establishment of a medical research board for the fledgling American air service with "discretionary powers to investigate all conditions affecting the physical efficiency of pilots, to carry out experiments and tests at different flying schools, to provide suitable apparatus for the supply of oxygen," and finally "to act as a standing organization for instruction in the physiological requirements of aviators."

Lyster's request was realized with the appointment of the recommended board in October 1917, and the establishment early in 1918 of SAM's predecessor, the Central Medical Research Laboratory. Major William M. Wilmer (after whom the world-famous Wilmer Eye Institute is named) was made Officer-in-Charge. By June 1918, the laboratory was training army doctors to conduct programs designated "care of the flyer" in aviation units to which the newly trained physicians, designated "flight surgeons," were to be assigned. Despite its name, education soon became the laboratory's major emphasis, institutionalized in 1922 by a change of name to the School of Aviation Medicine.

In 1926, when logic dictated that the school should be relocated to the area where air training was predominantly conducted, it was moved to Brooks Field, the Air Corps's primary flying training base at San Antonio. When the new Army Air Corps primary flying training base, Randolph Field, was completed there in 1931, SAM was again collocated.

Sharply increased aircraft performance soon prefaced a potentially vast expansion of the envelope within which combat operations could take place, clearly requiring deeper investigation. While SAM continued its research, a separate new physiological research laboratory was established at Wright Field, Ohio, in 1935, marking a new complexity in aviation medicine. The school moved back to Brooks in 1959 as part of the new Air Force Medical Center complex and in 1962 was given its present name to reflect possible expansion of the combat envelope into space.

SAM remains the U.S. Air Force's training center for aerospace medicine and the professional education of flight surgeons. However, since World War II, it has acquired other functions, including in-flight nursing, military public health, bioenvironmental engineering, and aerospace physiology, all of which reflect the evolution of research required for care of the flyer in the aerospace age.

Sources:

Ann Hussey, Robert Browning, Ed Alcott, et al., *A History of Military Aviation in San Antonio* (San Antonio, TX: AETC History Office, 1996).
Mae Mills Link and Hubert A. Coleman, *Medical Support of the Army Air Forces in World War II* (Washington, DC: Office of the Surgeon General, USAF, 1955).
Brig. Gen. Theodore C. Lyster, "The Aviation Service of the Medical Department of the Army," *Annals of Otology, Rhinology and Laryngology* 27 (September 1918).
Lt. Col. E. G. Seibert, "Activities of the Medical Research Laboratory," *Transactions of the Twenty-Fifth Annual Meeting of the American Laryngological, Rhinological and Otological Society, Inc.* 15 (1919).

Thomas A. Julian

SCHOOL OF APPLICATION FOR CAVALRY AND LIGHT ARTILLERY. Created by the War Department in 1892 to train army officers and units in cavalry and field artillery tactics and the combined operations of the two arms.

After delays in constructing facilities and finding troops to attend, the War Department opened the School of Application for Cavalry and Light Artillery in 1892, at Fort Riley, Kansas, as authorized by a congressional act of 1887. Divided into a subschool for cavalry and a subschool for light artillery, the school's principal instructional objective centered on providing practical training for officers and units of each arm in the combined operations of cavalry and light artillery, also called field artillery.

The school initially met supporters' expectations. During its first year, training in combined arms operations attracted the attention of many army officers, received favorable comments, and proved valuable. This prompted Major William F. Randolph, commander of the subschool for light artillery and later Chief of Artillery, to write in a report to the War Department in December 1894 that effective training in the combined operations of the two arms displayed the wisdom of establishing the school.

Although the school set high standards, focused on practical instruction, and offered much promise, unforeseen complications interfered with its program of instruction over the years. In 1894 the commandant of the school, Brig. General James W. Forsyth, complained to the War Department about the frequent disruptions in training caused by personnel shortages and the unnecessary amount of detached service for units that took them away for other duties. The chronic shortage of men and the practice of detached service continued, plaguing the school through 1898, and hindered proper instruction. Although the school remained opened during the Spanish-American War, personnel shortages stopped effective training in 1898.

Following the war, the problems persisted to impede training. From 1899 to 1901, the high turnover in personnel and units caused the training program to be suspended. In 1902 the War Department established garrison schools at all Army posts, including Fort Riley, to train officers in their basic duties as part of a progressive education system. For the next two years the rotation of personnel through the garrison school at Fort Riley took officers away from the School of Application for Cavalry and Light Artillery and frustrated its training.

Renamed the School of Application for Cavalry and Field Artillery in 1904 and still divided into subschools for cavalry and for field artillery, the renamed school faced virtually the same aggravations that its predecessor had encountered. Understrength units, detached service, and high turnover in personnel seriously restricted its program of instruction in 1904–5. The provisional field artillery regiment, created in 1905 at Fort Riley by the War Department to furnish field artillery officers with opportunities to lead large units but disbanded three months after its formation, also prevented training in the combined operations of cavalry and field artillery. During its short life, the regiment frequently took batteries away to meet its requirements. In 1906 the War Department further undermined the school's reason for being by stationing complete cavalry and field artillery regiments at Fort Riley to practice combined arms operations. As a result, the War Department closed the school and created the Mounted Service School at Fort Riley in 1907, with the mission of teaching equitation and field artillery. By focusing on equitation, however, the Mounted Service School failed to furnish effective instruction in field artillery. This situation left the War Department without a school for field artillery training. Although the Artillery School at Fort Monroe, Virginia,* existed, it concentrated its energies on coast artillery drill and practice and devoted little time to field artillery training.

As its short history suggested, the School of Application for Cavalry and Light (Field) Artillery never achieved the lofty goals of its founders. The perennial problem of insufficient personnel, the disruptive practice of detached service, and the frequent rotation of units and personnel through the school to meet the other pressing needs of the War Department hindered decisive progress in combined arms training and branch training.

Sources:

Annual Reports of the School of Application for Cavalry and Light Artillery.
George H. Cameron, "The Mounted Officers' School at Fort Riley," *Journal of the U.S. Cavalry* (January 1906).
John C. Gresham, "The School at Fort Riley," *Journal of the Military Service Institution* (May 1896).
Woodbury F. Pride, *The History of Fort Riley* (Fort Riley, KS: Cavalry School, 1926).

Boyd L. Dastrup

SCHOOL OF APPLICATION FOR INFANTRY AND CAVALRY. The U.S. Army's original designation of the school for commissioned officers at Fort Leavenworth, Kansas, which evolved into an internationally acclaimed institution for command and staff instruction.

In 1881 the Commanding General of the Army, William T. Sherman,* established the School of Application for Infantry and Cavalry at Fort Leavenworth, Kansas.* For the next century and a quarter "Leavenworth" has been synonymous with the advanced tactical and operational training of several generations of U.S. Army officers. Leavenworth has evolved over time to meet the changing needs of the Army, with a succession of school designations: School of Application (1881–87), Infantry and Cavalry School (1887–98, 1904–7), General Service and Staff College (1902–4), School of the Line (1907–16, 1919–23), Army Staff College (1904–16), General Staff College (1919–23), Command and General Staff School (1923–47), and Command and General Staff College* (1947–present).

Sherman's ultimate goal was an advanced professional school, a war college in fact if not name. But the initial School of Application course was remedial, aimed at overcoming significant educational and professional deficiencies of junior lieutenants. The quality of students in the first classes was so poor and the curriculum, which included reading, grammar, and arithmetic, so elementary that the school became known as the "kindergarten." By the late 1880s, however, with better-prepared student officers, full-time instructors, and reform-minded commandants, the curriculum had improved, and the school began to approach Sherman's original intent.

Two instructors, Arthur L. Wagner, who joined the faculty in 1886, and Eben Swift, who arrived in 1893, had a marked impact on Leavenworth. Wagner, an excellent writer and teacher, provided modern historical examples upon which to base tactical instruction. Swift assisted by developing standardized techniques for solving tactical problems, principally by means of an estimate of the situation expressed in a five-paragraph order. By 1898, when the War Department closed the school because of the Spanish-American War, the Leavenworth curriculum embodied an advanced course in military art. But the small class size, low ranks of students, and lack of a systematic means to utilize its graduates all served to limit the school's impact on the Army.

When Leavenworth reopened in September 1902, reforms initiated by Secretary of War Elihu Root* to correct several Army organizational problems also affected the school. In order to improve professional qualifications throughout the officer corps, Root established a progressive system of Army schools.* Only the best graduates at one level would proceed to the next. Leavenworth was to be a mid-level institution to prepare field officers for command of regiments and divisions and to serve as general staff officers with troops.

But for the first two years after it reopened in 1902, Leavenworth reverted to a remedial role; it trained two 100-man classes of recently commissioned lieutenants in organization, tactics, and other basic military subjects. Beginning in September 1904, however, the school began to serve the role Root had envisaged. A new commandant, Brig. General J. Franklin Bell, planned an increasingly sophisticated curriculum, selected able instructors, and sought well-prepared officers as students. The course consisted of the first-year School of the Line, in which tactical instruction was on combined arms formations of regimental and division size. The best students from the first year, usually somewhat more than half of the 40-man classes, went on to the second-year Army Staff College. Instruction the second year emphasized general staff duties and the operations of larger formations to include field armies. In both years, military art dominated the course, with the solution of tactical problems in map exercises and staff rides the principal means of instruction.

Because of their experience and training, Leavenworth graduates, the most distinguished of whom was George C. Marshall, dominated general staff positions in the American Expeditionary Forces (AEF) during World War I. Because they were too junior in rank and age, only a few graduates reached division command or above in that war. In 1916 when operational commitments grew, principally as a result of the dispatch of the Punitive Expedition to Mexico, the Army curtailed the annual course of study. The school remained closed for the duration of World War I.

Sources:

Boyd L. Dastrup, *The U.S. Army Command and General Staff College: A Centennial History* (Manhattan, KS: Sunflower University Press, 1982).

Timothy K. Nenninger, *The Leavenworth Schools and the Old Army: Education, Professionalism, and the Officer Corps of the United States Army, 1881–1918* (Westport, CT: Greenwood Press, 1978).

John W. Partin, ed., *A Brief History of Fort Leavenworth, 1827–1983* (Fort Leavenworth, KS: Combat Studies Institute, U.S. Army Command and General Staff College, 1983).

Timothy K. Nenninger

SCHOOL OF INSTRUCTION OF THE REVENUE-MARINE. The first shore-based institution for the education and training of young officers for the U.S. Revenue-Cutter Service.

The origins of the School of Instruction go back to 1876, when the Congress authorized provision of a school ship dedicated to the training of young Revenue-Cutter Service officers. After replacement of the original training vessel by the bark, *Chase* in 1878, that ship became the home of a succession of cadet classes for most of the remainder of the century. However, the cadets' two-year instruction program, essentially seagoing and practical in nature, allotted only five months annually to academic studies, while the *Chase* was tied up dockside in winter quarters. As specified by the Secretary of the Treasury, first-year cadets studied algebra, geometry, English composition, navigation, and seamanship, but the contract instructor added history and French as well. The second-year winter quarters program included solid geometry and trigonometry, natural philosophy, steam engineering, and international law.

The training program was shut down completely in 1890 because of congressional concern over the growing surplus of naval officers, and for several years a number of U.S. Naval Academy* graduates were given Revenue-Cutter Service commissions. But it was resumed essentially as before, four years later, until the school acquired its first facilities ashore. Late in 1900 the service purchased 75 acres of land near Curtis Bay, Maryland, and erected a modest collection of buildings, including a carpenter shop, a boat shed, and a classroom building where cadets could study during the winter. At the time, the school had a faculty of seven Revenue-Cutter Service officers and a student body of about 40 cadets, still selected on the basis of competitive examinations. The cadets continued to live on board the *Chase* until, in 1906, the service acquired a retired Navy sloop, the *Oriole*, and fitted her out as a floating barracks— complete with a drill hall and dance hall. Meanwhile, in 1903, Congress had extended the course of instruction to three years.

The home port of the *Chase* continued as the school's location until three years after the sailing ship was replaced by a steam-powered naval vessel renamed the USRC *Itasca*. In 1910, the *Itasca* was relocated from Curtis Bay to New London, Connecticut.* On September 10 of that year, the Army transferred Ft. Trumbull, near New London, to the Revenue-Cutter Service, and some of the School of Instruction's facilities moved ashore. Here, the emphasis remained on professional studies and the utility afloat of the knowledge to be gained. But the additional year permitted the addition of new courses. In 1906, general courses in both chemistry and physics were introduced, and courses in English composition and history returned to the first-year program, having disappeared from the regular two-year curriculum.

In 1914 the school superintendent, Captain Frederick C. Billard, renamed it the Revenue-Cutter Academy. In the following year an act of Congress amalgamated the Revenue-Cutter Service with the Life Saving Service, creating the U.S. Coast Guard. In the same year the school was officially designated the U.S. Coast Guard Academy.

Sources:

Stephen H. Evans, *The United States Coast Guard, 1790–1915* (Annapolis, MD: Naval Institute Press, 1949).

Riley Hughes, *Our Coast Guard Academy, A History and Guide* (New York: Devin-Adair Co., 1944).

Irving H. King, *The Coast Guard Expands, 1865–1915: New Roles, New Frontiers* (Annapolis, MD: Naval Institute Press, 1996).

John A. Tilley

SEA POWER. A term that refers to the means by which a state extends its military power at sea and uses that power, both in peacetime and in war, to achieve its national goals. In terms of professional military education, the term "sea power" is most closely associated with Alfred Thayer Mahan's four-part series of books on *The Influence of Sea Power*, which originated from his lectures at the U.S. Naval War College in the late 1880s and early 1890s.

According to the *Oxford English Dictionary*, the first recorded use of the term "sea power" appeared in Grote's *History of Greece* (1849) and Sir John Seeley's *Expansion of England* (1883). Before this, the term "the maritime powers" was common in diplomatic correspondence in the late 17th and early 18th centuries to refer to England and the Dutch Republic, both of which were allied and used their joint and combined forces in operations against France. In other languages, words such as the German *Seemacht* have a history of earlier usage but were also not originally used in precisely the same sense as that of modern English.

The term was brought into common currency with Alfred T. Mahan's* widely read book *The Influence of Sea Power Upon History, 1660–1783* (1890). Through the *Influence of Sea Power* series of books and in a number of articles, Mahan argued, as he did in his Naval War College* lectures, that sea power plays a continuing and decisive role in world history that had often been overlooked. Setting out to explore this in the history of the Anglo-Dutch/Anglo-French wars in the period between 1660 and 1815 and in contemporary terms of the United States at the beginning of the 20th century, he focused on international relations, political, economic, government, and professional issues. Among his principal ideas, he argued that external maritime trade was a key factor in the national prosperity and that such trade depended on the security of a strong navy that could remove opposing threats from the sea. In looking at this issue, Mahan believed that there were continuing principles that one could gain from historical study and that professional naval officers, in particular, benefited from the analysis of naval history for this purpose.

In 1897, Mahan explained his use of the term in a letter to a director at his London publishers. In that letter, he wrote:

The term "sea power" which now has such vogue, was deliberately adopted by me to compel attention and, I hoped, to receive currency. Purists, I said to myself, may criticize me for marrying a Teutonic word to one of Latin origin, but I deliberately discarded the adjective "maritime," being too smooth to arrest men's attention or stick in their minds. I do not know how far this is usually the case with phrases that obtain currency; my impression is that the originator is himself generally surprised at their taking hold. I was not surprised in that sense. The effect produced was that which I fully proposed; but I was *surprised* at the extent of my success. "Sea Power," in English at least, seems to have come to stay in the sense that I used it. "The Sea Powers" were often spoken of before, but in an entirely different manner—not to express, as I meant to, at once an abstract conception and a concrete fact.

Because of these associations, the term was also associated later in the 20th century with general ideas about the broad strategic use of navies. It has also been used in a negative sense by critics of Mahan who equated sea power with "Mahanian Doctrine," an oversimplification of Mahan's thought that stressed supremacy of the battleship fleet, the navalist quest for large battleships, and decisive and climacterical naval battles.

Mahan's use of the term led to its widespread use by other authors. In one of its most common usages, it has also come to be used as a synonym for the history of naval operations in general. This developed through a series of text-books used for teaching naval history at the U.S. Naval Academy.* The first of these, entitled *A History of Sea Power* was written by two academy instructors, William Oliver Stevens and Alan Wescott. First published in 1920, it remained in use in the academy's prescribed curriculum until 1955. Shortly after World War II, Wescott published a volume he had edited, entitled *American Sea Power Since 1775*, which focused on operational history. This volume was followed in 1955 by another which Wescott and his history department colleague, E. B. Potter, entitled *The United States and World Sea Power*, focusing on a narrative of World War II naval operations. In 1960, this textbook was followed by an extremely influential book edited by Potter and Fleet Admiral Chester W. Nimitz, entitled *Sea Power: A Naval History*. In 1972, the German naval historian Jürgen Röhwer published a translation, with massive expansion and numerous factual corrections, entitled *Seemacht: Eine Seekriegsgeschichte von der Antik bis zur Gegenwart*. In 1980, a condensed version of the English textbook was published to replace the original 1960 English edition. In 1991, a further nuance was added to the term with the title of Naval Academy Professor Kenneth J. Hagan's general history of the United States Navy, *This People's Navy: The Making of American Sea Power*.

Sources:

Kenneth J. Hagan and Marc R. Shulman, "Putting Naval before History," *Naval History* 9 (1995).

John B. Hattendorf, ed., *Mahan on Naval Strategy: Selections from the Writings of Rear Admiral Alfred Thayer Mahan.* Classics of Sea Power series (Annapolis: Naval Institute Press, 1991).

A. T. Mahan, letter to Roy B. Marston, 19 February 1897, in Robert Seager II and Doris Maguire, eds., *Letters and Papers of Alfred Thayer Mahan*, vol. 2 (Annapolis, MD: Naval Institute Press, 1975).

Jon T. Sumida, *Inventing Grand Strategy and Teaching Command: The Classic Works of Alfred Thayer Mahan Reconsidered* (Baltimore: Johns Hopkins University Press, 1997).

John B. Hattendorf

SERVICE ACADEMY BOARD. Board of inquiry, composed of military officers and civilian educators, appointed by Secretary of Defense James Forrestal in 1949 to study and recommend the general system of basic education by which officer candidates could best be prepared for careers in the armed services.

In 1948, former President Herbert Hoover's first Commission on the Organization of the Executive Branch of the Government was actively engaged in its work. Its Task Force on National Security Organization undertook to study various means for strengthening unity and cooperation among the armed services. Based on its collective opinion that "real unification must come from within," the task force, headed by Ferdinand Eberstadt, gave considerable attention to officer education. After recommending that joint education be provided for officers at all grades, it expressed urgency regarding the task of determining the proper approach to postwar service academy education, citing the currency of various proposals advocating a new academy for the U.S. Air Force. Remarking that "establishment of an air academy would mark a fork in the educational road of the services [from which] there can be no turning back," the task force recommended a thorough study of the undergraduate education of military officers.

The Eberstadt group's enthusiasm for a solution other than a third service-oriented academy was not shared by Secretary of Defense Forrestal, who decided to support legislation authorizing an air academy soon after the task force's report was issued. However, he apparently saw merit in its recommendation to undertake a study of undergraduate precommissioning education. On March 14, 1949, the secretary appointed the Service Academy Board, under the chairmanship of Robert L. Stearns, president of the University of Colorado. Retired General Dwight Eisenhower, then president of Columbia University, was named vice chairman. Its other members included four outstanding civilian educators, the serving superintendent of the U.S. Military Academy,* the recent superintendent of the Naval Academy,* and a former deputy commandant of the Air University.*

Forrestal charged the board with recommending "that general system of basic education which it believes is best adapted to . . . the needs of the regular armed services" and urged that it not allow the distinctive service rendered in the past by West Point* and Annapolis* "to interfere with its freedom of recommending changes in their roles." He asked the board to consider: (1) the moral, mental, and physical attributes needed in future officers; (2) the general fields of instruction that basic officer education should include; (3) the degree of specialized branch and joint military instruction needed in service academy programs; (4) the roles of and relationships between the academies within the overall precommissioning system; and (5) the manner of selection for officer candidates. The secretary also solicited recommendations on means for providing the Air Force with well-educated officers prior to construction of its academy and on special provisions to be included in the air academy legislation being proposed to the Congress.

In a preliminary report requested by Forrestal, the board provided a unanimous endorsement for the creation of a new four-year academy for the Air Force. In part, the board was responding to its newly acquired understanding of that service's unique shortage of academy-trained officers and of the limited capability of the existing academies to help fill the void even if they were expanded in size. But the board's opinion was also shaped by a change in viewpoint from its civilian members, almost all of whom had brought preconceived attitudes favoring some kind of system whereby career officer candidates for all the services would begin their education in a common academy. After interviewing witnesses and participating in discussions with the military members, however, the civilian educators became convinced that separate four-year academies were necessary for securing "an early devotion to a military career" and setting "the highest professional standards" for the other commissioning sources to emulate. "It seems unlikely," the board stated, "that the excellence achieved in the ROTC programs* would be maintained without this benchmark of comparison."

The Service Academy Board also assembled panels of subject-matter experts who met throughout the summer to examine the content of the academy programs. Separate panels were formed for science and engineering, the social sciences, language and area studies, teaching methods, physical education, and military education. Although most of their recommendations to the board were unique to their respective subject matter issues, a number of commonly expressed observations are of special note, especially in view of subsequent service academy developments. Several panels criticized the academies' excessive routine in their classroom and laboratory procedures for not "stimulating initiative, originality, and that healthy independence in thinking which is so necessary for real leadership." Several urged more opportunities for independent study through such devices as greater use of the libraries, more comprehensive laboratory problems, and closer linking of social science and humanities course work with a student's foreign language concentration. Four of the panels, largely made up of civilian educators, also made strong recommendations in favor of the current system of separate academies.

By the time of its final report, in December 1949, Secretary Forrestal had resigned and been replaced by Louis A. Johnson, who was opposed to maintaining separate service academies. However, the board provided a ringing endorsement of the existing academy system, praising "the integrity and the service identity" of West Point and Annapolis and recommending once again the establishment of an Air Force academy. It even examined four alternative concepts of career-oriented precommissioning education in detail and found them "inadequate." By joining all of the service secretaries and the Joint Chiefs of Staff in opposing fundamental changes in the academy system, the Service Academy Board made it virtually impossible for the new Secretary of Defense to implement his personal preferences.

Sources:

John W. Masland and Laurence I. Radway, *Soldiers and Scholars: Military Education and National Policy* (Princeton, NJ: Princeton University Press, 1957).

Service Academy Board, "A Report and Recommendation to the Secretary of Defense," Department of Defense, Washington, DC, 1950.

William E. Simons, *Liberal Education in the Service Academies* (New York: Bureau of Publications, Teachers College, Columbia University, 1965).

SHERMAN, WILLIAM T. William Tecumseh Sherman (born 1820, died 1891), General, U.S. Army, graduate of the U.S. Military Academy, while serving as the Army's commanding general from 1869 to 1883, recast and expanded the Army's postgraduate school system into its enduring form while fostering a broader renaissance of professionalism within the Army.

Sherman graduated fourth academically (sixth overall) in a West Point* class (1840) that initially numbered over 100 members. He was undistinguished in the military virtues at the academy, accumulating many demerits and attaining no cadet rank, but he remained a lifelong believer in the academy's educational system, including the regimentation of daily life, the engineering-ordered curricula, small classes, and frequent grading. Indeed, when Sherman became the founding superintendent of the Louisiana Military Seminary in 1860–61, he imposed many aspects of the West Point system. (Once, when one of the school's professors gave a long speech too erudite for the students, Sherman corrected the professor and made sure that he became, as one observer wrote, "a practical, useful instructor.") Later, as the Army's commanding general, Sherman made it clear that the distinctive features of the West Point system were not to be changed but rather made stronger. "Our country abounds in Scholars," he informed the academy's superintendent in 1879. "We want men of action." He enjoyed speaking at the West Point graduations where he was warmly received by the cadets.

Sherman believed in the supreme value of field (preferably combat) service in the education of an officer, but he also was far ahead of most of his contemporary officers in advocating intellectual study of the military art. Indeed, his wartime generalship unmistakably reflected his early studies under West Point professor Dennis Hart Mahan,* who corresponded with Sherman during and after the war. Later, when Sherman listed prescribed reading material for students at Fort Leavenworth,* Mahan's classic, *Outposts*, headed the list.

Sherman was also an unfailing patron of Emory Upton,* the postwar Army's foremost intellectual figure. Sherman repeatedly used his influence to help Upton and to advance the younger man's proposals for reform of the Army's field tactics and the nation's higher military policy. There was frequent correspondence and interaction between the two men, and both men borrowed and articulated one another's ideas. Under Sherman, Upton was commandant of cadets at West Point (1870–75) and became, in 1877, superintendent of studies at the Army's Artillery School of Application* at Fortress Monroe, Virginia—then the nation's principal postgraduate military school. Sherman encouraged Upton to broaden the school's curriculum by adding courses in military history, strategy, and logistics.

Sherman and Upton saw eye to eye on strengthening West Point* and on developing postgraduate education to, as Sherman wrote in 1879, "qualify officers for any duty they may be called upon to perform, or for any position however high in rank or command." By general order of May 7, 1881, Sherman founded the School of Application of Cavalry and Infantry* at Fort Leavenworth, to operate in the pattern of the artillery school. One lieutenant from each regular infantry and cavalry regiment were to be assigned for two-year tours as students, "for the gradual dissemination of the school's precepts throughout the Army."

During preparations to open the school, Sherman in Washington corresponded with Lt. General Philip H. Sheridan, the Army's commander in the West. Sherman wrote that he did not intend to meddle in school affairs, but soon afterwards he disapproved as too "onerous" much of the code of regulations proposed by the school staff. By general order of January 16, 1882, Sherman prescribed the school's organization and curriculum. The order called for practical instruction in such matters as army organization, tactics, and discipline and for remedial instruction of those students lacking strong basic education. But another objective was education in "the science and practice of war, as far as they can be acquired from books." Officer-students should prepare essays from their reading, Sherman wrote. Sherman sent his own copy of the British work *Soady's Lessons of War, as Taught by the Great Masters* with his own comments hand-written inside the book for benefit of the school staff. "This book, better than others, recognizes the force and effect of modern inventions, of steamers, railroads, and breech-loading rifles," he wrote on the flyleaf.

The school was to be no ivory tower. Sherman wrote that the officer-students were to be closely evaluated, and a final order of merit would be reached. Drill, discipline, and fieldwork were to be organized as if in active line units. When the school staff in late 1882 recommended expansion and upgrading, Sherman ruled against "pushing this school into the clouds."

Besides the schools at Leavenworth and Monroe, Sherman fostered an engineering school* that had originated shortly after the war at Willet's Point, New York, among a society of engineering officers. Sherman encouraged the founding of professional societies and the journals *Army and Navy Journal* and *Journal of the Military Service Institution*, and he detailed officers to land-grant colleges as instructors. His own *Memoirs* are regarded as more perceptive than most. Sherman often railed against politics and politicians, and for a time he moved the Army's headquarters away from Washington, to St. Louis, rather than contend for authority with a difficult Secretary of War; he wanted the Leavenworth school to be kept from political influence or control (in contrast to West Point, he wrote).

Sherman remained first of all a soldier, only secondly an intellectual-educator. He believed that instruction with books was less important than practical, "out-of-door" officer education with horse and rifle. Biographer John Marszalek notes that Sherman's intellectual curiosity was largely limited to buttressing what was already believed. Still, as the dominant figure in the post–Civil War Army, Sherman made lasting contributions, both in outlook and in formal ways, to professionalism and education in the American Army.

Sources:

John F. Marszalek, *Sherman: A Soldier's Passion for Order* (New York: Free Press and Macmillan, 1993).

Timothy K. Nenninger, *The Leavenworth Schools and the Old Army: Education, Professionalism, and the Officer Corps of the United States Army, 1881–1918* (Westport, CT: Greenwood Press, 1978).

Henry Shindler and E. E. Booth, *History of the Army Service Schools Fort Leavenworth, Kansas* (Fort Leavenworth, KS: Staff College Press, 1908).

Russell F. Weigley, *History of the United States Army* (Bloomington: Indiana University Press, 1967, 1984).

Ray L. Bowers

SIMS, WILLIAM S. William Sowden Sims (born 1858, died 1936), Admiral, U.S. Navy, graduate of the U.S. Naval Academy and U.S. Naval War College, served as president of the Naval War College, 1917 and 1919–22. His influence lastingly shaped the nature of the War College, its characteristic methods, and its status and roles within the Navy.

Sims graduated from the Naval Academy* (1880) at the middle of his class. He became a serious and hard-working officer, interested in self-education to an unusual degree. His mind was attracted to far-ranging topics, including, for example, the new ideas on biological evolution from Charles Darwin. Assigned as a junior officer to the school ship *Saratoga*, he organized the navigation teaching and wrote his own textbook, but soon afterwards he declined an opportunity to teach ordnance and gunnery at the Naval Academy. As naval attaché in Europe, his intelligence reports won the notice of high officers including the Assistant Secretary of the Navy, Theodore Roosevelt.

Assigned to the new battleship *Kentucky* in 1900, Lieutenant Sims sent missives to Washington severely criticizing the vessel's design, especially its gunnery systems. His chafing challenged the reputations of several senior officers, but Sims was later vindicated when, as the Navy's inspector of target practice, 1902–5, his efforts drastically improved the fleet's gunnery performance. One of several younger officers urging reform of the Navy's top structure, Sims gained the confidence and protection of President Roosevelt and served as the president's naval aide 1907–9.

Sims became one of four students assigned to the Naval War College's* first 16-month "long course," 1911–12. He had not especially wanted the assignment, professing interest in things "practical" rather than theoretical, but he quickly realized that the college represented the "main current of professional thought." At Newport, Rhode Island,* he drafted a letter to the Secretary of the Navy on how to make the college more effective and wrote an essay, "The Practical Naval Officer," extolling the study of naval strategy and tactics; Sims himself paid for the essay's publication and distribution. As commander of the Navy's destroyer flotilla in the Atlantic, he established "conference" meetings among his subordinate commanders to work out tactical problems, imitating how things were done at the War College. Sims pressed President Woodrow Wilson's Secretary of the Navy, Josephus Daniels,* to support the War College more strongly, and in 1916 testified similarly before a congressional committee. Newly selected as rear admiral, Sims asked for the War College presidency, which he briefly assumed in early 1917, prior to his wartime role as commander of U.S. Naval Forces operating in European waters. During the war, Sims relied heavily on his staff's planning section, which consisted almost entirely of graduates of the Naval War College.

Sims returned to Newport in 1919. He stressed that the Naval War College should be seen first as an educational institution, whose mission was not to prepare war plans but rather to train future war planners and commanders. Just as the officers of his old Atlantic flotilla had studied situations collegially to develop a shared doctrine, he wrote, graduates of the War College would form a corps of higher officers within the Navy accustomed to applying their minds to problems from a common viewpoint. Sims brought individuals from university life to the War College's staff and improved recognition within the officer corps that an assignment to the college was important professionally. He preserved, indeed strengthened, the college's historic use of wargaming and systematic analysis in studying strategy and plans.

Sims took a direct hand in applying Naval War College gaming to questions about aviation and reached the personal view that the aircraft carrier would become the capital ship of the future. Later, in retirement, Sims appeared for the defense in the trial of General Billy Mitchell.* (Sims, however, disagreed with Mitchell's view that aviation should be separated from the Navy.)

Sims never lost his iconoclasm. Appointed a member of the Naval Academy's board of visitors* in 1933 and unwilling to go along with the board's findings, he signed his own minority report contrasting the prescribed life and technical studies at the Naval Academy with the kind of searching intellect fostered in civilian universities. He noted that faculty members at the academy had no training or experience as educators and were replaced every few years. He recommended that the academy be made a two-year professional school for graduates of civilian colleges.

William Sims is today venerated in the lore of the Naval War College. He followed the tradition of the college's earlier leaders Stephen B. Luce* and Alfred T. Mahan* in viewing the college as a scholarly place for exploring the essence of conflict. Sims, however, emphasized that the theoretical study of war had a higher, practical purpose—the education and training of the Navy's future leaders toward the ultimate effectiveness of the Navy in war. Sims remains a remarkable individual, whose personal warmth and professional expertise allowed him rise to leadership in the organization he sometimes rashly challenged.

Sources:

John B. Hattendorf, B. M. Mitchell III, and J. R. Wadleigh, *Sailors and Scholars: The Centennial History of the U.S. Naval War College* (Newport, RI: Naval War College Press, 1984).

Elting E. Morison, *Admiral Sims and the Modern American Navy* (New York: Russell & Russell, 1942, 1968).

William S. Sims, "Naval War College Principles and Methods Applied Afloat," *Proceedings of the U.S. Naval Institute* (March–April 1915).

Ronald Spector, *Professors of War: The Naval War College and the Development of the Naval Profession* (Newport, RI: Naval War College Press, 1977).

Ray L. Bowers

SKELTON PANEL. Congressional panel appointed in November 1987, chaired by Congressman Ike Skelton, which recommended changes to joint professional military education in both service and joint schools to implement the explicit and implied joint education provisions of the Goldwater-Nichols Department of Defense Reorganization Act of 1986.

The chairman of the House Armed Services Committee, Les Aspin (D–Wisconsin), established the Panel on Military Education in recognition that rigorous, high-quality, professional military education is vital to national security. Following passage of the Goldwater-Nichols Act,* improving the nation's military capabilities for joint operations assumed an importance not reflected in the composition, curricula, or faculties of the individual service and joint colleges. To assure "that this [joint professional military education] provides the proper link-

SKELTON PANEL

age between the Service competent officer and the competent joint officer," the panel was charged to review service and joint plans for implementing the joint PME provisions of Goldwater-Nichols, as well as the ability of the Department of Defense to develop professional military strategists, and to report its findings and recommendations to the House Armed Services Committee.

The panel was chaired by Ike Skelton (D–Missouri) and included Solomon Ortiz (D–Texas), Buddy Darden (D–Georgia), Owen Pickett (D–Virginia) Jack Davis (R–Illinois) as ranking minority member, John Rowland (R–Connecticut), and Jon Kyl (R–Arizona). The panel staff was led by Dr. Archie Barrett from the permanent committee professional staff and supported by four officials assigned from the DoD for one year, representing the Office of the Secretary of Defense and the Departments of the Army, Navy, and Air Force.

Because both jointness and strategy combine the military capabilities developed and fielded by the services at higher levels of command, Skelton directed that the panel focus on intermediate and senior professional military education, the ten U.S. command and staff and senior service colleges, rather than the more service-specific education provided in basic and advanced tactical schooling. Further, he clarified that the panel should address professional development of military officers competent to contribute to both national military and national security strategy. During preliminary research, it became readily apparent that the quality of education imparted to student officers varied among the colleges. Consequently, quality of education joined strategy and jointness as the panel's third major focus. Skelton also directed that the staff consider the historical evolution of U.S. military education in its research and that it obtain the broadest possible perspectives from active and retired senior officers, defense experts, and civilian leaders and academicians.

The panel conducted extensive research into all past service and joint studies of professional military education and interviewed past leaders of those studies. The panel and staff interviewed over 10 defense and education experts and conducted 28 hearings in Washington, D.C., and at each of the 10 colleges. They also visited counterpart educational institutions in Germany, France, and the United Kingdom.

The panel determined that PME is becoming increasingly important to national success in peace and war; that the services' best officers should have both operational experience and education, which cannot be mutually exclusive; and that although the basic DoD military education system is sound, significant improvements can be made. The panel found that DoD lacked a framework for PME that linked the different levels of schooling, the focus of learning objectives at each level, the unique characteristics and capabilities of each school, and progressive learning within an overall structure. It recommended that the DoD "develop and implement a clear and coherent conceptual framework for the professional military education system."

The panel urged several changes aimed at improving PME quality: It recommended (1) that current laws be amended to facilitate hiring of civilian faculty; (2) that the chairman of the Joint Chiefs of Staff (CJCS) and service chiefs place greater emphasis on acquiring quality officers for faculty positions; (3) that students at intermediate and senior colleges be required to write frequent essay examinations and original papers; and (4) that faculty should be expected to thoroughly review and grade these written efforts. These last recommendations emerged from discussions with a wide range of military and civilian educators, as well as students at the Naval War College* where a rigorous academic program employed frequent grading to sustain high-quality academic effort.

A two-phase Joint Specialist Officer education program was recommended, with Phase I taught in service colleges for all students and Phase II in a shortened and restructured Armed Forces Staff College* course for both midgrade and senior officers en route to a joint assignment. The panel also urged changes in service assignment policies for intermediate-level schooling so that student bodies could achieve the desired service mix to address joint issues and operational challenges in a realistic, rigorous manner.

A related and special panel concern was the apparent cultural bias of the Navy regarding the importance of professional education for career development. The panel recommended that the Navy investigate whether naval officers can and should attend both intermediate and senior colleges and whether the Naval War College's intermediate and senior curricula should be more clearly differentiated to accommodate this approach. The panel did not endorse the Navy's proposals to accredit as joint education attendance at either civilian institutions or the Naval Postgraduate School,* believing that neither could or would meet the requirements for joint education.

To structure the colleges in a logically consistent framework, the panel recommended that the senior service colleges focus on national military strategy, leaving operational level of war to the intermediate colleges. These senior service colleges should have a greater mix of service faculty and students to create a joint learning environment.

The panel recommended that a National Center for Strategic Studies, configured as a research and education institution, replace the National War College.* This institution would focus on national security strategy rather than national military strategy and operational level of war then being taught at the senior service colleges. The curriculum would focus on senior officers destined for three- and four-star rank and federal officials from branches, agencies and departments involved in national security matters. This recommendation was supported by the incumbent CJCS but was not implemented. In a related matter, the panel urged that the existing CAPSTONE course* for flag officer selectees should be reinforced, and lengthened if required, to include national security and national military strategy.

The panel report has had a profound impact on joint PME, leading to the creation of a DoD education framework, changed joint curricula at service and joint colleges, improved service mixes of faculties and student bodies, and specialized joint educational programs. Naval education programs have gained increased emphasis, and opportunities are provided to a wider, more selective range of officers than in the past.

Sources:

Les Aspin, Chairman House of Representatives Committee on Armed Services, letter to Honorable Ike Skelton, November 13, 1987.

Professional Military Education, Hearings before the Panel on Military Education of the Committee on Armed Services, House of Representatives, One Hundredth Congress (Washington, DC: Government Printing Office, 1989).

Report of the Panel on Military Education of the One Hundredth Congress (Washington, DC: Government Printing Office, 1989).

John W. McDonald

SOLEY, JAMES R. Professor James Russell Soley (born 1850, died 1911), graduate of Harvard College, headed the Department of English Studies, History, and Law at the U.S. Naval Academy, taught at the new Naval War College, served as Assistant Secretary of the Navy, and received acclaim as a respected international lawyer.

Soley was a remarkable, if half-forgotten, figure, who had important influence in several areas of the modern Navy. In education, he did much to bring the Naval Academy* in line with the universities of his time, and also helped found the Naval War College.* In administration, he promoted his friend [Alfred Thayer] Mahan's* concept of a "Big Navy," as well as curbed some of the worst features of the political "spoils system" in the Navy's civilian employment. In history, he produced some six books on our Tripolitan War and Civil War, but, even more important, he began the collection and publication of the invaluable *Official Records of the Union and Confederate Navies in the War of the Rebellion.*

He had little naval background, other than being born in 1850 in Roxbury, Massachusetts, of a family that had been in New England since the seventeenth century. A few years too young for the Civil War, he went to Harvard, graduating in 1870. His inclination was towards teaching. After a year's experience at a boys' prep school, he came to the Naval Academy. In 1871, he became an Assistant Professor of Ethics and English.

He swiftly made his mark. By 1873, when he was scarcely 23, Soley was so well esteemed by the Superintendent, redoubtable Commodore John L. Worden . . . , that a new Department was created upon the vacating of the post in the area of English. Soley was promoted to acting Professor and made Head of the Department of English Studies, History, and Law, with full voice on the Academic Board. . . .

[In 1876], Soley was confirmed as Professor in the now defunct Naval Corps of Professors of Mathematics, and put on a lieutenant's uniform, ultimately rising to rank of commander. As a Department Head, Soley was perceptive and energetic. A report of his *(An Historical Sketch of the United States Naval Academy)* in 1876 sounded a modern plaint in speaking about the poor quality of candidates: "The large majority of rejections must be referred to the insufficient training of the schools. If the schools of the country, primary and secondary, do not teach their pupils between the ages of seven and fifteen to spell, to cipher, to answer simple questions in geography and grammar, what in those eight years do they teach?"

He held strong views about the mission of the Academy, after making a tour of European naval schools in 1878. A year later, while presiding at a meeting of the Naval Institute* to discuss three Prize Essays on the subject of Naval Education, including an entry by his friend Mahan, Soley shrewdly observed: "it should not be the commanders of the future whom we seek to train at the naval school. In all other branches of study the University course is preliminary and never final. At its close the student goes to the law school, scientific school, etc., to complete his education. If we could say that it *is* the midshipman alone . . . whom we seek to train at the naval school we should make a stride in advance—for we would then only attempt to lay the groundwork for a scientific education and could prepare him thoroughly to perform the duties of a subordinate officer . . . and I hold that when a naval college for officers is established we shall have found the place to educate the commanders of the future." Is it any wonder that he was among the first three naval officers invited to the faculty of the Naval War College in 1885?

Soley gradually grew and as [member of the Corps of Professors] of Mathematics could shift duty stations. He went to Washington in 1882 as a commander in charge of naval war records. The Army was collecting and publishing its documents for the Civil War, and so, in 1884, Soley succeeded in obtaining the appropriation that launched the Navy series. He took time out the following year to take a temporary appointment in the founding of the Naval War College at Newport.* He was the only one of the original three naval officers appointed to the faculty who appeared in time, and had to share the burden of instruction with Army Lieutenant Tasker H. Bliss.* . . .

In 1890, he received a law degree from Columbian University, (the ancestor of George Washington [University]) and resigned his commission as commander to take up the post of Assistant to Secretary of the Navy Benjamin F. Tracy. In this office, he introduced business methods into naval administration, revising the system of purchases and accounts. . . . Soley was an ardent advocate of a big battleship navy, and did much to secure the 1890 appropriation for the *Iowa, Indiana, Oregon* and *Massachusetts*. He would, however, probably have deserved a modest footnote in our naval history if all he did was sponsor and create the Naval Militia on a realistic basis . . . the forerunner of our present Naval Reserve.

The return of [Grover] Cleveland to office threw Soley, at 43, directly into the practice of [international] law. Entering the New York firm of his erstwhile chief, Secretary Tracy, Soley settled down to a lucrative and interesting career.[5]

SOUTHARD, SAMUEL. Samuel Lewis Southard (born 1787, died 1842), as Secretary of the Navy, 1823–29, was responsible for key improvements in that service's infrastructure ashore and its personnel administration. His efforts to establish a naval academy, though unsuccessful, were important in bringing the need for formal education of its officer candidates to the attention of the Congress.

[5]Reprinted, with permission, from Robert W. Daly, "James Russell Soley (1850–1911)," *Shipmate*, May 1957, Copyright 1957 by the United States Naval Academy Alumni Association. (Asterisks added.)

Samuel Lewis Southard . . . entered the College of New Jersey (i.e., Princeton) and completed the course in two years, graduating in 1804 at the age of seventeen years. Next he went to Virginia, where he struck up his friendship with James Monroe. . . . In 1811 he returned to New Jersey, with strong Southern sympathies indelibly fixed in his character, and was admitted to the state bar in the same year. . . .

Southard was county prosecutor at Flemington, New Jersey, in 1814. In 1815 he was . . . appointed an associate justice of the state Supreme Court. . . . In 1820 he was an elector for Monroe; in 1821 he was appointed to the U.S. Senate. His father, still in the House, and he worked on the Missouri Compromise, and an anonymous biographer stated flatly, "Samuel L. Southard was the author of these resolutions, although Henry Clay was given the credit."

The fact that Southard knew nothing about the sea provoked some merriment about his appointment as Secretary of the Navy. Yet Leonard D. White, who surveyed naval administrators from 1801 to 1829, regarded Southard as "perhaps the ablest of the group. . . ."

Southard's interest in the medical care of naval personnel developed when Commodore Porter's squadron, based at Thompson's Island (modern Key West), was so stricken with illness, most likely yellow fever, that it could not operate. Late in September 1823 Southard sent four surgeons to Porter, and soon the squadron was able to operate again. The occurrence also provoked two decisions: to establish a navy yard at Pensacola rather than Key West, and to provide surgeons and surgeon's mates who would be ready to go to sea. . . .

Meanwhile Southard pushed the construction of naval hospitals. The first site, in Chelsea, Massachusetts, was purchased in September 1823. He then acquired sites in Brooklyn, Philadelphia, and Norfolk, leaving actual construction to his successors.

"Our whole coast ought to be surveyed," Southard announced in 1825. "There is scarcely a mile of it which is thoroughly known." At that time he had already begun surveys of Charleston and of St. Mary's, Georgia, the first presumably under Lieutenant Lawrence Kearny, early in 1825. In his report for 1826 he stated that additional surveys of the harbors of Baltimore, Savannah, and Brunswick, Georgia; and Beaufort, South Carolina, were being completed. . . .

Southard lacked funds with which to draft a naval criminal code, or articles for the government of the Navy. Nor was he able to obtain additional ranks for the Navy. However, he succeeded in unfreezing the rank of captain. Only one captain had been appointed between 1818 and 1824. In 1825 nine were so appointed. Appointment as a midshipman also became easier during Southard's regime. . . .

Southard's plan to reorganize the Marine Corps stemmed from his desire to found a naval academy. Unless such an academy was provided the only source of properly trained Marine officers was West Point.* "Instruction is not less necessary to the navy than to the army," he told Congress in 1824. In 1825 he stated his position even more clearly. Because officer candidates came from poor families, were very young, and were too occupied to obtain an education:

> It is the formation of a school which shall combine literary with professional instruction, a competent portion of common learning with a profound knowledge of everything connected with military science, seamanship, and navigation, the theory with the practice of their profession, that is needed.

Southard felt that little was needed beyond $10,000 and the Army's willingness to transfer some buildings to the navy [sic]. A year later Annapolis* was strongly recommended to him as a possible site, but in 1825 his attention was focused on Governor's Island in New York Harbor. . . . As late as November 1828 Southard was pushing the Secretary of War to transfer Governor's Island to the Navy. Although the Army declined, Southard had recommended virtually the same method of creating a naval academy that George Bancroft* was to use successfully in 1845. . . .

Another reform Southard implemented was speeding up communications to and from the Pacific Squadron. In 1826 he told the House Committee on Naval Affairs that the passage from the United States to Valparaiso took from eighty to 120 days. That time could be cut in half (a slight overstatement) if a messenger traveled by fast schooner to Chagres on the Isthmus of Panama, crossed the Isthmus, and found another fast schooner waiting on the Pacific side. . . .

Southard was the first Secretary of the Navy to propose that the navy yards be located and operated in accordance with some general plan rather than as temporary expediency dictated. His recommendation that the location of the navy yards be reexamined was adopted in 1827, and in his final report he announced proudly that a board of officers had been considering the question. Nevertheless, as late as May 1828, the Senate asked him whether a new yard somewhere between Cape Hatteras and Florida was desirable. Southard's reply was blunt: "Our error is in having too many."

Because better ships were built in naval yards than by private contractors, in 1825 Southard abandoned private building. . . .

Southard had strict views on discipline in the Navy. He subjected two heroes of the War of 1812 to courts-martial and in the process apparently earned the undying enmity of Andrew Jackson. The two officers involved were Commodore Charles Stewart, the captain of the *Constitution* when she took H.M. ships *Cyane* and *Levant*, and Commodore David Porter, whose Pacific cruise in the *Essex* had virtually destroyed the British whaling industry. The two cases were heard in 1825, apparently by the same court-martial board. . . .

At the instigation of Captain Jesse Duncan Elliott, Southard was the first naval secretary to seek potential seamen inland rather than only in seaports. He also recommended that Congress enact regulations to make the Navy more attractive, stimulate recruiting, and stop the rapid turnover of personnel. Two approaches to solving the problem might be, he said, "to admit more boys, in the character of apprentices, and to enlist robust and healthy landsmen in the interior."

When the recommendation went unheeded, in 1828 Southard authorized Elliott to establish headquarters at Carlisle, Pennsylvania,* and "enlist healthy, able bodied men between 18 and 25 years of age for General Service." Two lieutenants and two midshipmen were sent to assist him. Apparently the experiment worked well, though it ceased to be taken seriously before Southard left office. However, as Langley says, it was "a preview of some of the practices that are now routine."

Southard welcomed technological change. While he believed that steamers might be useful as coast-defense vessels, he was also alive to the necessity of building conventional ships. During his first months in office he wrote to the chairmen of the House and Senate Committees on Naval Affairs, pointing out that there were only four sloops of war and that at least ten should be built. In January 1824, the House Committee approved the recommendation. . . .

Southard went out of office with the rest of Adams' Cabinet in March 1829. His work had been well done. In addition to the accomplishments detailed above, the number of ships in the Navy had grown from thirty-five to fifty-two, with sixteen on duty. The number of personnel had grown from thirty-four hundred to fifty-six hundred and the operating cost from two to three million dollars. In addition to his work as Secretary of the Navy, Southard had found time to serve briefly as *ad interim* Secretary of the Treasury in 1825 and *ad interim* Secretary of War in 1828. . . .

By 1829 [when Southard retired as secretary], the Navy had permanent stations for the protection of American interests in the Mediterranean, the Caribbean, the South Atlantic . . . and the Pacific.[6]

STAFF OFFICER PREPARATION. Formal instruction provided for experienced military officers by their governments, beginning in the 19th century, to qualify them to serve in general staff and lesser staff positions.

Perhaps the earliest example of a state's provision of special instruction for officers selected as potential members of a commanding general's staff occurred in the 18th-century court of Prussia's Frederick the Great. Each year, twelve of Prussia's best young officers were selected to spend the winter months in Frederick's suite to learn the arts of war directly from him. Soon after termination of the Seven Years War, Frederick turned toward development of a regular military school, at Berlin, but it was a school of precommissioning education designed to concentrate the finest available instruction on fifteen of the ablest products of Prussia's basic cadet schools.* A true staff school did not exist in that country until the reforms instituted by General Gerhard von Scharnhorst,* beginning in 1808.

Europe's first school devoted to the preparation of staff officers appeared in England in 1799. By Royal Warrant of King George III, the school became the senior department of the Royal Military College* in 1801. A second warrant that same year established a course of study and fixed its student body at 30 officers. The senior department's first commandment, a General Jarry, had served on the personal staff of Frederick the Great during the Seven Years' War, had returned to the French army after the war, and defected to England in 1795. He soon found, however, that the basic military knowledge possessed by British officers of the time was too thin to profit from his lectures on the art of war. He was instrumental, thereafter, in shifting the course content to mathematics and fortification.

Initially located in its own facility at High Wycombe, it was joined to the college's junior department for administrative purposes in 1808 and, twelve years later, actually moved to a common location at the Royal Military College at Sandhurst.* In the course of its relocation, the senior department lost its separate military staff, had its student body cut in half, and lost all but two of its faculty, both civilian theoreticians. Without military instructors, the school offered little in the way of professional instruction based on field experience. This condition remained until army reforms following numerous shortcomings in the British performance in the Crimean War included creation of a separate staff college in 1858.

[6]Excerpted, with permission, from Edwin M. Hall, "Samuel Lewis Southard, 16 September 1823–3 March 1829," in Paolo E. Coletta, ed., *American Secretaries of the Navy, Vol. I, 1775–1913* (Annapolis, MD: Naval Institute Press, 1980), Copyright 1980 by United States Naval Institute. (Asterisks added.)

France lacked a staff college until after Napoleon's defeat at Waterloo. The restored Bourbon monarchy's minister of war, Gouvion St.-Cyr, approved a recommendation to create a general staff corps and a school to prepare officers for staff positions. Accordingly, the École d'Application d'État Major was established in Paris in 1818. At first, Marshal Saint-Cyr intended that only graduates of the staff school were to enter the staff corps and that the school would accept as students annually only the 25 top-performing newly commissioned products of l'École Spéciale Militaire.* However, by the time Henry Barnard* reviewed the school, in the late 1850s, at least three students were admitted each year from l'École Polytechnique,* and another four or five from among second lieutenants in the regiments. By then also, officers from the regiments in the rank of captain or below might qualify for entry into the staff corps by passing the staff school's final leaving examinations.

The École d'Application d'État Major provided a two-year curriculum of both theoretical and practical instruction, followed by at least two years of regular service as a lieutenant in both infantry and cavalry regiments. The first year of study included astronomy, applied descriptive geometry, military topography, military administration and legislation, an introduction to field fortifications, military art and tactics, drawing, and German. Second-year students continued with drawing, German, and the military subjects with field fortifications, in particular, receiving a much heavier concentration. Since reconnaissance sketching and mapping and the supervision of logistical provisions, supply routes, and encampment security were important aspects of a staff officer's duties, drawing, both on foot and from horseback, received major attention during both years.

The pinnacle of staff corps development and education in 19th-century Europe was achieved in Prussia and, after 1871, in the newly unified state of Germany. The initial move in this direction was made under the tutelage of General Scharnhorst, who, even before the pivotal defeat of the Prussians at Jena, had separated the *Militarakademie* for commissioned officers from the upper cadet school, of which it had originally been part, and strengthened its program. Following Jena, in the midst of the civil and military reforms it triggered, Scharnhorst reorganized the academy, renaming it the Allgemeine Kriegsschule,* and established a new nine-month program of applied mathematics and science, military geography, tactics, mess administration, and language study. After his death and the return of peace to Europe, with more officers available for advanced schooling, the program was extended to three years. And it became almost the only avenue of entrance into the Prussian staff corps which, unlike its French counterpart, was regarded highly by the rest of the army. At first, an appointment to the staff, limited to 64 members, was coveted because of the prospects for more rapid promotion than in other parts of the army; but later in the century, after the dazzling Prussian successes over the Austrians and French, the staff corps was respected for its superior professional knowledge and its acknowledged contributions to the successful Prussian campaigns.

The three-year Kriegsschule (later called the Kriegsakademie) could be entered only by passing a comprehensive written examination prepared annually by a board of examiners in Berlin and requiring 10 to 12 days to complete. Any officer with three years' commissioned service was able to apply, with an affirmative endorsement from his commanding officer. Only 40 candidates were selected for entrance each year, and of those successfully completing the three-year course—usually at about age 28 or 29—only about eight were selected for duty in the Topographical Department that led to eventual consideration for a staff appointment. Those not selected returned to their regiments and served as adjutants or instructors in the army's divisional schools. The school program covered 11 months each year: eight of these in formal lectures and related written exercises; the remaining three in practical summertime fieldwork. The first year's summer was devoted to practice in military drawing and surveying; the second to temporary duty in branches of the army not their own; the third to daily field assignments of typical staff work, i.e., surveying Prussia's frontiers, reconnoitering a division's route of march or a fortress, etc. In both the lecture halls and field exercises the work was rigorous, and the student-officers were held to a high standard by highly competent civilian and military instructors.

Particularly after the Austro-Prussian and Franco-Prussian Wars, it was the Prussian staff system and staff school that attracted the attention of American military leaders. Commanding General of the Army William T. Sherman* instructed a team of officers, headed by Colonel Emory Upton,* to return from a tour of Asia by way of Europe to examine educational practices among the major military powers. Upton's enthusiasm over his observations of German institutions in 1876, shared by Sherman, led to the upgrading of professional instruction in the few existing American military schools and the creation of new ones, including what evolved into the U.S. Army's first staff school at Fort Leavenworth, Kansas.* Later, under the administration of Secretary of War Elihu Root,* similar admiration for German staff practices helped encourage formation of the War Department General Staff* and establishment of the Army War College.*

Sources:

Henry Barnard, *Military Schools and Courses of Instruction in the Science and Art of War*, rev. ed. (New York: Reprinted by Greenwood Press [original in 1872], 1969).

Martin van Creveld, *The Training of Officers: From Military Professionalism to Irrelevance* (New York: Free Press, 1990).

T

TEXAS A&M UNIVERSITY. Organized in 1876 as the Agricultural and Mechanical College of Texas, it soon acquired a commitment to education for military leadership which, along with its development as a major university, it still retains today.

Texas A&M began operation on October 4, 1876, as an all-male institution organized under terms of the [Justin] Morrill* Land-Grant College Act of 1862: "where the leading object shall be, without excluding other scientific and classical studies, and including military tactics, to teach such branches of learning as are related to agriculture and the mechanic arts." Military training and its Corps of Cadets remain distinctive elements of the school's culture and traditions.

To a very great extent, for the first 100 years of Texas A&M's operation, student life was shaped, molded, and directed by the Corps of Cadets. All students were required to enroll in the Corps of Cadets, wear military uniforms, and conduct themselves in accordance with the *Rules and Regulations.* Cadets awoke to reveille at 6:30, answered sergeant's call, marched to breakfast, fell into troop formation, and marched to classes. Inspections were held every Sunday morning. Students could not leave campus without permission and received demerits for breaking the rules. Cadet officers were charged with command of the cadet companies under the authority of a commandant of the Corps of Cadets.

Lawrence Sullivan Ross reinvigorated the military regimen when he became president of the college in 1891. Ross had begun his military career in 1858 at the age of 18, leading friendly Indian and Texas ranger troops against marauding Comanches. During the Civil War, Ross became a Confederate brigadier general, in command of a brigade that distinguished itself in battles in Missouri, Mississippi, and Georgia. He served as a county sheriff, state senator, and from

1887 to 1891 as Governor of Texas before coming to the A&M College as its president. Ross brought new funding, new faculty, new facilities, considerable prestige, and a renewed commitment to military discipline and training.

Students of Texas A&M subsequently became prominent in every war and military engagement. Eighty-nine Texas "Aggies" served in the Spanish-American War, 63 of those as officers or noncommissioned officers. Texas A&M was the first college in the United States to offer its facilities and equipment to the government for military training at the onset of World War I. By July 1918, Texas A&M had a larger percentage (37.5) of its graduates in military service than any other college or university in the United States, including 1,233 officers. Forty-nine Texas Aggies died in combat. Of those, four received the Croix de Guerre posthumously, and six were awarded the Distinguished Service Cross.

On October 3, 1916, Texas A&M officials applied to the War Department for permission to establish a senior Reserve Officers' Training Corps (ROTC).* The program was established in September 1917. Participation in the military training program of the ROTC was mandatory. Texas A&M students put away the old gray-and-black uniforms worn in the past and adopted the army khaki with campaign hats. The student yearbook for 1919 described student life as including, "Military duties from reveille until taps along with academic studies. . . . It was indeed a problem for mere human beings who require sleep to find sixteen hours a day to devote to military activities and duties." World War I reconfirmed the commitment, permanence, and respectability of military training at the Texas A&M College and prepared the school for an expanded role during World War II.

Almost 20,000 Texas A&M students and former students served in the Armed Forces during World War II, 14,000 as officers, with 29 of these in the rank of general. Texas A&M furnished more officers in World War II than did the United States Military Academy,* 46 of them serving in the Philippines in December 1941 when Japanese forces attacked. Twenty-five former Texas Aggies surrendered to the Japanese at Corregidor in May 1942 after a bitter defense and prolonged siege. Men from Texas A&M fought and died on every battlefield of World War II. General Dwight D. Eisenhower remarked that "No more convincing testimony could be given to the manner in which the men of Texas A&M lived up to the ideals and principles inculcated in their days on the campus" than is evidenced by those who took part in the heroic defense of Bataan and Corregidor, those 700 who died in combat, and those (seven) former students awarded the Congressional Medal of Honor.

Military training and the Corps of Cadets continued to dominate campus life after World War II, although returning veterans were exempted from participation. Expansion, the admission of women, and military training became increasingly critical issues in the years following. The Board of Directors made military training noncompulsory in 1954, but reinstituted it in 1957. James Earl Rudder, who was among the first ashore at Omaha Beach on D day and commanded a daring ranger attack on German gun emplacements at Pointe du Hoe, became vice president and then on July 1, 1959, president of the college.

The character of the college changed throughout the 1960s, during Rudder's administration. Although some women students had been admitted to the college on a special basis even before the turn of the century, the school remained essentially an all-male military institution until 1963, when the Board of Directors agreed to admit women on a limited basis. Effective August 23, 1963, the Texas legislature approved the change in name to Texas A&M University. Then, in September 1965, the Directors abolished the compulsory enrollment of all freshmen in the Reserve Officers Training Corps and in the Corps of Cadets.

Student enrollment rose slightly until 1971, when women were admitted on an equal basis with men. Thereafter, enrollment rose rapidly—from 14,221 students in the fall of 1970 to more than 29,500 students in 1977. Women were admitted into the Corps of Cadets in 1974. By 1990 more than 40,000 students attended Texas A&M University, the admission of women annually exceeding that of men.

The School of Military Science at Texas A&M University now includes departments of aerospace studies, military science, and naval science. While the number of students enrolled in military studies and in the Corps of Cadets has declined to comprise about 5 to 10 percent of the student body, the Army, Navy and Marine, and Air Force ROTC programs nonetheless are among the nation's top producers of officers. The Army ROTC program produces more officers than any other college or university with the exception of the service academies. Freshmen and sophomore students in the military programs generally advance from the general or basic military course to the professional or advanced courses. Many are recipients of four-year scholarships, and most at the advanced level receive full scholarships and become commissioned officers.

Texas A&M University offers many diverse academic and professional studies in ten academic colleges: the traditional programs in agriculture and engineering, architecture, business, education, maritime studies, liberal arts, medicine, science, veterinary medicine, and law. Its student body numbers approximately 43,000, and it maintains a research effort of more than $350 million annually (1995–98) and a strong commitment to military training. Despite the lower numbers of students in the Corps of Cadets, the Corps embodies the Texas Aggie spirit, reflecting, in part, the university's military history and traditions.

Sources:

John A. Adams, Jr. *We Are the Aggies: The Texas A&M University Association of Former Students* (College Station: Texas A&M University Press, 1979).

Henry C. Dethloff, *The Centennial History of Texas A&M University, 1876–1976* (College Station: Texas A&M University Press).

Henry C. Dethloff, *The Texas A&M University, A Pictorial History, 1876–1996, 2nd Ed.* (College Station: Texas A&M University Press).

George Sessions Perry, *The Story of Texas A&M* (New York: McGraw-Hill, 1951).

Henry C. Dethloff

THAYER, SYLVANUS. Sylvanus Thayer (born 1785, died 1872), Colonel, U.S. Army, graduate of Dartmouth College and the United States Military Academy, exerted a lasting influence on the curriculum, methods, and organization of the Military Academy as its superintendent (1817–1833).

Prior to Thayer's appointment as Superintendent in 1817, the U.S. Military Academy* at West Point was disorganized, had had an unimpressive record, and had received little support from the government and from the Army. The methods and techniques he introduced, the course of studies he outlined, and his disciplinary measures and honor system remain the basis for those in effect up to the present time, while the goals and aims he instituted are those of the present West Point. He truly was the Father of the Military Academy.

Thayer had been appointed a cadet at West Point during his senior year at Dartmouth in 1807. The curriculum of the fledgling and struggling Military Academy was not set firmly at that time. Cadets were examined when they were considered ready by the superintendent and were graduated and commissioned as lieutenants as soon as they were able to pass the examination. Because of his background at Dartmouth, Thayer was examined, graduated, and commissioned in the Corps of Engineers in 1808, after having been at West Point for only one year. He was the thirty-third graduate of the fledgling academy.

Thayer compiled a credible record in the War of 1812 and was duly rewarded. At the end of that war, President James Madison and Secretary of State James Monroe, alarmed at the almost catastrophic lack of military leadership demonstrated in that war, resolved to revitalize the Military Academy. Thayer was sent to Europe with the brevet rank of major to make a comprehensive study of military education and engineering. In France for two years, Thayer spent one of those years studying the methodology of the École Polytechnique.* He mingled with the best scientific brains in France and gathered for West Point a library of approximately a thousand technical volumes on military art, engineering, and mathematics.

Thayer returned in 1817 and was appointed by the newly elected President James Monroe to be superintendent at West Point with carte blanche to reorganize the school. Thayer found the academy in disarray and was welcomed by the small permanent faculty. He overhauled, reorganized, and reshaped all aspects of the Military Academy. Thayer felt that the honorable and faithful discharge of duty had to be the essential quality of the military profession. Honor was seen as the basis for military performance without which a professional education and the exercise of leadership could not be effective. The new system he instituted has been compared to a triangle, with honor at its base, and equilaterals respectively of education and discipline pointing to the end product, military leadership, at its apex. The Honor System he installed remains the basis of a West Point education to this day.

Thayer established a four-year educational program, with the firm principle that every cadet must have a graded recitation every day in every subject he was required to study. Cadets would be ranked by this daily classroom performance. This system was designed to encourage competition and eliminate favoritism. Graduates would be assigned to branches of the Army based upon their merit roll standing. A commandant of cadets was placed in charge of military instruction and discipline.

Under Thayer's direction, the Military Academy became preeminent both in science and in military affairs. His influence spread far beyond West Point. Every engineering school in the United States founded in the 19th century copied West Point, and most found their first presidents and professors among USMA graduates. Textbooks written by West Point faculty dominated American mathematics, chemistry, and engineering. In this way, Thayer is also recognized as the father of engineering education in the United States.

Sources:

Stephen E. Ambrose, *Duty, Honor, Country: A History of West Point* (Baltimore, MD: John Hopkins Press, 1966).

Ernest Dupuy, *Sylvanus Thayer: Father of Technology in the United States* (West Point, NY: Association of Graduates, United States Military Academy, 1958).

George Fielding Elliot, *Sylvanus Thayer of West Point* (New York: Julian Messner, 1959).

George S. Pappas, *To The Point: The United States Military Academy. 1802–1902* (Westport, CT: Praeger, 1993).

Herbert Y. Schandler

TRAINING AT SEA. The system by which virtually all navies and other maritime forces trained officers and enlisted men before the middle of the 19th century. The U.S. Navy and Revenue-Cutter Service operated without shore-based training facilities prior to the creation of the U.S. Naval Academy and the U.S. Coast Guard Academy.

The American sailing navy initially modeled its officer procurement system on the British tradition. Teenaged boys of "respectable" parentage were appointed to midshipmen's warrants by the President, the Secretary of the Navy, and members of Congress and were sent off on cruises on board warships. The ship's chaplain served as schoolmaster, teaching grammar, arithmetic, and, to the extent that he understood it himself, navigation. During the War of 1812, Congress specified that each newly constructed naval vessel should bear an individual labeled "schoolmaster" on her rolls. By 1815 fifteen warships had schoolmasters, and in 1819 a professional examination for promotion to lieutenant was instituted.

Few competent scholars showed any inclination to be ships' schoolmasters, and as nautical technology progressed the concept of the warship as classroom became less satisfactory. Several attempts by secretaries of the Navy to get authorization for a shore-based naval school died in Congress. The best the Navy could manage were four eight-month "cram schools"—at Boston, at the Phila-delphia Naval Asylum,* and on board the frigates *Guerriere* and *Java*—that tried to prepare the midshipmen for the lieutenancy examination by drilling them in navigation. A passing grade was no guarantee of an appointment. Congress established the number who would hold each of the four officer ranks (mid-shipman, lieutenant, master commandant, and captain), and the Secretary of the Navy promoted someone whenever a vacancy materialized.

Officers could stay in the service as long as they liked, and because of the meager pension system, few ever retired. The rank of "passed midshipman" was created for those who had passed the examination and were waiting for vacan-cies.

The U.S. Navy enlisted man of the sailing ship era is a shadowy figure, largely because the government regarded him as transient hired help and kept scarcely any records of his existence. He usually "signed on" a warship at the beginning of a cruise. Federal law limited his enlistment to three years, at the end of which he was dumped ashore wherever his ship happened to be. The salary ($12 per month for able seamen during most of the century) was lower than most Amer-ican merchant shipowners paid, and many warships' complements were made up mainly of foreigners.

In the 1820s, the Navy began the practice of stationing a worn-out frigate, ship of the line, or sloop of war at each of the major ports to accommodate enlistees who were awaiting berths in the few commissioned warships. The "receiving ships" were supposed to be fitted out and run like warships. In prac-tice, they became refuges for sailors who could not find jobs in the merchant marine.

In 1837, President Andrew Jackson signed a congressional act giving the Navy permission to enlist, with parental consent, apprentices (generally referred to simply as "boys") aged 13 through 18, with the intention of training them in the arts and skills of the seaman. The ships of the line *North Carolina* and *Columbus* and the frigates *Hudson* and *Java* were designated "school ships," on board which the boys would be isolated from sinful influences. By 1841, the program had recruited more than a thousand apprentices.

A year later Captain Matthew Calbraith Perry, commandant of the Brooklyn Navy Yard, conceived a scheme that he hoped would create an influx of ap-prentices from the midwestern states. A newly commissioned brig, the USS *Somers*, was to be fitted out for a cruise in the South Atlantic and the Caribbean with a crew composed largely of apprentices.

The *Somers* put to sea on September 13, 1842, with a total of 121 men crammed into her meager living spaces. Seventy-four were apprentices. A hand-ful of veteran enlisted sailors and petty officers provided a nucleus of trained manpower. There were four commissioned officers and seven midshipmen. One of the latter was 17-year-old Philip Spencer, son of John C. Spencer, Secretary of War of the United States. The *Somers*'s commanding officer was Perry's brother-in-law and close friend Lieut. Alexander Slidell MacKenzie.

After a leisurely Atlantic crossing, the *Somers* sailed from the Madeira Islands for the West Indies. She was several days away from the nearest land when MacKenzie began to hear frightening rumors: Midshipman Spencer and several seamen were plotting to slaughter the officers and turn the *Somers* into a pirate ship.

Whether the "*Somers* mutiny" was a genuine conspiracy or an adolescent fantasy is still unclear. MacKenzie ordered the four wardroom officers and the three senior midshipmen to investigate the matter and give him their advice. They concluded that Spencer, boatswain's mate Samuel Cromwell, and steward James Wales were guilty of mutiny. MacKenzie thereupon ordered the three men hanged from the *Somers*'s main yardarms.

The *Somers*'s return to New York touched off a Navy inquiry, a court-martial, and a wave of media criticism. Secretary Spencer wanted MacKenzie indicted for murder, but the Navy's investigation concluded that he had acted properly. Perry's apprentice cruise program died, and the Navy returned to the receiving ship system. Midshipman Spencer had his defenders, but it was clear that the system for appointing midshipmen was flawed. The *Somers* affair was prominent in the mind of Navy Secretary George Bancroft* when he launched the campaign that, in 1845, resulted in the establishment of the U.S. Naval Academy.*

For the first 86 years of its existence, the U.S. Revenue-Cutter Service drew most of its officers from the merchant marine, sometimes hiring unemployed naval officers. In its early days the "Revenue-Marine" took little interest in military discipline. Credit for giving it a military scheme of organization usually is given Captain Alexander Fraser, who also took an intense interest in officer training. In 1848, Fraser took the revenue cutter *Lawrence* from Washington to San Francisco, establishing the service's first base on the West Coast. He recruited a crew of young, energetic officers, purchased a sizeable library of books for them to study, and operated the *Lawrence* as a training ship.

In 1876 Sumner Kimball, chief of the Revenue-Cutter Service, persuaded Congress to authorize the creation School of Instruction of the Revenue-Cutter.* Unlike student selection for the two service academies, the Treasury Department was to appoint, on the basis of a competitive examination, "fairly educated young men who possess the necessary qualifications to enter upon the course of study." The course of study was to last two years, and graduates would be commissioned as third lieutenants.

The newly authorized school was located on board the revenue-cutter *Dobbin*, home-ported at New Bedford, Massachusetts, and its first class came aboard in May 1877, consisting of eight cadets (a ninth was rejected at the last minute because of his "general deportment and a manifest disposition to prevaricate"). The following summer, the *Dobbin* was replaced by the *Salmon P. Chase*, a handsome three-masted bark built for the purpose. The cadet program was divided into a summer cruise, from May to October, and dockside winter-quarters instruction. The curriculum for the latter included English, mathematics, history, international law, and astronomy, most of these taught by a single instructor,

Professor Edwin Emery. While at sea, the cadets learned the rigging and handling of sails, the knotting and splicing of lines, the use of navigation instruments, and ship handling. Two hours per week were devoted to theoretical instruction, using standard navigation and seamanship texts. By 1885 the school had produced 31 graduates.

Five years later the government abruptly shut the school down. The Naval Academy at Annapolis was producing more graduates than the Navy could absorb, and for the next few years the Revenue-Cutter Service was able to draw its officers from that source. The mid-1890s, however, saw an expansion of the Navy, and in 1895 an act of Congress provided for the retirement of Revenue-Cutter Service officers who were too ill or too old to perform their duties. The result was a *shortage* of junior officers—and a new lease on life for the service's training school. The *Chase* was taken into dry dock, cut in half, and lengthened by 40 feet to accommodate additional cadets.

In 1900, the *Chase* was moved to a new home port in Curtis Bay, Maryland, just outside Baltimore. During the next decade she visited most of the East Coast ports and made annual summer cruises to Europe, staying at sea for about seven months each year.

Meanwhile, steam had made its way into the Revenue-Cutter Service; and in 1907 the Navy transferred the USS *Bancroft*, a steam-powered gunboat with a two-masted sail rig, to the Revenue-Cutter Service as a replacement for the *Chase*. The *Bancroft*, renamed the USRC *Itasca*, offered training in both steam and sail, as well as a variety of modern weaponry. This essentially sea-based training of young men aspiring to be Officers continued until 1910, when the *Itasca* changed her home port to New London, Connecticut, and the school acquired what was to become a permanent location ashore.

Sources:

Riley Hughes, *Our Coast Guard Academy, A History and Guide* (New York: Devin-Adair Co., 1944).

Irving H. King, *The Coast Guard Expands, 1865–1915: New Roles, New Frontiers* (Annapolis, MD: Naval Institute Press, 1996).

Christopher McKee, *A Gentlemanly and Honorable Profession: The Creation of the U.S. Naval Officer Corps, 1794–1815* (Annapolis, MD: Naval Institute Press, 1991).

Samuel Eliot Morison, *"Old Bruin": Commodore Matthew Calbraith Perry, 1724–1858* (Boston: Little, Brown and Co., 1967).

John A. Tilley

TURNER, STANSFIELD. Stansfield Turner (born 1923), Admiral, U.S. Navy, a graduate of the U.S. Naval Academy and Oxford University, as president of the U.S. Naval War College (1972–1974) formed a professional faculty to teach a revolutionary new curriculum that has influenced all of the American war colleges and a generation of flag and general officers they have educated.

When Admiral Elmo Zumwalt (as Chief of Naval Operations) focused his reforming eye on the Naval War College,* he found that for a long time it had produced few new ideas or flag officers. To take a hard look at the Naval War College and to make it a source of new naval thought and leadership, Admiral Zumwalt in January 1972 recommended the promotion of Stansfield Turner to vice admiral, to become president of the Naval War College on July 1, 1972. Having issued a mandate for reform, Admiral Zumwalt provided unwavering support for the far-reaching changes that Turner's two-year tenure brought to the Naval War College.

Stansfield Turner had strong qualifications for this assignment. Entering Annapolis after two years at Amherst College, he graduated as commander of the Brigade of Midshipmen in 1946 and won a Rhodes Scholarship in 1947. His experience at Oxford, where he took a degree in Politics, Philosophy and Economics in 1950, significantly influenced his war college reforms. After Oxford he distinguished himself in assignments afloat and ashore and rose rapidly to rear admiral in 1970.

Steeped in tradition, the Naval War College remains today on the hill of Coaster's Harbor Island in Newport, Rhode Island,* where it was founded in 1884. After World War II, two new war colleges were added to it and the existing Army War College*: an Air War College* and, as the apex of the defense education system, a joint services National War College* in Washington, D.C. Although the three service war colleges only briefly accepted the National War College as a senior and superior institution, to claim parity they soon patterned their curricula on its year-long round of daily lectures on international relations, governmental organization, and current defense policy. In the year before Turner's arrival, students in the senior course at Newport—some 200 Navy commanders and captains and equivalent officers of other services—heard from over 155 outside lecturers. Although students were tightly scheduled in daily lectures and seminars, writing requirements were rare, assigned readings were seldom discussed, and no examinations evaluated the students' performance.

Turner began work immediately in January 1972, while still serving as the Navy's director of systems analysis at the Pentagon. Convinced that the Naval War College's curriculum and teaching methods both needed a thoroughgoing revision, he decided to discard the entire projected 1972–73 curriculum that was already in the final stages of preparation at Newport. He formed a small planning group (four of whose members were Oxford graduates), which met with him in Washington to devise an entirely new kind of war college education. Since Turner did not expect to remain as president for more than one or two years, there was no time for gradual change or for building consensus in the faculty and staff at Newport.

Working rapidly, Admiral Turner and his planning group designed an entirely new curriculum, whose teaching method was patterned after the Oxford tutorial system of writing regular essays after intensive reading. Still not fully completed when Turner assumed the presidency in July 1972, the new curriculum divided the year into three courses, Strategy, Management, and Tactics. With few formal lectures, these courses focused the students' work in weekly three-hour seminars led by professional faculty. Students were given large blocks of time to complete the heavy weekly reading assignments and to prepare seminar essays. Recognizing the need for a trained academic faculty to teach Strategy and Management, Turner recruited a number of new civilian professors for those departments. The Tactics Department was staffed principally with officers already serving on the faculty.

While the Management and Tactics courses have been regularly revised and renamed, the Strategy and Policy course endures today, over 25 years later, in a form recognizably based on its 1972 prototype. This Strategy and Policy course, which Turner has called "the jewel in the Naval War College crown," largely explains the new academic program's lasting success and influence.

In the spring and summer of 1972, Turner's planning group raced to prepare the syllabus, buy books, and organize a faculty for the Strategy and Policy course before it began in late August. The course's intellectual father was William R. Emerson, who conceived the idea of using a series of historical case studies, beginning with Thucydides' *Peloponnesian War* and a close reading of Clausewitz's* *On War*, to examine how nations have coped with recurring problems in the planning and conduct of war. In its first year, the Strategy and Policy course also focused on such topics as the role of British sea power in the Napoleonic Wars, Bismarck's limited wars, and the origins of World War II.

Of Turner's planning group, three joined the strategy department—Philip A. Crowl as chairman, and J. Kenneth McDonald and Josiah Bunting III as professors. Robert D. (Rusty) Williams chaired the management department, while Captain Hugh Nott, as Turner's chief of staff, performed miracles in organizing support for the new courses.

In his speech to the new class at the opening convocation, Admiral Turner attacked the "creeping intellectual devitalization in all of our war colleges since World War II," caused by their efforts "to add piecemeal to their curricula in a fruitless quest to cover everything of relevance." In sharp contrast, the new curriculum examined topics in depth in a coherent progression of seminars. The three courses, demands for extensive reading, frequent writing, and regular examinations were designed to open students' minds and stimulate new habits of creative thinking. How far an academic program achieves such objectives is hard to measure, but Turner's rigorous curriculum unquestionably continues to challenge and engage Naval War College students. It has left a legacy not only at Newport but also at the other three war colleges, which soon began to read Clausewitz, to rely more on civilian academics, and to require more writing and fewer lectures. In the post–Vietnam War reforms that prepared the American military for the Gulf War victory, the "Turner Revolution" at the Naval War College played an important role.

After leaving the Naval War College in 1974, Admiral Turner got his fourth star, held top naval and NATO commands, and served as director of the Central

Intelligence Agency until 1981. Since then he has published books on intelligence, terrorism, and nuclear weapons, taught at Yale, West Point,* and the University of Maryland, and chaired the special board of visitors* committee that assessed the Naval Academy in 1997. In a long career of service and achievement, however, it is his transformation of the Naval War College—and the enduring influence of his innovations—that have earned Admiral Turner his place as one of the preeminent American military educators of this century.

Sources:

Philip A. Crowl and J. Kenneth McDonald, "New Courses at the Naval War College," Conference Paper, Inter-University Seminar on Armed Forces and Society, Chicago, Illinois, October 12, 1973.

John B. Hattendorf, B. Mitchell Simpson III, and John R. Wadleigh, *Sailors and Scholars: The Centennial History of the U.S. Naval War College* (Newport, RI: Naval War College Press, 1984).

Williamson Murray, "Grading the War Colleges," *The National Interest* (Winter 1986–87).

J. Kenneth McDonald

U

UNITED STATES AIR FORCE ACADEMY. The four-year precommissioning institution of the U.S. Air Force, located just north of Colorado Springs, Colorado, designed specifically to produce dedicated, regular career officers for that service.

The process to create the Air Force Academy began in 1948 within the USAF's Air Training Command at the urging of the first Chief of Staff, General Carl A. Spaatz, shortly after the Air Force became a separate service. In September 1948, the service's new chief, Hoyt W. Vandenburg, decided that the academy would be a four-year institution (recommendations had been made to make it a five-year program so as to incorporate regular pilot training), and he appointed an Air Force Academy Planning Board within the Air University* to prepare the way. As the Air Force board neared completion of its work, the Secretary of Defense appointed a national Service Academy Board* to study the whole issue of federally supported undergraduate education for military officers. Its work led Secretary James Forrestal, in 1950, to support legislation authorizing a separate "air" academy.

Repeatedly shelved during the early years of the Korean War, legislation for the new academy finally bore fruit during the second session of the 83rd Congress. On April 1, 1954, the Air Force Academy Act was signed into law by President Dwight Eisenhower. The act stipulated that the Secretary of the Air Force would determine the location of the academy by establishing "a five-member commission to advise him in connection with the selection of a permanent location." The commission consisted of Dr. Virgil M. Hancher, president of the University of Iowa; Lt. General Hubert R. Harmon;* Charles Lindbergh; Merrill C. Meigs, vice president of the Hearst Corporation; and retired General Carl A. Spaatz.

On June 3, 1954, the commission recommended that the academy be permanently established at one of the following sites without preference or priority: a site on the Mississippi River about ten miles west of Alton, Illinois; a site about eight miles north of Colorado Springs, Colorado; and a site on the south shore of Lake Geneva, Wisconsin. On June 24, 1954, Secretary of the Air Force Harold E. Talbott, announced the Colorado Springs site as the chosen location.

The site of the Air Force Academy has a rich history. Originally, Plains Indians like the Comanche, Cheyenne, Arapaho, and Kiowa inhabited or passed through the area. The first whites in the area were explorers on the Zebulon Pike expedition in 1806. The first permanent settlements came to the area with the "Pikes Peak or Bust" gold rush in 1858. Most of the present-day academy property consisted of cattle ranches. One of the oldest standing structures in the Pikes Peak region, a log cabin built before 1870 by rancher William Burgess, still stands on the academy grounds.

The Air Force Academy, with its 18,500 acres, is one of the largest collegiate campuses in the world. The site encompasses five main valleys. A broad valley, close to the north boundary, is where cadets do their fieldwork during basic training. Lehman Valley, the next to the south, slopes gently away from the mountains and contains the main cadet academic and living area. Two of the remaining valleys contain large housing areas and public elementary schools, the Air Academy High School, and other support facilities. The site itself contains almost one hundred miles of paved roads, many with steep grades that present special problems during heavy snowstorms. It is one of the nation's highest campuses, with altitudes varying from 6,380 to 8,040 feet. During the academy's early days of sports competition, many visiting coaches and athletes feared that playing in such a high altitude would have adverse effects on the performance of their teams. Experience has shown, however, that the effects appear to be minimal.

The main cadet area holds numerous educational and athletic complexes. It has two large dormitories, a chapel, an administration building, and a planetarium. The cadet area also features a vast array of athletic fields and a military parade ground. The classrooms in Fairchild Hall, the main academic building, have been equipped with over 100,000 square feet of blackboard space so that cadets could write out their exercises. It also contains the library, which has thousands of books, journals, periodicals, government documents, and numerous computer databases to access as well as a large and ever growing airpower archive. All the cadet rooms in the dorms are linked to the Air Force Academy's computer network, giving cadets access to the school's numerous databases, e-mail, and the World Wide Web.

The Air Force Academy also has a small airstrip to support the flight indoctrination, soaring, and parachuting programs. The cadet flying team also trains at this facility. The academy's navigation training program, however, never used this airfield because of the limited size of the runways. Despite its size, though, the academy airstrip, during the summer training periods, is one of the busiest airports in the country, based on the number of daily takeoffs and landings.

The Cadet Wing moved from Lowry Air Force Base* in Denver to the permanent site in late August 1958. The first class to graduate, in the following spring, were seniors; and the second superintendent, Maj. General James E. Briggs, had some formidable goals to accomplish in a limited time. General Briggs had to pave the way for accreditation of the academy by the North Central Association of Colleges and Secondary Schools. The academic and military programs had already been established; but without accreditation, the degrees granted would be meaningless, and the opportunity for officer graduates to be admitted to postgraduate schools would be limited. For the new academy it meant attaining very high standards in a short time. Every aspect of the institution was to be subject to examination: educational programs, the degrees, teaching experience of the faculty, the quality and coverage of the library collection, the laboratory equipment the administration, the philosophy of the school, and hundreds of other related items.

To prepare for accreditation, Briggs relied on the academy's first Dean of Faculty, Brig. General Robert F. McDermott.* Once given the task, McDermott intended to create for the Air Force Academy an academic program that allowed graduates to better meet the educational and technological challenges demanded by the needs of the United States. His major thrusts were the enrichment program and academic majors in several program areas. The first was introduced in the 1956–57 academic year, offering some cadets opportunities to elect extra courses in addition to the accelerated work made available to them from the prescribed subject areas. A year later, opportunities for a major in either the social sciences or engineering sciences were provided. The prime objective was to challenge the cadets to advance academically as far and as fast as he was able. The program broadened the fields of study and afforded the cadet an opportunity to concentrate in areas of special interest and usefulness to the Air Force. Originally offered only in two areas to cadets with advanced academic preparation, majors were added, by academic year 1960–61, in the basic sciences and in the humanities. In later years, the academy would adjust the academic program to include several interdisciplinary majors and to create opportunity for all cadets to participate. Notably, by the time the first class graduated in 1959, the academy had received accreditation.

The introduction of the curriculum enrichment program was the Air Force Academy's first major departure from the traditional service academy philosophy that all students should pursue and be limited to a prescribed course of study. It was a vanguard program for American service academy education. At first, officials at West Point* were skeptical about the Air Force Academy's experiment; those at the U.S. Naval Academy* adopted a cautious attitude but soon provided limited opportunities for elective courses. However, the success of the Air Force Academy's program eventually encouraged both of these other academies to follow suit.

In 1956, Dean McDermott had also devised and enacted the "whole man" concept in selecting cadet candidates for appointment. He created a system that gave weighted recognition to the physical, athletic, moral, and leadership attributes of a candidate as well as his academic potential and his registered scholastic achievements. This innovation soon became part of the standard admissions policy of all service academies.

The mission of the Air Force Academy reflects the traditional service academy emphasis on the development of career officers. The official statement reads as follows: "The mission of the Air Force Academy is to provide instruction and experience to all cadets so that they may graduate with the knowledge and character essential to leadership and the motivation to become career officers in the United States Air Force." This emphasis on career motivation explains the special features of the academy and is the rationale behind the practice of maintaining a predominately military faculty. The academy has wanted faculty members to "to teach by what they are as well as by what they say." Besides having master's and doctoral degrees from civilian universities, the academy's military scholars have had practical professional experience in the Air Force during both war and peace. To obtain further continuity, selected members of the faculty were scheduled by the dean and the heads of departments to return to teaching duties after having served intervening tours elsewhere in the Air Force.

The Air Force Academy aims to provide a combination of academic education, professional orientation, and skill training in an environment conducive to motivating a cadet to devote his or her career to the service of the United States and the Air Force. Cadets must balance their time between academic and military duties. However, in the classroom, cadets must maintain proper military decorum at all times, thereby instilling in them a greater sense of professionalism.

To maintain its academic and military excellence into the twenty-first century, the Air Force Academy continues to improve its faculty and upgrade its facilities. Each academic department has begun hiring permanent civilian professors to provide stability as well as continuity in the educational process. The Air Force has begun a major renovation of the dormitories, upgrading the heating, plumbing, and electrical systems as well as upgrading the computer network to give cadets larger and faster access to the World Wide Web. Through educational and facility improvements the academy plans to continue to produce intelligent, well-educated, and motivated officers to lead the Air Force into the new millennium.

Sources:

M. Hamlin Cannon and Henry S. Fellerman, *Quest for an Air Force Academy* (Colorado Springs, CO: U.S. Air Force Academy, 1974).

George V. Fagan, *The Air Force Academy: An Illustrated History* (Boulder, CO: Johnson Books, 1988).

Edgar A. Holt, M. Hamlin Cannon, and Carlos R. Allen, *History of the United States Air Force Academy* (Colorado Springs, CO: U.S. Air Force Academy, 1957).

William E. Simons, *Liberal Education in the Service Academies* (New York: Bureau of Publications, Teachers College, Columbia University, 1965).

Major Timothy J. Matson, USAF

UNITED STATES COAST GUARD ACADEMY. The principal precommissioning educational institution for officers of the U.S. Coast Guard.

In 1915 President Woodrow Wilson signed an act of Congress amalgamating the U.S. Revenue-Cutter Service and the U.S. Life Saving Service to create the U.S. Coast Guard. Shortly thereafter the U.S. Revenue-Cutter Academy,* located at Ft. Trumbull, Connecticut, was renamed the U.S. Coast Guard Academy.

In its early years the school was small, producing about half a dozen graduates each year. Its three-year curriculum was heavily oriented toward practical training, though there were also courses in mathematics, physics, English, history, and French. All but a few of the instructors were Coast Guard officers. Cadets spent much of their time on board the training cutter *Itasca*, learning seamanship and gunnery. A separate course of instruction trained officers for the engineering branch.

In 1917 its Board of Instruction made a formal recommendation that the academy be developed into a technical school "in every way comparable in its completeness of courses, instruction, and educational facilities with either West Point or Annapolis." World War I and the Prohibition era, during which the Coast Guard took on the responsibility for stopping the smuggling of liquor into American seaports, saw an increase in the demand for new Coast Guard officers. By 1921 the corps of cadets outgrew the little *Itasca*'s living spaces, and the Coast Guard acquired a new, larger training vessel, the *Alexander Hamilton*. In 1926 Congress authorized the Secretary of the Treasury to require that cadets serve four years before being commissioned, and in 1931 the school officially adopted a four-year curriculum. Three years later the academy moved to a 45-acre reservation in New London, Connecticut,* overlooking the Thames River.

Over the next few years the school's academic quality and its enrollments improved dramatically. An advisory committee of professors from Columbia, Harvard, Yale, and M.I.T. undertook a detailed study of the curriculum. At that body's recommendation a distinguished permanent academic faculty was hired, and a board of visitors* made up of congressmen was established. In 1941, with enrollment at 199, the academy began awarding Bachelor of Science degrees in addition to ensigns' commissions.

The Second World War saw the most massive expansion in the Coast Guard's history, from a strength of 19,000 in 1941 to 171,000 in 1945; most wartime enlisted and officer inductees were accepted into the newly created Coast Guard Reserve. The four-year curriculum for regular cadets was reduced to three for the duration, and the Coast Guard Academy took on the responsibility for training reserve officers.

The first reserve officer candidates were required to hold college diplomas prior to swearing in, and to attend a four-month Reserve Officer Training Course at the academy. As the Coast Guard found it increasingly difficult to compete with the other services for qualified officer candidates, it dropped the stipulation that all its candidates hold college degrees. In the fall of 1942, the number of reserve officer candidates outstripped New London's ability to accommodate them. The overflow went to the Coast Guard training station at St. Augustine, Florida.

World War II also saw the Coast Guard setting some service academy precedents in the realm of civil rights. A presidential order of January 1942 mandated that the armed forces accept black recruits, and in April 1943, Ensign Joseph C. Jenkins, having completed the four-month reservist's course at New London, became the Coast Guard's first African-American officer. On November 23, 1942, President Franklin D. Roosevelt signed an act of Congress creating the Women's Reserve of the Coast Guard. The SPARs (named after the Coast Guard motto: "Semper Paratus–Always Ready") were to be modeled on the women's reserve the Navy had created a few months earlier. On June 28, 1943, the Coast Guard Academy opened its doors to women when a class of fifty SPAR officer candidates reported for indoctrination. The SPAR officer candidate course lasted six weeks (later lengthened to eight). In using its service academy to train women the Coast Guard was taking a step that none of the other armed services emulated. More than 700 of the 955 SPAR officers commissioned during the war received their training at New London.

When the German army overran Denmark, in April 1940, the square-rigger *Danmark*, training ship of the Danish merchant marine, was tied up at a pier in Jacksonville, Florida. The ship's captain offered the services of her and her crew to the U.S. government, and on the day after Pearl Harbor the *Danmark* was assigned to the Coast Guard Academy. She became the flagship of a small fleet of training vessels that also included the 65-foot schooner yacht *Curlew*.

The end of the war brought the academy an unexpected dividend. Four large-sail training ships of the German navy became available as war prizes, to be allocated to Great Britain, the United States, and the Soviet Union. The American representative secured the finest vessel of the four, the three-masted bark *Horst Wessel*. This ship, with the new name *Eagle*, became the academy's new cadet training vessel. During the next 50 years the *Eagle* became one of the Coast Guard's best-known symbols, serving not only as a training aid but as a recruiting and public relations tool. A refit in the late 1980s ensured that the *Eagle* would remain in service well into the twenty-first century.

The early postwar years were unhappy ones at the Coast Guard Academy. With the restoration of the peacetime four-year curriculum came an increased emphasis on technical training courses, as the Coast Guard tried to keep its cadets abreast of the new technology in engineering, weaponry, and electronics. A management specialist hired to analyze the academy's efficiency in the late '40s recommended that it be shut down and that the Coast Guard draw its officer candidates entirely from civilian universities. Enrollment during the 1950s ranged from 400 to 500—all male again; the SPARs virtually ceased to exist with the end of the war. The retention rates were alarming. Fewer than half of the cadets who showed up for their introductory "swab summer" graduated four years later, and a substantial percentage of those who did receive their commissions resigned after serving the mandatory three years. In 1951 the academy opened an officer candidate school, offering a four-month indoctrination course to Coast Guard warrant officers and enlisted men and to selected graduates of civilian colleges. By 1954 the officer candidate school was producing more than three times as many officers as the academy's regular four-year program. The Eisenhower administration toyed with the idea of merging the Coast Guard Academy with the U.S. Merchant Marine Academy*.

In 1957, Rear Admiral Frank A. Leamy was appointed Superintendent of the Coast Guard Academy and initiated an effort to improve the school's appeal, starting with the cadets' morale. Leamy divided the cadets into four "companies," each with a commissioned officer as "company commander." The companies were encouraged to compete with each other academically and in intramural sports. Cadets were given some exposure to Coast Guard aviation, with each year's second classmen (juniors) spending three weeks at the Coast Guard Air Station in Elizabeth City, North Carolina. Leamy also established the title of Academic Dean for the senior permanent faculty member and hired a famous professional athlete, Otto Graham, as varsity football coach. Leamy's successor, Rear Admiral Stephen Hadley Evans, instituted a number of academic reforms, getting the academy its first computers and increasing the number of full-time civilian faculty members with postgraduate degrees.

In January 1961, President John F. Kennedy noticed that the contingent of Coast Guard Academy cadets in his inaugural parade consisted entirely of white men. Kennedy promptly notified the Commandant of the Coast Guard, Admiral Alfred C. Richmond, that the academy was to begin recruiting African Americans. Richmond responded that the academy had no racial policy; it was, in fact, a point of pride in the Coast Guard that its academy admissions were based entirely on competitive examinations. Kennedy agreed that the current admission policy should continue. In the following autumn, following efforts to broaden the academy's recruiting of qualified young men, the first African Americans arrived at New London as regular cadets.

The early 1960s saw a major revision in the Coast Guard Academy's curriculum. Traditionally all cadets had taken the same courses, which heavily emphasized technical training; beginning in the late 1950s, electives in the liberal arts had been available only to those who were willing to carry an overload. Beginning in 1965–66, however, cadets were offered the option of choosing a "concentration" in either "science and engineering" or "management and social sciences" during their last two years, including at least five electives. The number of full-time faculty with postgraduate degrees steadily increased during the '60s, as the Coast Guard not only hired more civilian professors but encouraged officers assigned to academy positions to earn doctorates.

On October 7, 1975, President Gerald Ford signed a law requiring that the armed services admit women to their service academies the following year. The Coast Guard Academy had already announced that it would accept female applicants for the class entering in July of 1976. Female cadets would receive the same training as males—including summer cruises on board the *Eagle*.

By 1990 the academy was again the principal source of Coast Guard officers. Average annual enrollment in the 1990s was about 900, with a full-time faculty of about 110. A typical entering class numbered about 250 cadets, 24 percent of them women, 5 percent African-American, 6 percent Hispanic, and 7 percent Asian-American. Cadets could choose from eight academic majors: civil engineering, electrical engineering, mechanical engineering, naval architecture and marine engineering, marine science, mathematical and computer sciences, government, and management. New London remained the only U.S. armed service academy that did not accept congressional appointments; admissions continued to be based on SAT and ACT scores, high school class rank, and such factors as motivation, leadership potential, personal perspective, and physical fitness, as rated by a Cadet Candidate Evaluation Board.

Sources:

Irving Crump, *Our United States Coast Guard Academy* (New York: Dodd, Mead and Co., 1961).

Riley Hughes, *Our Coast Guard Academy: A History and Guide* (New York: Devin-Adair Co., 1944).

Robert Erwin Johnson, *Guardians of the Sea: History of the United States Coast Guard, 1915 to the Present* (Annapolis, MD: Naval Institute Press, 1987).

John P. Lovell, *Neither Athens Nor Sparta?: The American Service Academies in Transition* (Bloomington: Indiana University Press, 1979).

John A. Tilley

UNITED STATES MERCHANT MARINE ACADEMY.

For more than a half-century, the United States Merchant Marine Academy (USMMA) has supported both the economic and defense interests of the nation by training and graduating officers for America's merchant marine and Armed Forces.

The graduates of this academy, operated in Kings Point, New York, by the U.S. Department of Transportation's Maritime Administration, have served on seagoing merchant ships in peace and in war, in the military with ranks from ensign to admiral, and as the business leaders of America's maritime and transportation industries.

The USMMA is the product of Federal Government involvement in maritime training that dates back to just after the Civil War. In 1874, the U.S. Congress, concerned with the decline in the nation's merchant fleet, approved legislation that provided federal funds for "schoolships" operated by a number of states for training merchant marine officers. Over the next 50 years, various federal programs were enacted to bolster and support maritime training. None were particularly successful, however, since the programs lacked uniform training standards and central oversight.

Leading the drive in the 1930s for improved maritime training was Richard R. McNulty, a young shipping company executive with seafaring experience.

McNulty wrote a series of articles in the maritime journals of the day advocating standardized, disciplined, and federally supported merchant marine officer training.

His work was well received, but the catalyst for federal action was a tragic fire in 1934 aboard a passenger liner, the *Morro Castle*. In this incident, 134 lives were lost. An investigation determined that crew incompetence and negligence contributed to the scope of the disaster. Congress, prodded by this fiery tragedy, undertook a review of the nation's maritime training practices and subsequently passed the Merchant Marine Act of 1936. This landmark legislation enunciated a national policy that America's merchant marine should be "manned with a trained and efficient citizen personnel."

A U.S. Maritime Commission was created and tasked with establishing a reliable training system. In 1938, the commission created the U.S. Merchant Marine Cadet Corps. Its members reasoned that with the complexity of modern ships, the challenge of foreign competition, and the need for merchant officers with defense skills to meet any national emergency, a federal cadet training system was necessary. The next step was locating a shore-side facility for a merchant officer school. In March 1942, Congress purchased property on Long Island's north shore as the site of the USMMA. Construction began immediately, prompted by the immediate wartime need for seagoing officers. The academy was officially dedicated in 1943.

The U.S. Maritime Commission chose a professional military system for the academy, modeled to a degree after the U.S. Naval Academy's* program. The commission valued the qualities of leadership and discipline that a military system would instill in the USMMA students. The need for merchant ship officers to interact with Navy vessels also prompted the USMMA's founders to include naval science as a part of the training program.

World War II required that the USMMA produce its officers quickly, so the length of the program of study was set at just 24 months. This included a period of training at sea in wartime convoys, during which 142 academy cadets were lost to enemy action. By war's end, the USMMA had produced 6,634 licensed merchant officers.

In 1945, the academy switched from its abbreviated wartime curriculum to a four-year program. In 1949, the curriculum was accredited, and Congress authorized the USMMA to confer a Bachelor of Science degree. Seven years later, Congress designated the academy as a permanent federal institution. In 1974, admissions requirements were amended to permit the USMMA to enroll female students, the first federal academy to do so.

The academy's ability to serve the national defense came to the forefront once again during the Korean and the Vietnam Wars. Graduating classes were accelerated to meet a shortage of merchant marine officers needed for the immense sealift of wartime supplies to Asia. In the 1960s, the USMMA also served as a training site for officers of the first U.S. nuclear powered merchant vessel, the *Savannah*.

Events in the Persian Gulf in 1990 required a "breakout" of reserve fleet cargo ships to ferry military supplies to the Middle East. Some 150 USMMA students were assigned for training to vessels supporting Operations Desert Shield/Desert Storm. These young midshipmen proved to be valuable crew members and subsequently received Merchant Marine Expeditionary Medals for their service in a war zone.

Midshipmen enrolled in the academy's four-year program receive training in such professional maritime subjects as navigation, transportation logistics, and marine engineering, as well as a full program of naval science courses. In addition, each student spends a year at sea on various U.S. flag merchant ships gaining practical seafaring experience. This is followed by a two- to six-week shore-side internship with a shipping or transportation company.

The academy's regimental system instills its some 950 midshipmen with the traits of leadership, discipline, and dedication to duty required for a career that typically may include service at sea, maritime employment ashore, and participation in the U.S. Naval Reserve. Graduates receive Bachelor of Science degrees, merchant marine licenses, and U.S. Naval Reserve commissions. However, what distinguishes the U.S. Merchant Marine Academy from other federal service academies is that graduates may also apply for active duty commissions with any branch of the Armed Forces. In recent years, some 18 percent of graduating midshipmen have entered the U.S. Navy, Marine Corps, Army, Air Force, and Coast Guard as commissioned officers on active duty.

As the size of the Armed Forces diminishes in the 1990s, the military services have taken a new look at the USMMA. Academy graduates, with their professional military training, their understanding of transportation logistics, and their practical shipboard experience, have been recognized as a cost-effective source of officers for all branches of service. The U.S. Merchant Marine Academy enters the 21st century committed to its multipurpose role in support of the Armed Forces, the seagoing merchant fleet, and the nation's transportation industry.

Sources:

"Kings Point Roots Grow from U.S. Maritime History," *Journal of Commerce*, September 30, 1983.

Rear Admiral Thomas T. Matteson, *Tell America: The United States Merchant Marine Academy* (Exton, PA: Newcomen Society of the United States, 1997).

C. Bradford Mitchell, *We'll Deliver: An Early History of the Merchant Marine Academy* (Kings Point, NY: U.S. Merchant Marine Academy Alumni Association, 1977).

Martin P. Skrocki

UNITED STATES MILITARY ACADEMY. A four-year government-supported and sponsored undergraduate institution, founded in 1802, which confers upon its graduates the degree of Bachelor of Science. A highly esteemed source of officers for the Regular Army of the United States, it has had a marked

328 UNITED STATES MILITARY ACADEMY

influence on the development of the nation and of a defense establishment devoted to civilian control.

From the very beginning of the American Revolution, leading statesmen had realized that some professional training was necessary for American military leaders. The founding of a military school at the strategic location of West Point, New York,* had been proposed by General Henry Knox* in 1776, and George Washington and Alexander Hamilton had repeatedly urged adoption of this suggestion. A small informal school for "artillerists and engineers"* had been established at West Point shortly after the war, but lack of resources had kept it ineffective.

The leaders of the new nation anticipated that the major portion of the armed forces would come from the armed citizenry, the militia. Thus, they reasoned, a trained professional officer corps must come from the society as a whole, must be open to all men of ability whose sole qualification was merit, who would be obedient to civil authority and unwilling to use their monopoly of military knowledge for their own ends, and would be able to train and lead citizen soldiers in time of war.

The genius of the U.S. Military Academy (USMA) lay in meeting those requirements. Washington, John Adams, and the others who contributed to the formation of the school hoped to build an academy controlled by, and with students appointed by, civilian political leaders. The academy would impart to its cadets the military knowledge that had to be kept alive in America if the country were to retain its independence.

On March 16, 1802, the Congress authorized President Thomas Jefferson to organize a Corps of Engineers which "shall be stationed at West Point . . . and shall constitute a military academy." Thus, the United States Military Academy, or West Point, as it is generally called, was established with the Army's engineer corps having first claim on its graduates and control over their education. At this early point, the American government recognized, however feebly, that the military art required specialized training, and the government accepted the responsibility for providing that training.

In its first decade and a half, however, West Point was neglected and mismanaged. Public indifference, official hostility, and lack of resources from the Congress combined to defeat its ambitious educational and military goals. By 1812, it had graduated only 71 cadets. Its graduates took little part in the War of 1812, and at the end of that war it could be considered a failure.

Although some efforts were made after the war to correct obvious deficiencies, little was done, and disorder and lack of support continued until 1817, when Major Sylvanus Thayer* was appointed Superintendent. Known as the Father of the Military Academy, Thayer brought order out of chaos, making the academy one of America's great scientific and engineering institutions. Under his leadership and direction, the Military Academy became vibrant and imaginative, famous for its engineering program and its creative faculty, and a model for civilian schools to copy. The methods and techniques Thayer pioneered, the course of study he introduced, the disciplinary measures and honor system he instituted are the basis for those in use at West Point today.

The influence of Thayer and West Point on engineering education in the United States made the years from 1840 to 1860 the Military Academy's greatest age. During this period, the country fought its first successful war of expansion and subsequently settled all the continent east of the Mississippi River and a large part of the area to the west of it. West Point officers protected the settlers moving west while drawing the maps and building the transportation systems that moved them. West Point engineers built an enormous number of roads, canals, and railroads. Almost to a man, the Army engineers who worked on these projects were USMA graduates. Until the Mexican War, with one single exception, West Point was the only institution in the country training civil engineers. Many USMA graduates who did not themselves become civil engineers became the teachers of students who did.

The academy's influence in the pedagogic aspects of civil engineering at least equaled its influence in the actual building process. In academic affairs, the Military Academy remained preeminent in science and civil engineering. USMA graduates founded most of the major engineering colleges established in the nation during the 19th century and became presidents or faculty at those institutions. All these schools used the methods and textbooks developed at West Point. In matters scientific, the small military academy led the nation and was proud of its outstanding program and faculty.

West Point graduates distinguished themselves in the Mexican War. Nearly all the men who would rise to high command positions in the Civil War fought in Mexico and with scarcely an exception performed admirably. General Winfield Scott, Chief of the Army and not an academy graduate, stated, "I give it as my fixed opinion that but for our graduated cadets, the war between the United States and Mexico . . . probably would have lasted some four or five years, with, in its first half, more defeats than victories falling to our share."

In the Civil War, a significant number of southern officers who had been educated at West Point joined, formed, and led the Confederate Army. In that war, USMA graduates served as senior commander on each side in every major battle. The victorious Union commander, General Ulysses S. Grant, became the first West Point graduate to be elected President of the United States.

After the Civil War, however, and until the third decade of the 20th century, the academy stagnated. It became a small, forgotten, narrowly professional college tucked away in a corner of New York state, enamored of its success in the Civil War, paying little attention to the outside world and receiving little attention in return. Moreover, it became resistant to attempts to change the system under which it had achieved past success. By the end of the century, the unique recitation method—originally developed for and extremely successful in the teaching of mathematics—was rigidly required for all other academic subjects, regardless of its suitability for the new subject matter rapidly proliferating in higher educational curricula. West Point, whose scholarship and methods before the Civil War had been ahead of the Army and the nation, was after that conflict increasingly irrelevant to both.

However, this academic stagnation, which continued until the 1930s, was offset by an emphasis on military professionalism. The academic curriculum in the physical sciences, except for the top-performing class sections, became less theoretical as more time was devoted to practical applications in such fields as optics and mechanics. These same years saw increased time devoted to professionally relevant courses in the social sciences and required instruction in infantry, cavalry, and artillery tactics for all four cadet classes.

The impact of this emphasis was well demonstrated by West Point graduates who dominated the high command of the American Expeditionary Force in World War I even more than they had during the Civil War. In 1919, a hero of that war, Brig. General Douglas MacArthur* became superintendent and embarked on a campaign of innovation and inspired leadership. In academic affairs, he encouraged experimentation with teaching methods other than the academy's traditional classroom recitation, and he urged introduction of additional courses in the humanities and social sciences. Convinced of the need for a more enlightened type of troop leadership befiting an Army manned by citizen soldiers, he insisted on more realistic forms of military training and increased opportunity for cadet contacts with the outside world. He and his successors returned the academy permanently to the mainstream of American life, as a well-esteemed institution of undergraduate preparation for public leadership.

The quality, character, leadership, and proficiency of USMA graduates, as well as the worth of the institution to the nation, were well demonstrated during World War II—in expanding the small American Army and Army Air Corps, in training, equipping, and transporting that massive force, and then leading it to victory on two fronts. After the war, General Dwight D. Eisenhower, Class of 1915, and the allied supreme commander in Europe, became the second West Point graduate to be elected President of the United States.

During the cold war years, the U.S. Military Academy evolved with the times and prudently adjusted its program. Having raised entrance standards and strengthened its curriculum sufficiently by the mid-1930s to become accredited to grant the Bachelor of Science degree, it had already achieved a solid foundation on which to build after 1945. By the 1980s, the movement toward liberalization of the West Point curriculum, initiated years earlier, culminated in the provision of academic majors. This was accompanied, of necessity, by the development of a better academically trained faculty and the encouragement of less rigid classroom routines. Thus, the U.S. Military Academy maintained its front rank among American undergraduate institutions while continuing to graduate highly qualified and highly motivated officers for the U.S. Army.

Sources:

Stephen E. Ambrose, *Duty, Honor, Country: A History of West Point* (Baltimore: Johns Hopkins Press, 1966).

George S. Pappas, *To the Point: The United States Military Academy, 1802–1902* (Westport, CT: Praeger, 1993).

William E. Simons, *Liberal Education in the Service Academies* (New York: Bureau of Publications, Teachers College, Columbia University, 1965).

Herbert Y. Schandler

UNITED STATES NAVAL ACADEMY. Between 1850 and 1925, the primary and nearly the only source of young officers for the U.S. Navy, and still the major precommissioning source for officers who rise to senior and flag rank.

The U.S. Naval Academy was created in October 1845, when Secretary of the Navy George Bancroft* ordered two civilian professors and two naval officers from the teaching staff at Philadelphia's old Naval Asylum* to resume their duties at Annapolis, Maryland.* In the following summer, the academy received its first congressional appropriation. Chief among the public pressures leading to congressional approval were (1) concern over the harsh discipline administered to midshipmen being trained aboard naval vessels and (2) recognition of the need for a thorough technical education for officers responsible for the newer steam-propelled naval ships.

Existing laws, reflected in Bancroft's initial plan for the Naval School as it was first called, limited the provision of naval education only to officers (e.g., midshipmen) already on active service. But he did not wish to propose new legislation to change this practice until the academy was well established. Rather, as he instructed Commodore Franklin Buchanan,* his designee as the academy's first superintendent, Bancroft intended "to collect the midshipmen who from time to time are on shore" and send them to Annapolis for appropriate study. Thus, the academy's first student body consisted of 36 older midshipmen who had been at the Naval Asylum preparing for their lieutenant's examination, 13 others awaiting their orders to sea, and seven acting midshipmen appointed that very year. Students could be called away for shipboard duty at almost any time, as many were during the war with Mexico (1846–48).

By 1851, after an extensive study of the academy by a board of distinguished naval officers, the program was expanded from two to four consecutive years, and admittance to the first year's course was limited to boys from fourteen to sixteen in age. Control over most appointments was taken away from the executive branch of government and allocated among the congressional districts and territories, with each member of the House of Representatives allotted two appointees within the student body at any one time. Of the 25 appointments allowed the President, 10 were reserved for the sons of army and navy officers. In 1850, the institution was officially designated as the United States Naval Academy.

The early program of instruction at Annapolis incorporated many of the academic and administrative features developed earlier by the U.S. Military Academy.* Disciplinary matters and military training were made the purview of a commandant. Control of academic instruction and examinations was vested in an Academic Board, composed of the superintendent, the senior civilian professors from most of the academic departments, and the commanding officer of the training ship *Preble*, which had been permanently stationed at Annapolis and used for summer practice cruises. Academic instruction was conducted as daily graded recitations by each of the students, with the grades used to establish a cumulative order of merit within each class. A program largely modeled after West Point's was maintained until and during the academy's temporary relocation northward to Newport, Rhode Island,* throughout the Civil War years.

Following the war and the academy's return to Annapolis, the earlier dominance of the civilian professors on the Academic Board diminished as control over the instructional program shifted to successive groups of outstanding naval officers. Commander Stephen B. Luce,* who had written a much-esteemed textbook on seamanship while teaching at Newport, returned to the academy as commandant and contributed mightily to the school's increasing emphasis on naval professionalism. An institutional ethos was spawned that a later graduate called a "Gospel" of government service. Under Superintendent (Rear Admiral) David D. Porter,* an official concept of "honor" was established for the first time. Midshipmen were assured that their statements would be accepted as truth, and they were encouraged to regard the performance of duty as a moral obligation rather than as an outcome of military discipline.

Beginning with Superintendent Porter and, a decade later, advanced even further by Commodore Christopher Rodgers* (1874–1878), the Naval Academy also expanded its theoretical studies. By the early 1880s, despite repeated protests from older naval officers on its board of visitors,* its academic program had advanced to the stature of a true college, particularly its courses in mathematics and physical science. The standard curriculum also included language and history courses and Ethics and Law. Textbooks for the latter emphasized such concepts as the divine origins of "The State," a "natural order" of mankind, and a disdain for materialism and commercial profiteering. Under Superintendent Rodgers, who was concerned by the wide range of educational preparation among the entering naval cadets, elective courses were offered beginning in 1876, at first consisting only of advanced calculus and analytical mechanics.

Rodgers's concerns reflected gradual changes in the academy's student body, which had become significant by the 1880s. Since the Civil War, the proportion of candidates appointed from the more heavily populated Eastern seaboard had dropped from over 80 to less than 45 percent, reflecting the growth of the newer states of the South and West. This change also resulted, in part, from the extension to each state's two senators the same appointment privilege previously reserved to the congressmen. However, westward expansion impacted the educational preparation of incoming classes less severely than these numbers suggest, as many candidates appointed from western states during this era had been educated in eastern urban centers or private schools.

In other respects, post–Civil War students at Annapolis remained very much like their predecessors. The hazing of first-year students by upperclassmen continued, acquiring a degree of ritualized brutality. The naval cadets of the late

19th century were also enterprising, forming their own athletic teams, both in-tramural and a few intercollegiate.

Perhaps the most significant impact on the Naval Academy of the late 19th century was made by the Navy's transition toward steam propulsion. According to Park Benjamin, the Navy's experience with its shipboard engineers (chiefly volunteers) during the Civil War had been "dismal," and it was ready, therefore, to have education in the handling of steam engines included in the academy program. Between 1871 and 1882, the Naval Academy experimented with a series of separate programs of instruction for students intent on engineering careers* and those preparing for line-officer duties. However, in the Navy Personnel Act of 1882, Congress intervened by abolishing the distinction between "cadet-engineers" and "cadet-midshipmen." (It also severely limited naval commissions but initiated opportunities for academy graduates to accept commissions in the Marine Corps.) Henceforth, all naval cadets were again exposed to a common curriculum which no longer permitted advanced students to enroll in electives.

The Naval Academy reached the turn of the century with an instructional program the scope of which was to change little until after World War II. After Congress finally incorporated the engineers into the Navy line in 1899, future graduates of the academy had to be equally well versed in engineering and the more general seagoing fundamentals; therefore, both elements assumed major roles in a curriculum common to all students. Coupling these elements with cultural studies believed essential for all men of affairs resulted in a tightly prescribed and highly regimented program of instruction. Nevertheless, having gained accreditation as an "approved technological institution" in 1931, from the Association of American Universities, the Naval Academy was authorized by Congress to grant the Bachelor of Science degree.

World War II brought about a program reduction to three years' duration, and it also brought on political concern over whether a single-service precommissioning school was best suited to meet national security needs—particularly the need for interservice cooperation, demonstrated repeatedly during four years of global conflict. However, in a 1944 report that foretold the findings of the postwar Service Academy Board,* a special Navy board affirmed that alternative patterns of officer preparation would be less able to motivate and properly train an officer candidate for service in his own branch. Meanwhile, a wartime influx of faculty members with civilian university teaching experience helped set the stage for a gradual liberalization of the academic program in the postwar period.

Movement away from a lock-step curriculum began in 1953–54. By the decade's end, under encouragement from a new superintendent, Rear Admiral Charles L. Melson, the academy offered opportunities for more advanced midshipmen to gain credit for introductory courses through examination and to substitute electives in the same fields.

Since the Naval Academy's expansion to over 1,000 full-fledged midshipmen early in the 20th century, movement toward a more diversified academic curriculum had been hampered by a large number of professional military faculty who lacked graduate education in their respective teaching fields. In May 1962, Secretary of the Navy Fred Korth announced his decision to appoint a civilian Dean of Faculty and directed that the academy faculty be upgraded. In response, Navy officials accelerated efforts already under way to recruit more civilian faculty and identify active duty officers already holding advanced degrees. Meanwhile, they also moved to attract an appropriate civilian dean. The first scholar to hold that post, Dr. Bernard Drought, joined the academy staff beginning with academic year 1963–64.

While these changes in faculty policy were being implemented, substantial effort to expand the electives program was also under way. During the tours of superintendents Charles Kirkpatrick and James Calvert,* the opportunity for midshipmen to participate in the electives program was increased, and full-fledged academic majors became a regular program feature. Under Kirkpatrick (1962–64), plans were set to make at least six electives available to all students beginning with academic year 1964–65. The march toward full-fledged academic majors was consummated on Calvert's watch (1968–72). Although the number of majors has varied over the ensuing years (as of 1997–98, it had been reduced to 18), the basic structure of the Naval Academy's academic curriculum has changed but little since then.

Paralleling, and in a sense responding to, these postwar changes was a general strengthening of the academy's practical training. Through a succession of leaders, the Navy's enthusiasm for liberalization of the academic curriculum has both waxed and waned, but commitment to the primacy of the Naval Academy's professional military mission has been constant. This commitment has been reflected in a number of postwar superintendents' attention to program features such as the training cruises, the honor system, and the indoctrination of first-year students. In the mid-1960s, formal assessments of a midshipman's performance while training at sea* were initiated and included in the overall order-of-merit rankings. In the next decade, the midshipmen's first training cruise became more structured, in specially designated training craft where more uniform experiences and standards could be assured. Representative of the academy's emphasis on professional instruction and motivation is the fact that, since the introduction of full-fledged academic majors, professional courses have formed the bulk of the required core element of the overall program.

Sources:

Peter Karsten, *The Naval Aristocracy: The Golden Age of Annapolis and the Emergence of Modern American Navalism* (New York: Free Press, 1972).

John P. Lovell, *Neither Athens Nor Sparta?: The American Service Academies in Transition* (Bloomington: Indiana University Press, 1979).

William E. Simons, *Liberal Education in the Service Academies* (New York: Bureau of Publications, Teachers College, Columbia University, 1965).

Jack Sweetman, revised by Thomas J. Cutler, *The United States Naval Academy: An Illustrated History, 2nd Ed.* (Annapolis, MD: Naval Institute Press, 1995).

UNITED STATES NAVAL INSTITUTE. Since 1873, a forum for the exchange of ideas, a historical depository, and a "university press" for the Naval Academy and the sea services, serving its members and the Navy, Marine Corps, and Coast Guard. Founded to act as a catalyst for "the advancement of professional, scientific, and literary knowledge," this nonprofit, non-government-affiliated organization has been an important contributor to professional military education and development.

At its genesis, the Naval Institute was established as a forum for the original members who were concerned about the future of the Navy. Serving in a navy bogged down in the doldrums of the post–Civil War era, when advancements in technology were being ignored for the sake of fiscal frugality, the founding members hoped to stimulate interest in bringing the Navy into the industrial age. A product of the 19th-century American Lyceum system of adult education, the Institute began when 15 naval officers of various ranks met in one of the lecture rooms at the U.S. Naval Academy* in Annapolis, Maryland,* to (in the words of then Naval Academy Superintendent Rear Admiral John L. Worden) "organize a Society of the Officers of the Navy for the purpose of discussing matters of professional interest." The first meeting followed the Lyceum pattern by including the reading of a paper on "The Battle of Lepanto," written by one of the attendees, and a subsequent discussion of the proffered paper by those attending. Subsequent meetings, held monthly in the early evenings of October through June, continued in the same manner. The idea caught on and new members began joining; five years later, the membership had grown to 245.

Less than two years after the Institute's founding, a volume of the proceedings of previous meetings was published and included the papers previously read and discussed at the early meetings. The lead paper focused upon the need for apprentice training in the U.S. Navy, while others covered such diverse topics as "Experimental Determination of the Center of Gravity," "Compound Engines," and "The Armament of Our Ships." Soon, other volumes of proceedings followed until, in 1879, it was announced that the *Proceedings* would be published on a quarterly basis. Other papers, submitted by members but not discussed at the meetings, began to be included so that the publication ceased to be a mere reflection of what had occurred in the meetings and became a professional journal instead. In 1914, it became a bimonthly publication and then, in 1917, it took on its current *monthly* regularity. *Proceedings* magazine has served as an open forum since its earliest days, presenting the various sides of many important issues, such as the need for a naval reserve force, needed improvements in gunnery training, and the role of women in the Navy. What makes the magazine unique is that it is not subject to government control and does not reflect an editorial point of view. The ideas and opinions expressed are those of the contributors, not the editors. This open forum has led to some controversies over the years but, overall, has served the Naval Institute, its members, and the sea services well.

In 1878, to encourage the members to put their thoughts on paper and submit them for possible publication, the institute created an essay contest that offered a variety of prizes, including a cash award. This tradition has continued. Today, the Naval Institute, with the aid of donations contributed by various sponsors, conducts seven different thematic essay and two photographic contests each year.

In the frugal years of the late 19th century, the U.S. Navy had neither the facilities nor the funding to produce professional books or instruction manuals for use in the fleet. The Naval Institute filled this void by devoting entire issues of *Proceedings* to single subjects. In 1885, one such issue was devoted to "Marine International Law" and in 1891 the subject was "Instructions for Infantry and Artillery, U.S. Navy." In 1898, the Board of Control authorized the publishing of books on naval and associated subjects and published its first work, an account of American naval exploits in the Spanish-American War. More books quickly followed including, in 1902, the first edition of *The Bluejacket's Manual*, an introductory "bible" for young sailors who must learn the unfamiliar ways of the Navy. That same manual is still published today, with its twenty-second edition currently in progress.

In 1907, a member of the engineering faculty at the U.S. Naval Academy wrote that, "from necessity, this Department has been experimenting for years in textbooks of foreign authorship and which were exceedingly inappropriate in teaching midshipmen the description, operation and management of American machinery." He added that books written by university professors were also objectionable because they were "bulky, well-padded, costly, and necessitating the omission of large quantities of text owing to the difference in the method of training at the Academy." These revelations provide some insight into the reasons behind the eventual unofficial, but important, role of the Naval Institute as the "university press for the Naval Academy." More and more specialized texts needed for instruction at the academy were published by the Naval Institute, which served not only the needs of the academy but the authors of these books as well. Because the Naval Institute is a nongovernment organization, it could copyright the materials it published, thereby providing protection for the authors that would not have been available had their books been published under the auspices of the U.S. government.

The publishing program at the Naval Institute grew through the years, evolving eventually into the Naval Institute Press, which has produced thousands of titles over the decades. Today's catalog offers more than 700 active titles. Some textbooks and manuals are still produced for the sea services, but the press has expanded in many other areas, most especially history, literature, and reference works. Although the institute has successfully published enough popular works to make the press financially self-supporting, emphasis has been placed upon a subvention program that ensures the publication of other works of academic importance. In 1984, the press produced its first original fiction work, Tom Clancy's *The Hunt for Red October*, which became a best-seller of extraordinary proportions. Since that time, the Naval Institute Press has produced a limited number of fiction works and continued to expand into other modern extensions of the publishing world, including audio books and CD-ROM versions of some of its reference works.

Through the years, the Naval Institute has expanded into other fields as well. A number of television documentaries and motion pictures have benefited from the institute's resident expertise, the photographic archives have grown into one of the world's foremost collections, and the oral history program has preserved a wealth of important historical information that might otherwise have been lost to posterity.

Borrowing from the tradition established in the earliest days of the institute—when topics of current interest were discussed and debated as part of the evening's proceedings—the Naval Institute began in 1985 to produce seminars in which single or multiple topics are discussed by panels of experts with interaction from the audience. These seminars have been held in Annapolis and at various fleet-centered locations around the nation and have focused on a wide range of topics including the Vietnam War, maritime strategy, media-military relations, and the bombing of Pearl Harbor.

In 1923, in an article celebrating the Naval Institute's half-century of existence, Lieutenant Commander Roy C. Smith, Jr. wrote that "with the possible exception of the Naval War College* at Newport, Rhode Island,* no other source has so greatly furthered the material development and professional advancement of the Navy as has the Naval Institute." Through its open forum, book and periodical publications, television documentaries, seminars, and photographic archives, the Naval Institute continues to serve the needs of the sea services in ways that are true to the original charter that called for its members to strive for "the advancement of professional, scientific, and literary knowledge."

Sources:

Nancy Kercheval and Kevin T. Gilbert, "Naval Watchdog," *Annapolis* (October 1993).

Fred L. Schultz, "The Naval Institute at the Forefront of World Maritime Issues," *Maryland Magazine* (Winter 1991).

Captain Roy C. Smith, III, "The First Hundred Years Are . . ." *U.S. Naval Institute Proceedings* (October 1973).

Captain G. V. Stewart, "The Admirable Servant, Occasionally Obsequious: Seventy-five Years of the Naval Institute," *U.S. Naval Institute Proceedings* (October 1948).

Thomas J. Cutler

UPTON, EMORY. Emory Upton (born 1839, died 1881), Brig. General, U.S. Army, graduate of the U.S. Military Academy, was the U.S. Army's most influential late-19th-century reform theoretician and an early advocate of comprehensive professional military education.

Upton, a native of upstate New York, attended Oberlin College for a year before entering West Point.* He graduated eighth in the class of 1861 and was immediately plunged into the Civil War. Commissioned a second lieutenant of artillery, he quickly displayed high competence as a troop trainer and combat leader. During the war he rose to the rank of brigadier general and commanded both infantry and cavalry divisions, thus gaining combat experience in all three arms of the service. An innovative tactician, Upton in 1864 devised an assault plan that nearly broke the Confederate line at Spottsylvania Courthouse. Deeply religious, idealistic, and intensely dedicated to his profession, Upton was disgusted by what he believed was needless battlefield carnage caused by untrained, ill-qualified commanders. His war experience thus impelled Upton toward military reform.

Upton's distinguished war service gained him powerful patrons. General Ulysses S. Grant personally promoted Upton to brigadier general after his Spottsylvania exploit, and the young officer also became a protege of William T. Sherman,* postwar Commanding General of the Army. Accordingly, while most officers spent the years after Appomattox administering Reconstruction or fighting Indians, Upton, except for brief field assignments, was able to devote himself to Army education and reform.

Immediately after the war, Upton drafted a new system of infantry tactics suited to the growing firepower of late 19th-century weapons. The Army adopted his system in 1867. From July 1870 to June 1875, Upton served as commandant of cadets and instructor in artillery, infantry, and cavalry tactics at the Military Academy.* In summer 1875, General Sherman dispatched Upton and two other officers on a two-year round-the-world trip to study the armies of Asia and Europe for possible lessons applicable to the United States. After his return from this tour, Upton spent the next three years at the Artillery School at Fort Monroe,* Virginia, then the Army's only advanced branch school, where he taught military theory and distilled his foreign observations into an agenda for Army reform.

On his trip, Upton, like many other officers from many other nations, had been most impressed by the Prussian army, then fresh from its decisive victories over Austria and France. He dedicated himself to persuading Americans to adopt those elements of the Prussian system which he believed applicable to the United States. In particular, Upton admired Prussia's employment in war of troops trained in peacetime and led by officers fully schooled in the science of command, as opposed to what he saw as the mistaken American practice of relying on hastily raised, untrained troops under equally untrained officers. Upton first publicized his views in *The Armies of Asia and Europe*, a report on his world tour published in 1878, which consisted of detailed descriptions of the armies he had visited and a section outlining a plan for American military reform. His plan called for an enlarged, expansible regular army backed by a nationally controlled trained reserve and for the creation of an American equivalent of the Prussian general staff.

Upton also advocated the expansion of professional military education. In *The Armies of Asia and Europe*, he recommended that the United States establish a comprehensive system to provide army officers the training in command and staff work, which their Civil War predecessors had so conspicuously lacked. The nation must create, he said, "a War Academy to educate officers in the art of war, and to prepare them for the staff and to hold high command." In a letter written in 1877, he elaborated:

West Point is, in my judgment, far superior to any academy abroad for preparatory training for officers. But, once in service, we have nothing to compare with the war academies of Europe, except the Artillery School. You know how ignorant our generals were, during the war, of all the principles of generalship. Here, I think, we can correct that defect and form a corps of officers who in any future test may form the chief reliance of the government.

Through personal correspondence, contact with influential military men and civilians, and advice to the congressional Burnside Commission on an abortive Army reorganization bill, Upton promoted the cause of military reform. In the late 1870s, he began work on his monumental *The Military Policy of the United States*, a history which would document the waste and folly with which the United States had conducted its previous wars and make a conclusive case for his reform program.

Upton's work on *Military Policy*, his career, and his life came to an untimely, tragic end. In March 1881, while Upton was commanding the 4th U.S. Artillery at San Francisco, the pain and growing irrationality caused by an inoperable tumor in his nasal passages became unbearable. At age 41, he committed suicide, leaving his manuscript and his work of reform unfinished.

After Upton's death, his influence lived on. Other Army reformers of his generation adopted Upton's program as their agenda. They broadcast his ideas through professional journals and, when they could, incorporated them into official policy. In particular, they advanced Upton's program of officer education. The U.S. Army in the decade after Upton's death gradually developed a network of postgraduate branch schools, including the Infantry and Cavalry School at Fort Leavenworth,* which took on features of a command and staff college. After the Spanish-American War, Secretary of War Elihu Root* secured publication of Upton's unfinished *Military Policy of the United States* in order to educate Americans about the need for military reform. Root took up Upton's crusade for an officer corps systematically educated for higher staff and command assignments. He revived the branch schools and incorporated them into a rationalized system of officer professional education culminating in the Army War College.* While Upton's accomplishments in professional military education in his lifetime were limited, he truly can be credited with laying much of the intellectual foundation for the modern Army's system of officer training.

Sources:

Stephen A. Ambrose, *Upton and the Army* (Baton Rouge: Louisiana State University Press, 1964).

Russell F. Weigley, *Towards an American Army: Military Thought from Washington to Marshall* (New York: Columbia University Press, 1962).

Graham A. Cosmas

USAF EDUCATIONAL REQUIREMENTS BOARD. Board of senior Air Force officers established in 1959 that supervised a multiyear study of the qualitative requirements for education needed in various officer career specialties and provided in the professional military schools.

In April 1959, Air Force leadership established the Educational Requirements Board (ERB), composed of senior officers from selected major commands, to identify and describe the current and future qualitative educational requirements of commissioned Air Force officers. Among the board's assigned responsibilities were (1) studying the specific fields of study and identifying the optional patterns of preparation most appropriate for the different officer career specialties, (2) determining the percentage of officers in each of these specialties who should receive specific levels of the appropriate education, and (3) updating these data with particular attention to future changes resulting from the development of new weapon and support systems. The overall intent was to develop a rational basis for devising and administering officer assignment policies.

Early in the board's history its Secretariat, located at the Air University* under initial direction of Colonel William H. Bowers, decided to divide the study effort into two phases: (1) educational objectives to guide student-officers toward the preparation needed for specific areas of career specialization and (2) educational objectives to guide planning for the service's professional military schools and the assignment of student-officers. For the first phase, ten panels were formed, one for each major career area in the USAF Officer Classification System: aerospace operations; the scientific area; research and development engineering; civil engineering; electronics and maintenance engineering; materiel; comptrollership; intelligence; security; and administration, including personnel and other normal administrative services. Each panel was composed of officers from different major commands who were serving in that particular career area. The second phase of the ERB study, which began in late 1961 as the career panels were finishing their work, was carried out by a single task group of officers that was representative of all major Air Force organizations.

The panels representing the major Air Force career specialties were assembled for their initial meetings in the early months of 1960. Each devised a research plan appropriate to its career area with guidance from the Secretariat staff. Several panels developed detailed attitude surveys which were distributed to officers serving in their respective career areas. Others relied on interviews with selected field practitioners using standard sets of questions developed by the panel. In any case, the panels sought information on typical job functions and their relationship to specific elements of formal education experienced by the incumbents, i.e., their relevance, their degree of importance, the anticipated impact of future technical developments, and the propriety of current position classifications.

Panels began submitting their formal reports for Secretariat and ERB review in the early summer of 1961. Subsequent submission of revised panel reports for review and acceptance by the Deputy Chief of Staff for Personnel was accomplished by most of the panels by July 1963.

The ERB's Professional Military Education Task Group was first organized late in 1961. It was charged with determining the proper philosophy and objectives of Air Force PME, providing a detailed description of the areas of study to be included in such programs, and determining the proportion of the officer force that should attend each of the service PME schools. Headed by Colonel Russell V. Ritchie, commandant of the Air Force's Extension Course Institute, the PME Task Group assembled at the Air University for a series of bimonthly meetings throughout most of 1962. Its early effort was focused on consulting various sources, including some PME historical material assembled by the chairman, and exploring the views solicited from the major commands concerning their recommended changes to the Air University schools.

The task group determined that then-current Air Force PME programs were deficient in their attention to both joint education and studies about war, particularly air warfare. They also found that the personnel actions affecting Air Force PME were inconsistent at best: The best officers were not being assigned to either student or faculty billets; classes varied widely in experience level and quality; the assignment of graduates had little apparent relation to their preceding course of study; and the utilization of non–air force military schooling followed no discernible career-oriented rationale.

By late in the fall of 1962, the task group had agreed on their assumptions for the study and were focusing on selecting appropriate PME objectives. Its initial focus on objectives was without regard to PME level or the nature of the student body. The group settled on seven general objectives that included (1) developing the student's understanding of such concepts as the military role in "achieving national goals in both peace and war" and "the technological, economic, political, and psycho-social factors which form the basis of international conflict"; and (2) developing the student's ability to "think creatively," to "solve military problems in a logical, systematic manner," and to "present findings in a manner permitting logical analysis and comparison of alternatives."

Later in 1963, effort was devoted to assessing the adequacy of the Air Force's then-current PME structure and sorting out content objectives for specific levels of schooling. Although initially assuming a three-tiered, service-oriented school structure, the task group had, following its April meeting, adopted the view that an Air Force staff college and war college were adequate. It then concentrated on formulating curricular objectives for each, using Benjamin Bloom's *Taxonomy of Educational Objectives* to distinguish between two major sets of cognitive values: (1) knowledge and (2) intellectual abilities and skills.

By midsummer, the task group had completed its initially assigned tasks and formulated its recommendations. Aside from its proposed two-tiered structure of Air Force PME, the task group recommended earlier exposure of officers to joint issues and operations—even urging greater utilization of the command and staff schools of other services. But it argued against awarding equivalent PME credit to an officer who attended a war college other than the Air Force's. Pointing out the prior lack of an officially endorsed system of PME, it proposed a system based on the group's stated philosophy of military education, an explicit set of system objectives, and official guidance to the schools regarding the kinds of student competence and areas of knowledge deemed appropriate for each level—even specifying individual course lengths.

The task group also recommended policies regarding student selection and career integration, urging that all officers receive first-level PME sometime during their fifth and sixth years of commissioned service but that selection for the war college be competitive. Completion of a preparatory correspondence course was advocated prior to both, with war college applicants taking a mandatory written examination as well. Final selection of the limited number of war college students would be accomplished by a special board based on performance in both the course and the examination and the candidate's periodic effectiveness reports. Correspondence and/or nonresident extension courses were recommended to provide war college study opportunity for those board-qualified officers not selected for the resident program. Failure to complete either Air Force War College course successfully by the end of his sixteenth year would terminate an officer's promotion opportunity. Further, completion of an Air Force War College program would be required before selection to attend either of the senior joint colleges.

The ERB forwarded the essence of the PME Task Group's report to the Air Staff in late July 1963; board modifications were mostly minor except for its urging attendance at both service colleges at earlier stages of an officer's career. A thorough review resulted in air staff acceptance of several of the board's recommendations, i.e., its statements of PME philosophy and PME system objectives, proposals for improving faculty quality, greater use of preparatory courses by correspondence, and universal attendance at a first-level staff college. But the Air Staff balked at denying equivalent PME credit for non–Air Force war college attendance and cutting off promotion opportunity for nonattendees, and it questioned the justification for abandoning the three-level PME pattern. It also asked the task group to restudy its proposal for competitive war college examinations and to develop more detailed and reasoned curricular guidance for the two proposed service colleges.

Air Staff actions took place in late October–early November 1963. Task group and ERB responses were given form in the early months of 1964. However, because of the buildup of forces in Southeast Asia later in 1964 and other cold war deployment actions, many of the Air Force PME and related personnel policies acquiring momentum from the ERB findings were not implemented until years later.

V

VIRGINIA MILITARY INSTITUTE. America's first state (public) military college, combining full-time professional military education with diverse academic and extracurricular programs.

Founded in 1839 in Lexington, Virginia, the Virginia Military Institute (VMI) drew on France's l'École Polytechnique* and the U.S. Military Academy* as its military educational models and was also influenced by the ideas of John T. L. Preston and Alden Partridge.* During VMI's formative years virtually all of its faculty were West Point–trained officers, but ultimately these were replaced by VMI graduates—who reached 50 percent by 1860 and exceeded that level for nearly 100 years. However, because of a need for more broadly based faculty, VMI graduates receded to approximately 25 percent by the 1980s. Throughout its existence, VMI combined full-time professional military education with an adversative educational system, which concentrated on character development through challenging daily cadet routine, academics, and athletics.

From its inception, VMI was intended to educate and produce citizen-soldiers who could provide peacetime leadership in civil pursuits and, when called in wartime, could serve in militia and volunteer forces. Democratic equality of opportunity at VMI was secured through provision of State Cadetships—in effect, need-based scholarships for cadets of limited means. Inclusion of "Pay Cadets" from more affluent segments of society and other states and countries made the cadet corps more cosmopolitan.

VMI's educational core was initially in mathematics and engineering, and later in chemistry, physics, and, eventually an expanding number of liberal arts disciplines. More than 16,000 graduates and a large number of "former-cadets" (the latter including such distinguished men as General George S. Patton, Admiral Richard E. Byrd, and General Lewis B. "Chesty" Puller) have entered business and finance, industries, government and military service, the arts, and the legal and medical professions.

VMI's citizen-soldier form of PME was immediately tested in the Mexican War. Although it had graduated its first class (of 16 men) only four years earlier, 25 alumni served in that war. At this time, VMI also became a model for other state military colleges. In the era before the Civil War, VMI also became a resource for military education of militia and volunteers officers—exemplified by VMI commandant William Gilham's comprehensive tactics, drill, organization, administration and military justice manual, used extensively by both Confederate and Union officers. By the start of the Civil War in 1861, there had been only 903 matriculates but, of these, 22 had served in the Regular U.S. Army. An additional 1,112 matriculates constituted VMI's wartime classes (1862–68). Of this total of 2,015 matriculates, some 1,796—constituting 89 percent of the alumni (and 94 percent of the living alumni)—joined the Confederacy, and at least 18 joined the Union forces. From April to July 1861, VMI cadet drillmasters trained units (approximately 15,000 troops), contributing greatly to early Confederate victories. VMI was then closed by Confederate authorities; however, officer losses soon mandated its reopening to continue producing junior officers. Prospective officers, selected from battlefield units, made their way to VMI for training. Graduates of other colleges, e.g., over 80 from the University of Virginia, a unit from Washington College, and local militia were also trained in VMI courses.

The VMI Cadet Battalion, itself trained in a special wartime course of instruction, participated in several military operations. Most notable was its participation in combat at New Market, Virginia (May 1864). At a cost of nearly 25 percent casualties, VMI contributed to the small but significant victory, marking its cadet corps in world history as the only one to fight as a unit in battle victoriously. Because of the corps's role in the battle, federal troops burned VMI (June 1864).

Despite postwar restrictions on military training and service, VMI rebuilt and reestablished its PME role. Regular Army professors of military science and commandants of cadets joined VMI's staff after 1891 and 1894, respectively (although both positions were also occasionally filled by staff members). In 1898, 136 alumni served in the Spanish-American War.

During the 20th century, VMI continued as a substantial source of citizen-soldiers; however, increasing numbers served as career soldiers. Typically, through World War II, less than 10 percent chose military careers; however, since 1945 (because of the larger sizes of modern classes), career officer percentages have increased substantially, 248 men achieving general/flag officer rank. World War I's U.S. Army contained over 1,048 officers (of whom 190 were in service before the war), and 143 enlisted men from VMI's alumni. Over 4,100 alumni—including Army Chief of Staff, General of the Army George C. Marshall and 61 other generals and admirals—served in the Second World War. Large numbers of VMI men served in the Korean and Vietnam Wars. Over 500 alumni—including a strong mixture of active and reserve soldiers—served in the Persian Gulf War. Over 300 have died in military service since World War I.

PME at VMI during this century was primarily embodied in its resident Reserve Officers' Training Corps* (ROTC) programs. Originally, VMI cadets received military training but were required to request and take examinations for direct commissions. After 1904, VMI graduates could be commissioned by the War Department. Prior to 1917, cadets could also attend the Plattsburg Camps, which provided officer training to civilian volunteers. In 1917, VMI created three units (infantry, artillery and cavalry) of the Officers' Reserve Corps. VMI also conducted military instructional camps (two in 1917 and one in 1918) to train volunteers. After 1918, paralleling development of the National Guard and reserves, VMI established its ROTC to provide engineer, infantry, artillery, and cavalry combat arms officers for the Army. VMI's first ROTC commissioned officers (1921) entered the Officers' Reserve Corps. This process continued until the Second World War. By 1924, VMI was equipped with the latest infantry, artillery, and cavalry weapons and equipment, reflecting improved technology, and modern combat arms integration.

World War II saw a major disruption in PME at VMI. ROTC was suspended from May 1943 to September 1946. The Class of 1942 was last to go through the regular ROTC program, receiving accelerated graduation and commissioning. Of the Class of 1943 (graduated May 1943) virtually all graduates were sent to officer training camps, and most were commissioned in the Army and Marine Corps. Nearly all the wartime classes (1944, 1945, and 1946) joined the Enlisted Reserve Corps. These classes entered the service as enlisted men (many were assigned to the Army Specialized Training Program [ASTP] and awaited Officer Candidate School assignments). VMI, with PME thus interrupted, managed to maintain a very small wartime cadet corps and administered an ASTP course (which trained 2,148 men by the end of the war). Army Air Forces training was added in 1945.

At the war's end, ROTC was reestablished. Reflecting the changes in the nation's military establishment in 1947, Army and Air Force ROTC were provided to cadets. Branch-material, Army infantry, artillery, and (until 1948) cavalry commissioning was reestablished. The Marine Corps component at VMI evolved from an informal adjunct to the Army program into a full-scale element of the Naval ROTC program (1970).

During the post–World War II era—including the cold war, Korean War, and Vietnam War—smaller American wars and the lessons learned in the world wars ensured minimal disruptions to PME during mobilizations. This allowed continuation of PME activities during those conflicts. During this period, PME was more directly complemented by VMI's expanding undergraduate education, and cross-curricular activities. Expanding degree-granting education in biology, chemistry, civil and environmental engineering, computer science, economics and business, electrical engineering, English, history, international studies, mathematics, mechanical engineering, and physics provided regular and reserve officers with a broad range of skills. Leadership opportunities within the cadet corps—extraordinary in comparison with virtually all American colleges and consisting of full-time cadet assignments—were a primary supplemental PME activity. Other cadet leadership roles in extracurricular activities, cadet government, and athletic (intercollegiate, club, and intramural) teams also contributed.

All cadets (including noncitizens and those not physically qualified for ROTC) participated in the officer training programs. As part of VMI's core curriculum, each cadet took eight semesters (12 semester hour credits) of ROTC. Enrollment requirements were specified by federal authorities. Initial choice of ROTC program was an individual cadet's option. After 1966, ROTC scholarships were available through competition. Most scholarships were awarded before matriculation, but some were also made available to upperclassmen based on merit. Qualified ROTC cadets received uniform allowances, subsistence allowances, and pay during summer training (required of all programs). Cadets were also allowed to participate in simultaneous membership in military reserve units.

In the post-Vietnam era approximately 50 percent of VMI cadets participated in Army ROTC. Thirty percent joined the Navy and Marine Corps programs in Naval ROTC, and the remaining 20 percent participated in the Air Force ROTC program. These were strongly complemented by a wide variety of PME-related extracurricular activities (e.g., army aviation, ranger, tanker, and artillery units; ranger challenge; and field training exercises) and the general cadet regimen. Substantial numbers of cadets were also allowed to compete for cadet professional development training and for attendance at airborne, ranger, and other service school training. ROTC summer camp was a part of the Army program, most recently at Fort Bragg. Army cadets were also selected for cadet troop leader training with Regular Army units following the camp. Navy and Marine Corps officer training programs in Naval ROTC included a four-year program that provides familiarization with Navy surface, subsurface, nuclear, aviation, and special warfare forces. Summer training for Naval ROTC cadets was on fleet ships; and, for Marines, was at Quantico Marine Base.* Air Force ROTC oriented cadets for pilot, navigator, nonrated operations, technical and nontechnical officer career fields. Air Force field training was included during the summer between sophomore and junior years. Additionally, cadets competed for an advanced training program serving with an Air Force unit in their chosen career fields. Commissioning requirements have been controlled by the respective military services and vary over time. Enrolled cadets who successfully complete the ROTC programs are commissioned as reserve officers. Those who meet service requirements for career status are commissioned accordingly.

Based on the recognition that PME in an ever-shrinking world requires greater breadth of knowledge and experience, VMI has developed a rigorous foreign study, training, and travel program, which has complemented PME and general educational programs. Exchange programs with the Royal Military College of

Science (United Kingdom) and the Bundeswehr University (Germany) have been included, as were cadet delegations visiting France, Estonia, and the Republic of China. VMI has also sent cadets abroad for full semesters through its membership in the Institute of European and Asian Studies and the Beaver College Center for Education Abroad. It has also sponsored summer programs at Oxford University and at the Athens Centre in Greece.

Although not an official part of the VMI, the George C. Marshall Research Foundation was based on the VMI campus after 1964. The foundation sponsored undergraduate scholars and internships that provided access to its extraordinary collection of 20th-century national security archives. VMI hosted the Marshall Awards Seminars for the nation's top ROTC students. This seminar featured lectures by senior military officials and guest lecturers. A variety of other VMI-sponsored lecture series, oriented to topics on international affairs and national security, have complemented PME activities.

From 1839 to 1997 VMI was a male-only institution of higher learning. In June 1996, the U.S. Supreme Court declared VMI's all-male admissions policy unconstitutional. Subsequently VMI's state-appointed governing body, the board of visitors,* voted to convert to coeducation while remaining a public institution. The VMI's administration implemented that policy with a methodology programmed to ensure that VMI men and women share common PME standards of performance.

Sources:

William Couper, *One Hundred Years at VMI* (Richmond, VA: Garrett and Massie, 1939).

Thomas W. Davis, ed., *A Crowd of Honorable Youths: Historical Essays on the First 150 Years of the Virginia Military Institute* (Lexington, VA: VMI Sesquicentennial Committee, 1988).

Maj. General Francis Henney Smith, *History of the Virginia Military Institute: Its Building and Rebuilding* (Copyright 1912 by the Virginia Military Institute) (Bay Shore, NY: Evergreen Press, 1988).

Jennings C. Wise, *The Military History of the Virginia Military Institute from 1839–1865* (Lynchburg, VA: J. P Bell Company, 1915).

Albert Z. Conner

VOROSHILOV MILITARY ACADEMY. *See* MILITARY ACADEMY (VOROSHILOV) OF THE GENERAL STAFF.

W

WAR DEPARTMENT GENERAL STAFF (1903–47). A planning and co-ordination agency created to rectify problems in command, control, and administration that surfaced in the War Department during the War with Spain in 1898. Until 1947, the General Staff was the only Army agency with oversight of the entire range of military education.

Before 1903 a number of precedents ensured that the new War Department General Staff would have some involvement in military education. Successive commanding generals became associated with the establishment of individual schools, most notably General William T. Sherman's* role in founding the Infantry and Cavalry School* at Fort Leavenworth, Kansas.* American reformers seeking to change staff relationships in the War Department looked to the Prussian General Staff* and its control of the *Kriegsschule** as a model. In addition, the Military Information Division of the Adjutant General's Office, which became a part of the War Department General Staff, included among its responsibilities the inspection of departments of military art established under War Department auspices in civilian colleges and universities. But these precedents did not mandate that the General Staff would have comprehensive coverage. This outcome was the direct result of the attitudes of the two men most responsible for its creation—Secretary of War Elihu Root* and his chief military advisor, Colonel (later Maj. General) William H. G. Carter. They sought central control over a linked system of professional education.

The first chief of staff, Lt. General Samuel B. M. Young (August 1903–January 1904), organized the General Staff into three divisions, loosely based on the Prussian model. Eventually, the First Division coordinated the War Department bureaus and in time of war acted as an operations center; the Second (Military Information) Division collected military intelligence; and the Third Division prepared war plans. Members of the Second Division also inspected military departments in colleges, while members of the Third Division also doubled as instructors for the Army War College.* They also exercised oversight of the early Army educational system.*

When Maj. General J. Franklin Bell (April 1906–April 1910) consolidated the three divisions into two sections in 1908, one of the outcomes was that the Second Section, formed by combining the Second and Third Divisions, became responsible for all aspects of military education. Bell focused upon filling gaps in officer education left when Root and Carter created a system. Under his leadership, the General Staff was heavily involved in the creation of the School of Musketry in 1907 (forerunner of the Infantry School) and the preliminary work for the establishment of the School of Fire in 1911. Bell also sought to expand the small percentage of officers who actually attended these schools. Bell was compelled to shift emphasis to education—often remedial—simply as a matter of expediency, when Army War College attempts to use officer-students to supplement the efforts of the planners in the Third Division, demonstrated their lack of advanced professional education.

From 1910 until 1918, Army energies shifted away from professional education to focus on training. Under Maj. General Leonard Wood (April 1910–April 1914), the staff's greatest concern in this area was creation of a pool of trained officers in the event the army had to mobilize. Beginning in 1913 he sponsored a series of summer training camps that attracted college students and young business and professional men, called the Plattsburg Movement. They featured rudimentary military evolutions and patriotic speeches that sometimes shaded over into political statements after the outbreak of World War I in Europe, earning the profound suspicion of President Woodrow Wilson's administration. When Pancho Villa raided Columbus, New Mexico, in 1916, the Army's PME and branch schools were closed in order to obtain officers to muster the National Guard into federal service. After American entry into World War I in April 1917, the Chief-of-Staff was dissuaded by the staff from his intention to allow officers to learn their business "on the job" in France, and he permitted the creation of a series of divisional schools for both company and field officers modeled after the Plattsburg program. In the first series commencing in May 1917, the General Staff established sixteen divisional schools, one for each new tactical division. Three subsequent series of mobilizations with accompanying divisional schools followed. Unfortunately, instruction was minimal, student officers learned no common doctrine, and equipment was often nonexistent.

Meanwhile, events had conspired to limit the supervisory effectiveness of the General Staff. A provision in the National Defense Act of 1916 inserted by its opponents reduced the number of General Staff officers in Washington to 19 by April 1917. Amid the staff's chaotic wartime expansion, a training committee of twenty officers was created, with no clear authority and apparently little support from the Chief-of-Staff. It was supposed to coordinate the entire wartime program and failed. Moreover, the need for technical training led the General Staff to reopen some of the schools—most notably the School of Fire at Fort

Sill, Oklahoma, in 1917—and the newly appointed chief of field artillery, Maj. General William J. Snow, who led the critics of divisional schools, secured permission to establish a central Field Artillery Officers' Training School for all aspiring field artillery officers. General Peyton C. March, the last wartime Chief-of-Staff (March 1918–June 1921), allowed the chief of field artillery, a member of the General Staff during the war, and his counterpart as chief of coast artillery, an ex officio member of the General Staff, to exercise day-to-day control over their branch schools just as the War Department bureau chiefs already did for their branch schools. This meant that the General Staff exercised little influence over all but two branches, the infantry and cavalry. As conditions on the Western Front were not conducive for the employment of mounted troops, the staff spent most of its time involved with issues concerning the education of infantry officers, ultimately adopting the field artillery model for their training.

The post–World War I military education system represented a distinctly new phase in officer education in the U.S. Army. General March and his successor, General John J. Pershing (July 1921–September 1924), were convinced that the relatively small number of officers with advanced professional education in the wartime army had provided the difference between victory and defeat. March sought to make advanced professional education the norm for all regular and reserve officers in all branches. Under Pershing, budget pressures forced the consolidation of schools within the branches and the establishment of basic and advanced courses at those schools for company-level and battalion-level positions respectively. The Leavenworth Schools, reopened as the General Services School (renamed the Command and General Staff School* in 1928) focused on combined arms training at division and corps; while the Army War College, prohibited by the National Defense Act of 1916 from planning, educated officers for service at field army and theater headquarters and on the War Department General Staff. In 1923, at the urging of the Assistant Secretary of War, the War Department created the Army Industrial College* to train Army officers to plan during peacetime for the mobilization of materiel and industrial resources in the event of emergency and to supervise the procurement of supplies in wartime.

General Pershing reorganized the General Staff along the lines of his General Headquarters in France during World War I. He introduced the G-system of functional organization to the War Department. G-3, Operations and Training, took over responsibility for education from the War Plans Division, which remained on the General Staff as a theater headquarters staff in embryo in the event of a future war. The end of the war and the postwar legislation ensured that the G-3 Division's relationship to the Army schools was very different from its predecessor's. With the country reverting to normalcy, G-3, along with the rest of the staff under General Pershing, adopted the prewar posture of an advisory and coordinating agency.

The Army school system expanded during economic good times in the 1920s and contracted with the economy in the 1930s. When the Army mobilized again for war in 1940, the increased complexity of weapons and equipment led to an even greater expansion of branch and specialist schools. As in World War I, the Army War College closed for the duration. The Army Industrial College closed briefly but then reopened to focus on the problem of demobilization once the fighting ended, while the Command and General Staff School stayed open continuously, offering abbreviated courses to prepare officers for service on the staffs of divisions and corps. Entry-level officer training again proved controversial. The Chief-of-Staff, General George C. Marshall, Jr., even threatened to resign to protect the General Staff's preferred solution—officer candidate schools. The G-3 Division continued to exercise staff supervision over Army education, but it became increasingly circumscribed in size, influence, and prestige as other agencies acquired portions of its mission, notably Headquarters, Army Ground Forces, and Headquarters, Services of Supply (later Army Service Forces), created in 1942.

Marshall and other senior Army leaders drew one major lesson from their experiences in World War II, even while the conflict still raged: Wars of the future would require the services to work together closely. In the immediate postwar period the General Staff focused more on joint than service education. General Marshall and his successor, General Dwight D. Eisenhower (October 1945–February 1948) pressed for the establishment of the National War College,* created in February 1946, that would prepare officers for duty on theater and combined staffs. At the same time, Marshall and Eisenhower pressed for unification of the armed forces. Their efforts led to the creation of a single National Military Establishment (later Department of Defense) in 1947. The War Department became two subcabinet departments, the Department of the Army and the Department of the Air Force. The War Department General Staff, in much reduced form, became simply the General Staff, part of a larger entity known as the Army Staff, consisting of all staff officers assigned to Headquarters, Department of the Army (other than those working directly for the Army Secretariat). Over time this became a distinction without a difference, and in the wake of the 1986 Goldwater-Nichols Department of Defense Reform Act* the term "General Staff" disappeared from the statute books. Although not without missteps, the War Department General Staff's stewardship of military education over the 44 years of its existence was one of its most impressive and enduring accomplishments.

Sources:

Harry P. Ball, *Of Responsible Command: A History of the U.S. Army War College* (Carlisle Barracks, PA: Alumni Assoc. of the U.S. Army War College, 1984).

Hanson L. Ely, *A Series of Lectures and Addresses Delivered by Major General Hanson L. Ely, U.S. Army* (Ft. Leavenworth, KS: General Service School Press, 1927).

Otto Nelson, *National Security and the General Staff* (Washington, DC: Infantry Journal Press, 1946).

U.S. War Department, *Annual Reports, 1919*, 3 vols. (Washington, DC: Government Printing Office, 1920).

Edgar F. Raines, Jr.

WEST POINT. *See* UNITED STATES MILITARY ACADEMY.

WEST POINT, NEW YORK. Historic and current site of the U.S. Military Academy, on the west bank of the Hudson River, approximately 45 miles north of New York City. "West Point" is often used interchangeably with "the Military Academy" when referring to that institution.

The recognition of West Point as an ideal location for a military post first became a matter of public record on the eve of the American Revolution and resulted in its fortification during 1778–79. First laid out by a French engineer, Lt. Col. Louis Dashaix de la Radière, but constructed largely under the supervision of Colonel of Engineers Thadeus Kosciuszko, the post was protected by two main fortifications, Forts Clinton and Putnam. George Washington, Commanding General of the Continental Army, had recommended construction of a "strong fortress" on the site and, upon completion of its main fortifications, transferred his headquarters there. It was from West Point that he conducted the defense of the Hudson highlands through November 1779.

By the end of the Revolutionary War, West Point had become the site of a major military encampment. In 1781, for example, with the army in winter quarters in the Hudson highlands, its garrison included six Continental brigades and a detached regiment from three different colonies and several companies of provincial militia. It also stored great quantities of powder and ammunition, primarily at Fort Putnam. In 1782, the entire Corps of Invalids was moved there; formed initially by the Continental Congress to provide guards for key cities and arsenals and to "serve as a military school for young gentlemen previous to their being appointed to marching regiments," the Corps of Invalids set an early precedent for West Point's ultimate mission. However, with the depletion of the army following the war's end in 1783, the post became primarily a quartermaster and ordnance supply center. Only about 100 officers and men were retained at West Point to guard the major portion of weapon and ammunition stores, including many captured arms, left from the Revolution.

In 1794, with British troops still garrisoned in forts along the northwest frontier of the fledgling United States, Congress reacted to the threat of renewed conflict stemming from a diplomatic crisis over neutrality rights and moved to strengthen a rather neglected U.S. military establishment. One of its measures was the creation of a Corps of Artillerists and Engineers,* which was garrisoned at West Point. It also created the new junior officer rank of cadet for posting among units of the regular U.S. Army. Four battalions were authorized for the new corps with eight cadets assigned to each. In that same year, work began on the repair and improvement of Fort Putnam on the heights overlooking West Point's plain. In February 1796, the commandant of the Artillerist and Engineer Corps, Lt. Colonel Stephen Rochefontaine, established a school of fortification at the post; all junior officers and cadets were ordered to attend. Later that year, the original school building and books were destroyed by a fire of mysterious origin. However, practical instruction in the art of fortification became a regular feature of the post routine for the young officers and cadets of the corps until another school was opened in 1801.

Sources:

Edward C. Boynton, *History of West Point* (New York: D. Van Nostrand, 1863).

Sidney Forman, *West Point: A History of the United States Military Academy* (New York: Columbia University Press, 1950).

Edward S. Holden, "Origins of the Military Academy," *The Centennial of the U.S. Military Academy, Vol. I* (Washington: Government Printing Office, 1904).

WILSON, HENRY B. Admiral Henry Braid Wilson (born 1861, died 1954), graduated from the U.S. Naval Academy in 1881 and served as its superintendent from July 1921 until his retirement in February 1925. He wrote the first official statement of the mission of the U.S. Naval Academy and codified the ascending system of privileges, or "rates," used at the academy to this day.

In his *Annual Report of the Superintendent* for 1921–22, Wilson said the mission of the Naval Academy* was to "mould" midshipmen "into educated gentlemen, thoroughly indoctrinated with honor, uprightness and truth, with practical rather than academic minds, with thorough loyalty to country, with a ground-work of educational fundamentals upon which experience afloat may build the finished naval officer, capable of upholding . . . the honor of the United States and withal giving due consideration that healthy minds in healthy bodies are necessities for the fulfillment of the individual missions of the graduates." These goals, he added, "can only be attained if, through humane yet firm and just discipline, the graduates carry into the Service respect and admiration for this Academy."

Wilson had reason to believe the "respect and admiration" of the midshipmen for the academy to be at low ebb when he became superintendent. The abbreviated, three-year curriculum adopted during World War I did not end until June 1919, while the regiment of midshipmen, instead of returning to its pre-1916 ceiling of 1,094, now numbered close to 2,500. Adding to the disruption caused by these and other factors, Wilson's predecessor, Rear Admiral Archibald H. Scales, had responded to a hazing scandal in 1920 by asking the seniors in the first class to promise in writing not to haze members of the fourth class, or "plebes." When the "firsties" refused, Scales had physically separated the plebes from the rest of the regiment and even posted guards at the entrances to their quarters, thereby alienating the midshipmen and attracting unintended national attention.

Wilson—who had received the Distinguished Service Medal for his wartime actions as Commander, U.S. Naval Forces in France and later commanded the Atlantic Fleet—attributed these events to the misplaced loyalties of the midshipmen. As superintendent he insisted that their loyalty to the Naval Academy and its standards should always come before their loyalty to classmates and class traditions. On September 1, 1921, Wilson sent a letter to the regiment codifying a number of unwritten customs having to do with seemingly minor, but actually very important, aspects of midshipman culture. He designated certain walkways and areas of the academy, for example, for use only by upperclassmen in order to relieve "the congestion of midshipmen traffic." He said that plebes should "proceed to formation on the double" in order to teach them the value of "promptness." Wilson thus transformed privileges and obligations previously thought to belong to each class into a system that belonged to the academy. In the same letter, he banned hazing and listed practices to be avoided by seniors when dealing with juniors—thus clarifying the law that had made hazing a court-martial offense but had not adequately defined what hazing meant.

Although interested in academic matters, Wilson placed more weight on the training midshipmen received to become junior officers. He ended the policy of appointing midshipman officers from the senior class only at the beginning of each academic year, instead choosing a new group of officers each month during the first six months of school. Those judged to have made the best officers were selected to lead the regiment of midshipmen during the final three months of classes. In 1922 Wilson also directed the Department of Seamanship to offer the first course in naval leadership taught at the academy. The Naval Institute* solicited suggestions for a textbook, and by the next year the academy had complied "a mass of data" combining "advice and actual experiences" for use in the textbook especially prepared for the course.

Together with his fair but firm way of dealing with subordinates, these and other contributions to the Naval Academy enabled "Uncle Henry," as Wilson was affectionately called behind his back, to earn the lifelong respect of the many midshipmen who knew him.

Sources:

General Correspondence. Office of the Superintendent. Superintendent's Annual Report, 1911–35. Records of the United States Naval Academy. Record Group 405. National Archives-Affiliated Archives: Record on deposit at United States Naval Academy Archives, Annapolis MD.

Jack Sweetman (rev. by Thomas J. Cutler), *The U.S. Naval Academy: An Illustrated History (2nd Ed.)* (Annapolis, MD: Naval Institute Press, 1995).

Henry B. Wilson Scrapbooks. United States Naval Academy Museum, Annapolis, MD.

William R. Roberts

Editor's Postscript

The changes American PME has experienced over the years have been diverse, since it is really a collection of several different educational endeavors—as demonstrated in the preceding dictionary entries. Improvements affecting the service academies, for example, have not impacted on and would not necessarily be appropriate for the war colleges. Each type of institution has different objectives and performs a different PME mission for the American people. Changes among the service academies have been quite measured and under the reliable scrutiny of appropriate academic accrediting agencies and each school's board of visitors.* But developments at the war colleges paint a different picture.

Over the years, changes among the PME programs conducted for commissioned officers often have been made largely in response to external pressures and have tended to be more mercurial. However, whereas changes frequently reflected the judgments and policy preferences of a service chief-of-staff or chief of naval operations (CNO) or the predisposition of the current school commandant (both of these influences will continue to some extent), recent change—particularly at the war colleges—has been responsive to a more general sense of educational purpose. In the late 1990s the war colleges seem to acknowledge the need to focus on fostering the analytical skills and disciplined judgment required to think critically about war and to advise higher authority on the most effective ways of employing military force in support of national objectives.

This difference has been especially true since the Goldwater-Nichols legislation* in 1986 that prescribed standards and procedures for a greater attention to preparation for directing joint operations and since the report of the Skelton panel* three years later. However, institutional responses have varied, and the different impacts of the Skelton report on specific schools and on the PME system in general suggest a continuing need for periodic assessment of how close specific schools are coming to achieving the acknowledged goals. Mere acknowledgment of a worthy purpose does not insure that an institution is, in fact, moving in that direction.

But in providing for program reviews, the all-too-frequent practice of bringing together a special committee of flag officers and/or prominent citizens for a few concentrated sessions of reviewing earlier reports or hearing selected presentations on the whole range of existing PME programs is inadequate. Many of the principal participants are chosen for the office they now hold or because of noteworthy performance in a perhaps marginally related field rather than because of demonstrated expertise in the educational process (not that it is uniform!) or in a significant element of PME. Sincere and smart as they may be, their recommendations too often take the character of "tinkering at the margins" rather than grappling with some of the really serious issues of professional education for the nation's military leaders. For example, do elements of the program reflect a central purpose that is appropriate for the professional context and the kinds of tasks in which graduates will need to perform? Do the academic calendar and scheduled student activities of a school provide ample opportunity to encourage the particular skills and habits of mind stipulated in its stated objectives? Are the subject matter and methods of instruction appropriate for achieving those objectives?

A frequently voiced recommendation at conferences on the future of PME and in most exchanges of written opinion on the subject is for some panacea like "put war back in the war colleges." The doctrinal developments at the interwar Naval War College* are extolled; more attention to Clausewitz* and German PME practices is urged; the careers and innovations of the Great Captains are cited; more studies of military history are recommended—all as if the conditions that made each of these contributions to PME noteworthy in the past continue to exist with the same impact today and possibly into the future.

In considering such recommendations one should note the arguments presented by Thomas C. Hone, at a February 1998 PME symposium hosted by the Naval Postgraduate School,* regarding doctrinal contributions at the Naval War College. Hone points out that the significance of those contributions resulted largely from the context in which the War College operated at the time. Doctrine developed at the War College and tested in its wargaming* exercises was needed because fleet staffs and that of the CNO at the time were too small to develop doctrine from the infrequent fleet exercises of a small, budget-starved, interwar navy. Following the World War II fleet and staff expansion and amid the continuous cold war forward deployments, however, doctrine was developed by the operational force, and strategic concepts were formed in the Pentagon; "the War College slipped to the periphery." Moreover, in part because of this change, the War College innovations of 1972 under Admiral Stansfield Turner,* strongly supported by the CNO, moved far afield from the mission of doctrinal development. Hone presented these facts (in substantially more detail than shown here) in cautioning against acceptance of the superficial proposition, advanced by some, that the post-1972 Naval War College program should be used as the model for revamping war college curricula in order to develop joint operational doctrine.

Teaching war at the "war colleges" (and the academies) is certainly a worthy recommendation. But with what functional purpose with respect to the contemporary and future military profession—to provide graduate-level study of military affairs for senior officers? To prepare them for serious staff work in the Pentagon? To enlist their participation in the development of timely doctrine? (These *alternative* PME formulations are Hone's.) And which wars? War under what kinds of conditions? One of the more unfortunate choices of phraseology to creep into the military literature (and official documents) in recent years is "operations other than war." As if "real war" could be of only one type!

The point with regard to PME is that, given finite course durations, the inclusion of "more war"—military history, etc.—means the elimination of something else. For the service academies, there are sound philosophical and practical arguments, unique to undergraduate institutions, for providing ample opportunity for theoretical and intellectually liberalizing studies. But the higher levels of PME require different considerations. It is at these levels that critics like to use the term "frills" when referring to subject matter that is not strictly military in character. Aside from being of shorter duration, the PME schools for commissioned officers have different central purposes. It is the relative potential contribution to each institution's central purpose that should determine a proper balance between so-called "academic" studies and those with strictly military content. I would be very leery, for example, of eliminating an "academic" study that would help today's student appreciate the complexity of the evolving world scene and could help illuminate the kinds of war that he or she might be called upon to fight or the kinds of constraints our military might be required to observe. One of the real lessons of the Vietnam War, however unpleasant it may be, is that in a democracy the military doesn't get to choose the conditions under which it must fight or even to set the rules of engagement.

Future reviews, like that of the Skelton panel, need to assure serious, competent evaluation—preferably within clear parameters and according to relevant criteria that enable systematic evaluation and in-depth analysis of specifically acknowledged problem areas. From time to time, some of these problems are likely to result from events and policy decisions outside the immediate realm of PME, such as the abrupt end of the cold war or a decision committing the United States to take a prominent role in international peacekeeping operations. As the dictionary entries show, reactions to such developments within institutions of officer education have varied, all the way from initiatives to restructure the program so as to make the new development a new central "theme" for a substantial portion of the academic year to pretending that it doesn't really affect the central purposes of the U.S. military profession and "getting on" with the "real" business of PME. Those readers with experience on PME faculties will readily recognize these reactions by recalling institutional responses to such temporal influences as "massive retaliation," "counterinsurgency," and "management."

For some time, it has become almost routine for review boards and individual observers to recommend increasing the presence of civilian academics on the faculties and staffs of PME institutions. And several of the schools have dutifully complied. But it is important to focus on—and reflect in academic policy—the reasons for such a recommendation. Schools at several levels of PME acknowledge as one of their purposes the encouragement and critical examination of new concepts and ideas regarding the military profession. The war colleges, in particular, stress the principle of academic freedom and, within understandable limits, their effort to achieve and maintain it is an honest one. But the respective weights of service doctrine and of readiness to step lightly around issues that might affect a brother officer's career prospects are ever present. And, given the need for a faculty that still must be heavily professional military and the officers' disciplined attitudes of a lifetime, there is still a tendency within PME faculties to salute and say, "Aye aye, sir" when higher authority expresses a preference for some academic direction or faculty practice. In the process, of course, possible public or interservice controversy may be avoided, but it can also close off opportunities for timely innovation. Moreover, when what is agreed to is one or more additional tasks that have little to do with the central purpose of the school, one result can be insufficient attention to the quality of the internal educational process. For example, such excursions can result in a lack of effort on the kind of faculty research and writing demanded uniquely for the production of teaching materials needed by a professional school.

The appointment of competent civilians, including military retirees, to key academic and administrative positions can help. A post comparable to that of the academic dean of a liberal arts college or of a professional department within a university, *with comparable responsibility and authority* as well, is one such position. True, the institutions of PME are *military* schools and necessarily must observe fundamental and relevant military values. But the purposes of professional military schools, as distinct from training bases or operational units, is not to instill disciplined behavior and obedience to higher authority. The kind of discipline that is relevant to their missions is the mental discipline to respect truth and reason and to apply recognized standards of analysis and judgment to professional issues.

Establishing these standards and assuring their application comprise what has been called "the domain of the faculty." Maintaining the kind of climate wherein the faculty can perform this mission is the central responsibility of the institutional administration, and unless institutions of PME can establish and maintain such an atmosphere, they are not worthy of being called institutions of higher education. This is precisely where a competent and dedicated civilian dean can best do the job. There have been a prominent few military commandants who possessed the insight and sensitivity to perform this function as well as their other strictly military or politically sensitive roles—but *very few*. These are not the functions for which ranking military leaders have been trained; nor should they be!

Those who are familiar with the history of service academies are all too aware of the issue of proliferating courses and training regimes, and the problems created by this overcrowding of the academic program are not unknown at other levels of PME either. But the potential problems of proliferating addressed here can result from proliferating schools. One is particularly well known to administrators of officer personnel assignments: By the time a young, operationally experienced officer has demonstrated his or her potential for high-level command and staff assignments, there is precious little time left in all but a few "star" careers for all the kinds of career building assignments and PME experiences that the officer "must have." In the first place every military enterprise with a need for highly qualified people—the Pentagon; the service academies; PME postgraduate faculties; NATO staffs; attaché posts—all recruit this kind of officer during the seven-to-sixteen-year commissioned service period. And many of these kinds of assignments entail periods of special preparation and/or extensive fixed tours of three or four years' duration. Adding new "must-have" PME courses at the command and staff or war college level only compounds the problem.

This problem is related to another because of the finite availability of well-qualified faculty resources for instruction in professional schools. Through the years, as related in several of the dictionary entries, most reviews of officer education practices have stressed the need for better-qualified faculty members and for officer personnel policies designed to assure their continuing availability. Encouraging and evoking development of the kind of intellectual discipline and habits of analysis that are desired in the products of PME institutions require instructional skills, personal qualities, and subject matter mastery not widespread throughout the military officer corps. This kind of resource is finite. Maintaining more than the optimum number and types of PME institutions can only insure that several will be without adequate numbers of professional faculty qualified to produce the desired results.

The most recent cases of the installation of new "must-have" courses involve individual service creations—the "advanced" warfare schools supported by three of our four armed forces. The worrisome aspect of service school proliferation is the tendency toward perpetuating a service-oriented doctrinal emphasis that counters the desirable encouragement of better joint planning and operational cooperation. Not that beginning new service-sponsored programs is necessarily to be avoided! One can see certain advantages to setting up new schools on an experimental basis to test the effectiveness of new instructional approaches and

new subject matter emphases, looking toward possible adoption of these innovations and the absorption of their faculties in the regular command and staff
or war colleges.

In one of the "summing-up" chapters of their monumental 1957 study of
military education, John Masland and Laurence Radway decry officer assignment policies that tend to emphasize the quantitative aspects of PME at some
cost to qualitative considerations. In particular, they lamented policies that
tended to obscure the unique purposes of individual institutions, in this case the
National War College. If this was a matter of particular concern in the midst of
the cold war, it is an even more urgent issue in the relatively ill-defined international context leading into the 21st century!

As demonstrated in the U.S. involvement in a number of UN peacekeeping
operations and in the NATO operations around Kosovo, American military leaders are increasingly being called upon to plan and carry out military operations
in complex political environments and under uncharacteristic constraints. Such
challenges demand the intellectual discipline to analyze complicated situations,
a willingness to recognize the inappropriateness of parochial solutions, and the
capability to think creatively in changing circumstances. Our higher-level PME
institutions and their governing agencies must strive continually to assure that
such strategically important educational outcomes remain central to the academic
program development, reviewing processes, student and faculty assignment policies, and overall system design that actually define the PME contribution to our
national security.

General Bibliography

Artz, Frederick B. *The Development of Technical Education in France, 1500–1850*. Cambridge, MA: Society for the History of Technology and the M.I.T. Press, 1966.

Ball, Harry P. *Of Responsible Command: A History of the U.S. Army War College*. Dallas, TX: Taylor Publishing Company, rev. ed., 1994.

Barnard, Henry. *Military Schools and Courses of Instruction in the Science and Art of War* (rev. ed., 1872). New York: Reprinted by Greenwood Press, 1969.

Bassford, Christopher. *Clausewitz in English: The Reception of Clausewitz in Britain and America, 1815–1945*. New York: Oxford University Press, 1994.

Converse, Elliott V., III (ed.). *Forging the Sword: Selecting, Educating, and Training Cadets and Junior Officers in the Modern World*. Chicago: Imprint Publications, 1998.

Creveld, Martin van. *The Training of Officers: From Military Professionalism to Irrelevance*. New York: Free Press, 1990.

Eddy, Edward D. *Colleges for Our Land and Time: The Land-Grant Idea in American Education*. New York: Harper and Brothers, 1956.

Ennels, Jerome A., and Wesley Phillips Newton. *The Wisdom of Eagles: A History of Maxwell Air Force Base*. Montgomery, AL: Black Belt Press, 1997.

Fagan, George V. *The Air Force Academy: An Illustrated History*. Boulder, CO: Johnson Books, 1988.

Finney, Robert T. *History of the Air Corps Tactical School, 1920–1940*. Washington, DC: Center for Air Force History, 1992.

Forman, Sidney. *West Point: A History of the United States Military Academy*. New York: Columbia University Press, 1950.

Hattendorf, John B., B. Mitchell Simpson III, and John R. Wadleigh. *Sailors and Scholars: The Centennial History of the U.S. Naval War College*. Newport, RI: Naval War College Press, 1984.

Huntington, Samuel P. *The Soldier and the State: The Theory and Politics of Civil–Military Relations*. New York: Vintage/Random House, 1957.

King, Irving H. *The Coast Guard Expands, 1865–1915: New Roles, New Frontiers*. Annapolis, MD: Naval Institute Press, 1996.

Kreidberg, Marvin A., and Merton G. Henry. *History of Military Mobilization in the United States Army, 1775–1945.* Washington, DC: Center of Military History, 1989.

Lovell, John P. *Neither Athens Nor Sparta?: The American Service Academies in Transition.* Bloomington: Indiana University Press, 1979.

Lyons, Gene M., and John W. Masland. *Education and Military Leadership: A Study of the R.O.T.C.* Princeton, NJ: Princeton University Press, 1959.

Masland, John W., and Laurence I. Radway. *Soldiers and Scholars: Military Education and National Policy.* Princeton, NJ: Princeton University Press, 1957.

Moncure, John. *Forging the King's Sword: Military Education Between Tradition and Modernization: The Case of the Royal Prussian Cadet Corps, 1871–1918.* New York: Peter Lang, 1993.

Nenninger, Timothy K. *The Leavenworth Schools and the Old Army: Education, Professionalism, and the Officer Corps of the United States Army, 1881–1918.* Westport, CT: Greenwood Press, 1978.

Reeves, Capt. Ira L. *Military Education In The United States.* Burlington, VT: Free Press, 1914.

Simons, William E. *Liberal Education in the Service Academies.* New York: Bureau of Publications, Teachers College, Columbia University, 1965.

Sumida, Jon Tetsuro. *Inventing Grand Strategy and Teaching Command: The Classic Works of Alfred Thayer Mahan Reconsidered.* Washington, DC: Woodrow Wilson Center Press/Johns Hopkins University Press, 1997.

Sweetman, Jack, revised by Thomas J. Cutler. *The U.S. Naval Academy: An Illustrated History, 2nd Ed.* Annapolis, MD: Naval Institute Press, 1995.

Weigley, Russell F. *History of the United States Army.* New York: Macmillan, 1967.

Weinert, Richard P., and Robert Arthur. *Defender of the Chesapeake: The Story of Fort Monroe.* 3rd rev. ed. Shippensburg, PA: White Mane Publishing Co., 1989.

Index

Boldface page numbers indicate location of main entries.

Milling, Thomas D., 106, 202

Mitchell, William, **201–3**; air combat commander in France, 201; Air Service Field Officers' School, founder of; 201, 202; Air Tactical School, influence on, 106, 202; concepts of PME for airmen, 201–2; views on air power, 201. *See also* Command of the Air

Moltke, Helmuth von, 172–73, 237

Monroe, James, 302, 310

Monroe, Keith L., 239

Montana, University of, 30

Montgomery, Alabama, 26

Moore, Harry, 37

Morrill, Justin S., **203–5**; Land Grant Act of 1862, sponsor of, 8, 59, 203, 244; requirement for military training, different interpretations of, 8, 204; requirement for military training, his rationale for, 203–4; subsequent augmentation of the law, 204. *See also* Army Reserve Officers' Training Corps

The *Morro Castle*, 326

Mountbatten, Louis, 274

National Defense Act of 1916: Army War College performance of General Staff functions prohibited, 64, 80, 350; General Staff officers in D.C. reduced, 349; mechanism for mobilizing industry provided, 55; Reserve Officers' Training Corps established, 8, 32, 59, 100, 203

National Defense Act of 1920: Air Service established as Army combat arm, 34; CGSS graduation made prerequisite for Army War College attendance, 50; for General Staff appointment, 50, 64; mobilization and procurement functions assigned, 55; Regular Army officers and NCOs authorized as ROTC instructors, 8, 59

National Defense University, **206–9**; accreditation of degree-granting programs, 208, 212; administrative structure, 145, 207; auxiliary programs, proliferation of, 207, 208; colleges within, 47, 48, 150, 160, 206, 210; De-

fense Acquisition University, relation to, 208; research and educational support activities, 206–7

National Security Act of 1947, 13, 39, 65, 150, 151, 163

National Security Act of 1949, 13, 150

National War College, **209–12**; academic program, evolution of, 211–12; faculty, evolution of, 15, 210–11; master's degree, 212; origins, 12, 144, 152, 209–10; student body, changes in, 210

Naval Asylum, Philadelphia, **212–13**; William Chauvenet, influence of, 97, 213; establishment, 97, 213; shore-based study, need for, 212. *See also* Chauvenet, William

Naval Command Course, 224, 235

Naval Personnel Act of 1882: "cadet-engineer" rank eliminated, 9, 333; USNA graduates commissioned in Marine Corps, 333

Naval Personnel Act of 1899: Engineer vs. Line dispute, resolution of, 9, 10, 214, 252, 333

Naval Postgraduate School, Annapolis, **213–16**; accreditation of degree-granting programs, 216; antecedents at USNA, 9–10, 214–15; earlier postgraduate study, 214; formal recognition of, 215; non-engineering programs, inclusion of, 215; tensions with USNA, 215

Naval Postgraduate School, Monterey, **216–19**; accreditation, 217; early structure, 217; move from Annapolis, reasons for, 216–17; officers' civilian graduate study, role relative to, 217; warfare-oriented interdisciplinary studies, development of, 218

Naval Reserve, 11, 219, 221, 301, 327

Naval Reserve Officers' Training Corps (NROTC), **219–22**; early curriculum, 219; establishment, reasons for, 219; Holloway Plan, revised under, 220–21; a non-USNA source of career officers, advantages of, 220; scholarship program, growth of, 221; scholarship program, required courses in, 221

About the Contributors

MAJ. JOHN J. ABBATIELLO, USAF, formerly Assistant Professor of History at the U.S. Air Force Academy, is training to fly the new JSTARS command and control aircraft. He is editor of *Forged by Fire: Military History for the Profession of Arms* (1988) and *Armed Conflict in Human History* (1997).

ALAN C. AIMONE is archivist at the USMA Library, U.S. Military Academy, and has contributed to *American Civil War: A Handbook of Literature and Research* (1996). He is author of *A User's Guide to the Official Records of the American Civil War* (1993).

ARCHIE D. BARRETT, Colonel, USAF (Ret.), formerly on the staff of the House of Representatives Committee on Armed Services and staff director for its Subcommittee Panel on Military Education (the Skeleton Panel), served as Deputy Assistant Secretary of the Army for Manpower and Reserve Affairs. Now retired from government service and an active consultant, he is author of *Reappraising Government Organization* (1983).

CHRISTOPHER BASSFORD is Professor of Strategy at the National War College and has taught at civilian universities, the Marine Corps Command and Staff College, and the Army War College. He is author of *Clausewitz in English: The Reception of Clausewitz in Britain and America, 1815–1945* (1994) and the forthcoming *On Waterloo: The Exchange between Wellington and Clausewitz.*

DONALD F. BITTNER is Professor of History at the Marine Corps Command and Staff College and a Fellow, Inter-university Seminar on Armed Forces and Society. He has contributed articles to the *Journal of Military History* and is author of " 'Soldiers of the Sea' in the Last Days of the Age of Sail: Officers of Royal Marines, 1815–1866. Part I—An Institutional Overview," *Selected Papers, 1997—The Consortium on Revolutionary Europe, 1750–1850* (1997).

MAJ. MICHAEL A. BODEN, USA, is Assistant Professor, Department of History, U.S. Military Academy at West Point. He is completing his dissertation on "Friedrich Engels and the Art of War" for Vanderbilt University.

RAY L. BOWERS, Colonel, USAF (Ret.), formerly Associate Professor of History at the U.S. Air Force Academy, served as chairman of the Southeast Asia Histories Project in the Office of Air Force History. He is author of *The USAF in Southeast Asia: Tactical Airlift* (1983).

ROBERT A. BRACE, Colonel, USA (Ret.), formerly Dean of Academic Affairs, U.S. Army War College, is Director of Instructors, Science Applications International Corp.

EVELYN M. CHERPAK is Head, Naval Historical Collection, Naval War College and teaches at Salve Regina University and the University of Rhode Island (Continuing Education). She is author of "Sources on World War I in the Naval Historical Collection," *Relevance* (Summer 1998) and "Mary Robinson Hunter: Reminiscences of Her Life in Brazil," *Documentary Editing* (March 1997).

ALBERT Z. CONNER, formerly a career civilian in the Department of Defense, is a freelance writer. He has contributed several articles to the "VMI at War" series in the *VMI Alumni Review* and several more in *Armor, Military Review*, and *Soviet Military Studies*. Conner is author of *Red Army Order of Battle in the Great Patriotic War* (1985).

GRAHAM A. COSMAS is Chief, Histories Branch, at the U.S. Army Center of Military History and an officer in the Society for Military History. He is co-author of *The Medical Department: Medical Service in the European Theater of Operations* (1992) and *U.S. Marines in Vietnam, Vietnamization and Redeployment* (1986).

LTC. CONRAD C. CRANE, USA, is Professor of History at the U.S. Military Academy. He is author of *Bombs, Cities, and Civilians: American Airpower Strategy in World War II* (1993) and co-author of *The Prudent Soldier, the Rash Old Fighter, and the Walking Whiskey Keg: The Battle of Valverde, New Mexico, 13–21 February 1862* (1987).

THOMAS J. CUTLER is Associate Director of Membership and Development at the U.S. Naval Institute. He is author of *The Battle of Leyte Gulf: 23–26 October 1944* (1994) and *Brown Water, Black Berets: Coastal and Riverine Warfare in Vietnam* (1988).

BOYD L. DASTRUP is Command Historian, U.S. Army Field Artillery Center and Fort Sill. He is author of *The Field Artillery: History and Sourcebook* (Greenwood Press, 1994) and *King of Battle: A Branch History of the U.S. Army's Field Artillery* (reprint 1994).

HENRY C. DETHLOFF is Professor of History at Texas A&M University. He is author of *The United States and the Global Economy* (1997) and *Texas A&M University: A Pictorial History* (1996).

LTC. A. JAMES DIEHL, USMC, Former Deputy Director, CAPSTONE Program at the National Defense University, is author of "The Goldwater-Nichols DoD Reorganization Act: Quo Vadis?" an unpublished master's thesis for Auburn University, 1988.

JEROME A. ENNELS is Director, Office of History at the Air University, and co-author of *The Wisdom of Eagles: A History of Maxwell Air Force Base* (1997). He has contributed articles to *Airpower Journal* and its predecessor and authored Air University historical studies, including "A Strange New Bird: The Genesis of Powered Flight in Montgomery, Mar–May 1910" (1998) and "Those Daring Young Men: The Role of Aero Demonstration Teams in the Evolution of Pre–World War II Pursuit Tactics" (1994).

DANIEL B. FOX is Senior Research Analyst at The RAND Corporation, where he has employed computer simulations in research on various national security problems. He is author of "Not Merely Planning for the Last War," in Paul K. Davis (ed.), *New Challenges in Defense Planning* (1994) and co-author of "Theater Analysis and Modeling in an Era of Uncertainty," R-380-NA (1994).

KENNETH W. FRITZ, Lt. Colonel, USAF (Ret.), and former F-111 pilot, is Chief, College Programs Division at the Armed Forces Staff College. Before taking this position in 1994, he taught joint staff functions and protocol at the college.

DAVID M. GLANTZ, Colonel, USA (Ret.), is Editor of *The Journal of Slavic Military Studies*. He is author of *Stumbling Colossus: The Red Army on the Eve of War* (1998) and *Kharkov 1942: The Anatomy of a Military Disaster* (1998).

JOHN W. GORDON, Colonel, USMCR (Ret.), formerly a visiting professor of military history at the U.S. Military Academy, is Professor of History at The Citadel. He is author of "Orde Wingate," in John Keegan, ed., *Churchill's Generals* (1992) and *The Other Desert War: Special Forces in North Africa, 1940–1943* (Greenwood Press, 1987).

DOMINICK S. GRAHAM, a cadet at Royal Military Academy-Woolwich, in September 1939, and an officer-instructor at the opening of Royal Military Academy-Sandhurst, in 1947, is Professor (Emeritus) at the University of New Brunswick, Canada. He is author of *Against Odds: Reflecting on the Experience of the British Army in Two World Wars* (1998) and *Coalitions, Politicians, and Generals* (1993).

JAMES R. GRAHAM, Colonel, USAF (Ret.), is Director of Conferences at the National Defense University. He is editor of *Non-Combat Roles for the U.S. Military in the Post–Cold War Era* (1993).

ALAN L. GROPMAN, Colonel, USAF (Ret.), is Chairman, Department of Grand Strategy at the Industrial College of the Armed Forces. He is author of *The Air Force Integrates, 1945–1964* (1998) and *Mobilizing U.S. Industry in World War II* (1996); and editor of *The Big L: American Logistics in World War II* (1997).

GRANT T. HAMMOND is Professor of International Relations at the Air War College. He has contributed articles to a number of professional journals and is author of "America and Regional Conflict in the Post–Cold War/Gulf War Era: Some Implications for the Future," in Sharyl Cross et. al., *Global Security Beyond the Millennium: American and Russian Perspectives* (1998) and "The Perils of Peacekeeping for the U.S.: Relearning Lessons from Beirut to Bosnia," in Edward Moxon-Brown, *A Future for Peacekeeping?* (1998).

LEE S. HARFORD, JR., is Chief Historian, U.S. Army Reserve Command and, as LTC, USAR, served during 1996–97 as theater historian for U.S. Army forces in Bosnia. He is co-author of *U.S. Army Cadet Command: The 10-Year History* (1996) and contributed articles to the *Proceedings* of both the 22d and 23d consortia on Revolutionary Europe (1992; 1993).

JOHN B. HATTENDORF is the Ernest J. King Professor of Maritime History at the Naval War College and adjunct director of the Munson Institute of American Maritime Studies. He has written or edited more than 30 books on maritime and naval history, including *Doing Naval History: Essays Toward Improvement* (1995) and *Mahan on Naval Strategy: Selections from the Writings of Rear Admiral Alfred Thayer Mahan* (1991).

THOMAS L. HENDRIX is Assistant Director for Educational Services, U.S. Army Military History Institute at the Army War College.

HAROLD L. HITCHENS, Colonel, USAF (Ret.), formerly Assistant Professor of History and Faculty Secretary at the U.S. Air Force Academy, recently retired as Senior Research Associate, University of Pittsburgh. He has contributed articles to several military and scholarly journals and is editor of three historical series of *Executive Session Hearings, Committee on Foreign Affairs, U.S. House of Representatives* (1976–1990).

THOMAS A. JULIAN, Colonel, USAF (Ret.), formerly Associate Professor of History at the U.S. Air Force Academy, is completing a history of aeromedical evacuation in the U.S. Air Force. He is author of "The Role of the United States Army Air Forces in the Warsaw Uprising, Aug–Sep 1944," *Air Power History* (Summer 1995) and "Operations at the Margin: Soviet Bases and Shuttle Bombing," *Journal of Military History* (October 1993).

THOMAS A. KEANEY, Colonel, USAF (Ret.), formerly Associate Professor of History at the U.S. Air Force Academy, served as Professor of Military Strategy at the National War College until 1998 when he became Executive

Director of the Foreign Policy Institute at the Johns Hopkins School of Advanced International Studies. He is co-author of *Revolution in Warfare?: Air Power in the Persian Gulf* (1995) and two reports of the *Gulf War Air Power Survey: The Summary Report* and *The Effects and Effectiveness of Air Power*, (1993).

LTC. TONY KERN, USAF, is Associate Professor and Director of Military History at the U.S. Air Force Academy. He is author of *Flight Discipline* (1998) and *Redefining Airmanship* (1997).

EUGENIA C. KIESLING is Associate Professor of History at the U.S. Military Academy at West Point. She is author of *Arming Against Hitler: France and the Limits of Military Planning* (1996) and editor and translator of R. Castex, *Strategic Theories* (1994).

THEODORE A. KRACHT, formerly Captain, USAF, served as Assistant Professor of History at the U.S. Air Force Academy before leaving active service.

GARY T. LORD is Charles A. Dana Professor of History at Norwich University and a member of the editorial advisory board of *Vermont History*. He has contributed articles to that journal and the *New England Quarterly* and is author of the historical text of *Norwich University* (1994).

MARK D. MANDELES is President of the J. de Bloch Group, a research organization specializing in public policy analysis. He is author of *The Development of the B-52 and Jet Propulsion* (1998) and co-author of *Managing "Command and Control" in the Persian Gulf War* (1996).

MAJ. TIMOTHY J. MATSON, USAF, formerly Assistant Professor of History at the U.S. Air Force Academy, is training to Fly KC-135 aerial refueling aircraft in the USAF's Air Mobility Command.

J. KENNETH McDONALD is former Chief Historian of the Central Intelligence Agency and held endowed chairs in National Security and Foreign Affairs and in Maritime History at the Naval War College from 1972 to 1974. He is General Editor of the *C.I.A. Cold War Records* series, 5 vols. (1992–1996) and author of "Secrecy, Accountability and the C.I.A.: The Dilemma of Intelligence in a Democracy," in Richard H. Kohn, ed., *The United States Military Under the United States Constitution* (1991).

JOHN W. McDONALD, Colonel, USA (Ret.), is Vice President at the Science Applications International Corporation and former military staff member for the House Subcommittee Panel on Military Education (the Skelton Panel).

DAVID R. METS, Colonel, USAF (Ret.), who has taught history at both the U.S. Air Force and U.S. Military Academies, is Professor of History at the School of Advanced Airpower Studies, Air University. Formerly Editor of the *Air Univer-*

sity Quarterly Review, he is author of *Master of Airpower: General Carl A. Spaatz* (1988) and *Land-Based Airpower in Third World Crises* (1986).

DENNIS P. MROCZKOWSKI, Colonel, USMCR, is Curator of the Casemate Museum, Fort Monroe, Virginia. He is author of *The U.S. Marines in the Persian Gulf: With the 2nd Marine Division* (1993) and *Fort Monroe: A Walking Tour* (1995) and has served as Field Historian with U.S. military units deployed to Bosnia, Haiti, Somalia, and the Persian Gulf.

RICHARD R. MULLER, a member of the Air Command and Staff College faculty since 1991, is Vice Dean for Academic Affairs. He is co-author of *The Luftwaffe's Way of War* (1998) and author of *The German Air War in Russia* (1992).

TIMOTHY K. NENNINGER is Chief of Modern Military Documents at the National Archives. Most recently, he authored "Leavenworth and Its Critics: The U.S. Army Command and General Staff School, 1920–1940," *Journal of Military History* (April 1994) and "American Military Effectiveness in the First World War," in Alan R. Millet & Williamson Murray (eds.), *Military Effectiveness*, Vol. F (1988).

ROBERT G. POIRIER, formerly an intelligence officer and manager with the CIA, is now a consultant. He is author of *By the Blood of Our Alumni: Norwich Citizen-Soldiers in the Army of the Potomac* (1999) and *They Could Not Have Done Better: The 3rd Vermont Volunteer Infantry in the War of the Rebellion* (forthcoming).

COL. DAVID E. PRICE, USAF, who formerly held the USAF Chief of Staff Chair at the Industrial College of the Armed Forces, is Director of Budget Programs in the Office of Deputy Assistant Secretary (Budget), Secretary AF. He is author of "Color of Money: Foundation for Budget Execution" (July 1998) and "The Budget Process—The Basics in One Short Lesson" (January 1997), both in *The Air Force Comptroller*, and "Leadership: Some Thoughts on the Military, Circa 2025," *Joint Forces Quarterly* (Autumn 1996).

EDGAR F. RAINES, JR. is Historian at the U.S. Army Center of Military History and formerly served in a similar capacity in the Office of the Deputy Chief of Staff for Plans and Operations, Army Staff. He is author of *Eyes of Artillery: The Origins of Modern Army Aviation in World War II* (1999) and "Beyond the Green Books: A Prehistory of the U.S. Army in the Cold War Series," in William W. Epley (ed.), *International Cold War Military Records and History: Proceedings of the International Conference on Cold War Military Records and History Held in Washington, D.C. 21–26 March 1994* (1996).

ALEXANDER W. RILLING, Captain, USN (Ret.), served for eighteen years as Associate Adjunct Professor of Management at the Naval Postgraduate School, Monterey. He is author of "The First Fifty Years of Graduate Education in the United States Navy, 1909–1959," an unpublished Ph.D. dissertation, University of Southern California, 1972.

LARRY D. ROBERTS is Command Historian at the U.S. Army Engineer Center. He has published numerous reviews on the Frontier Army and the U.S. Army Corps of Engineers and is author of "The Bailey Bridge" and "The Engineer Replacement Training Center at Fort Leonard Wood, Missouri," both in Barry Fowle (ed.), *Builders and Fighters: U.S. Army Engineers in World War II* (1992).

WILLIAM R. ROBERTS is Associate Professor of History at the U.S. Naval Academy. He is co-editor of and contributor to *Against All Enemies: Interpretations of American Military History from Colonial Times to the Present* (Greenwood Press, 1986).

JOHN SANDERS is Public Affairs Officer at the Naval Postgraduate School. He has authored articles in *Aerospace America*, *Defense* magazine, *Navy Times*, and other publications.

HERBERT Y. SCHANDLER, Colonel, USA (Ret.), who formerly taught at the U.S. Military Academy and served on both the Army and Department of Defense staffs, is Professor of History at the Industrial College of the Armed Forces. He is author of *The Unmaking of a President: Lyndon Johnson and Vietnam* (1977).

DENNIS E. SHOWALTER, formerly Visiting Professor of History at both the U.S. Air Force and U.S. Military Academies, is Professor of History at Colorado College. He has authored many books and published reviews in the field of military history; among his recent works are *What If?: Strategic Alternatives of World War II* (1997) and *Tannenburg: Clash of Empires* (1991).

WILLIAM E. SIMONS, Colonel, USAF (Ret.), formerly Assistant Professor of History at the U.S. Air Force Academy and Senior Staff member and Consultant at the RAND Corporation, has published articles related to PME and other national defense issues in *Defense and Diplomacy, Armed Forces Journal, Air University Review, Military Affairs*, and *Naval Institute Proceedings*. He is co-author of *Soldiers for Peace* (2 vols., 1996) and co-editor of *The Limits of Coercive Diplomacy, 2nd Ed.* (1994).

MARTIN P. SKROCKI is Public Information Officer at the U.S. Merchant Marine Academy, where he has served in a related capacity for 25 years. He collaborated with George Wedemeyer in preparing *Wireless Man: Story of a Great Lakes Radio Officer* (1987) for publication.

FRANK M. SNYDER, Captain, USN (Ret.), formerly a member of the teaching faculty at the Navy War College, is Research Scholar at the college's Center for Naval Warfare Studies. He is author of *Command and Control: The Liter-*

ature and Commentaries (1993) and prepared the "Introduction" for republication of *Sound Military Decision, 1942 Edition* (1992).

CAPT. GEORGE L. STAMPER, JR., USAF, formerly Assistant Professor of History at the U.S. Air Force Academy, has entered training to fly the B-1 bomber aircraft. He is author of "The Sikorsky S-16 and Russian Aviation During the Great War," to be published in *War in History*.

LT. MICHAEL A. STEEN, USN, who has returned to Navy line officer duties, is a former instructor in history at the U.S. Naval Academy.

JON T. SUMIDA teaches history at the University of Maryland. He is author of *Inventing Grand Strategy and Teaching Command: The Classic Works of Alfred Thayer Mahan Reconsidered* (1997) and *In Defence of Naval Supremacy: Finance, Technology, and British Naval Policy, 1889–1914* (1993).

JOHN A. TILLEY is Associate Professor of History at East Carolina University. He has published several articles on Coast Guard history for the *Commandant's Bulletin* and other U.S. Coast Guard publications and is author of *The British Navy and the American Revolution* (1987).

GREGORY N. TODD, formerly an editor and writer with *Army Logistician*, is Associate Editor of *Parameters*, the quarterly journal of the U.S. Army War College, where he has served on the staff for over twenty years. His articles also have appeared in *Airpower Journal, Military Media Review*, and *Golden Seal*.

JAMES E. TOTH, Colonel, USMC (Ret.), is Chairman, Department of Military Strategy and Logistics, at the Industrial College of the Armed Forces. He is co-author of "Building Victory's Foundation: Infrastructure," in Alan L. Gropman (ed.) *The Big "L": American Logistics in World War II* (1997) and author of "Winning War and Peace," in Stephen J. Cimbala (ed.) *The Soviet Challenge in the 1990s* (Praeger, 1989).

DAVID F. TRASK, formerly Chief Historian at the U.S. Army Center of Military History, is author of *The AEF and Coalition Warmaking, 1917–1918* (1993) and *The War With Spain in 1898* (1981).

FRANK UHLIG, JR., formerly Editor, *Naval War College Review*, 1981–93, is Research Scholar at the Naval War College. He has published articles in the *Review* and the *U.S. Naval Institute Proceedings* and is author of *How Navies Fight* (1994) and editor of *Vietnam: The Naval Story* (1986).

JAMES A. WINNEFELD, Rear Admiral, USN (Ret.), formerly Senior Staff member at the RAND Corporation, is co-author of *A League of Airmen: Air Operations in the Gulf War* (1993) and *Joint Air Operations: Command and Control* (1992). He has also published a novel, *An Ace in Masquerade* (1998).

HAROLD R. WINTON, Colonel, USA (Ret.), currently Professor of Military History and Theory at the School of Advanced Airpower Studies, formerly taught at the Army's School of Advanced Military Studies at Fort Leavenworth. He is author of *To Change an Army: General Sir John Burnett-Stuart and British Armored Doctrine, 1927–1938* (1988) and "Partnership and Tension: The Army and Air Force Between Vietnam and Desert Shield," *Parameters* (Spring 1996).

ISBN 0-313-29749-5